Fixed aerials
All-metal wing
Port navigation light
Freight hatch
International registration marking
Mail, freight and baggage hold
Adjustable chairs
Aft cabin
Flaps fitted to trailing edges of the wing
Promenade cabin
Wing tip float
IMPERIAL AIRWAYS
EUROPE • AFRICA • INDIA • THE FAR EAST • AUSTRALIA • U.S.A. - BERMUDA

CHALLENGING HORIZONS

CHALLENGING HORIZONS
QANTAS 1939-1954

John Gunn

University of Queensland Press

ST LUCIA • LONDON • NEW YORK

First published 1987 by University of Queensland Press
Box 42, St Lucia, Queensland, Australia

© Qantas Airways Limited 1987

Typeset by University of Queensland Press
Printed in Australia by Globe Press Pty Ltd, Melbourne

Distributed in the UK and Europe by University of Queensland Press
Dunhams Lane, Letchworth, Herts. SG6 1LF England

Distributed in the USA and Canada by University of Queensland Press
250 Commercial Street, Manchester, NH 03101 USA

Cataloguing in Publication Data

National Library of Australia

Gunn, John, 1925–   .
 Challenging horizons.

 Bibliography.
 Includes index.

 1. Qantas Airways — History. 2. Aeronautics, Commercial
 — Australia — History. I. Title.

387.7'065'94

British Library (data available)

Library of Congress

Gunn, John, 1925–
 Challenging horizons.

 Bibliography: p.
 Includes index.
 1. Qantas Airways — History. 2. Air lines — Australia —
History. I. Title.

HE9889.Q33G865   1987   387.7'065'94   86-4294

ISBN 0 7022 2017 5

To Cedric Turner

chief architect of the postwar Qantas

Contents

Illustrations

Preface

The international air route between Australia and England through Singapore, around which was structured the flying boat fleet and commercial basis of Qantas operations, was severed in World War II. In a little over one month, in 1942, Qantas lost five flying boats as a result of enemy action or in other war service (two while under charter to the RAAF). By May 1942, with only two flying boats under their direct control, operations had been restricted to Darwin and New Guinea. "We now find ourselves struggling to keep operating", wrote Hudson Fysh at the time.

Qantas had become an international airline with no route and only the remnants of a fleet. With the breaking of the Empire route to England after the Japanese advance south to Singapore, the Australian Department of Civil Aviation assumed financial responsibility for Qantas operations, though much work was done and paid for (through the department) by the United States forces. Qantas in fact ceased functioning as a major airline and became an integral part of the Australian war effort.

Challenging Horizons covers the history of the Qantas wartime operations, losses and casualties, and their uneasy relationship during those years with a Department of Civil Aviation that was not always interested in their survival as an organization. It tells how Qantas initiative, opposed by the department, established a new and remarkable air link for Australia from 1943 across the Indian Ocean from Perth to Ceylon, flying Catalina flying boats on nonstop flights of some thirty hours without incident over a period of two years. From that tenuous wartime route came the early postwar air links with Britain by modified wartime landplanes — slow, unpressurized, uncomfortable, and uneconomic. This volume describes the emergence of an international framework for airline operations, Britain's struggle to establish an aviation industry in a world dominated by American transport aircraft, and Australia's unwilling but unavoidable swing to US airliners with the Qantas choice of Lockheed Constellations. It ends as Qantas, with a fleet of modern, pressurized airliners, flew eastward as well as westward from Australia and operated across the Pacific to San Francisco and Vancouver.

As in *The Defeat of Distance*, which told the history of Qantas from its beginning to 1939, I have had long discussions with many people who were closely involved in the events with which this volume deals. Their advice and perspectives have guided me in my judgments but I have, however, continued to rely on the written word of the day and the detailed primary sources available for the substance of this volume.

Many of those who helped in the preparation of this history were acknowledged in the preface to the first volume. Research for this second volume was greatly facilitated by many others. In the United States I have to thank John Gamble, Boeing Aircraft Company; Anne Millbrooke, corporate archivist for United Technologies; Lockheed Aircraft Corporation's public affairs department and Peter Mingrone, now retired from Lockheeds but intimately concerned with their Australian activities in former years. In England, Ralph Robins, managing director of Rolls-Royce, made it possible for me to meet and talk with many past and present executives of that company. Ron Wilson, on behalf of British Airways, greatly helped with locating research material from the archives of the RAF Museum, Hendon. In Australia I am grateful for the help given by the Department of Prime Minister and Cabinet, the Department of Aviation, the Australian Archives, and the Mitchell Library, Sydney. I must again thank Edgar Johnston for lending me his papers and John Fysh, as trustee of the papers of the late Sir Hudson Fysh, for allowing me access to them. Above all, I must thank the many people who served or are now serving Qantas who gave their time and willing assistance.

Part 1
1939 to 1945

Introduction
The Indivisible Crown

Britain's declaration of war against Germany on 3 September 1939 meant, for an Australia that considered itself unquestionably a part of the British Empire, an automatic declaration of war by Australia. Neutrality, with Britain under threat, was unthinkable; the Crown was indivisible.[1] The war, as Italy and then Japan became involved, was to sever the airline links between the two countries — links that had had their roots in the first epic flight from England to Australia by Ross and Keith Smith in 1919.

After this flight, the courage and ambition of the pioneers and the long efforts and arguments of governments and fledgling airline companies culminated in a safe and predictable mail and passenger service in December 1934 that linked Australia by air with the other side of the world. Britain's Imperial Airways, founded in 1924, flew through Egypt, the Middle East, and India as far as Singapore; Qantas Empire Airways, a partnership formed in 1934 between the original Q.A.N.T.A.S. (Queensland and Northern Territory Aerial Services Limited) and Imperial Airways, operated the route between Singapore and Brisbane. Founded in 1920 by World War I airmen Paul McGinness and Hudson Fysh, with the backing of pastoralist Fergus McMaster (its first chairman) and other Queenslanders, Q.A.N.T.A.S. had painstakingly built a reputation for reliability and integrity that had won for Qantas Empire Airways, despite intense and prolonged competition, the support of the Australian government in conducting Australia's first regular overseas airline services.

1

Fergus McMaster, as Australian as the soil of the western Queensland plains where Q.A.N.T.A.S.* began, was like most Australians of his day a devout and loyal supporter of the cause of Empire. Though there had been disagreements, disappointments, and at times bitter argument with Imperial Airways, the concept of Empire was always central to McMaster's thinking. With Hudson Fysh as its tenacious and able managing director, the small, inland airline became the base on which the international Qantas Empire Airways was built. The Australian section of the England–Australia service, between Brisbane and Singapore, was operated until 1938 with the British DH86 biplane which, in construction, was a plywood box with spruce stiffening and fabric outer covering. The four Gipsy VI engines were mounted on the lower wing and it would carry up to ten passengers and a crew of two at 145 miles an hour. (QEA carried fewer passengers to permit high mail loadings.)

In 1938, the small DH86 landplanes were replaced by the handsome Short S.23 C-class flying boats. With an empty weight of 20 tonnes, they had four Bristol Pegasus XC engines of 920 horsepower and could carry fifteen passengers, three cabin crew, and two aircrew at a cruising speed of 165 miles an hour. The flying boats had been urged on an unwilling Australian government (but a willing QEA) by Britain, as part of Imperial Airways's plan for a revolutionary and visionary Empire Air Mail Scheme under which mails to all parts of the British Empire were to be carried by air without surcharge. The scheme was never fully put into operation. (From the outset the Australian government decided to retain a surcharge for airmail from Australia, though much lower than that charged previously.)

Operationally, the flying boats were popular and successful. Their QEA route from Singapore took them to Darwin, then across the Gulf of Carpentaria and northern Queensland and down the eastern coast of Australia to Sydney. In their first year of operation with QEA, operating three times a week in each direction, they carried 4,900 passengers; in their first nine months from 4 August 1938 they carried substantially more mail than the DH86 landplanes had carried in all their four years of operation.

On 1 September 1939, as war with Germany loomed, QEA was instructed by the Australian government that their service

* As in the first volume, Q.A.N.T.A.S. is used when referring to the holding company for the Australian share in Qantas Empire Airways.

to Singapore would cease. The flying boat *Champion*, on its way north from Sydney, was recalled from Townsville. Five days later, when it was judged that Italy and Japan would not immediately enter the war and that Imperial Airways would be able to continue on its route across the Mediterranean, the service was resumed, though only on a twice-weekly basis. To discourage mail loadings, Britain introduced a surcharge for mail and Australia increased its surcharge.

By 15 September 1939, QEA had adjusted to the reduced schedules. Though uncertain of its future, it had just completed its own workshops at Mascot, Sydney, capable of overhauling the flying boat engines and was sufficiently self-contained as an airline to carry on if the Empire route to Britain was broken. With the outbreak of war, the airline retained one immediate objective — somehow to keep the QEA organization intact. QEA now set about rendering maximum service to the country.[2] It would, said Fergus McMaster on 27 September, stand firm by the Empire.[3]

The Outbreak of War
1939 to 1940

1 "All our planning ahead has gone by the board for the duration", Hudson Fysh wrote to McMaster on 9 October 1939. "My main work here looks like that of arguing with the government about charters etc. and seeking adjustments with Imperial Airways." He asked his chairman what would be the reaction if he left Qantas for more active war service "in view of the position on the Board, which is not altogether normal".[1]

It was far from normal. Fergus McMaster had suffered a heart attack late in 1938 and was still very unwell. Fysh had carried the main burden of leadership since, in a period that had seen the growth of the new flying boat services; the almost intractable problem of proper bases for the boats; intense political argument over the establishment of a flying boat terminal in Sydney's wealthy harbourside suburb, Rose Bay; the vital acquisition of emergency engine spares from a hard-pressed England; and the completion, on 18 August 1939, of a new engine overhaul workshop at Mascot. (The Rose Bay hangar was not completed by the government until October 1939, well over a year after the start of flying boat operations.) Overshadowing all these pressing operational demands was the threat of a war that would cut Australia's air links with the world.

For Fergus McMaster personally the possibility of losing Fysh was greatly disturbing but he advised his managing director that it was a matter for the board. His personal view, he said, was that there were many more people offering to assist than the government could cope with. "Your first duty

4

The facade of the QEA engine overhaul workshop at Sydney's Mascot airport. Completed in August 1939, it was still in use as a storage facility in the 1980s.

is to the aviation companies and . . . the successful operation of the services from Sydney to Singapore and the inland services." They had a bearing, said McMaster, on the war effort.[2] The two men, who together had built the now threatened airline over two decades from an outback joy-riding and charter company with two small aircraft, no premises, and a staff of three, paused to exchange personal letters in the unreal but disturbing atmosphere of the opening weeks of the war. To McMaster in his illness Fysh wrote: "This is just a simple straightforward few words of genuine old friendship . . . I realise what a tough and worrying time you are having. There may be nothing I can do, but there may be. You have some very true and staunch friends, but I would like you to feel I am also there if required. Keep the old fighting spirit going."[3]

McMaster said the letter was touching and helpful. "I do not wish to leave Qantas after so many years so closely woven in this work", he replied. "But if you can see your way clear to relieve me for, say, two or three months, the doctor seems confident that it would make a big improvement in my health." The doctor, he said, seemed satisfied that the heart condition had cleared up satisfactorily. "My trouble is with arthritis, and with practically a breakdown of the nervous system. Do not worry about me, for you have a lot on your shoulders."[4]

Fysh wrote to Sir John Reith, chairman of the new British Overseas Airways Corporation and their partner company in Qantas Empire Airways. (On 12 June 1939 the British Overseas Airways Corporation bill went before the House of Commons in England, incorporating Imperial Airways and British Airways in a new, government-owned organization. The bill received Royal Assent on 4 August and provided that the new BOAC would officially take over as operator on 1 April 1940.) McMaster "had asked to be relieved of worries for the next two or three months until his gold injection treatment is completed", Fysh told Reith. He used the occasion to comment on the relationship between the English and Australian companies. "I often think we take too much for granted and are apt to forget what we owe to Imperial Airways in regard to financial and other major matters of assistance", wrote Fysh. "As a matter of fact this . . . applies to most activities in Australia and . . . to defence. We are reliant on the Mother Country, but in some Australian quarters this is not admitted." Fysh told Reith that he was a little more reconciled to staying on in his present work, though he had felt restive and anxious to be of use.[5]

There was a real possibility that Fergus McMaster, for so long the man whose clear mind and solid integrity had guided Qantas in political and business high policy, might not be able to resume the chairmanship. Hudson Fysh had never disguised his own ambition to succeed McMaster if that should happen and had said so in March 1939 in a letter to Sir John Reith adding, however, that it had hardly been possible to discuss the question with McMaster.[6] That Fysh was anxious to stake his claim now and assert his competence is clear from a letter he wrote on 24 November to F. J. Smith, who represented the interests of Imperial Airways on the Qantas Empire Airways board. Referring to McMaster's illness, Fysh then wrote:

> I myself have naturally been the one to greatly take the lead under the conditions which have pertained during the last year, and I have had to take the final action. . . My position under existing conditions was sometimes difficult. . . . There are going to be a lot of considerations ahead which demand the closest insight into the intricate make-up of QEA and its associations with Imperial Airways and the governments, and I do not feel that the Board are going to suffer from any unsound advice or decisions from myself. Mr McMaster and I have worked together closely for very many

years and he has been a tower of strength as chairman. We have both been responsible for many of the big moves, but in common fairness to myself you should understand that though Mr McMaster was the main force behind Qantas during the formation and in the early years, I consider myself mainly responsible, from the Qantas side, for moving into Brisbane from "the bush", and for the link with Imperial Airways — and I negotiated the first agreement in London.[7]

It was not altogether an unreasonable attitude, though McMaster had in fact clearly remained "the main force" behind Qantas well beyond the early years, and was the dominating influence right up to the time of his heart attack in 1938. Despite the ability, integrity, and sheer tenacity that Fysh brought to his work, McMaster's maturity in all political and business matters and his powerful character established him always as the undoubted leader. Hudson Fysh, however, had every claim to succeed him if illness forced his retirement, though in no way did Fysh hint that this time had come. "I feel the present position on the Board must definitely continue," he told F. J. Smith, "and if it is a little difficult at times for myself, it is certainly nothing to complain about."

Conscious that Qantas could be disbanded as a civil organization and taken over in its entirety by the air force, Fysh wrote directly to the prime minister and treasurer, R. G. Menzies, on 5 December.

> I have received a personal letter from Sir John Reith [British Overseas Airways Corporation] which shows that there has been considerable pressure on the part of the Royal Air Force to take over Imperial Airways, but this has been successfully objected to . . . along the lines that Imperial Airways could continue to carry out the communications work required of it — if anything more

When Australia declared war on Germany in September 1939, a number of civil aircraft were impressed by the RAAF for transport and sea patrol duties. Two BOAC owned Empire flying boats, *Centaurus* and *Calypso*, were in Sydney when war was declared and they were quickly modified for military use in the newly completed Qantas hangar. *Centaurus* is seen at its moorings in Rose Bay after its handover to No. 11 Squadron, RAAF.

satisfactorily than the RAF. In regard to the work of Qantas Empire Airways, we are in much the same position. Our organisation has been built up over a period of nineteen years . . . and [we] feel well fitted to deal with the air transportation requirements of your government, having in view all the time the very important developments which must take place after the war in conjunction with British Overseas Airways Corporation.

Fysh warned the prime minister against possible exploitation of the war situation by the Dutch and American airlines. "I feel sure it is the desire of the government to see that such neutrals do not capitalise on our wartime preoccupation and obtain a footing which would not have been possible in peace time, and which might cause lasting damage to British interests." If a trans-Tasman service did not start, Fysh wrote, great pressure could be expected from Pan American to operate to Sydney.[8] Fysh also asked the prime minister for confirmation that the Qantas landplane services from Brisbane to Daly Waters in the Northern Territory would be continued in the coming year.[9]

The East Indies Dutch airline KNILM had operated between Batavia and Sydney from 3 July 1938 and Fysh did not want it, or KLM from Holland, to make further inroads into Australia. Pan American, after a false start in 1937, was preparing to link Honolulu with New Zealand by flying boat. Already Pan American had demonstrated its reach and competence with flying boat routes from Miami to Buenos Aires and from San Francisco to Manila and Hong Kong. QEA's partner, Imperial Airways, was using its new flying boats to operate to Durban in South Africa as well as to Singapore. The pressures for international competition were in place.

The new year of 1940 began calmly enough for Qantas Empire Airways. Fysh told McMaster on 8 January:

> There is a great deal going on in the office but nothing much out of the ordinary, or requiring high policy decision. Financial adjustments as a result of the war are perhaps our biggest work. Although we appear safe, actual detailed finality regarding a new financial basis with Imperial Airways, the charter of flying boats and engine overhaul in Australia is a very long way off yet. Mr Corbett, the director-general [of civil aviation] told me here last week that Cabinet had approved of indemnifying us against King's Enemy Risks. He also told me that Cabinet had agreed to the trans-Tasman service.[10]

From Imperial Airways there was unsettling news. Sir John Reith, chairman of Imperial Airways since July 1938 and first chairman of its successor BOAC, was to become Britain's minister of information. "Sir John Reith's new post is rather a bombshell [and] most unfortunate after the friendly contact established", wrote Fysh. "I have personally had many assurances from Sir John which might not fully stand in the case of a new chairman . . . "

The chairmanship of Qantas Empire Airways and of the original Q.A.N.T.A.S. was also a matter of concern in the first weeks of 1940. McMaster wrote to Fysh: "It has been provisionally decided that I should go for a trip (to Sydney), I have had electro-cardiographs of the heart [sic], X-rays of the heart, and other tests. The doctor yesterday, in a general overhaul, told me to knock myself about as much as I can physically — the more exercise I take, the better it will be . . . The real trouble is that my nerves have completely broken down." He asked Fysh to arrange accommodation for him in a convalescent home or private hospital and said that, although he could attend the directors' meeting due in Sydney, he could not do so as chairman.[11] On 11 January, McMaster tackled the possibility that it might be necessary to appoint his successor as chairman in a letter to Qantas director F. E. Loxton.

> Some time ago, you brought up the question regarding the future chairmanship of Q.A.N.T.A.S. and QEA, and Hudson Fysh was mentioned as my possible successor, I take it that neither yourself nor Mr Templeton are in a position to accept the chairmanship if and when it may become vacant. As you know . . . my progress towards better health has been very marked, but none of us knows what is round the next corner. Hudson Fysh was one of the principal founders of Q.A.N.T.A.S. and it is my confirmed belief that he should be my successor, both as chairman of Q.A.N.T.A.S and QEA. I wish to place this decision on record . . .

McMaster then suggested that Fysh be made vice chairman, as a first step.

> Mr Fysh has had long experience of Q.A.N.T.A.S. and QEA and, during my illness, I feel we can agree that he has handled all the negotiations — both overseas and with the Commonwealth — satisfactorily. Although Mr Rudder, as vice chairman of QEA, has acted as chairman during my illness, I understand he agrees with the principle that the chairman of Q.A.N.T.A.S. should be chairman of QEA, and that he himself definitely would not accept the chairmanship of QEA.[12]

In his usual open manner he sent a copy of this letter to Qantas director Ainslie Templeton and Fysh. "I do not like any backhand negotiations regarding Board adjustments", he told them, adding in his letter to Fysh: "I feel that you are the logical successor to myself . . . I well remember the old pioneering company, and the work you did in founding that company and pushing it through those difficult years. It is my wish . . . that you should succeed me as chairman."[13]

Loxton replied promptly to McMaster's letter. "I have no other comment to make than that, in view of the very prominent and highly important part played by Mr Fysh in the formation and successful operation of the company and his long association with yourself, he is logically the director to assume the chairmanship in the event of your retirement . . . "[14]

For Hudson Fysh, McMaster's action was generous and reassuring. "I do appreciate your attitude and what you have done", he wrote, "and cannot overstress my feeling . . . I am genuinely happy in my position under your chairmanship but should you drop out through any cause, I would not like to be superseded. Your name will live and your wishes carry weight after you are gone, and your support is therefore valuable."[15]

Within a week of this exchange about the leadership of Qantas between two of its three founders, McMaster received a short telegram from the third founder, Paul McGinness. Recognized by both McMaster and Fysh as the driving spirit behind the creation of the airline — "the bravest of the brave", Fysh had called him — the restless McGinness had left them after the very first scheduled service had been flown from Longreach in western Queensland in 1922. McGinness had resisted the board ruling that pilots should not drink, and had shown little enthusiasm for what were to him the dreary details of management and routine. He left Queensland for Western Australia but the small farm on which he at last settled failed miserably after ten years and was, in the mid thirties, assigned to his creditors. He had tried, without success, to obtain through a sympathetic Edgar Johnston, controller of civil aviation, a position in the department, bitterly regretting that he had ever left aviation. Now, after unsuccessfully trying to rejoin the air force when war broke out, he sought McMaster's assistance in getting a recruiting post. "Have wired Sir Donald Cameron [MP] for appointment in new air recruiting scheme", he telegraphed McMaster. "No vacancies in air force over the age limit. Will you see Cameron?"[16]

McMaster responded generously to McGinness's wire but Fysh saw only difficulties. "I am writing Sir Donald supporting the application", McMaster told Fysh. "McGinness has a lot of faults but, in the RAAF drive, I cannot see that he can do any harm, and it is possible that he, with his splendid war record, would make a very much more effective appeal than

10

others . . . I suggest that, if you can do so conscientiously, you should support his application also."[17]

Fysh found himself unable to support the pilot with whom he had flown in action as observer, and the man whose initiative and enthusiasm had brought into being the airline he now directed. He wrote to McMaster:

> In regard to McGinness I am sorry, Fergus, to have to write that you will be well advised not to recommend him for any job, as he is quite unreliable and uncontrollable — and will only land up in a mess. Mac has had chance after chance but always ends up the same way. I have seen him lately and Arthur Baird and I both realise it is useless trying to do anything for him which entails employment in a job where average commonsense is required. In a fighting aeroplane he would be good even yet, if his health would stand it.[18]

Qantas Empire Airways had now, since its inception in 1934, flown over six million miles in both landplanes and flying boats without any injury to passengers or crew. "I maintain that a record like this, seeing that it covered organising and training for four-engined landplanes which were new to us, flying overseas under great initial difficulties, and then organising and training for flying boat operations, is a record which has never been equalled in any part of the world", Fysh wrote to McMaster on 23 February. "It reflects the highest credit on Captain Brain, who has been in charge of flying operations during this time."[19]

McMaster's period of rest greatly restored his health and spirits. By mid-March he was able to tell A. E. Rudder that he would resume his work. "Had I thought my illness would have tied me up for so long I would, and should, have resigned", he wrote. "I have appreciated all that you and Mr Fysh have done for me, particularly yourself in carrying on the chairmanship over such a long period without complaint."[20] McMaster told Fysh that his health was definitely better than at any time since his heart attack in November 1938.[21]

Their old partner, Imperial Airways, now had as its new chairman Clive Pearson; W. L. Runciman (who had become the senior executive under Sir John Reith when he took up his appointment on 1 July 1938) continued in office. On 1 April 1940, "the appointed day" under the legislation, British Overseas Airways Corporation came into being as the actual operator and Imperial Airways was no more; but the effect on QEA was, wrote Fysh, little more than the substitution of BOAC for IAL in all their agreements.[22] One of the principal

11

questions that had to be resolved between them as a result of the outbreak of the war, however, was that of return on capital during the wartime period. McMaster told QEA board member W. A. Watt: "The basis of the partnership is that each shall work for a 'square deal', and we can say that Imperials have honoured the letter and the spirit of the undertaking." Fysh, in an official letter to Dismore, assistant general manager of Imperial Airways, had suggested a net return on capital of 7.5 per cent after tax, with tax estimated at 1.5 per cent, making a target of 9 per cent for their gross return on capital. "We feel if we got 8.5 per cent gross for the duration of the war we would be on a very good wicket", he told McMaster.[23] McMaster proposed using his influence in political circles to break the deadlock that existed with the government on the terms of QEA's inland contract and to press for a reasonable return on the capital invested in the internal landplane service that QEA operated between Brisbane and Daly Waters and told Fysh:

> Since Cabinet made the decision [on QEA operation of the route] the Country Party has joined with Mr Menzies and holds considerable influence. I have been very directly associated with the Country Party for a long period and . . . I could write to Mr Thorby, Deputy Leader of the Federal Country Party, Mr A. W. Fadden — also a Country Party member — and Senator Foll, who is a Brisbane member but represents the United Australia Party. The company is faced with either accepting a very unsound contract, or the people of the outback losing the air services which have operated in the West since 1920. The position directly affects the Country Party, and no doubt pressure can be exerted in that quarter.[24]

Fysh encouraged him. "An approach to the new Country Party members of the Cabinet cannot fail to be beneficial", he wrote. "I am afraid the position still exists that pressure outside the actual ministry concerned is very often the only way to secure proper attention. Press criticism perhaps helps more than anything."[25]

The extension to New Zealand of the England–Australia flying boat service was now imminent under what both McMaster and Runciman thought was a very clumsy arrangement.[26] In early April, representatives of the British, Australian, and New Zealand governments met in Wellington to try to finalize agreement and a financial formula under which the trans-Tasman service would operate. Both Australia and New Zealand had opposed Britain's original wish that Imperial Air-

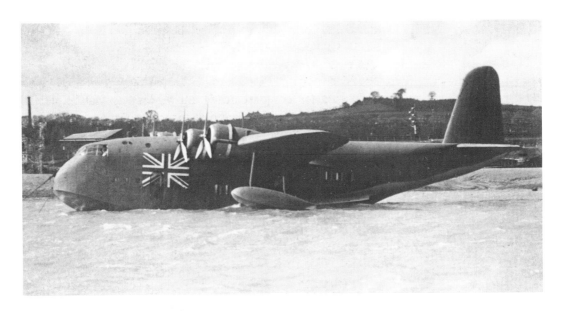

ways operate the route, though New Zealand lacked funds to do it and Australia had no particular interest in the service at all. Australia and New Zealand, suspicious of one another, were united only in their opposition to a British monopoly. All three governments had had differing views on aircraft types and capital commitments. The Wellington discussions dragged on until 25 April, only five days before the start of the service, when agreement on a financial formula and subsidy levels was reached.[27] In essence the agreed formula provided a subsidy of £95,000 sterling for the first year, with the first year dividend not to exceed three per cent. (Subsequent dividends were to be limited to six per cent.) Any payments to the three operators were to be subject to the approval of the all powerful Tasman Air Commission (representing the three governments), located in Wellington. It was an unwieldy and inefficient structure for a new airline but McMaster commented: "I have no doubt that good, honest, clear thinking by all concerned will eventually iron out many of the clumsy conditions that are necessary at the outset."[28]

The Tasman Empire Airways regular weekly service between Sydney and Auckland was inaugurated on 30 April 1940, when the Short S30C flying boat *Aotearoa* left Auckland at 6 a.m., arriving nine hours and fifteen minutes later at Rose Bay, a distance of 1,348 miles. It carried nine passengers and about 40,000 letters. Hudson Fysh, A. E. Rudder, and Edgar Johnston were among the passengers. Australia's share of the annual subsidy for the service was estimated at £21,850 plus

This official photograph of *Clifton*, one of the last Empire flying boats built for BOAC, was taken for inclusion on its Certificate of Airworthiness issued on 20 April 1940. The C of A document is now in the Qantas archives. The large Union Jack was necessary to prevent attack by Allied aircraft.

provision at Sydney of landing areas, hangars, maintenance facilities, slipways, wireless aids, and meteorological services. The agreement among the three governments for the service was limited to the duration of the war.[29] Johnston wrote privately to McMaster saying he had been missed at the Wellington discussions where final agreement "would have been simplified by your quiet and effective methods of persuasion".[30] Fysh formally reported to the board on 16 May that the whole formation and constitution of Tasman Empire Airways had many features that did not occur in other contracts. Its commercial future was greatly bound up with government policy, he wrote, but given efficient management it should be possible to pay small dividends, with the safety of the capital invested appearing secure.[31] McMaster's original optimism about the service soon faded and he told Fysh: "The whole organisation is so unwieldy and overweighted in overheads for the amount of flying done and revenue expected that I feel some less expensive organisation should be attempted."[32] Fysh agreed that TEA was a sick organization but recommended only gradual changes.[33]

McMaster had also been concerned about the reliability of the engines on all the flying boats.

> There definitely seems a weakness in the engine unit. In commercial aviation comfort, reasonable speed and dependability are necessary if you are to attract passengers. The engines used on the flying boats give good power for their weight but they seem very intricate and it is questionable whether it would not be more sound to get greater stability from the engines by sacrificing a certain amount of load, if by doing so you could avoid these expensive hold ups that so frequently occur . . . The engine for commercial aviation should be designed for one purpose only and reliability should be its objective.[34]

Engine problems had been one of many difficulties in settling down the QEA flying boat service from Singapore. Fysh told McMaster:

> The pressure down here [Sydney] has been great. For the past year I have set myself the task of calming down on things without losing efficiency — not getting bottled up about details. I have been fairly successful and this, plus regular exercise through the week as well as at weekends, has kept me fitter than usual and I seem to have got over most of my troubles of a year or more ago. A very great deal of work has fallen on Harman and Turner since the war started owing to the many extra matters involving agreements and estimates and I was glad the board awarded them the rise in salary that they did.[35]

14

Their worries were increased when H. V. C. Thorby (now postmaster-general) told McMaster: "The subject has been raised as to whether better use can be made of the services, both British and Dutch, now operating to and from Australia. [It is] essential that we should avoid any waste of fuel or effort at a time like this if we can in any way strengthen the Allied cause by utilising aircraft space which may now be going to waste."[36] McMaster responded with a strongly worded telegram to his friend Senator Foll, minister for the interior and information. Qantas, he said, was now operating a very unsound contract on the inland Brisbane–Daly Waters service that could necessitate a loss or withdrawal from a route that the company had pioneered and operated since 1922. Further Dutch competition on this Qantas inland service would, he warned, make the position much worse. McMaster said that the inland route was adequately served, while on the flying boat service (with the exception of Sydney–Townsville where at times some passengers were turned away) there was ample accommodation. Further Dutch competition with the Empire flying boat service would mean additional taxation on the United Kingdom and would hit QEA's Australian shareholders. "I contend that foreign services are a danger and should be restricted rather than encouraged," he said.[37] McMaster also had family worries as both his sons (one only seventeen) wanted to join up. "Great sacrifices will have to be made by all sooner or later", he wrote to Fysh.[38]

Fysh now heard from England that his friend Dismore, who had done so much for Imperial Airways and Qantas in helping establish Qantas Empire Airways in 1934, had applied to be released from BOAC to join the Royal Air Force. "My unhappiness was greatly accentuated by the way things became so impossible for the old Imperial Airways people", Dismore wrote to Fysh on 4 June. "I feel like the last branch waiting for the axe. But it never fell. Instead, the last vestige of authority was taken away and put in the hands of the late British Airways people. You know, Hudson, Imperial Airways was more than a job — it was a life's work. I put all I had into it and gave more than health and social life could probably stand. But the new gang will never realise this . . . "[39]

QEA's relationship with the new BOAC management was good. Fysh wrote to BOAC's director-general, W. L. Runciman, on 24 June: "No doubt the future of the flying boat service is in the lap of the gods. Out here my object is to keep at least a portion of the QEA organisation together, consistent with the maximum service to the Empire in this critical time,"[40] Runciman's reply was flattering. He congratulated Fysh on his efforts to get the engine overhaul shop at Sydney established. "I do not know how we should be faring without it today", he wrote.[41]

McMaster now made a surprising proposal to Fysh. On 18 June he wrote: "When you were in England there was a definite urge by Sir John Reith for you to remain [there] to assist with the reorganisation of the Empire Airways. . . . Myself and other directors objected, but under the present dangerous conditions of the Empire I feel that the Board would be unanimous for you to go overseas if you desire . . . I am quite prepared to go down and live temporarily in or near Sydney."[42]

Fysh responded at length:

It was a surprise to receive your suggestions that I should go overseas . . . I would not fit into the picture there — the possibility of such a move is too late. QEA is facing the most difficult time in its history when all we know about the future is that it is going to be difficult . . . This is assuredly the time when a steady hand is required and when by my knowledge and vital contacts I can be of most value to the company. I feel that I can only serve better by taking on a responsible position in the RAAF . . . and such a position is definitely not offering at the moment. You are, of course, aware that last year I was offered the position of Director-General of Civil Aviation, but here again the time for acceptance is past. [Regarding] physical fitness — I am certainly not A1 these days. Another matter in regard to service is remuneration. I am willing to make personal sacrifices to the limit but I would be reluctant to reduce my family to a beggarly state of existence and . . . eliminate even the chance of the continuance of the present schooling my children are receiving. I am obviously not situated at this stage to make such a sacrifice. Would QEA make up the difference of my salary if I went into the RAAF? As you are well aware, the policy of the company has precluded the accumulation of capital to any extent despite my being one of the founders of the company . . . So far as I can see, Fergus, none of us can really do much except to hold ourselves ready to serve to our utmost when called on to do so. Bold and vigorous leadership is what we want, and ruthless cutting away of the wretched red tape . . . which is clogging the efforts of the country. In my view it is the politicians, not the people, who are to blame. One thing we can take as certain — that the present political system here in Australia will be swept away or drastically modified within the next few years; but our first job is to win the war. I realise to the full your splendid offer to come down and keep things going here, and know what a sacrifice this would mean to you . . . but I feel that the time for this has not arrived yet.[43]

16

Fysh concluded less than tactfully:

> Some of us have given our lives to the company to the exclusion
> of all other outside interests and are deeply involved in the com-
> pany's future. Baird and I have given twenty years of our lives . . .

His last sentence stung Fergus McMaster who sent him a
handwritten note: "I have re-read your letter, and I take the
slap in the face. At one time you held . . . that I had done
something for Qantas and QEA but your letter . . . refutes any
feelings of that kind now."[44]

An extraordinary general meeting of Q.A.N.T.A.S. was called
on 4 July to discuss the effect of the world situation and the
recasting of the Empire airmail service. In his chairman's address, McMaster explained that the United Kingdom government by act of Parliament had taken over the whole of the
organization of their partner in QEA.

> The Empire routes are now under direct control of the British
> Overseas Airways Corporation, which is being financed and back-
> ed direct by the UK government through the Air Ministry . . .
> The changeover, under present world conditions, perhaps gives
> greater security to Qantas. In regard to finance, the Corporation
> will pay to QEA by way of subsidy any deficiency between reve-
> nue and expenditure. This is a simplification of the old subsidy
> conditions. In addition to this subsidy the Corporation will pay to
> QEA interest at the rate of 7.5 per cent gross per annum on the in-
> vested capital. QEA will continue to benefit from any revenue
> obtained from its investments or other sources. The funds which
> QEA has available for investment are mainly represented by accu-
> mulated obsolescence reserves. The Company's revenue from
> other sources is mainly from the operation of the internal services
> under contract with the Australian government . . . It is impossi-
> ble to give you any detailed forecast of the possible gross earnings
> of QEA . . . [45]

McMaster remained doubtful about the usefulness of the
Tasman flying boat service. He wrote to Fysh:

> As you know, I have never been a keen advocate of the New
> Zealand–Australia service and am wondering if this could be given
> over to Pan American Airways for a definite term of lease, and the
> New Zealand flying boats used in a Brisbane–New Caledonia
> connection, or some other way in which they would be able to give
> greater service to the Empire than they are giving in their present
> capacity. Perhaps I am pessimistic but I feel that the closer the
> connection we can make with America, the safer we will be.[46]

It was a sentiment that was to be expressed dramatically by
the Australian prime minister in the following year but neither

17

Fysh nor the minister for civil aviation, J. V. Fairbairn, supported the idea of an Australian link by Pan American. On 6 July, Fysh wrote to the minister commenting on a story that had appeared in the *Sydney Morning Herald* about a supposed invitation from the government for Pan American to fly a Boeing Clipper aircraft from Auckland to Sydney on a courtesy visit. The Tasman flying boat service, said Fysh, would not have been commenced except as the final link with Pan American at Auckland. "The service was also commenced as the first link of a future Pacific service . . . Later on, when the Empire Services are ready to connect up between Canada and New Zealand, the situation may be changed in that it may be necessary to allow Pan American the right to visit Australia in exchange for the landing rights in the Hawaiian Islands and any other American bases."[47] The minister agreed with him. "No request whatever has been received from either the United States government or Pan American to pay a courtesy visit to Sydney, which would undoubtedly be the thin end of the wedge", he told Fysh. "With the Trans-Tasman airways in operation there would be no reasonable argument for allowing Pan American to continue from Auckland to Sydney."

Fairbairn was angered by a novel Pan American proposal to put pressure on the Australian government. "I am more concerned about the proposal for [Pan American] making alternate trips to [Auckland and] Noumea [then] carrying passengers on by yacht [from Noumea to Australia]. This is obviously to create the absurd position of flying people across the Pacific and then taking four days to bring them on by yacht [on the last leg] to Brisbane, which would raise a public clamour for the [Pan American] service . . . to be permitted to come on to Brisbane and Sydney."[48] McMaster, however, was not convinced. "From a personal view and the interests of QEA perhaps the [Pan American] proposal should be fought . . . The question is whether a greater good would not be done to Australia and the Empire by giving out a friendly gesture to the Americans . . . I feel that there are bigger things than QEA or TEA in the balance at the present time."[49] Fysh replied: "If Pan American are allowed to operate to Australia without the granting of watertight reciprocal rights for a British company to use American bases, plus the right to alight in America, it is just definitely goodbye to a future Pacific service."[50]

Although QEA's services to Singapore had been limited to two per week instead of the prewar three, the total number of passengers carried for the financial year ending 31 March 1940 exceeded those of the previous year by almost ninety per cent. A total of 5,417 passengers travelled on the route, compared with 3,024 in the preceding year. The company's landplanes in Queensland carried 2,550 passengers, bringing the total number lifted by QEA aircraft to 8,454 (compared with 5,854 to 31 March 1939), an increase overall of fifty-six per cent. In addition, total freight carried increased by sixty-eight per cent to 123 tons. Mails, however, because of the surcharge rate, fell. Only 21 services out of 256 operated arrived one day or more late, giving a terminal punctuality rate of ninety-two per cent.[51]

In Europe, as the German war machine overran Denmark and a stagnating military situation on the Continent forced the resignation of Chamberlain after bitter debate in the House of Commons, a new leader emerged in Britain. On 10 May, as German forces moved into Holland, Belgium, and Luxembourg, Winston Churchill became prime minister. By 26 May, as annihilation of both the British and French armies seemed likely, the order was given for the evacuation from Dunkirk to begin. On 22 June, France accepted Germany's armistice terms and on 24 June capitulated to Italy, which had entered the war on 10 June. Churchill made his momentous speech of resolve and resistance: "The whole fury and might of the enemy must soon be turned on us . . . Let us therefore brace ourselves to our duties, and so bear ourselves that if the British Empire and its Commonwealth lasts for a thousand years, men will still say 'This was their finest hour'." Britain itself was now threatened with invasion.

The airline link across the Mediterranean was cut and plans were immediately implemented for a weekly service to link Sydney, via Cairo, with Durban. It commenced on 19 June and the mails, flown from Sydney to Durban, were then taken on by ship to England. (The frequency was doubled on 17 August.) There were sixteen flying boats south of Italy when the Mediterranean was cut and all were used on the new "Horseshoe" service until this, too, was cut by the Japanese advance southward in February 1942. Maintenance of the flying boats was to be carried out completely either at Durban or Sydney, and a programme begun by QEA to make long-range tanks for them.

Air communications across the Pacific posed different problems. In the context of world events, there were elements of farce in Cabinet Agenda 406 put to the Australian War Cabinet by Fairbairn on 11 July. Pan American Airways service to

BOAC transferred its base for Empire flying boat operations from Poole in Dorset to Durban in South Africa following Italy's entry into the war. The Durban–Sydney link was christened the "Horseshoe Route" after the shape it produced on a map and services began on 19 June 1940. Heavy camouflage was no longer necessary as this photograph of *Clifton* at Rose Bay in late 1940 clearly shows.

operate from San Francisco via Honolulu, Canton Island, and Noumea to Auckland commences next week (12 July) and thereafter on a fortnightly basis, the agenda item read. "Mr Casey has advised that the Company proposes to operate a yacht to carry passengers and mails between Noumea and Sydney but . . . would not proceed with this proposal if the necessary permissions were given for them to extend their service from Auckland to Sydney." (R. G. Casey had resigned his Cabinet portfolio and seat in Parliament to become Australian minister to Washington. He presented his credentials at the White House on 5 March 1940.) Casey, Cabinet was told, had advised Pan American that such negotiations should be conducted between governments.

The item continued:

> The yacht journey between Sydney and Noumea will take four days, whereas with a suitable connection which can be arranged between the Trans-Tasman and the Pan American services at Auckland, the air journey between Noumea and Sydney would be two days. The yacht connection therefore serves no useful purpose for either mails or passengers and is obviously designed to bring pressure upon the Commonwealth Government to permit an extension of the Pan American Airways service to Australia by public criticism of a four day yacht journey at the end of a three day air journey. Although under the existing international position there may be many advantages in fostering good relationships between the United States and the British Dominions in the South

Pacific, it is to be remembered that the right to land in Australia is now our last bargaining counter to secure rights for landings in Hawaii for a British Trans-Pacific service, which it is the agreed aim of the United Kingdom, New Zealand and Commonwealth Governments to establish as soon as possible ... The [Pan American] suggestion that the permission ... to come to Australia should be revocable at any time is quite inadequate as a safeguard because once the Pan American Airways service was established, the pressure of public opinion would make it very hard if not impossible for the Commonwealth to revoke the permission.

The possibility of establishing an Australian service to Noumea with QEA flying boats was proposed as a counter to the Pan American pressure. "I would stress my view", said the minister, "that it should never be necessary actually to operate the Australian air service to Noumea, but our ability to do so at any time should counter the Pan American proposal for a yacht connection."[52] His recommendation was approved by the War Cabinet. The prime minister, R. G. Menzies, had received a quite different proposal for Pacific operations on 4 April from Capt. P. G. Taylor. (In June 1939, Taylor had undertaken a remarkable survey flight across the Indian Ocean by flying boat to explore, as a defence precaution, the possibility of an alternate air route from Australia.) Menzies put

The proposal submitted by Capt. P. G. Taylor for Pacific services in April 1940 recalled his survey flight across the Indian Ocean in June 1939. This photograph was taken at the Rose Bay flying boat base prior to the departure of Taylor and his crew. The aircraft, named *Guba*, was a civil version of the US Navy PBY-1 owned by Dr Richard Archbold from the American Museum of Natural History and chartered by the Australian Government.

Taylor's proposal before the War Cabinet, with Admiral Sir Ragnar Colvin and Air Chief Marshal Sir Charles Burnett present (heads of the navy and air force). Taylor's suggestion was that the government acquire a large flying boat costing £22,000 and with a range of 4,000 miles "for the establishment of air bases in the Fiji Islands, Cook Islands, Marquesas Is., Ellice Is. and Gilbert Is." and for the purpose of carrying out air patrols and compilation of an air survey. Taylor also outlined his ideas for a trans-Pacific air service with onward links to Canada and Europe. "Captain Taylor offered his services", said the Menzies agenda item.

Neither Colvin nor Burnett approved. The service proposed was "well outside the Australian sphere of influence and . . . a dispersal of effort". Bases so established could, without adequate protection, become a potential danger. "Our strategy in war, they said, must be directed primarily towards the defence of trade and the guarding of the approaches from where the enemy is likely to come."[53] Despite condemnation by the service chiefs, the War Cabinet remained interested in the idea of an all-British route across the Pacific. On 11 July, Fairbairn wrote to the chief of Air Staff: "Subsequent to the [government] decision to purchase . . . PBY aircraft [Catalina flying boats], War Cabinet decided [Taylor] should be commissioned to combine a delivery flight of the first of the PBYs [from America] with his originally proposed survey flight."[54] To Taylor, Fairbairn confirmed the War Cabinet decision "that you should be commissioned to make the delivery flight of the first of the PBY Flying Boats which have been ordered by the Commonwealth and, in carrying out such delivery flight, undertake a survey of a proposed all-British air route across the Pacific".

On 23 September 1940, however, Edgar Johnston wrote to Fairbairn: "Air Chief Marshal Sir Charles Burnett has asked the Civil Aviation Department to arrange delivery of the PBY flying boats . . . no doubt prompted by Mr Casey's advice that crating and ocean freight would cost about $47,000 for each boat. Also that the United States require flight delivery ex-Hawaii by an Australian civil crew . . . with no armament to be carried." (The United States was, of course, not yet at war.) Captain Taylor, said Johnston, was not licensed to act as pilot of any flying boats and it had been decided in consultation with the chief of Air Staff that Qantas Empire Airways "should be asked if they could assist . . . Qantas pilots are most experienced in the operation of large flying boats and the Chief of

Air Staff is anxious to have QEA deliver them . . . in view of the probability that the Qantas organisation would be asked to undertake all necessary major maintenance and overhaul work" on arrival in Australia.[55] Johnston told the minister that QEA was eager to carry out this work and was prepared to place Capt. Lester Brain, superintendent of flying operations, in charge. (Scottie Allan, QEA's most senior and experienced pilot, had already left them for service in the RAAF.* In August 1940 he took charge of the RAAF's Rathmines Seaplane Training Flight in New South Wales, later name No. 1 O.T.U.) Referring to Taylor's idea for a trans-Pacific route survey, Johnston pointed out that "the best route for the British air service across the Pacific has already been selected and agreed by representatives of the United Kingdom, the Commonwealth and New Zealand and certain preparatory work . . . has been undertaken".

The prime minister also agreed that Qantas should be used for the PBY Catalina flying boat deliveries, if charges were reasonable. Captain Taylor would act, not as pilot, but as navigator; Captain Taylor had seen him and accepted these arrangements. Johnston said that Qantas's quotation for each delivery was reimbursement of expenses plus five per cent, to cover costs of organizing and financing. The five per cent margin was estimated at £100 to £150 per trip and was considered reasonable.[56] Johnston estimated the total delivery costs for the first seven aircraft at £2,500 to £3,000 each which compared "very favourably with the £15,000 advised by Mr Casey for crating and shipping". Johnston wrote to the chief of Air Staff mentioning a Qantas suggestion of bonuses for the crew of each flight which, he thought, his department could agree to.[57]

On the Pan American problem, Fysh told Fairbairn on 11 July that Tasman Empire Airways would find it difficult to operate an Auckland–Noumea service because of maintenance troubles and "it would certainly not be possible for them to operate from Brisbane to Noumea". QEA could, he said, easily operate a fortnightly service between Sydney or Brisbane and Noumea if it was necessary to do this in order to hold the British interest in the Pacific, "but we are hoping . . . that no such necessity arises. . . . I emphatically feel that if Pan American are allowed to operate to Australia without the

---

* There has been confusion over the spelling of Captain Allan's sobriquet, Scottie. Others have spelt it "Scotty" and it was spelt thus in the first volume. However, Captain Allan uses the "ie" ending, which is used in this volume.

American government first granting definite British rights to use the necessary American bases, plus the right to land in America when required, the Pacific will be closed to our air expansion in that direction, and the dream of a world encircling air route would have been abandoned."[58]

Fysh also wrote to Arthur Fadden (who was to become prime minister for a brief period in the following year) that QEA wanted to combat the possible danger "of Pan American forcing their way into Australia" as a result of Tasman Empire Airways being unable to handle the connecting traffic from Noumea. "We are naturally anxious that should a service come into operation between Brisbane and Noumea this should be operated by QEA", he wrote. To Pan American's president, Juan Trippe, Fysh expressed only corporate cordiality at Pan American's new air link with Auckland. He sent a message of goodwill on what he described as the opening trip of the first regular air connection between Australia and the United States across the South Pacific. "I have watched with interest and admiration the expansion of Pan American, which is a kindred movement to that carried out by BOAC, Qantas Empire Airways and Tasman Empire Airways", he wrote. "The object of this letter is to offer on behalf of the Board of Qantas Empire Airways the fullest measure of cooperation."[59] In the QEA gazette, *Empire Airways*, Fysh wrote that the American service showed the desire of American people for harmony in the Pacific and brought Sydney within seven days transit time of New York. "Sydney becomes an air junction of great importance, a halfway house on the longest continuous aerial trail in the world."[60] (In that same issue of the gazette, QEA expressed its profound regret at the death of J. V. Fairbairn, killed when an RAAF Lockheed Hudson aircraft crashed approaching Canberra airport on 13 August. Arthur Fadden became the new minister.)

McMaster maintained his national perspective on the American moves to fly into Australia. He told Fysh:

> We have, I feel, to accept realities . . . Britain has not now — and I feel will never — regain control of the seas which made for safety for Australia and the other Dominions in the past. America . . . should be encouraged to spread her interests in the Pacific and come as close as possible to Australia. The great democracies must be brought together for safety, not only for the safety of Australia and the other Dominions, but for Britain herself. Much as we may dislike this re-arrangement, it is simply an evolution that time will bring about sooner or later.[61]

24

J. V. Fairbairn, appointed Australian Minister for Air on 26
April 1939, was killed in the
crash of an RAAF Hudson
bomber near Canberra airport
on 13 August 1940.

It was a far-sighted view for the time, and one which was to
dominate Australian government perspectives for many ensuing decades. It did not, however, influence either Fysh or
Runciman, at BOAC, in their corporate view of the Pan
American ambitions.

"QEA and Australia would be rather upset if through the
complicated make-up of Tasman Empire Airways and some
touchiness on the part of New Zealand, Pan American were
enabled to cash in and operate a service between Noumea and
Sydney via Brisbane — which would hurt TEA interests to an
even greater extent than an operation by QEA", Fysh told
Runciman.[62] He was just as concerned about the Dutch. "Our
feeling here is that while the greatest degree of friendliness
should be cultivated with the Dutch, they should not be will-

ingly conceded a portion of our very basis of existence while Empire services are still able to do the job. Our experience with the Dutch shows that they are ready to take and encroach all the time, and are past masters at this without giving something in return."[63] Runciman was equally concerned. "It is important nothing be conceded . . . until definite assurance [is] obtained [for the] reversal of the United States government refusal to permit use of Hawaii and California by a British Pacific air service", he cabled Rudder. The time had arrived, he said, for Tasman Empire Airways to apply officially for the trans-Pacific service in accordance with the recommendations of the Pacific Defence Conference, in order to defend a position that seemed extremely dangerous to British interests.[64] Rudder relayed the BOAC view to Edgar Johnston and Fadden. Clearly the conflict with Pan American was now intensifying.

The chairman of the board of Pan American, C. V. Whitney, and party arrived in Australia on 5 September. Fysh told Runciman: "We found them quite disinclined to discuss any airways matters . . . Their one objective seemed to be to avoid all contact. This was, of course, plainly indicative that Pan American are not going to be content to sit down at Auckland but are doing all possible to come to Australia." McMaster, on the same day, told Fysh: "Speaking privately, I consider it most absurd that Pan American services come within seven hours of Australia but are forced to go past and make the Australian contact in New Zealand. Pan American must eventually come to Australia direct."[65] McMaster met Whitney in Brisbane and told Fysh on 9 September that he was "easy in discussion and open regarding his wishes for the extension of the Pan American services direct to Australia. It is definite", said McMaster, "that the yacht service will be placed in operation as soon as ground facilities permit. I feel we can count upon this yacht connection between Noumea and Brisbane as temporary only, for the pressure for a direct service will be too great."[66]

Runciman saw nothing absurd in resisting Pan American. "The experience of the last twenty years has shown the extreme folly of failing to stick up for ourselves in the misguided opinion that concessions will buy goodwill", he wrote from England, possibly with his country's recent experience of German diplomacy in mind.[67] (In summer skies the Battle of Britain was at its height as the German Luftwaffe planned its final, massed assault for mid-September.)

I am more than ever convinced that the precise opposite is the truth and that our relations with our friends and competitors are not only the better from our point of view, but also much more harmonious if they are based on recognising the other fellow's rights and aspirations but, at the same time, insisting firmly on our own. It is difficult not to resent the transparent manner in which the Dutch in the East Indies are seeking to cash in on their ally's misfortunes. Nobody wants to stop them from being prosperous, but they should not be allowed to do so at our expense. . . . Similarly in the Pacific, while we cannot and indeed should not try to deny to the Australian people the advantages of a South Pacific air service, here also some allowance should be demanded for difficulties occasioned by a war in which the Americans have not yet thought fit to engage themselves.

Their anxieties were partially quelled when the director general of civil aviation, A. B. Corbett, set out the official position of the Australian government on the Pan American manoeuvres in a memorandum on 12 November.

No official request has been made by the USA government or Pan American Airways to operate to Australia, but if and when made the Australian government would demand reciprocal rights in Hawaii and the United States. It is conceivable that the Australian government might not be able to maintain this position for political reasons but, in any case, it would not grant a permit without reciprocal rights without consulting the Home Government . . . [68]

There were lighter, if transient, moments for McMaster and Fysh. McMaster's doctor wrote to him from Brisbane: "In our 23,400-odd patients I think you have the unique record of paying for professional services before an account has been submitted . . . " He was encouraging on McMaster's health. "We see no reason why, with reasonable care, you should not have many years of useful citizenship, during which period your wise judgement will be of great service to the community. This is our hope and expectation."[69] Fysh, in turn, had a letter from his friend in London, C. G. Grey, founder of *The Aeroplane* magazine in 1911 and its editor for twenty-eight years. "What a fool one is to pioneer", wrote Grey. "Imagine how rich you and I might have been if we had turned our undoubted talents to plain commercial swindling instead of being idealists and trying to do things for the good of humanity. Still, it has been a lot of fun, hasn't it?"[70]

As 1940 ended, QEA's experienced ground engineer, Dudley Wright, left in early December for the United States to pre-

Arthur Fadden was appointed Minister for Air following the death of J. V. Fairbairn. Fadden is seen here with the Governor General, Lord Gowrie after being sworn in as prime minister on 29 August 1941.

pare for the delivery to Australia from the Consolidated Aircraft plant in San Diego the Catalina flying boats ordered by the Australian government. Lester Brain, in charge of the delivery programme, QEA's senior radio technician, A. S. Patterson, and P. G. Taylor joined him four weeks later (with Taylor to act as navigator) to make the first delivery flight, a flight that would be only the third in aviation history to accomplish the direct flight across the South Pacific Ocean. (Kingsford Smith and Ulm had made the first crossing from east to west, in the *Southern Cross*; Kingsford Smith and Taylor had made the second crossing, from west to east, in the *Lady Southern Cross*.)[71] In the 1941 New Year's Honours List, Fergus McMaster was created a Knight Bachelor in recognition of his long services to Australian air transport and the pastoral industry.

Pacific Precision 1941

The new year brought an urgent request from the Commonwealth government for QEA to commence a service to Dili, in Portuguese Timor, as an alternative stopping point to Koepang on the Empire route. The massive prewar Japanese commercial penetration of the Pacific area had, in October 1940, extended to Dili when they flew the first of a number of survey flights from Palau, in the Caroline Islands, using a Kawanishi flying boat. Hudson Fysh, following agreement by the Portuguese government in Lisbon in December for British landing rights, visited Dili to complete arrangements for the start of a QEA service and took the opportunity to report on Japanese activity there. He wrote to the prime minister, R. G. Menzies, after returning from Dili on the first eastbound QEA service (on the *Cambria,* with Capt. Russell Tapp in command), which left for Sydney on 21 January. (The first fortnightly service to Dili from Sydney began on 17 January 1941 with the flying boat *Coriolanus,* commanded by Captain Hussey.)

Fysh wrote:

> The Governor is apparently pro-British, but states that he must trade with whoever will buy the products of the country, and the Japanese have filled the bill in this direction . . . The Japanese penetration has been carefully planned and had been most effective, supplying the colony with a navy which it was in desperate need of . . . The Japanese at Dili are annoyed at the concessions granted the British flying boat service . . . Summarised, the Japanese can be expected to increase their hold on the country unless Australia is prepared . . . to put money [in] . . . [1]

In the United States, Lester Brain did not find it easy to have in his team the accomplished but highly individualistic P. G. Taylor. He wrote to Edgar Johnston: "I took much pains to keep peace with P. G. and succeeded in maintaining happy relations. It was not easy."[2] They had arrived in Los Angeles on 1 January, after crossing the Pacific on Pan American's Clipper service. Brain reported that Pan American extended every help and they were able to study the entire flight operation of the service. At Consolidated's main factory, in San Diego, Brain saw something of the United States's vast industrial muscle as it geared up for hostilities. Some 20,000 employees were producing Catalina flying boats (PBY5s and PBY2s) and four-engined B24 bombers at such a rate that it was difficult to find places to put them. The PBY5s were being produced at the rate of eight a week, with plans to increase this considerably. Altogether this one factory was turning out about sixty big aircraft a month, Brain reported. "In some sections," he wrote, "work on semi-complete machines was progressing in buildings still in course of erection. It is common to complete assembly in the open. At this moment there are literally acres of aircraft under construction out of doors. As far as the eye can see there are lines and lines of big, modern war planes. The sight is one I shall never forget." (Brain was impressed with the B24 wing loading which, at 56 pounds per square foot, was the highest he had ever heard of for any aircraft.)[3]

Diplomatic considerations had led to the decision that the Catalina should be delivered as a civilian operation and it was one of the conditions of purchase that each aircraft should be flown as far as Honolulu under American command, where they would then become the property of the Australian government. The Catalina aircraft that they had come to collect was not a new design but had been proved in service by the United States Navy since introduction of its predecessor, the PBY1. Engine power and loading in the PBY5 (called the Catalina after an island off the US coast) had been improved. The 24,000-pound all-up weight of the original aircraft had been improved by internal strengthening of the hull to provide a normal service loading of 27,000 pounds, an overload of 29,200 pounds, and a specially approved weight for take-off in calm water of 34,500 pounds. The small, low hull was undersized for the higher weights, Brain noted, with take-off qualities substantially affected at anything over 30,000 pounds. For

the planned departure from San Diego the weight was 32,600 pounds.

There was now a setback. Brain was told that the first Australian aircraft would not be ready until the first week in February. There were, however, four British machines waiting on the ramp to be flown away, but the delivery crew organization could not presently cope with them. Since the Australian and British machines were identical in almost every detail, even to camouflage and markings, it was suggested that Brain accept one of them. After long negotiations, Brain reported, the British authorities asked if the Australians at San Diego could take two of the aircraft immediately to Australia, one of which could remain the property of the Australian government, the other to be flown on for the British to Singapore. As Scottie Allan, now in the RAAF, was also in San Diego with RAAF radio technicians and engineers, Brain was able to agree. The two aircraft were prepared for departure on 24 January.

Unsuitable weather on 24 January postponed take-off for the following afternoon. On the morning of 25 January, however, the British decided that they were not yet ready in Singapore for the second aircraft. Rapid crew rearrangements were made and Brain reverted to his original plan. Taylor, Wright, Patterson, and Brain himself, plus three Americans made up the crew, with Scottie Allan and two RAAF sergeants as super-

The first Catalina flying boat built for the RAAF taxying at San Diego during acceptance trials in January 1941. Flown by Qantas crews, nineteen Catalinas were delivered to Australia between January and October 1941.

numeraries. At 3.40 p.m. local time on 25 January, with ten on board, the Catalina turned into a seven-knot head wind for take-off. The little hull, Brain commented, took green water over the cockpit at first but lifted into the air after a run of forty-seven seconds.

They took an indirect route for Honolulu, dictated by weather, and covered 3,000 statute miles in just over twenty-two hours, with sufficient fuel left for a further four or five hours flying. Throughout, they worked with the flight organization, radio, and meteorological facilities of Pan American, who assisted without reserve. At Honolulu they were joined by Capt. Orme Denny as co-pilot, and the Americans left them. Their route now took them via Canton Island and Noumea to Sydney. There were, said Brain, no mechanical troubles. "The engine cowlings and wing were spotless on arrival in Sydney, in marked contrast to the British engines of similar type, which have four to six times the oil consumption and throw oil and grease all over the place."[4] Taylor's navigational work was "tireless, methodical and efficient", he commented, while his own flying task was relieved by Captains Allan and Denny. (Denny left them at Noumea to return to Honolulu to command the next delivery flight.) Brain thought the aircraft was well fitted out for the crew, with an electric stove on which water could be boiled, four comfortable bunks, and lockers. Smoking was allowed anywhere on board. Though the trip was without incident, Brain noted: "It need scarcely be pointed out that for an arrival at night in a minute coral island such as Canton, a crew is absolutely dependent on radio to guide the aircraft in ... It is highly recommended that duplicate radio transmitters and receivers be installed." The flight marked the beginning of a sustained programme in which nineteen Catalinas were flown across the Pacific without incident. (Lester Brain commanded the last of these delivery flights, which arrived in Sydney on 22 October 1941.)

The generous help and co-operation of the American airlines in general were contrasted with the attitude of the Dutch in a letter from Runciman to Fysh. Referring to "that narrow commercialism which we find too often associated with the reputation of the Dutch", he wrote:

> Difficult as it is to bear with patience what at times seems an almost unscrupulous exploitation of the position by Pan American, it is nevertheless true that the airlines in the United States are being asked to make, and are willingly making, considerable

sacrifices to provide transport and other aircraft for the Imperial Air Forces. Nobody, as you and I well know, can drive harder bargains than the Americans, but we are finding here that once their generous instincts are aroused, no one can give more without asking anything in return.

Runciman added that everyone there was "deeply stirred by the magnificent exploits of the Australian troops in Crete".[5]

Pan American had, indeed, not slackened in their efforts to fly into Sydney and had brought in the heavy guns of their government. The Australian Department of External Affairs was concerned, and forwarded to the prime minister, who was then in London, a cable received from the Australian minister, Casey, in Washington.

> As you know, the question of our granting landing rights in Australia to Pan American Airways has been the subject of many representations on behalf of Pan American and has frequently been referred to by the State Department. According to instructions, I have always replied that Australian landing rights are dependent on reciprocal landing rights at Hawaii being granted when requested.
>
> There are signs that our standing fast on this attitude is having the effect of magnifying the whole question and it is possibly doing us harm in other and more important directions. Whilst the subject as such has not been officially raised with me lately, our virtual refusal to reopen the question has been brought into conversation on more important matters by the Secretary of State . . . The implication has clearly been that whilst we are seeking very whole-hearted American co-operation in certain future eventualities, at the same time we steadily refuse to grant landing rights in Australia, despite their importance from a defence point of view. Compared with the great issues that are at stake, I submit that this matter is relatively trivial . . . In any event, we cannot want reciprocal landing rights until after this war. When we emerge successfully from this war I am inclined to believe that America will have no scruples in granting us landing rights in Hawaii and denying them to Japan. I think it is significant that the United States has freely co-operated in facilitating the flight delivery of Catalinas across the Pacific . . . [6]

The director general of civil aviation, Corbett, advised his minister (and acting prime minister), Fadden, that Casey "has stated a case which is, in my opinion, correct because of the changes in relationship between the United States and the British Empire, and the time has come to settle this matter which is of grave importance to Australia". Fadden cabled the prime minister in London:

> For reasons of high policy touched on in Casey's telegram, Cabinet has been considering desirability of reopening question

of extension of Pan American Airways South Pacific service to Australia. As you are aware, the Commonwealth government, besides maintaining reciprocity in landing rights as basic principles of policy in this matter, has also consistently held the attitude that an approach for extension of the Pan American service could only be entertained if made by the United States government. Furthermore, we have regarded ourselves as fully bound by agreement confirmed at Wellington Conference April 1939 for consultation between United Kingdom, Commonwealth and New Zealand governments on matters affecting trans-Pacific services.

Fadden asked Menzies to raise the question with appropriate United Kingdom authorities and explain that

the Commonwealth government considers that it would be of advantage to intimate of its own accord to the United States government that it is ready to discuss extension of Pan American service to Australia. Such an offer would preserve the condition that the granting of terminal rights in Commonwealth territory would be conditional on reciprocity in United States territory on behalf of any future British trans-Pacific service [but] ... the United States government could be given to understand that for various practical reasons rising out of present war conditions, such a service could naturally not be established for some time ...

Fadden pointed out that this new initiative was an advance on Australia's side "in that we have hitherto taken the line that approach should come from the United States government itself".[7]

The prime minister replied on 26 April that Britain was agreeable, providing that New Zealand was safeguarded by stipulating that Pan American should operate alternately to an Australian and New Zealand terminal; that negotiations be between the governments; and that the initiative would come not from Australia but from the United States.[8]

Fergus McMaster now became much more directly and closely linked with acting prime minister Fadden's party organization by accepting the presidency of the Queensland Country National Party. He did so with misgivings, writing to A. E. Rudder on 8 May:

This so close linking of myself in politics could have possibly an embarrassing effect should there be a change of Commonwealth Government on strictly party political lines ... I did not know that the move was contemplated by the Queensland United Australia Party–Country Party parliamentarians. A special messenger called on me on behalf of the Acting Prime Minister and the whole of the parliamentarian [sic] members concerned, asking me to accept the presidency of the new organisation. I refrained to accept

[*sic*], giving primarily my health as a reason. Later in the day a further deputation waited on me and I also received a telegram from Mr Fadden asking as a personal favour for me to accept, if only temporarily, the position. Under the circumstances . . . I feel that to stand out in the face of this personal appeal . . . would not be doing the right thing in our Company's interests.[9]

The first American built aircraft to be purchased by Qantas reached Sydney in June 1941. It is seen here leaving the Sydney wharf area for Mascot airport. The Lockheed 10A had been previously owned by an American manufacturing company and carried the name *Que Sera Sera* on the nose.

Although Qantas Empire Airways had begun a new service to Dili in Timor as part of the Empire route, and was now fully involved on the important Catalina delivery programme, there were other developments closer to home. QEA's provision of maintenance for the Horsehoe route flying boats had been eased by the transfer from Hythe, England, to Durban of BOAC's workshops, but the Qantas workshops at Rose Bay, Mascot, and Archerfield (Brisbane) had been increasingly occupied with maintenance and servicing work for the RAAF. Staff numbers had risen to 409 and a new through service from Brisbane to Darwin was inaugurated on 3 July 1941 to alleviate a bottleneck caused by increased overseas traffic commitments on the flying boat service.[10] Negotiations for the new Darwin service, mainly involving QEA secretary Harman and chief accountant Turner, had been underway since February. It was to use the Lockheed 10A aircraft, bought by QEA for US$41,250. The Lockheed 10A could carry ten passengers and a crew of two at 180 miles per hour and marked the company's first operation of a non-British aircraft. Agree-

35

Qantas's first American built aircraft, the Lockheed 10A, being assembled at Mascot airport Sydney in June 1941. Lester Brain is standing behind the port engine, discussing the assembly operation with a ground engineer.

Lockheed 10A *Inlander* at Archerfield airport, Brisbane on 3 July 1941

ment had been reached on 15 May between Edgar Johnston (as chairman of the government's subsidy committee) and C. O. Turner on a total subsidy for QEA's inland routes for Brisbane–Mt Isa, Brisbane–Darwin, and Cloncurry–Norman-ton of £22,327 per annum, a modest increase of £1,675 over the previous contract. The Lockheed was to do a weekly ser-vice to Darwin and the QEA DH86 aircraft was to replace the DH90 on a twice-weekly service between Brisbane–Cloncurry

and Mt Isa. "Both from a national point of view and that of the company's progress, the . . . [Darwin] service is felt to be of the greatest importance", Fysh wrote in his June managing director's report.

Dutch persistence in their efforts to gain access to Australian passenger traffic and airmail increasingly angered McMaster.

> The pressures which they have exercised directly and indirectly on our Government and private members of the Government, and through our Press, have been absolutely improper . . . [Their] service to Australia is purely commercial and [without] the intention to assist the Empire. I definitely feel [they] are not playing a clean, fair, international game. It is a different matter regarding the Pan American service, where that service comes to within 900 miles of Brisbane and is debarred entry to Australia. Although I favour Pan American coming to Australia, that company is not the United States Government and no doubt Pan American . . . will urge for every worthwhile concession, and we do not want to be asleep.[11]

He had the opportunity to put his views to Prime Minister Menzies, who visited Brisbane from 20 to 23 August. "As President of the political organisation here, I have the responsibility of looking after the Prime Minister and the arrangements", he told Harman.[12] Runciman appreciated this political link. "The Pacific question is not easy, particularly in view of Pan American's expansionist attitude and the opportunities which the war has given them", he wrote. "I am glad that you have been able to ensure that the right people in Australia are correctly informed on these matters."[13]

McMaster's close political contact with the federal government was, however, to end abruptly. Five days after his visit to Brisbane, on 28 August 1941, the prime minister announced his intention to resign. There were, Menzies said in a public statement, differences of opinion within the government parties that might not exist under another leader; many of his Cabinet colleagues felt he was unpopular with large sections of the press and the people and this handicapped the effectiveness of the government.[14] Menzies expressed his readiness to serve under Arthur Fadden, leader of the Country Party, who formed a ministry on 29 August (with Menzies holding the portfolio of defence co-ordination). The Fadden ministry survived only throughout September but was defeated during budget discussions with the help of two independent Victorian members. John Curtin, leader of the Australian Labor Party, was commissioned on 3 October to form a government. Curtin

The RAAF impressed another two of Qantas's Empire flying boats in mid 1940 for use by No. 11 Squadron based at Port Moresby. They were *Coogee* and *Coolangatta* and they joined the former BOAC boats *Centaurus* and *Calypso*, searching for German surface raiders off North Eastern Australia. This photograph of *Coolangatta* taking off from Port Moresby in late 1941 shows the bomb aiming cupola installed in place of the mooring hatch door in the nose and two 500 pound (227 kg) bombs beneath the wing.

himself took on the additional portfolio of defence co-ordination, so briefly held by R. G. Menzies. The new minister for civil aviation was Arthur Drakeford. (Labor continued in government until December 1949, with important consequences for Qantas and Australian domestic civil aviation.)

On 8 August Corbett had warned Fysh that "in the event of hostilities with Japan occurring without warning, flying boats west of Darwin will be recalled to Darwin and those between Darwin and Sydney will be recalled to Sydney". The maintenance of air communication with Singapore was considered of primary importance, said Corbett, and Qantas services to Singapore should be continued until it becomes impossible to operate owing to enemy action. "It may be necessary . . . for Qantas to carry on to Calcutta or other Indian port to link up with BOAC, proceeding there by an alternative route omitting Singapore."[15] Corbett told Fysh that the Netherlands East Indies government had granted permission to land at Sabang, Sibolga, Padang, and Benkoelen, if the route had to be diverted. (QEA in August carried out a survey of a reserve route through the Andaman Islands from Rangoon through Port Blair and Sabang to Singapore.) On 15 August, Corbett modified his instructions.

> The Chief of Air Staff has informed me . . . that flying boats actually at Singapore on the outbreak of hostilities with Japan should continue their journeys eastward or westward as long as the routes remain open, but if the westward route is closed from Sydney, flying boats at Singapore should be instructed to return to Australia. The only circumstances under which flying boats

could come under the orders of the Commander-in-Chief Far East would be when no possible return route to Australia remains available.[16]

Corbett also had time to write a tart note of criticism. "I understand that at least one flying boat on the Qantas service has been stripped of interior fittings and that the results are very seriously inconveniencing passengers on long journeys. The resulting cold and noise is stated to make this stripped aircraft very inferior to KNILM for passenger service. You will recall that this Department did not approve of this procedure."[17] Fysh replied that Qantas had "had practically no complaints" and that almost the whole fleet had been stripped (with the work in the main carried out at Durban). Stripping, he said, allowed "something like 600 lb extra for the carriage of mails, passengers or freight . . . and is a worthwhile contribution to the war effort".[18]

Fysh, with no little optimism, arranged discussions with Harman, Brain, Baird, and Turner on possible postwar air route operations to and from Australia if the war should end quickly. There would, he said, be thousands of aircrew available, large stores of bombers and equipment, and unprecedented demand for travel.[19] Lester Brain, however, had seen promise of a revolutionary new civil airliner in the United States. "The outstanding machine apparently being developed for post-war commercial use is the Lockheed Constellation. This I understand to be a four-engined pressure cabin landplane, said to have a range of 4,000 miles with sixty-four passengers." Fysh had some mild criticism of his senior engineer, Arthur Baird's, organizing abilities. "He has had a great deal on hand and is doing great work," wrote Fysh to his chairman, "but I am still acutely up against the old trouble with him, which is organisation. There is a lot of wheedling and battling going on at the moment in an attempt to get him to install and organise [Dudley] Wright as his Number 2, and so relieve him of some of the pressure, but I am not finding it easy."[20]

Fergus McMaster was now asked to attend the modest wartime ceremony that would confer on him his knighthood. He wrote to Fysh:

I have received a letter from the secretary to the Governor-General asking me to be present at Admiralty House, Sydney on Saturday 27 September at 10.45 a.m. when His Excellency will be pleased to confer the accolade of a Knight Bachelor upon me. Owing to the war, the ceremony has been made a very simple one and supporting knights are not required; and, further, the recipient may be accompanied by two relatives or friends only. Edna [his wife] is to attend the ceremony with me and I am asking J. A. J. Hunter, but if he is unable I would sincerely wish you to be with me. [J. A. J. Hunter, MHR was one of McMaster's principal helpers in establishing the early Qantas.] We have had a long association and it is principally due to that association that the honour has been conferred.[21]

McMaster told the shareholders of Q.A.N.T.A.S. on 14 October that Qantas Empire Airways was playing an important part in assisting the war needs of Australia. Four of the company's flying boats, with highly trained crews to operate them, had been taken over by the government. The company had also, on behalf of the government, been doing overhaul and maintenance work on aircraft and engines at Rose Bay, Mascot, and Archerfield workshops. The Catalina delivery programme had been undertaken and, because the war had left BOAC short of flying staff, QEA had agreed to provide aircrews to operate a through service from Sydney to Karachi from 16 October, a distance of 8,000 miles. He warned that the competitive spirit in civil aviation had not been dulled by the war and that the various members of the Commonwealth would have to stand together on the operation of the main trunk routes.[22] Two weeks later, Fysh was able to report to Air Chief Marshal Sir Charles Burnett, chief of Air Staff: "With the arrival of Captain L. J. Brain at Rose Bay on the morning of the 23rd, in command of a Catalina flying boat, the last of these deliveries has been completed. Captain Brain was placed in charge of the delivery operations . . . and commanded on four deliveries, including the first and last. The deliveries have gone off with clockwork precision."[23] Burnett replied expressing the great appreciation of the Air Board and himself: "[It] reflects great credit on the company and those concerned."

Australia now received its greatest ever shock to its security as two seemingly impregnable bastions of defence were stripped of credibility. Both the fortress Singapore and the might of the Royal Navy were to be humbled by Japanese arms.

In Singapore, on 2 December, British troops took up their battle stations as reports of heavy Japanese troop movements by sea were received. Unaware of what lay ahead, Hudson Fysh left Sydney by flying boat on 4 December for talks in Singapore with Walter Runciman. On 7 December, the Japanese attacked Pearl Harbour and the United States entered World War II. At 4.14 a.m. on 8 December, Fysh was awoken

By December 1941, only two of the original six Qantas Empire flying boats delivered in 1938 remained in Australian registration markings. These were VH-ABA *Carpentaria* and VH-ABF *Cooee*; both were operating on the Horseshoe Route between Sydney and Durban. *Cooee* is shown on the slipway at Singapore carrying the red, white and blue stripes required for recognition when flying near war zones.

in Raffles Hotel by the noise of anti-aircraft guns and bombs falling on Singapore. On 10 December the two greatest battleships of the Royal Navy, the *Prince of Wales* and the *Repulse*, were attacked at sea by the Japanese air force and sunk. For the first time in its history, Australia was immediately and directly imperilled.[24]

Severed Links
1942

3 At the outbreak of war with Japan, Qantas Empire Airways was flying a million and a half miles a year, almost all on airline operations. By far the main route was the flying boat service between Singapore and Sydney, which carried 7,600 passengers, 260 tons of freight, and 296 tons of mail in 1941. Though the QEA service was to Singapore, QEA crews were assisting BOAC by flying through to Karachi, 8,062 miles from Sydney. (Commanders operating the route were L. J. Brain, W. H. Crowther, H. B. Hussey, O. D. Denny, R. B. Tapp, C. R. Gurney, L. R. Ambrose, E. C. Sims, A. A. Koch, R. S. Adair, O. F. Y. Thomas, W. B. Purton, and S. K. Howard. M. Millar of Mansfield & Co. was in charge of operations at Singapore.) Airline staff had grown to over 400, from the 290 employed when war with Germany was declared. With the Japanese advance, the company was now to lose its main route and most of its flying boats. It would be left with two flying boats for its own operations and two chartered to the RAAF. Increasing pressure from the air force to take over even the two remaining aircraft threatened QEA with virtual extinction.[1]

QEA calls at Bangkok and Penang were eliminated immediately following the Japanese bombing of Singapore. On 11 December, Fysh received instructions to implement a withdrawal plan which omitted the Burma coast and operated Rangoon–Port Blair–Sabang–Medan–Singapore. (Air raids on Medan made it unattractive and most commanders operated direct from Sabang to Singapore. Dili was abandoned as a stopping place, the last service calling there on 6 December.)

Contact was established in Singapore with the Royal Air Force headquarters that controlled the area between Rangoon and the Darwin area. As the time of full moon was close, the RAF recommended that night stops and dawn operations at Singapore be avoided when possible. QEA commanders were given full discretion to modify their Rangoon–Batavia schedule. Fysh flew out of Singapore on 14 December for Batavia, where arrangements were made with KLM and KNILM to share all mail and other loadings available to maximize their joint effectiveness.[2] Fysh left for Sydney on 21 December and found time to write a personal note to McMaster. "We have been together a long time and we have seen Qantas grow to a grand thing", wrote. "Now we face greater difficulties than ever and I would like to say that you can rely on me to be a trier — and to back you up and the Board in every way."[3]

As the Japanese advanced down the peninsula and occupied the west coast of Malaya, Singapore and the Malacca Straits came within range of close-range air attack. The movement of ships from the docks at Singapore became uncertain. Further south on the route, Japanese advances on Kuching and the subsequent fall of Cavite and Manila were to make Batavia, where a standby QEA flying boat was stationed, vulnerable to attack. QEA crews now frequently sighted hostile aircraft and were, reported Capt. John Connolly, "in a constant state of uneasy vigilance".[4] Airmail was still carried to Rangoon and Singapore, but the load was increasingly one of arms and ammunition. Return trips from Singapore carried mainly refugee women and children.

On 6 January, a shuttle service started between Singapore and Batavia and daylight air raids on Singapore became heavy. Flying boats adopted a "funk hole" procedure when raids were in progress or threatened, and landed among the Dutch islands to the south of Singapore, waiting for an "all clear" before completing their flight. The civil airport was heavily bombed and arrangements were made to operate from the Inner Road, using Clifford's Pier, and so shorten the time that passengers would have to spend in the danger area.[5] On 15 January, the stand-by flying boat was sent from Batavia to Australia and on 26 January, staff began transferring from Singapore to Batavia. During the night of Friday 30 January, all possible British and Allied forces were moved into the island of Singapore and parts of the Johore Causeway (the connection with mainland Malaya) were blown up. Roads were barricaded; for Singapore, the end was near. On that same day, Japanese fighter aircraft shot down the QEA flying boat *Corio*, with the loss of ten passengers and three crew members.

The *Corio*, under the command of Capt. A. A. Koch and First Officer Lyne, set out from Darwin on Friday 30 January on a special flight to bring back women and children refugees from Sourabaya. Their crew was senior radio officer A. S. Patterson, purser W. G. Cruickshank, and steward S. C. Elphick and there were thirteen passengers. As they neared the shore of the island, Patterson had just completed sending a radio message when, Captain Koch reported, "we heard a peculiar rattling in the fuselage of the aircraft and at the same time saw the air become filled with tracer bullets from an aircraft attacking overhead and a batch behind . . . I opened the throttle and dived to water level, steering for the nearest beach, which was about fifteen miles away. The noise of the bullets crashing through the machine became terrific and I tried swerving . . . I continued this manoeuvre at a height of about one foot above the water." Inside the aircraft, incendiary bullets streamed through the fuselage with intermittent cannon fire. Two engines were on fire and the cabin filled with smoke. Passengers, some of them now dead, were thrown about violently by the avoiding action. The aircraft's speed fell away and Koch put it down on its badly holed planing hull. "The nose of the aircraft plunged underneath the water", he wrote, "and I was thrown over the instrument panel and out through an opening caused by the impact. I then came to the surface. The aircraft was floating with the wings . . . on the water. There were seven Japanese Zero fighters circling about 1,500 feet overhead."[6] The fighters watched for some minutes, then departed.

First Officer Lyne received a bullet graze in the neck and was also thrown clear of the aircraft. He clung to a floating basket but when he sighted Patterson, who was seriously injured with a cannon shell through the knee, he gave the basket to him. The aircraft was now burning to the waterline and Lyne set out to swim for the shore.[7] Koch and a passenger, Moore, also set out for the beach (though Koch had one injured leg). Three hours later they reached the breakers and Moore dragged Koch clear of the water, binding up his arm and leg. Some time later they were reunited with Lyne and two others passengers, Westbrook and Fisher, who had reached land. Of the eighteen people on board, seven had survived the crash but of these only five had made it to the shore. Eventually Moore reached Koepang (on the following Monday) and the small band of survivors was rescued by Dornier flying boat.

Earlier in January, Hudson Fysh had cabled Runciman at BOAC that the director-general of civil aviation had submitted to QEA far-reaching official proposals from the American government for a worldwide extension of Pan American Airway's operations. Pan American, said Fysh, were now stated to be the United States government organization providing for the military service between the United States and Sydney. Pan American now wished to provide this link by way of the Atlantic, not the Pacific. They would themselves, it was proposed, flying from the United States to Bahrain; the Dutch would fly from Bahrain to Bangalore; Pan American would fly Bangalore–Batavia; then Qantas Empire Airways would fly Batavia–Sydney. The primary objective of the service, said Fysh, was to serve US forces in the Pacific. Pan American demanded full control of traffic and scheduling, but it was understood that Qantas would otherwise still operate without alteration (though under an agreement with Pan American). "In the absence of any counter proposals from the Air Ministry," said Fysh, "the Australian government is fully behind the scheme."[8]

Runciman had his suspicions about the Pan American objective. "The Americans seem to have made up their minds that they will not be able to re-open the Pacific route effectively . . . for some time to come", he wrote. "They are giving much attention to connecting Australasia with the U.S. via the South Atlantic, Africa and India . . . Our Pan American friends are still a little too keen on pushing commercial advantage under the guise of military necessity."[9] Runciman received a report from BOAC's John Brancker (in charge of the India and Burma regions) that the United States, using Pan American as its instrument, planned a world service using Qantas on the Java–Australia link. The sympathy of the Australian government (with Britain) had been lost, Brancker said, due to the complete lack of constructive proposals from the Air Ministry. "I suggest vigorous action be taken to preserve the identity of QEA and ourselves. It appears Pan American are taking the opportunity of forcing the issue as quickly as possible in order to secure all available aircraft for American supply purposes. If the scheme as suggested by PAA is adopted, they will inevitably destroy the identity of other operators, securing rights and prestige at the end of the war."[10]

McMaster was quick to point out to the minister for civil aviation, Arthur Drakeford, that such a Pan American domination might deprive Australia of the ability to support the Australian forces, which had no other long-distance aircraft available.[11] Drakeford countered:

> I realise your apprehension . . . but the war makes it necessary to deal with facts as they exist — not as we should like them to be. The U.S. government needs a ferry service from the United States to Australia for the prime purpose of supplying munitions to the U.S. armed forces assisting in the defence of this country . . . The U.S. government purchased the whole of PAA's fleet. It is proposed to use Qantas and BOAC to supply one section, from Java to Australia. The Commonwealth government will, in agreement with the U.S.A., use Qantas to operate that portion of the service from Java to Sydney. Pan American will issue instructions as to priority of loading, frequency of operation, and general traffic management to fit into the whole scheme, but Qantas will continue to operate as an entire organisation and continue to own its own aircraft etc. In that respect, Qantas is better off than Pan American . . . The interests of your company will be carefully watched by the Commonwealth Government and, when the war is won, your company will . . . still be intact.[12]

On the same day that the minister wrote so bluntly to McMaster, his departmental head wrote in even more authoritarian terms to Fysh.

> There is no Pan American project to be considered [said Corbett haughtily]. It is a U.S. Army project . . . I assume the co-operation of Qantas. If that is not forthcoming, the service will still operate . . . I know you have always wanted to do something worth while in the war effort. Surely this is a great opportunity. Can you think of anything more vital to the defence of Australia than this [US] service pouring munitions and men in as fast as possible. Let us first win the war, and we will get on the with the prestige business later.[13]

(Fergus McMaster later made handwritten comments on this Corbett letter: "Corbett was assured time after time that QEA would co-operate fully but would not sell itself to either Pan American or Australian National Airways." The statement that the projected US service was no Pan American project was, wrote McMaster, found to be incorrect. "Corbett was always up against QEA. To perhaps be unjust, both Mr [Harold] Gatty representing Pan American, and Holyman [ANA] entertained him a lot and it was common understanding that the three — Corbett, Gatty and Holyman — worked as a team in so far as Corbett could, for I threatened him at one stage to get

46

the whole position [aired] at Canberra, and I had many friends there."

There was, indeed, a first class row in progress. Fysh replied to Corbett on 16 January assuring him that QEA would do anything in its power to further the war effort.

> Sir Fergus McMaster is a man who has the highest sense of patriotic and moral duty . . . QEA are in the hands of the Government in these matters but as a company we obviously cannot move till we have heard from British Airways [*sic*], with whom we have a contract . . . The proposed military service which envisages use of not only QEA but BOAC flying boats and equipment has the very greatest bearing on any plans which may have been formulating in London for a continuance of the Empire Service.[14]

Corbett now wrote a personal and confidential letter to Fysh hoping "it will assist you in gaining a clear picture of the present position and its difficulties and that it will help you to avoid adding to those difficulties". (McMaster's comment on this letter was that "it was Corbett who was adding to the difficulties".) The plans for setting up the US ferry service were proceeding, as far as the United States and Australia were concerned, wrote Corbett with finality. "It is recognised that the [UK] Air Ministry could withdraw BOAC support but to do so would create a situation which would be extremely tense . . . I shall . . . use whatever influence I have to override with complete ruthlessness any difficulty which might retard armed assistance to this country at the present time. This is no time for trying to pull both ways at once." (McMaster commented: "Corbett was trying to pull three ways.") Corbett told Fysh: "It is not necessary to remind you that the Government has very wide powers and means to implement the decision already made."[15]

Fysh wrote to McMaster:

> Corbett's letter is somewhat in the raw but, to be honest, there is much in what he says and I am quite certain he reflects the views of the Australian Government. If only British Airways could have secured four Catalinas the position would have been very different as they could then have guaranteed to keep the route open to Australia. I see no other alternative than for British Airways and QEA to throw all the weight they can behind the American proposals . . . I think we all agree further delay and indecision by the people in England will be fatal.[16]

(McMaster, in a pencilled comment, later wrote at the foot of Corbett's letter: "Fysh was not a good mixer or negotiator. He would leave Sydney for Melbourne in the morning and be back in Sydney that night. I often advised him to stay down in Melbourne for two or three days and get to [mix] with these people and entertain a bit, but it was not his nature, with the result that he would have his official interview with Corbett for twenty minutes or an hour and [come] back again.'')

Late in the afternoon of the day Corbett's letter was received, Fysh heard from England by cable. "Apparently the British Air Ministry have agreed in part or in whole to the USA plan", he told McMaster, "but have difficulty in transferring any further Empire flying boats to this end. Whether this means any boats in addition to what we normally have in our section [five or six boats] or any boats in addition to the two we own I am not sure."[17] It now seemed that, in effect, QEA was to become a subcontractor to Pan American and be paid by Pan American on behalf of the US government.[18] On this issue, McMaster would not, however, budge; he fought Corbett and obtained agreement that QEA should be paid through their own government.[19] Then, quite suddenly, the whole issue of the proposed Pan American service evaporated. Brancker wrote to McMaster from BOAC that the Clipper aircraft proposed for the Pan American link between Java and India were not immediately available and not likely to become so. "It seems, therefore, that . . . QEA cannot aid the war more than by carrying on as they are at present, operating services between Australia and Java", he wrote.[20] Far greater issues than air transport were now, however, looming. The Japanese southward advance was to make any ferry service through the Middle East, India, and Batavia impossible.

On 31 January, following the loss of the *Corio*, the Commonwealth government gave the order for suspension of the Batavia–Darwin section of the Empire route and for rapid reorganization, to replace it with a shorter, direct link between Tjilatjap (on the south coast of Java) and the port of Broome in Western Australia. From the beginning of February, Batavia came under air attack and flying operations down Sumatra's west coast were risky. Heavy shipping in the ports of Sabang and Padang made them attractive targets for bombing and QEA flying boats avoided them as much as possible. Flights down the coast were made at hours when the Japanese were unlikely to appear, arriving at Sibolga after 4.00 p.m. and leaving before 8.30 a.m. the following day.[21] If boats were delayed, they were hauled close inshore, where a natural break in the coral islands behind Saroedoet Island had been widened and dug out, and covered with vegetation. Sibolga was now a key point, with Port Blair and Batavia, for night stops.

On 3 February 1942, Captain Crowther left Batavia for the last shuttle flight to Singapore, timing his departure to arrive in late afternoon when all Japanese aircraft were likely to have returned to base. They flew low over the Sumatran jungle, below the level of the hills when possible, to avoid being sighted and were about half way along the route when a radio message from Singapore said there could be no guarantee of any facilities for their arrival. Crowther decided to proceed, then thought he should let his crew express their feelings. There would have been no difficulty in turning back at that moment, but all agreed to continue and their arrival at Singapore was uneventful. In the early hours of the following morning. Crowther was taken out onto the crowded harbour by the director of civil aviation to decide a take-off path that would avoid the minefields, the many ships, and the fish traps. There was just enough moonlight filtering through the clouds to provide sufficient visibility as Crowther opened the throttles and, heavy with refugees, the aircraft lifted from the water on the last flying boat service to leave Singapore.[22]

On 10 February, a strong enemy convoy was reported approaching down the South China Sea and enemy air patrols and raids were reported through the Sunda Straits and over Batavia in the early afternoon. The dangers from enemy air attack were intensifying over what remained of the tenuous air route that still inked Darwin with Karachi, though not with Singapore. (The first service from Batavia to Australia through Tjilatjap left on 8 February under the command of Captain Thomas and, two days later, Captain Denny left Sydney for Tjilatjap.) General Wavell had himself visited Singapore for three days from 11 February and it seemed increasingly clear that the island could not be held. In these hazardous conditions, on 8 February, Capt. Russell Tapp set off from Karachi for Batavia on the last through service of the Empire flying boat route. Operation of the route had by now come to depend considerably on the extra fuel carried by the flying boats, which had to land each time it was necessary to transfer this extra fuel to the aircraft tanks. Tapp's route took him to Calcutta, Akyab, and on to Port Blair and here, where there were visits by Japanese aircraft almost daily, one engine gave trouble and take-off had to be abandoned. The temperature was high and the aircraft load heavy so there was no option but to return to the mooring and to correct the trouble. (On board as a passenger was BOAC's engineer superintendent for the Malayan area.) Just after midday, a Japanese reconnaissance aircraft flew directly overhead, but nothing happened. Late in the afternoon an engine run-up was tried and seemed satisfactory. A midnight departure was decided, to allow a 6.30 a.m. arrival at Sibolga and onward passage, after refuelling, to Batavia. When take-off was attempted, there was trouble. Tapp wrote:

> To our disgust, the trouble showed up again just before we were airborne. We were forced to return to the moorings, McMillan [the BOAC engineer] got straight back to work. He had had practically nothing to eat all day but within two minutes he had his coat off, and by 4 a.m. we had a satisfactory run down the take off area. It was too early to leave as we would arrive at Sibolga during the Jap bombing of that area.

They left at 9.00 a.m. and flew out to the west of the Little Andaman Islands and Nancowry, as it was not known if the Japanese had occupied them.

> Well out to sea we continued on southward till towards evening we turned back eastward to approach Sibolga. When we were close in there was an alert at Sibolga. We turned back out to sea and, after twenty minutes or so, the all-clear was given. We approached Sibolga again and the same thing happened. Back out to sea again we went until the all-clear was given the second time. We came in for the third time, only to have the same thing happen . . . We [reached] the conclusion that we must be the cause of all these alerts.

Wondering if they would be fired at by their friends, they decided to go in but landed without incident. Next morning, when they left, they again flew westward away from the land before turning south.

> We flew on until it was time to come back to pass to the north of Java in order to enter the prescribed corridor of entry. This was difficult, as enemy aircraft were reported over the sea off the east coast of Sumatra, Padang and Benkulen. A wait was essential. Off the west coast of Sumatra there are some small islands, the southernmost called South Pagi. Here we found a little backwater called Tio Bay with light trees and vegetation on all three sides; a good place to hide a camouflaged boat. We landed and threw out an anchor.

After three hours they continued on to the Sunda Straits and passed a large convoy headed for Java. "We passed very close to a small Dutch naval vessel which had been at Batavia for some time and one we all knew well. We were very low down and as we passed by, to our amazement we were greeted with two bursts of machine-gun fire . . . " They were not hit and flew on without further incident to Batavia, ending the last through Empire service from Karachi. Tapp handed over the aircraft for its onward flight to Australia. His own instructions were to wait for another aircraft and return to Karachi. "Before I got away from Batavia," Tapp concluded, "Singapore fell and the enemy overran Sumatra, making it impossible to carry out the return flight. Eventually I took a load of passengers to Tjilatjap and then on to Broome, and passed through Darwin two days after it had suffered from its first and biggest raid."[23]

On 14 February, a message was received at Sibolga from the director of fighter operations at Bandoeing. "Fying boats are to stop at Batavia and Calcutta until further notice as parachute troops have landed at Palembang . . . Flying boats are not to proceed east of Calcutta or west of Batavia until further advised." The Empire route was broken. On 15 February, Singapore surrendered to the Japanese. On 19 February, Capt. L. Ambrose flew the last service out of Batavia for Australia via Tjilatjap and the following day QEA's headquarters were transferred to Tjilatjap from Batavia.

On that same day, 19 February, the Japanese landed at Dili in East Timor and, in bright sunlight, launched their first and heaviest air attack on Darwin. The attack was commanded by Admiral Nagumo, who had been in charge of the massive raid on Pearl Harbour, and was led in the air by Commander Fuchida, who had led the air strike at Pearl Harbour. The Japanese had assembled a powerful task force of four aircraft carriers, four heavy cruisers, and nine destroyers 220 miles northwest of Darwin. From the carriers, 188 aircraft-fighters, bombers, and dive-bombers headed in radio silence for a completely unsuspecting Darwin. From Ambon, in the Celebes, 54 land-based bombers followed them.

Captain Koch, who had commanded the *Corio* when it had been shot down near Koepang three weeks before, was a patient in the Darwin hospital that morning. He described the attack:

> There was practically no warning. I heard the sirens and the roar of the Japanese planes almost simultaneously . . . Three [bombs] landed very close. The walls shook and pieces of the ceiling fell in. One of the bombs had hit a wing of the hospital . . . After the first wave of bombers had passed I decided to make for the beach. I could only just walk . . . Some of the Jap machines were diving low and machine-gunning buildings. I could heard the crunch of bombs in other parts of the town. The machines were sweeping over ships in the harbour . . . [24]

51

The first Japanese air raid on Darwin on 19 February 1942. The Empire flying boat *Camilla* floats unscathed at her moorings while the Australian coastal trading ship *Neptuna* burns alongside the wharf. Many small vessels were strafed and sunk by attacking Japanese fighters; while *Camilla* was hidden when the smoke from *Neptuna* drifted over her. Qantas Captains Hussey and Crowther managed to fly *Camilla* clear only eight minutes before the *Neptuna* exploded.

When the first wave of bombers arrived, the QEA flying boat *Camilla* was at her moorings southeast of the jetty. More bombers followed, again attacking the crowded harbour and the town. Two big ships were burning at the wharf and thick smoke was blowing over the still undamaged *Camilla*. The jetty that led to the wharf end was severed and oil and water from broken pipes poured into the harbour. When it became known that one of the burning ships was loaded with explosives, Captains Hussey and Crowther, who had made their way to the wharf, decided to attempt to get the *Camilla* to safety. The civil aviation launch, which had been landing survivors from the bombed ships, took them out to the flying boat. A check showed that there were only two small shrapnel holes in the elevators and that all tanks were full of petrol. As Hussey inspected the hull plates below the waterline for damage, Crowther started the engines. *Camilla* began to drift towards shallow water and, after considering and quickly abandoning a plan to hide the boat in nearby mangroves, it was decided to get into the air. They took off, all four engines operating, and flew south, keeping low. Eight minutes later, the burning ship at the wharf blew up and the QEA passenger

launch and all small craft nearby were sunk. Crowther and
Hussey flew on for twenty-five miles, then decided to land on
the Alligator River. That plan, however, was abandoned almost at once when they realized that radio communication
might become difficult and fuel supplies might not get them
there. Instead, they altered course and headed for Groote
Eylandt, about 420 miles away. Crowther, who had been shav-
ing when the first bombs hit Darwin, still had dried soap
around his ears when, just after midday, they landed.

The Japanese sank nine of the forty-five ships that were in
Darwin Harbour on 19 February and severely damaged thirteen others. The jetty was shattered, two Catalina flying boats
sunk at their moorings, and many major buildings hit. At Darwin aerodrome, in the later raid by the land-based aircraft, the
RAAF headquarters, hangars, and aircraft on the ground were
all hit.

Crowther and Hussey took on 1,400 gallons of petrol at
Groote Eylandt and late in the afternoon took off for Darwin,
flying the great empty flying boat in radio silence. At Darwin
they prepared for a dawn departure with their load of passengers including Captain Koch, who had been transferred to the
flying boat base. Their flight south to Sydney was completed

The Qantas hangar at Darwin
aerodrome after the bombing on
19 February 1942.

without incident and they were welcomed by reporters, waiting anxiously for the first eyewitness accounts of the massive Japanese air strike on Australia's northernmost city.

The day after the bombing of Darwin and the escape of *Camilla*, QEA lost its DH86 airliner, RMA *Sydney*. Under Capt. C. H. C. Swaffield, the aircraft took off from Brisbane on 20 February on its usual inland service to Darwin with L. S. Marshall as copilot and seven passengers. Soon after take-off it entered heavy cloud, losing control and crashing into a timbered area, with the loss of all on board. It was the first fatal DH86 accident in QEA's seven years of intensive airline operations with the type. (The departmental inquiry into the cause of the crash was inconclusive.)

Tjilatjap was chosen as the northern terminal for the rapidly improvised shuttle service to Broome in Western Australia as the enemy advance made it impossible to use Sourabaya. (The 1,210-mile crossing, with a payload limit of 1,800 pounds, took eight hours.) Malcolm Millar, who had transferred to Tjilatjap, extracted from Bandoeing headquarters the information that Supreme Command were evacuating Java because it was not considered possible to hold it against the Japanese. An extremely powerful enemy convoy was approaching from the east towards Sourabaya or Bali. Operations were considered feasible for only another five days, ending on 27 February.

At the Australian end of the shuttle service — the remote town of Broome — communications with Sydney were poor and unreliable. An epidemic of dengue fever was rife amongst the swollen population of refugees, who had arrived from Java on American, Dutch, and QEA civil aircraft as well as on military transports. People slept where they could, distressed and anxious, and plagued by swarms of mosquitoes in the hot, humid atmosphere. Lester Brain arrived there at 4.30 p.m. on 21 February, and was met by Doug Laurie, QEA station superintendent, who had come from Darwin.

> Capt. Denny and his crew were aboard *Circe* at its moorings in the harbour [Brain noted in his diary]. They had gone aboard and were spending the night there in order to avoid having to walk out through the mud carrying their baggage next morning . . . at low tide. [There was a 32-foot rise and fall of tide at Broome.] Capts. Ambrose and Purton were at the hotel, having arrived in from Java today . . . All the evacuees are anxious to push on from Broome as quickly as possible and have brought with them an atmosphere as though the Japanese were close behind them. Most of the locals are very jittery and drinking heavily.

Brain noted that his room-mate had in his custody one of the few submachine guns available and had been instructed that the aerodrome was to be defended to the last man. "[He] assures me it will have to be the second last man since he is not waiting." News came through that all women and children were to be evacuated next day on the ship *Koolinda*. That same afternoon, Captain Howard arrived with the flying boat, *Corinthian*, from Darwin and on the following morning Captain Denny departed for Tjilatjap in *Circe*. A US Army Air Corps colonel arrived from Allied Headquarters in Java and informed Brain that he would take charge of everything in Broome, including all aircraft. Brain telegraphed Corbett who replied next day that QEA flying boats would be controlled by the department, but "the fullest co-operation with the Air Corps was desirable where possible".[25]

Although it had been the original purpose of the QEA operations from Broome to ferry in urgent war supplies for the defence of Java, it soon became evident that Java would fall, and that the flying boats' main function would be to evacuate people. Shuttle flights continued and Broome became crowded with aircraft. Brain wrote: "I shall not be surprised if all this activity brings an enemy raid." As the situation in Java deteriorated, Millar sent a signal on 26 February for two flying boats to fly out QEA staff and stores. On the same day he was advised by Java Allied Headquarters that the last QEA shuttle service should leave on 27 February. Brain telegraphed Qantas:

22 February 1942, *Coriolanus* on one of the first shuttle flights refuelling at Broome before departure for Tjilatjap in Western Java. The vessel is a pearling lugger with the masts removed and the deck stacked with fuel drums.

> Denny arrived today . . . advises that Millar received confirmation
> . . . from Bandoeing of their previous advice that 27th would be
> latest date on which our boats should cease departure . . . How-
> ever, I am confident he will remain fast until instructed otherwise
> or things collapse . . . Spirit here excellent, all staff working really
> well. Pilots argue with each other for privilege of doing next trip.
> No radio contact yet possible from here to Tjilatjap . . . We will
> carry on while ever possible. Machines now depart here empty
> and return with evacuees . . . Bandoeing has advised us cease.
> The decision now rests with Aviat . . .

Although this information was dispatched to Sydney it did not
reach Aviat (the Department of Civil Aviation).[26] There were
tragic consequences. Lester Brain continued with the shuttle
and sent *Corinthian*, under Captain Howard, and *Circe*, under
Captain Purton, out from Broome on 27 February. On the following day Captain Denny was ordered to proceed to Tjilatjap
in *Coriolanus* but was recalled to Broome after taking off when
last minute orders were received from the Department.

Corinthian and *Circe* left Tjilatjap within minutes of one
another at dawn on 28 February from a harbour that was now
almost deserted. *Circe*, with first officer M. W. Bateman, radio
officer H. G. A. Oates, purser L. J. Hogan, and sixteen
passengers on board (mostly Dutch officials and their families)
was never seen again. A brief radio message was received when
she was about two hundred miles out from Java, then silence.
(Brain sent Captains Thomas and Ambrose out in *Corinna* on
2 March in a last search for the missing boat but after ten
hours in the air they found no trace of her.[27] Captain Denny,
in another search on the preceding day, was more successful.
He located and rescued the crew of an American DC3 in *Corinthian* on an isolated part of the coast known as Vansittart
Bay, north of Broome.)

On the last two shuttle services all remaining staff except
Malcolm Millar, ground engineer C. Short, and the QEA
Sibolga agent were evacuated. These last three were later
flown to Broome by US military aircraft. In all, three Empire
flying boat services came into Broome before the regular shuttles began on 22 February and seven shuttles were operated,
including that on which *Circe* was lost. On these ten trips from
Tjilatjap, eighty-eight passengers and seven tons of cargo were
carried. QEA flying boats also carried a considerable number
of passengers on to Port Hedland and Perth and carried out
search and rescue operations along the West Australian coast.[28]
Compared with the total number of people flown out of Java,
it was a small contribution, but for the QEA staff involved it

was an exhausting and dangerous operation. (Altogether, over 7,000 people passed through Broome. There were as many as fifty-seven aircraft landings there in one day.) On one of the last QEA shuttle services, the commander of the Australian forces in Singapore, General Gordon Bennett, was flown out.

Lester Brain's forecast on 28 February of a likely air attack on Broome proved accurate. On the morning of 3 March, Japanese fighter aircraft came in from the sea under a clear sky, their tracer guns and cannons shattering the silence. Fifteen flying boats of various types, mostly Dutch Dorniers that had been flown across from Java, were at their moorings waiting to use the primitive and inadequate refuelling facilities. The people on board included many Dutch women and children who had been evacuated. They were preparing for breakfast as their aircraft swung gently at anchor. Brain, still weak from dengue fever, recorded in his diary that at 9.30 a.m. *Corinna* was being refuelled while twenty-five passengers and crew waited on the wharf with their baggage to go aboard. From his hotel he heard the gunfire. Uncamouflaged Japanese Zero fighters, gleaming silver in the sun, were diving on the undefended harbour as he headed for the waterfront. There were shouts and screams from the burning boats. "The natives are in a great panic and will not assist me to drag a row-boat down the mud to the water", he wrote. "I . . . am not strong enough to do this alone owing to fever and absence of food for some days past. Malcolm Millar [Mansfield & Co] appeared at the right moment and between us we get [it] into the water. The Japs have finished off all the flying boats now and are proceeding over to the land aerodrome . . . " Half a mile from shore, Brain saw heads bobbing in the water and heard cries for help from a group of Dutch people. "We got the woman and baby, also the boy and three of the most exhausted men aboard the row boat and the remaining four men clung to the edge", wrote Brain. "We could not handle any more so returned to the nearest mangrove beach."[29]

The leading Japanese fighter had selected the flying boat *Centaurus* (under charter to the RAAF) as target and it burst into flames. The QEA boat, *Corinna,* was being refuelled by Captain Mathieson; Captain Ambrose was at the end of the jetty with the passengers. Ambrose later described what happened:

All hands were involved in attempts to rescue those who had already been loaded on to many of the flying boats . . . Evacuees included many Dutch women and children and although I have

57

little praise for the people of Broome who fled from their town by any means possible at the commencement of the raid, crews and other personnel involved in the evacuation teams deserve full commendation for the desperate efforts made to save personnel from drowning or being burnt to death as they struggled vainly to escape from spreading, flaming fuel which, in pouring from holed tanks, quickly formed a blazing scum on the surrounding sea. A Liberator bomber took off just as the raid began but fell a blazing wreck into the sea about eight miles off the coast . . . the sole survivor, a U.S. army sergeant, swam ashore thirty hours later. Seventy people were brought ashore, but many were already dead, and few had hope of survival due to extensive third degree burns . . . [30]

The Japanese destroyed all the flying boats in the harbour and six landplanes at the aerodrome, as well as the Liberator that managed to get airborne. A Douglas DC3 was shot down sixty miles north of Broome. A later estimate of the total loss of life was seventy, though many of the names of the Dutch civilians who died were not known. (Twenty-nine unidentified dead were buried in Broome cemetery.) There were no QEA casualties.

About one hour after the departure of the Japanese, *Camilla*, under Captain Sims, arrived at Broome. Sims had been on a rescue mission to pick up twenty-five passengers from the SS *Koolama*, which had been bombed and had run ashore on the coast west of Wyndham. Because of Brain's foresight he had been instructed not to return to Broome before 11.00 a.m., when it was anticipated that the second QEA flying boat, *Corinna*, would have left for Sydney. Brain had foreseen the danger of having two boats at Broome simultaneously and his foresight saved *Camilla* (aided by Sims's caution in flying an inland detour when he heard by radio that Broome had issued an air raid warning). Sims landed in the devastated harbour and was, wrote Captain Ambrose, "encouraged to taxi up a very inadequate creek. He knocked the extreme end of his wingtip on the mast of a lugger in so doing . . . Bill Bennett and I hand-pumped enough fuel for him to fly to [Port] Hedland."[31] Sims took wounded and other evacuees with him and returned to Broome on the following day to fly out Qantas, British Airways, and US Navy personnel.

Brain wrote in his diary:

The town is almost deserted this morning. Many people have packed their belongings and moved out permanently, heading south in a so-called "land convoy". Actually their convoy is a nervous rabble and includes a number of American deserters . . .

Many other townsfolk, particularly those with official or semi-official positions in Broome, have evacuated themselves from the town area for the day . . . This latter group comprises most of the more responsible citizens . . . These evauations were a surprising indication of the demoralising effect of air raids on the Australian public . . . I have always credited the man out back with possessing more moral courage than city folk. The result was that the town was undefended at its most vital points and practically deserted, except for the American troops awaiting evacuation by air.[32]

By 5 March, all the Americans had been evacuated.

After a trip south to Perth with wounded, *Camilla* returned to Broome on 7 March and next day flew Lester Brain and other Qantas staff to Port Hedland and south to Perth. Brain found that the capital city of Western Australia was in a poor state.

Lester Brain holds a piece of the steel structure from the Qantas hangar recovered after the air raid on 19 February 1942. Damage from bomb splinters and blast indicates that this section was part of the hangar door, blown outwards by a bomb which had come through the roof and exploded on the hangar floor.

> Perth [he wrote] had become a bottleneck, with people streaming in by air and sea, and all rail services to the eastern States booked out for weeks ahead . . . The general atmosphere is depressing. The streets and hotels are crowded with men, mostly in uniform — Americans, Dutch, English and Australian . . . many are without equipment and belongings. They are like a forgotten legion, without money, not knowing where they are heading for. Each of the services — Navy, Army, Air Force and Americans — is claiming priority for its own.[33]

He found a place for himself in a DC3 of Australian National Airlines and returned to Sydney.

The fall of Singapore and the withdrawal from Java had severed completely the Empire air route which had been the very basis of Qantas operations. The airline had lost three flying boats — *Corio, Circe,* and *Corinna* — by enemy action. Two more, *Centaurus* and *Coogee,* had been lost while under charter to the RAAF (one in the attack on Broome, the other in a landing accident at Townsville). All that were left were the *Camilla, Corinthian,* and *Coriolanus.* The airline operations of Qantas had been reduced to the Brisbane–Darwin landplane route and other minor services in Queensland.

An Obscure and Weak Position 1942

In only three months of war, the Japanese had been victorious at Pearl Harbour, and in Malaya, Singapore, Burma, and the Netherlands East Indies. Rabaul had fallen on 23 January and Japanese forces were advancing on Port Moresby, in New Guinea. Even before the attack on the American fleet at Pearl Harbour, Australians had been shocked by the sinking of HMAS *Sydney* in November 1941 by the German raider *Kormoran* only a few hundred kilometres northwest of Fremantle, with the loss of all those on board. Then, two weeks after the air raid on Darwin, another Australian warship, HMAS *Perth*, was lost in the Battle of the Java Sea. Britain, it was apparent, could no longer be regarded, as it had been since British settlement, as the powerful and reliable protector of Australian sovereignty. Old certainties had suddenly vanished; Australia, which had sent its own best fighting troops to the Middle East to help Britain, could expect no help now from the Mother Country. As the Japanese thrust south over the Owen Stanley Range in New Guinea towards Port Moresby, Australia faced the real and imminent threat of invasion and occupation. There was a pressing requirement for all available air transport to supply the front line areas.

The flying boats that remained were now, with the ending of the shuttle service, operated for the Department of Civil Avaiation, mainly between Sydney, Brisbane, and Darwin, carrying military loads. (There were fifteen special Darwin charters in March and April.) The Brisbane–Darwin landplane service, which had been operated by a Dragonfly air-

4

QEA Dragonfly at Batchelor, sixty miles (96.5 km) south of Darwin, while on charter to the US Army. The Dragonfly was based at Daly Waters about two hundred miles (321.8 km) further to the south. Taken in late 1942.

craft, the Lockheed 10 and the DH86 *Sydney* until the crash of the latter, was augmented by QEA DH86s that had been commandeered by the RAAF but were now lent back to the airline. (Three DH86s were delivered to QEA at the end of March but one of these was given back to the RAAF in May.) The old service frequencies were cancelled and, to maximize the military traffic, all stops were eliminated except those needed for refuelling. The inland Cloncurry–Daly Waters weekly service with Dragonfly aircraft was operated to all intermediate stops and the weekly service between Cloncurry and Normanton continued without interruption. A QEA Dragonfly was established at Daly Waters for use by US Army officials and at Cloncurry a Fox Moth light aircraft was used for US Army patrols of supply line roads across north Australia to Darwin. Because of the rapid drive south by the Japanese it was decided that a reserve flying boat base, in addition to that at Rose Bay, was needed and in March, in a *Seagull* amphibian lent to QEA by the RAAF, Lester Brain made a survey of possible sites. Lake Boga, fed by the waters of the Murray River that divided Victoria and New South Wales, was chosen. (Qantas were never to use Lake Boga but it became an import-

ant RAAF flying boat and overhaul centre, commanded for a considerable time by Captain Scottie Allan.)

With the breaking of the Empire route to England, the Australian Civil Aviation Department assumed financial responsibility for the operations of Qantas, though much of the work was to be done for (and paid for by) the US forces through the department. Harold Getty, who headed the Allied Directorate of Air Tranpsort, now pressed again for exclusive control over the operation of all QEA flying boats and civil aircraft. However, at a meeting on 4 March in Melbourne at which QEA, the department, the RAAF, and BOAC were represented, it was decided that as Australia's own forces were without effective air transport, control should continue under the Civil Aviation Department.[1] The new financial basis for all QEA flying, and for the planned expansion of engine and aircraft overhauls and repairs for the Department of Aircraft Production, was to be one of cost-plus. The agreement between QEA and BOAC was considered suspended as of 19 February 1942. BOAC's chief secretary, B.N. Gilpin, wrote to McMaster:

One of QEA's Fox Moths in north-west Queensland, late 1942. The heavy camouflage was a necessary precaution in the early years of the war. The upper surfaces of the wings are devoid of markings; the prewar red, white and blue stripes on the tail have had the red section removed and even the registration letters on the sides are difficult to see from a distance.

> Unhappily the Empire service has now been broken [and] we have to face the consequences of that break in the arrangements that have been in force between our two organisations and their respective governments. As you know, we are not free agents at the present time but are required to operate our aircraft to the requirements of the Secretary of State for Air. The Air Ministry is not prepared to let us continue our paymens to QEA as before, in

view of the changed circumstances on the Empire route; this seems also to be the attitude of your government, which discontinued from 19 February the subsidy and mail payment which you passed on to us. The unescapable conclusion is that our mutual agreements are, by a ruling of higher authority, suspended until the Empire route to Australia has been restarted. You can be sure that we dislike intensely this rupture . . . [2]

An internal BOAC memorandum to departmental heads noted: "Should circumstances arise where the Qantas organisation could not be usefully employed, the whole question would be reviewed, but the present arrangements may be considered as very satisfactory from the Corporation's point of view."[3]

On 22 March, on a charter flight to Darwin, one of the three surviving QEA flying boats crashed on landing and was completely wrecked. The *Corinthian* was under the command of Captain Ambrose, with Captain Tapp acting as first officer. There were twelve passengers on board, all US personnel, and a heavy military load of gun barrels, ammunition chests, tripod legs, and reels of insulating wire. A normal approach was made about one hour after midnight. Conditions for landing were good, said Tapp, though it was possible that Ambrose was blinded by a searchlight as *Corinthian* appeared to fly unchecked straight into the water.[4] (Both Ambrose and Tapp were highly experienced pilots and no blame was attached to either for the accident.) Hudson Fysh wrote that the landing was made a long way short of the laid-down flare path and, almost immediately on touching down, the planing hull of the aircraft broke up and it capsized. The most likely cause of the accident, he said, was that the flying boat struck some semi-submerged object, with a shift of the heavy load being a contributing cause.[5] A rescue launch picked up survivors almost at once, but two were missing, believed trapped in the rapidly sinking hull. Tapp, with great courage, re-entered the water and swam in the darkness into the interior of the subsiding wreck but the two bodies were never found.[6] Ambrose was seriously hurt on impact but Tapp and the other survivors suffered only superficial injuries. QEA was now left with two Empire flying boats.

With only the remnants of the original flying boat fleet, Hudson Fysh felt keenly what he believed was a broken undertaking by the government. When, early in the war, he wrote, four Qantas flying boats were placed under charter to the RAAF, "it was a definite undertaking that these aircraft would be handed back to the company on delivery of the nineteen Catalina flying boats. This promise has never been honoured and the company has been placed at a great disadvantage."[7] He also believed, in view of the nature of QEA operations, that Qantas aircrews and some heads of departments should be granted RAAF rank "or at the very least one or two of us at the top [should be]". QEA, though operating under the heading of commercial aviation, should, he wrote, really have been styled "air transport" as for practical purposes their activities were wholly of a military nature.[8] In a letter to Air Chief Marshal Sir Charles Burnett he pointed out that Harold Gatty had been appointed a group captain. Perhaps, he said, a useful start could be made by granting rank "to those of us who are on the RAAF Reserve now. I am afraid, however, that some of the ranks are very low in respect of the jobs that have been done. Captain Brain, Mr Baird and myself would need ranks higher than those under which we appear on the reserve list." If this was not acceptable, wrote Fysh, he suggested honorary rank.[9] "We have all given long service to aviation and several people such as Kingsford Smith and Ulm in the past have been accorded honorary RAAF rank." The official reply to this request, from Air Vice-Marshal G. Jones (now chief of Air Staff) stated:

> Those Qantas people on the RAAF reserve could not be permitted to wear uniform unless called up for service. It boils down to this; an organisation must be either civil or a service organisation. We cannot have an organisation which is half and half. There will, of course, be occasions when your staff, even though not called up for service, could be permitted to wear uniform . . . We would have to be very careful, though, in granting such authority.[10]

Though seeking the status of RAAF rank in QEA's now almost wholly military role, Fysh remained at the same time anxious that what remained of the airline should not disappear as a civil organization. Despite Fergus McMaster's constant references to the obstructionism of the director-general of civil aviation, Fysh wrote diplomatically to Corbett on 8 April expressing gratitude for the departmental assistance given to Qantas.

> We owe a great deal to you in fighting for our continuation. Every effort is being made to cut our expenses down. Our Traffic Section has practically been eliminated. Publicity has been eliminated [in terms of] staff. Our providoring, stewards and purser sections have gone . . . Owing to the intensive operation of the two flying boats and operation of the DH86 aircraft, which you so opportu-

nely handed over to us, there is no great surplus of crews, but a ferrying job would employ our senior captains on jobs to which they are best fitted . . . We are anxious, of course, to hear that approval has been officially accorded to your proposed recommendations for the carrying on of QEA work. This is . . . a very vital matter for us, and which we hope will ensure QEA carrying on as an organisation during the war period.[11]

Qantas was, Fysh noted, "in an obscure and weak position."[12] Four charter flights were made to Noumea and two of them (one carrying a ton of bullion) flew on to Vila. As the Japanese pressed inland from the coast of northern New Guinea, special charter flights were made to Port Moresby, with troops and equipment. Some semblance of stability returned when, on 1 May under instruction from the Commonwealth, QEA commenced a flying boat service to Darwin for priority passengers and freight, leaving Sydney every third day. (On 17 June it became a regular twice-weekly service.) At the same time QEA began a weekly service to Noumea. Both the Darwin and Noumea services were frequently interrupted when the flying boats were needed for more urgent trips[13] and the possibility of the complete demise of Qantas was so real that Fergus McMaster wrote to Fysh on 30 April: "From Turner's talks [in Melbourne] it seems that in the event of flying boat work ceasing, or in the event of the Commonwealth no longer desiring to keep QEA together against the day of reopening overseas operations, then the Commonwealth would not be prepared to pay all of our interest and other standing charges inescapably remaining. In fact, they might not pay anything at all." McMaster referred to the Darwin service that was to start the following day and continued: "Our next string should be Sydney–Brisbane–Noumea and this should be excellent if the Americans agree; it would be mostly their traffic . . . Withdrawal of the DH86 aircraft looks more than likely. The RAAF want them back as ambulances . . . It will leave us greatly overstaffed with pilots. I am again approaching Mr Corbett re ferry work for our surplus men, and if this can't be arranged it looks as if some of our men will have to go . . . "[14]

One faint hope for QEA renewal of sustained, major overseas operations was the possible opening of an air link to Britain across the Indian Ocean. On 16 February 1942, before BOAC knew of the break in the Empire route through Singapore, Runciman had cabled Fysh about Air Ministry proposals for Catalina operations on a reserve route between Ceylon and Australia using RAAF crews under naval control. Brain had interviewed Corbett about the BOAC cable and learned that the plan was to base six Catalinas in Ceylon and begin operating from 1 April using RAAF and QEA crews. Corbett, Brain had reported, did not think the proposal would assist the air transport problem from Java. "The proposed service was [then] six weeks away," Corbett had responded, "which is a long time these days . . . "

Brain and Crowther continued to study the possibility of such a service after the break in the Empire route and argued that a non-stop service of 3,513 miles was possible between Ceylon and Perth.[15] On 27 April, Fysh raised the matter with Corbett and was, somewhat melodramatically, rebuffed. Corbett replied:

> I am afraid you will obtain no support for a proposal to restart an Empire service via Cocos and Ceylon at present. The area is not regarded as safe for flying boats. The prospect of obtaining Catalinas is most remote. My reaction is that at present such a proposal would be a little short of murder and I would strongly oppose risking crews' lives. Wait until the position improves . . . I think a service to Noumea will be included in your activities shortly, but we are not yet ready to start.[16]

McMaster, in a handwritten comment on this letter, said that Corbett's opposition to Qantas was expressed "in every way he could obstruct".

In a further effort to get work for Qantas, Fysh wrote on 7 May to Air Vice Marshal W. D. Bostock, chief of staff to the commander of Allied Forces in the South-West Pacific.

> We have lost our overseas route and no less than six Empire flying boats have been lost — *Corio*, near Koepang, engaged on the Empire service; *Circe* and *Corinna*, engaged on the Broome–Tjilatjap shuttle when operating for the US Army through our Civil Aviation Department; *Corinthian* at Darwin during a night landing, again when operating for the US Army; *Centaurus* and *Coogee*, lost while on charter to the RAAF. This leaves us with two Empire flying boats and three under charter to the RAAF. The work we are undertaking at present comprises (i) operation of two flying boats between Sydney and Darwin (ii) operation of one Lockheed 10A between Brisbane and Darwin (iii) operation of two DH86 aircraft, at present engaged on urgent civilian evacuation work from New Guinea (iv) repair and overhaul of Empire boats on charter to the RAAF (v) Aircraft Production Committee work which mainly comprises repair and overhaul of *Seagulls* and *Walruses* at Rose Bay: *Pegasus, Pratt & Whitney, Genet Major, Cheetah* and *Warner Scarab* engines at Mascot; Avro *Ansons* at Archerfield; *Cheetah and Gipsy VI* engines at Archerfield. This work still leaves us in a position where our executive organisation,

trained crews and staff are not being fully utilised . . . We now find ourselves struggling to keep operating.[17]

The urgent evacuation work in New Guinea that Fysh listed had been referred to Qantas only days before, after a remarkable missionary from New Guinea, Father Glover, arrived in Melbourne at the end of a series of courageous personal rescue missions. Glover, who held a pilot's licence, had for some months previously been flying out people from Japanese-held beach areas in northern New Guinea to Ramu, a hill station inland. When he crashed his aircraft on one flight at Ramu, he set out on foot with an engineer for Alixishafen, behind the Japanese lines at Lae, where he knew a similar aircraft existed. They managed to take the aircraft and Father Glover flew it to Mount Hagen, a mission station in the heart of New Guinea. There were ninety people at Mount Hagen hoping to be evacuated and, aware that he could not possibly fly them out in his own aircraft, Father Glover set out for Australia to ask for assistance. He ran out of petrol on the south coast of Papua and made a forced landing. By canoe, lugger, then motor launch he somehow battled his way to Thursday Island and on to Melbourne. There he was promised that rescue would be attempted.[18]

The task of operating into Mount Hagen and bringing out the evacuees was given to Qantas. Four days after being approached, Capt. Orme Denny, who knew the country well, departed with Captains Sims and Nicholl and their crews in the DH86 aircraft *Melbourne* and *Canberra*, which had been quickly fitted with long-range tanks. Their immediate destination, already subject to air attack, was Horne Island, on the tip of Cape York Peninsula, from where the flights into Mount Hagen were to be made. With them were Father Glover and a veteran Guinea Airways pilot, Tommy O'Dea.

On 13 May, the two aircraft departed from Horne Island on the first run towards the Bismark Range, which runs along the central spine of New Guinea. Between the peaks, averaging 12,000 feet in height, were gaps over which, at 7,000 to 8,000 feet, it was possible to fly if they were clear of cloud. Both aircraft, though at times separated, managed to find the valley leading to the gap which brought them to Mount Hagen. There were cheers from the crowd awaiting rescue and from hundreds of locals when they landed and the engines were shut down.

With six to seven passengers per load, the evacuation began, but the soft aerodrome and the height made take-offs hazardous. Denny asked for help from the local population to harden the surface of the take-off strip. Soon he had two thousand people marching and singing, up and down, stamping their feet into the soft grass surface. For a night and most of the next day, they marched, sang, and stamped. There was no payment made and no food available to give to them. But the stamping was effective, the surface made firm, and the operations continued. Three days before the evacuation was completed, the Japanese, in a major raid on 21 May, attacked Port Moresby with thirty-four bombers. In all, the two DH86s flew out seventy-eight people, including forty-five troops, without loss of life or damage to aircraft. Captain Denny and his party were back in Brisbane fourteen days after they had set out.

QEA's earlier hopes for aircraft ferrying work, which would keep their senior pilots occupied, receded.

> I am afraid there is very little chance of getting a ferry organisation going [Fysh told McMaster on 5 May]. Gatty [ex-Pan American] has never helped us and I am quite sure never would, but he is reported as out of the picture at the moment . . . and Col. T. B. Wilson, Chief of Transportation Service, US Army, appears to be the man. He was president of Trans World Airlines till he took over this job. [But] it is increasingly difficult to get decisions.

In a second letter to McMaster that day he said that Ansett's

QEA DH86 *Melbourne* about to take off from Mount Hagen on 14 May 1942 during the evacuation of troops and civilians isolated by the Japanese advance.

chief pilot had come to Qantas trying to obtain crews to man American aircraft which, according to Ansett, they were taking over to operate on behalf of the Americans.

> I rang Corbett immediately. He was rather wrathful and said that Ansetts might think they were going to do the work but he, Corbett, knew they were not. He asked if we had been in touch with the US Forces and I was able to tell him "No". Corbett said we were not to get in touch with them. I said we had no intention of doing so as we were operating under his department. I will watch the matter carefully but, particularly as we are in the midst of financial negotiations with the Civil Aviation Department to keep us in existence, we can hardly contact our US friends. This is apparently all part of the gradual but sure USA intrusion.[19]

With Qantas firmly under the thumb of a wartime director-general of civil aviation who was sensitive about his authority, there was no possibility for initiative other than through the department and its minister. On 15 May, Fysh sent Drakeford a copy of a preliminary plan to establish an Indian Ocean service. "The prestige to Australia in being instrument in suggesting, working for and finally securing the operation of such a service . . . would be enormous", he wrote. "QEA is up against shortage of aircraft. We have two Empire flying boats and one Lockheed 10A in our fleet. In addition, at the moment, we have two DH86s on loan from the RAAF . . . QEA finds itself in a serious situation and must obtain replacement aircraft."[20] The minister replied with only a crumb of hope. "[There is] no immediate prospect of the RAAF returning any flying boats and [it is] quite certain the US Army will not make available any of their aircraft. I know of no immediate prospect of any PB2Y3 flying boats being made available . . . I know the director-general of civil aviation is considering a proposal regarding keeping intact your organisation as far as practicable, and when this is submitted to me I will give it careful consideration."[21]

Corbett was even more emphatic about aircraft shortages. Fysh told McMaster:

> Mr Corbett says it is quite impossible to obtain aircraft for an Indian Ocean service. The Lend and Lease [sic] people have just cabled from the USA that there are no more aircraft available for the RAAF or civil companies here until the end of 1945. I feel we should keep at it [the Indian Ocean proposal] just the same and cable BOAC putting the proposition up to them. The Dutch civil aircraft have been finally purchased by the USA and handed over to the US Army for operations by Mr Gatty. There was a proposal that Australia buy them and hand them over to the civil com-

panies . . . Mr Corbett thought he had secured this and was upset that the minister could not get this through. The Prime Minister decided that the USA could have them. Col. Wilson, Head of USA Army Transportation Service, was also upset at this decision as Mr Corbett was going to employ the aircraft in his service . . . However, there is major competition and disagreement in full swing between the USA Army Organisation and the USA Air Service. Wilson and Gatty are at loggerheads . . . Undoubtedly Gatty is thinking Pan American and is not co-operating with Australian civil organisations.[22]

Fysh sent McMaster performance data on the PBY2Y3 flying boats and the B24 Liberators as possible aircraft for an Indian Ocean route. "There is a real need for an air connection with BOAC through the Middle East . . . and [both] aircraft evidently would have sufficient range to give the connection via the Indian Ocean without having to use Cocos . . . " McMaster replied.

I am afraid, however, that the question is too big for men like Mr Corbett and the Minister . . . who evidently do not know where they are in connection with the USA Army complications. The influence of Mr Gatty would, I feel, be against such a development. It is possible that if anything is to be done it will need to be with the [UK] Air Ministry through BOAC . . . The future of the company depends upon the maintenance of its flying operations to a far greater extent than any other of its possible activities and we should try every means of establishing a Pacific ferry diplomatic mail service and the Indian Ocean connection.[23]

Fysh cabled BOAC for support for the Indian Ocean proposal at the end of May and at the same time wrote to Air Vice Marshal J. Jones, chief of Air Staff, pleading for the return of the chartered QEA flying boats. Both BOAC and Jones were unhelpful. Fysh received a cable from Runciman, in England, and told McMaster: "It does not look as if they [BOAC] are taking the matter seriously at all, or their view is that the prospects are so hopeless that it is no use taking the matter seriously . . . The ball is completely thrown back at us." With some courage, Fysh then asked: "Would you be willing for QEA to spend up to £200,000 for, say, two PBY2Y3 flying boats?"[24]

McMaster did not dismiss the proposal, but was noncommittal.

One of the questions is whether, commercially, the B24 Liberator compares favourably with the PBY2Y3. I am inclined to the opinion that after cessation of hostilities and the free opening of the normal air route from here to England, the service will be operated by landplanes . . . [but] it would seem a good long way in the

future before Japan is pushed out of the territory which is naturally on the Empire route.

Until then, he said, the air service would first connect via the
Indian Ocean. "I feel that neither he [the minister] nor his
government are sound on the larger national questions, especially on Empire questions."[25]

Though McMaster had clearly recognized the value to Australia of closer co-operation with the United States he remained, as a man of his time, a devout supporter of Britain and the
Empire. There were now (and had been since the entry into
the war of Japan) serious conflicts of interest between Britain
and Australia and the prime minister, John Curtin, was at
odds with Churchill. Six months earlier, on 27 December,
Curtin had stated publicly in an article in the Melbourne
Herald that the Australian government regarded the Pacific
struggle as one in which the United States and Australia
should have the fullest say. "Without any inhibitions of any
kind, I make it quite clear that Australia looks to America, free
of any pangs as to our traditional links or kinship with the
United Kingdom. We know the problems the United Kingdom faces . . . But we know, too, that Australia can go and
Britain can still hold on . . ."[26]

In late February, 1942, Curtin had opposed Churchill's
pressure that the 7th Australian Division, recalled from the
Middle East, should be landed in Burma. "The movement of
our forces to this theatre . . . is not considered a reasonable
hazard of war", Curtin cabled. Churchill, however, had already ordered the diversion towards Burma of the convoy
carrying the 7th Division, pending advice from Australia. He
now had to tell Curtin that the convoy could not reach Australia without refuelling. For the Australian government, it
seemed plain that their considered views had gone unregarded
by the British prime minister.[27] John Curtin was further
angered by a proposal from Churchill that R. C. Casey, the
Australian minister to the United States, should be made
British minister of state in the Middle East, with a seat in the
British War Cabinet. Curtin told Churchill that a change of
Australian representation in Washington was not considered
desirable. Casey, however (to whom the decision was left),
accepted the offer. The feeling in Australia that the country's
interests were of little consequence in England was not a pre-
rogative of the Curtin government; Menzies had come back
from England in 1941 with the view that Churchill "had no
conception of the British Dominions as separate entities and,

furthermore, the more distant the problem from the heart of the Empire the less he thought of it".[28]

On 18 June, Edgar Johnston, assistant director-general of civil aviation, prepared a Cabinet paper for Drakeford on the operations of Qantas Empire Airways Limited. It outlined the activities of the company from 19 February, when the Empire route was broken, and assessed the costs involved: "the proposal is that Commonwealth liability should apply to the whole of QEA's operations as from 20 February except the operation of flying boats from 20 February to 7 March, for which period Pan American accepts liability". (QEA's flying boats had operated under charter to Pan American on behalf of the US War Department from 20 February to 7 March, when they came under the direction of the Department of Civil Aviation.)

Johnston calculated that for the period from 20 February to 30 April "during the period the company was reorganising to meets its future operations" total costs for operation of the flying boats, the Lockheed 10A, and the DH86 aircraft were £65,400. Estimated costs per annum from 1 May for the flying boat, Lockheed, and DH86 Darwin services, plus the Noumea service, were £436,700. There was a policy, wrote Johnston, of not seeking reimbursements from other Commonwealth defence departments. Credits would accrue from 1 May to the department from commercial, US, and Commonwealth loadings at an estimated rate of £278,400 per annum, including a lump sum of £55,900 proposed to be made by the US forces in lieu of fares and freight charges. "There will be . . . an apparent loss of £158,300 per annum on the Qantas operations", said Johnston's paper. "This loss can be regarded either as the cost of maintaining the Qantas organization intact, or as being undercharge for service given by Qantas to its users, who are almost entirely the US and Commonwealth military defence forces." The proposed Commonwealth payments to Qantas did not include payments by the Department of Air for the charter of flying boats to the RAAF (which, from 1 May, were at the rate of £156,000 per annum); nor did they apply to the Cloncurry–Normanton or Cloncurry–Daly Waters services (which operated under subsidy), or to the Flying Doctor Service or the operation of QEA's small aircraft. The minister approved these recommendations for payment on 4 July 1942. The QEA organization, though depleted, was to continue to have the backing of the government.

In itself, this held no great prospects for any QEA future as an international airline. The Indian Ocean proposal remained moribund; Britain's civil aircraft manufacturing capacity was nil and her civil airline prospects bleak; and there was every prospect that the United States, rich in current transport types and well advanced with new civil designs, would dominate completely the postwar air routes of the world. In early July Runciman cabled the dismal British position to McMaster: "We maintaining all overseas services but have pointed out [to the government] that our aircraft are getting old and cannot continue indefinitely without replacements ... We have told the Air Ministry that if the British government unwilling or unable secure new equipment then the only alternative sooner or later will be to abandon air transport throughout the world to the Americans."[29] McMaster cabled S. M. Bruce, the Australian high commissioner in London:

> If America can make aircraft available to Pan American to operate established British services America should make such aircraft available to Britain or any allies for such purposes. Unless this support is fully implemented all must doubt the sincerity of the Atlantic Charter and professions of unity of our nations. The question is of grave national importance and we urge that Britain stand up to her Empire obligations, for the air services are part of our national structure ... Pan American are operating steadily and expanding and through development of Atlantic and Pacific ferry services their operations are growing to a vast scale. They alone are gathering rich experience and will alone be ready to inherit world air routes ... This is the equivalent to strategic defeat.[30]

McMaster broadened his attack. He lunched in Brisbane with Opposition leader Arthur Fadden and British journalist William Courtenay and briefed them. Courtenay sent cables to Allied Newspapers in London and direct to Britain's deputy prime minister, Clement Attlee. "Australia, Cairo and the Middle East could be linked by a new air service to operate a 44-hour schedule if plans revealed to me today mature", cabled Courtenay. Both Fadden and McMaster had stressed the importance of keeping open the Empire air routes. "Sir Fergus McMaster showed me with the aid of maps the new alternative routes his company has worked out for restoring the thread of Empire communications ... It is practicable using four-engined American flying boats for ... non-stop Australia–Ceylon."[31] To Attlee, Courtenay cabled: "American control of all ocean air routes would be the equivalent to strategic defeat for us and against the spirit of the Atlantic Charter."[32] Fysh, Mc-

Master told Fadden, had placed proposals for an Indian Ocean service before Corbett personally and had written fully to the minister.[33]

Drakeford's reply was unequivocally negative. "My advice at present", he told Fysh on 3 July, "is that you are hammering at the door of an empty house. The US Army has recently announced that it will start a world ferry service and all available information indicates that if this can be done it will make demands on available US aircraft . . . The US will certainly meet its own needs first and, when this has been done, there still remains the other difficulty that an Indian Ocean crossing by unarmed aircraft is not at present a practicable proposition."[34] Both the British and Australian governments seemed powerless to influence the future structure of overseas air routes or to check the might and influence of American air transport operations on which both depended so much. "It is to be hoped British civil aviation will ride out the war", Corbett wrote privately to Fysh on 13 July 1942. "We have been fighting here for a long time to keep things together. We have not always succeeded and, bit by bit, civil aviation has had to give up things which I think could have been used by us more efficiently in the war effort. There is not much support for these civil views in wartime . . . What fear is that when the time comes for our [US] eagle to become a dove, we shall not have a feather to fly with — and our dove may be labelled 'Pan American'." Corbett added with uncharacteristic humility: "Personally I am quite willing to stand aside if the operators think it would be helpful. Let me know quite frankly what you think."[35]

Financial as well as operational parameters for Qantas were also firmly in the hands of government. Edgar Johnston set out a summary of suggested profit margins on air charters for an interdepartmental committee: "The arrangements with Qantas — and all other air companies — could proceed on the basis of an interim profit margin of 4 per cent of agreed costs as being the minimum margin allowed by some other government departments." Qantas, wrote Johnston, argued for a margin of seven per cent on the capital cost of the assets involved for flying boats chartered by the RAAF and 7.5 per cent on fixed annual costs and variable costs (baed on hours flown) for their own operation of flying boats, the Lockheed 10A, and the DH86s lent by the RAAF. The War Cabinet had, he said, in general terms, set down an allowable profit margin principle of one per cent in excess of the market rate on government securities, assessed on the value of the asset. For aircraft charter the War Cabinet provided for, in rough terms, a profit of ten per cent of the net overall cost to the company. The interdepartmental committee, however, thought the question of margin for profit one which could be decided only as part of a general government policy to be applied to all organizations engaged in war activities and that formulation of such a general policy was outside its scope.[36]

The cumbersome processes of government, taxed to the limit by the immediacy and complexity of military events, seemed to both McMaster and Fysh to promise only the demise of British international aviation. Fysh wrote to McMaster on 24 July:

> I feel that right now, in weeks even, the future of British overseas aviation hangs right in the balance. Our leaders are either hopelessly deaf and blind or hopelessly tied up. Now is the time for decision and on the answer hangs the future of British aviation perhaps for decades. The papers are full of the great strides of American air transport, while the British remain silent and inactive. Unless we can obtain new aircraft and new routes, QEA will inevitably come to the end of its tether as an overseas operator.[37]

McMaster, in a speech in Brisbane some days later, predicted that unless a policy was formulated quickly, British air transportation must come to a standstill. He referred, he said, not merely to commercial or civil aviation but to air transport.

> QEA is not engaging in commercial operations. The company has lost its overseas routes and is operating on account of the Commonwealth government, transporting urgent war materials and personnel. Its workshops are overhauling aircraft engines engaged in this work and also service aircraft and engines. Its cost of operation is agreed with the government and its profit is fixed . . . However, QEA is still labelled "commercial". Lend Lease aircraft are not available for commercial operations. In the USA . . . the Navy and Army are co-operating to keep the internal and overseas civil airlines in existence, against the day of renewal of peacetime activities. This co-operation takes the form of labelling operations as either military or naval and thus allowing free expansion without any stigma or commercial flavour . . . men from former peacetime airline concerns have been accorded high positions in the Army and Navy transport organisations. For three years of war, Australian civil aviation has been carrying on labelled as such. Is it too late to change or reorganise?

McMaster urged creation of an Australian War Air Transport Auxiliary to function as a separate command carrying loadings for all the services.[38]

McMaster persevered with Drakeford, pressing for aircraft and the Indian Ocean service.

> Whatever action is taken by you now will determine the future, not only of Australian but of Empire ocean air services [he wrote on 29 July]. To relinquish British and Australian interests will not assist the war effort, but on the contrary will weaken the whole structure [and] be a definite exposure of weakness in our national fitness. There should be the same co-operation and singleness of aim between commercial and military aviation as that between the Mercantile Marine and the Navy. The Indian Ocean air link is an essential service and it will be operated at no distant date. The service is definitely a British–Australian right and responsibility and we as a people . . . have no right to surrender that right and responsibility.

McMaster then quoted from a cable from London.

> No transport aircraft at present in production in the United Kingdom, consequently Empire now dependent upon American transport types, mostly obtained under Lend Lease. Americans apparently consider this entitles them to start commercial operations on Empire routes by way of repayment, and they resent any attempt at control or co-operation. American Army, Navy seem willing assist American commerce often under cover of military service. Consider all Dominions should realise the extent of Empire problems.

The cable, said McMaster, came from a responsible authority in London whom he could not name. (It was probably Dismore, QEA's former close friend at Imperial Airways.) "We cannot escape the view that if the Atlantic Charter is not merely a piece of cant and humbug, it pledges cover for the future of the ocean air routes. I again stress that if British Airways and Qantas need new flying boats . . . they should be treated on an equal basis with Pan American."[39]

As if to underline McMaster's concern, the London *Times* published a statement on 3 August by General Harold Lee George, chief of the Army Air Transport Command, at a press conference.

> Air Transport Command has already assigned wartime routes to ten major United States airlines, and the intention is to incorporate the remaining eleven US airlines. Under [the] programme, American and TWA will fly to London at least twenty-four times every day. United and Pan American will fly to Australia and India twenty to thirty times weekly, in addition to other routes. To do this, the Army has promised to lend-lease new cargo planes to the airlines as fast as they come off the production lines — a minimum of three hundred by Christmas . . . The biggest immediate addition will be the twin-engined Douglas DC3s. Next will be the

25-ton DC4s, able to carry a 10-ton payload nonstop for 2,200 miles . . . [40]

This candid American declaration of strength was matched on 2 August by an equally candid British declaration of weakness. A British Airways official told the press: "The acute shortage of commercial planes precludes any immediate measures to restore trans-oceanic services as desired by Australia." His company, he said, had nothing like enough machines to cope with their own immediate services and the position was, if anything, worse than Australia's. They were using converted old-type bombers whose range, load, and carrying capacity made them useless for the Australia–India service given prominence on the day before by the *Times*. If anything were to be done, said the unnamed official, it had to be done by the Americans.[41]

BOAC's chairman, Clive Pearson, cabled Hudson Fysh supporting this grim British assessment and Fysh wrote to McMaster on the eve of a meeting between his chairman and Prime Minister Curtin: "It is depressing to note the change in tone. Apparently they can do nothing in England, and ask Australia if she has any influence with Uncle Sam." Fysh telegraphed McMaster: "Good wishes on your most important representations on which depends greatly our future sphere of usefulness". He stressed QEA's lack of aircraft, the urgent need for the formation of the proposed Transport Corps, and the dissatisfaction of Qantas crews as reported by Brain who were undertaking war trips under civil guise unarmed, though they were otherwise very willing to participate." In the event of capture the position of the crews may be dangerous as civilians."[42]

Both Fysh and McMasters let off some emotional steam in an exchange of letters on 20 August. "The whole position of air transport in Australia is . . . distressing when you think whose hands its destiny is largely in", wrote Fysh, referring to Corbett as "an average post office official, retired as having completed his usefulness, old, crochety, dogmatic, unwilling to listen to the advice of his subordinates or the old operators". Equally scathing, he assessed Ben Chifley, a future Australian prime minister of great stature:

> We have his [Corbett's] boss, who has no qualifications for anything that I have ever heard of, except that he may have been a good engine driver . . . The way our two remaining flying boats are being hustled backwards and forwards on the job that they are on, you would think that the Allied campaign in that area depend-

ed on them — and I am not sure that there is not a lot of fact in such a statement . . . The already extended troops may be extended further, and we may have difficulty in getting back to our regular runs.

McMaster, though just as critical of their political masters, was willing to lay the blame for poor government closer to home.

When the Prime Minister [Curtin] was here last Thursday, a mythical enemy plane was reported, the sirens blew and the Prime Minister and all the others of us went underground, knowing full well that there was not an enemy base within a thousand miles of Brisbane. Politics has got into the hands of a few union leaders and they govern the country today because you and I are too lazy and selfish to oppose them. Religion for you and I and millions like us does not exist, except as a cloak. You ask me what you can do? No one knows what they can do until they try to do it . . . It is a phase of our civilisation, which over the last twenty years, under our so-called democratic cloak, we have lived a selfish, decadent life. We have been devoid and are still devoid of a national ideal, for the Atlantic Charter so far is simply an empty drum. If the war terminated tomorrow there would be a rush and a struggle by a few, and in a flabby way by the whole of us, to go on from where we left off in 1939. We are lacking in political and religious responsibility and we are selfish and lazy . . . There is no Anzac spirit in us in that we are all content to pay someone else to fight for us.[43]

Fysh was also indignant about the tactics and motives of one particular Australian airline operator, Reginald Ansett. He wrote to Ivan Holyman at Australian National Airways of his concern that Ansett "does not seem to be playing it fair by the other Australian airline operators in a number of ways . . . I find that friend Ansett has been out after our pilots and is offering them jobs at advanced remuneration and position, not only for the war but after it, when his scouts say he is backed by unlimited American capital for big expansions in this country. Unless he can be trimmed he will be a big menace later on . . ."[44] Holyman replied: "I entirely concur. Ansett is not a bit concerned with any of the other operators; to the contrary, he is not even concerned with his own company — he is only interested in Reginald Miles Ansett and will sacrifice anybody and anything and go to any lengths to achieve notoriety and financial gain for himself. . . "[45]

Fysh thought Ansett had already reached an understanding with American interests.

If this is so [he wrote to Holyman], then the very greatest danger lies in its possible effect later on the purely British interests in

Australian aviation. Since the war started, one or two very serious blunders have been made by our official people, but what may yet prove the worst is the direct contract which was allowed between Ansetts and the USA Transport Organisation . . . I think we have got to ensure that there is a fair distribution amongst suitable Australian operators of the Douglas or other aircraft for internal operation when they eventuate . . . [46]

As these pressures of higher policy mounted on McMaster and Fysh, Qantas crews were being called on to operate an urgent priority service into the front line. Brain made the first flying boat trip to the base at Milne Bay (on the eastern extremity of New Guinea) early in August, taking in army cargo and bringing back stretcher cases and other personnel. (He flew out only fifty minutes before the first Japanese air raid on Milne Bay.)[47] In August, *Camilla* and *Coriolanus* operated charter flights from Townsville to the forward military area. Under the control of Air Transport Command, twenty-four trips were made to Moresby and seven to Milne Bay carrying troops, complete units of special aerodrome Defence Corps, light antiaircraft guns, ammunition, bombs, and equipment, as well as commandos and key Army personnel. The return flights brought out sick and wounded. On 25 August, the Japanese invaded Milne Bay in thick weather only an hour after one of the QEA flights (under Captain Denny) had left.[48]

While these operations were in progress, Hudson Fysh committed a major blunder in protocol in his anxiety about future QEA overseas operations. He wrote directly to the governor-general of Australia, Lord Gowrie, asking for his assistance in pressing for replacement aircraft and initiation of an Indian Ocean route. Though ill-judged and absurd, it underlined Fysh's deep concern. He wrote to the governor-general:

that British Air Transport is going through a very critical stage indeed because, if replacement aircraft cannot be secured to make good the war wastage being experienced, there will shortly be no British Air Transport worth speaking of . . . We have been pressing for the opening up of an Indian Ocean service from Port Hedland or thereabouts to Trincomalee in Ceylon, or to Bangalore in southern India. US aircraft, the PB2Y2 flying boat, for instance, are in production which can carry a load of nearly two tons over this great distance . . . We are continuing our representations to the Australian Civil Aviation Department, to the Minister for Air, Mr Drakeford, and Mr Curtin last week was interviewed by Sir Fergus McMaster, our chairman . . . I know you are vitally interested and respectfully suggest that your interest and assistance at this juncture may prove a very helpful factor.[49]

The reply from Admiralty House, Sydney, was cold and official. "The Military and Official Secretary is desired by His Excellency the Governor-General to acknowledge receipt of a letter dated 22 August 1942 from the Managing-Director, Qantas Empire Airways Limited, and to inform him that the subject matter mentioned therein is entirely one of Government policy."[50]

Corbett was angry and incredulous when he heard of the letter.

> In view of all the official information which has been supplied to you by the Minister and myself as to the present difficulties, and the replies you have received from England to similar representations, and the interview your chairman had with the Prime Minister, it appears rather extraordinary that you should address such a communication to the Governor-General. The inference must be that you do not understand the position and you are prepared to go beyond the responsible Minister and the Department to seek assistance in a way which appears to me improper . . . [51]

A contrite Hudson Fysh responded promptly: "I would never have dreamt of sending the letter had I thought that it would be accepted in the light in which it was . . . I realise my action was quite wrong . . . I greatly regret having given you the trouble that I have and will be more careful in future — but if His Excellency actually read the letter, which I doubt, then he would have read information which might not be unhelpful."[52]

McMaster's interview with Curtin had proved fruitless and there seemed no prospects for Qantas of either additional aircraft or an international operation that would help guarantee their postwar survival as a civil organization.

> There has been nothing from the Prime Minister [McMaster told Fysh on 25 August 1942]. I do not expect any help from him. In the first place, he has no strength of character or vision . . . The unfortunate conditions on the Russian and Near East fronts and the push going on in the Solomons make it almost impossible to expect any adjustment for the time being, even if we had a strong Prime Minister and Minister for Air. Messrs Fadden and Spender had an interview with General MacArthur but, again, I feel we did not get anywhere because there is too much immediate strain on the available aircraft in the war zones. All these interviews can do is help keep our position alive . . . [53]

Despite his anger and seeming despair, he kept trying. On 2 September he wrote to Sir Earl Page, a member of the War Advisory Council, urging the formation of an Australian Air Transport Corps and pushing for a Pacific ferry plan. He stressed also that there was no direct air connection in existence between Australia and Britain across the Indian Ocean, or between Australia, India, and the Middle East. PBY5 four-engined flying boats (Catalinas), said McMaster, could fly Port Hedland–Trincomalee nonstop and with sufficient fuel carry six to eight passengers, their luggage, and something better than a ton of freight. Two of them could operate a twice-weekly frequency each way and if necessary extend to Karachi or even Cairo. Using the airgraph letter system such a service could carry both military and ordinary mail; 32,000 letters normally weighed a ton, he pointed out, but by airgraph would weigh only 30 pounds. "We understand that one of the conditions under the Lend-Lease Act is that aircraft made available to Britain and Australia cannot be used for commercial purposes. We submit that the Indian Ocean service would not be commercial. If it becomes a question of QEA purchasing the aircraft, this could be arranged . . ."[54]

Hudson Fysh, just as concerned, pressed Corbett. "One wonders what the latest position is regarding the future utilisation of the QEA organisation, whether new routes or new aircraft are any nearer", he wrote on 15 September. Corbett, in his playful, mandarin prose responded: "The matters of which you wrote . . . are proceeding along their allotted course with a ponderous precision. It is all very irritating, I know, but I know of no way to accelerate those whom I can neither reach nor influence."[55] In a second letter, delighting in his effortless logic, he wrote:

> It is a fact that United Airlines has been awarded a contract to run four services daily from the USA to Brisbane within six months . . . So far this Department has received no official confirmation; neither has the Government, as far as I know, but that is the way things are done these days. I cannot follow your reasoning that all this strengthens the case for replacement of your lost flying boats. As a matter of fact it is the reverse. The USA will supply its own needs first. It needs six months to find twenty machines for United Airlines to begin with. What chance do you think you have until that need is supplied?

With utter reasonableness and blithe pessimism Corbett continued his pedantry:

> A proposal to cover overseas services by Qantas can only be made when there is a reasonable prospect of obtaining aircraft suitable for the job. It is no use firing at a dead target . . . Even when aircraft are available, it does not mean that Australia only has to ask for them. There are others clamouring too. If you knew all the difficulties you would know how utterly hopeless it is to do what you suggest at present. I have told the Government time after time that Australia is heading . . . for a post-war position in which

we may have no aircraft and not be able to operate our own internal services — while the USA may be here to take up the running. That danger is now recognised, I think, by the Government. Nothing is to be gained by continually writing on this subject . . . I appreciate your offers of help but, at the moment, I need help which you cannot give.[56]

McMaster's response to Corbett's negativism was brief. He told Fysh: "We cannot afford to let things drift simply because Ministers and officials do not like continuous pressure."[57]

McMaster was also concerned about QEA's own organization. After receiving from Fysh a list of the expenses of directors and executives, he wrote: "The amount disclosed is disconcerting. It is impossible to avoid the conclusion that the whole set up of QEA requires revision regarding costs, from that of the directors right through the executives and the staff." He was sensitive about his own expenses and thought them definitely heavy but unavoidable. "There would appear no escape from this other than by the appointment of a chairman resident in Sydney." He told his managing director that he had had helpful discussions with Turner

> in regard to the financial adjustments with BOAC. I hope no action will be taken without consultation with myself which would involve a question of policy, or admitting either directly or indirectly that we consider the Empire Scheme and Service as terminated in February last. We should avoid admission . . . for so long as there is life and the will to live . . . the impossible often happens. It must be our policy to keep our organisation together and instil confidence that the service will again become operative.[58]

In the midst of these preoccupations, QEA received a cable from Runciman, asking if they could assist with pilots. "My first reaction", Fysh told McMaster, "was one of astonishment that British Airways is still in such a low position as to again approach us for crews. It shows the pitiful state of British civil aviation. I do not think the Civil Aviation Department would be in favour of releasing any of our men . . . If we let any crews go it greatly weakens our position if work . . . does eventuate."[59]

Qantas had a strong and experienced pilot organization and did not want to lose it. McMaster, in a letter to QEA director W. A. Watt asking him to meet the prime minister and again urge the ferry plan idea, wrote:

> We have thirteen captains and acting captains whose aggregate flying times total 113,679 hours and twelve First Officers whose average is 2,800 hours each . . . As a body perhaps this is one of the finest groups available. There are good national reasons for

not breaking up such a team . . . We are in a very awkward position in that we have to work with a weak Minister for Air and a Director-General of Civil Aviation who has spent a long life and training in the administration of one particular utility only, and certainly has neither the outlook or the training for the position he holds. His main weakness is that he will not accept any assistance from his executives or people such as ourselves.

He commented on Corbett's recent defeatist letter to Fysh and concluded: "I feel I have every justification in asking your assistance to get to the directing heads — that is, the Prime Minister and General MacArthur."[60] On the same day that he wrote to Watt, McMaster again tackled the prime minister: "Unless we can secure aircraft operations, the company will have to face disintegration", he wrote. "There is no intention on our part to push commercial aviation as against military needs at this desperate phase of the war. What we do ask in effect is the raising of the status of civil aviation and full opportunity to take part in the war." He reminded Curtin that QEA had submitted a Pacific Ferry Plan by which they could ferry five hundred bomber aircraft a year from the USA to Australia. "This company is not a private company in the ordinary sense in its constitution and objectives."[61]

Though the future of flying operations remained uncertain, the QEA engineering base at Rose Bay was swamped with work. Arthur Baird (one of the three original Qantas employees, with McGinness and Fysh, and still in charge of engineering) wrote to McMaster: "Daily the requirements and the pressure on this Flying Boat Base increases. This is brought about by the pressure of our own two flying boats, the RAAF flying boats, RAAF combat marine aircraft, the USA Marine freighting aircraft and USA combat aircraft, together with the ever increasing RAAF Rathmines [flying boat] operations and the Dutch marine aircraft requirements."[62]

The same week, Fysh again raised his concern at manoeuvrings by Ansett in:

a definite build up . . . being attempted here in agreement with some USA interests. As you know, Ansett got around Mr Corbett, who allowed him to sign a direct contract with Colonel Wilson's USA Transport Organisation, though we were told we cannot do the same, even if we wanted to — because Mr Corbett has seen his mistake. I have always thought this just about the greatest blunder Mr Corbett has made so far, and it may have far reaching results yet . . . [63]

Fysh was well aware that QEA could not compete internally

in Australia after the war with the powerful Australian National Airways of Ivan Holyman.

> Holyman, with his overwhelming plant, route and connection advantages must predominate in Australia, and while we must do all we can to share in Dominion operations, our overwhelming need is to keep our overseas status alive. The first real danger signal will flip up if we go out of flying boat operations, so let's hope we can hang on . . . At this critical hour I don't see how we could find new friends to come to our rescue in a hurry; anyhow, they would surely wish to control us and they would have American interests to carry the sort of influence we require. Holyman represents a free enterprise, non-subsidised endeavour, backed by the old shipping companies. QEA, on the contrary, has been more bound to governments and owes allegiance to the Australian and UK governments. What will be the trend after the war? The American companies are obviously fighting for the right of commercial expansion anywhere, and Australian National Airways may be said to be in this category . . . It seems to me that the commercial interests in the USA will be impressing on their government the necessity for this free expansion and it may be that this will become an established USA principle . . . the USA, though frowning on geographical imperialism, has been one of the most ardent commercial imperialists in the world. In Russia, of course, all the big industries are owned by the people. In England the swing is decidedly that way. Here in our own country we have the threat of Dr Evatt and others to nationalise commercial aviation. Will things go that way? Obviously we are entitled to a lead from our partners, British Airways, and without the formation of a strong policy between us . . . I do not see any hope but that we will get badly trampled on.[64]

It was a sound and thoughtful letter. McMaster replied: "The future is most obscure . . . Our plain course at the present time is to secure any aircraft of any type worth flying and to constantly press our claim on the Indian Ocean link, even if that link is only of a token nature." The existence of Qantas, he believed, was imperilled.[65]

Unexpectedly additional aircraft became available, though not the flying boats they so desperately needed. In mid-October QEA was told that it would receive three Lockheed Lodestars, part of the mix of Lodestars, Lockheed 14s, and Douglas aircraft bought by the United States Army Air Corps from the Dutch after the collapse and evacuation of Java. (All these aircraft carried the usual Army Air Corps marking of a white star on a blue circle background and, though they were allotted call sign letters, they were not registered as civil aircraft.)[66] With that moderate good news came uncertainty about whether QEA would operate the Lodestars under the Department of Civil Aviation or under the authority of Gatty and his organization. Fysh put the general question of Gatty's authority to Corbett on 21 October 1942. "Gatty has asked Brain if we would go to Milne Bay with the Empire flying boats if required, and also to other centres . . . on the south coast of New Guinea. Should application be made to you in matters such as this, or will we simply go to places in New Guinea as directed by Gatty if in our opinion it is safe and proper to do so?"[67] Corbett replied with his usual tidy pedantry:

> It is the desire of this Department, and I know it is also the desire of QEA and every Captain in the Company, that the most efficient service be given to military air transport by the civil flying boats. However, there is a proper way of doing this. The Commonwealth Government, through this Department, has undertaken heavy financial liabilities with Qantas, as you know. I have no intention that your Captains should receive direct orders from Group Capt. Gatty or the Transport Command if such orders lead the flying boats into dangerous situations. This Department is responsible, not the Allied Air Transport Command, if a flying boat gets into trouble. This is how I want the matter arranged. Firstly, the Captain of a civil flying boat will take no orders from anyone contrary to his own judgement as to operations in the air . . . Secondly, orders are to be received by and given to Captains only by Qantas representatives at Townsville or Sydney who, in turn, must consult with the Air Officer Commanding, RAAF, Townsville . . . [68]

The arrangements for Qantas operations in New Guinea were agreed between Gatty and Corbett and set down "in a memorandum of agreement as between Qantas Empire Airways and the US Army and Air Forces".[69] Fysh commented: "From a company point of view this move is of the greatest importance and appears to remove the previous fear of having no aircraft to operate in the event of further losses." He added that since commencement of aircraft repair and maintenance work for the Department of Aircraft Production, shortage of ground engineers had been acute, and they were now in the same position regarding pilots.[70] McMaster thought the memorandum a satisfactory basis for an understanding but, he told Fysh, "QEA is located between the USA control and the Civil Aviation Department, not a position one would perhaps tolerate under more normal conditions". He advised Fysh that QEA's current policy should be to maintain the inland route and "hold on to the DH86s until something more stable is secured regarding replacement aircraft". Whenever operating the flying boats between Cairns and Sydney they were to try to carry the maximum load of civilian passengers, ordinary mail, and freight. Overseas, apart from pressing for the Indian Ocean connection, QEA should follow up if a breakthrough was made militarily for a route to the Philippines through Port Moresby and Rabaul. Referring to a BOAC cable, he commented: "BOAC has little or no influence and apparently the Empire policy for which QEA was established is not going to be either a present or postwar vital consideration by the British Government. We have to realise that a position is developing in which QEA must consider the possibility of new and strong associates for postwar reconstruction."

McMaster was scathing in his comments on Australia's political leaders and their policy that troops of the CMF (the Commonwealth Military Forces), unlike the volunteer AIF, could not be used outside Australia.

> One can hardly imagine anything more degrading or contemptible than for men such as Curtin, Forde and Evatt directing the war effort and appealing for self sacrifice and national effort, and to have the Army so divided [so that] a large proportion cannot be sent outside the three-mile limit of Australia — and at the same time have the Americans coming here by the thousands in the defence of our country, and under conscription . . . We are all parties [in] this drift and . . . must take responsibility attaching to a National Government under the leadership of such men . . . whose history has been wholly political and self-interested.[71]

The first of the Lodestars (also designated as a Lockheed 18 or, by the military, a C56) on loan from the US Army Air Corps was handed over on 26 October and departed for Townsville on 4 November. It carried the name "Qantas" on its nose. (The second was received on 5 November and the third on 1 January 1943.) With QEA's Lockheed 10A and the DH86s on loan from the RAAF, the first two Lodestars were to begin intensive operations in New Guinea from 21 November. Corbett and Hudson Fysh had a brief but bitter argument both on the supply of air crews and the nature of QEA's war work.

> Your view that the RAAF should supply you with pilots is interesting but I hold out no prospect of success [Corbett told Fysh on 9 November]. Their pilots cost the country a large amount to train. Their proper answer to your request for their pilots is that you, not being able to supply crews, should hand Qantas aircraft to the RAAF. I should then not attempt to combat such a solution and QEA would close down for the duration . . . There is no support for your view by the RAAF that Qantas operations are war operations. Qantas is doing exactly similar work to other airline companies.[72]

Australian troops wounded during the Buna–Gona campaign wait beside a Qantas Lodestar for evacuation from Dobodura to Port Moresby.

Two days later an irritated Corbett wrote again:

I refer to your telegram [that Allied Air Transport Command had agreed to supply copilots and wireless operators as a definite part of the agreement for QEA operation of their aircraft] . . . No arrangement was made by Air Transport Command with the RAAF to supply pilots. I am unaware of the alleged agreement with you, of which you failed to advise me . . . You evidently entered into some agreement with him [Gatty] that RAAF crews would be supplied. You also appear to have asked the RAAF to release pilots to your company without reference to me . . . You confused the whole matter, first by trying to obtain the release of pilots from the RAAF and, second, by making arrangements with Gatty unknown to me or the RAAF. The matter has now been straightened out. The RAAF will post sufficient pilots and radio operators to fly US transports by your company. They remain on duty in the RAAF and may not be used by you for any other purpose. Let that be clearly understood by all concerned.[73]

Fysh replied that he could not agree to the accusations made by Corbett. He had, he said, only approached the RAAF for consideration of the release of a former Qantas employee. He emphatically denied ever having made any arrangement with Gatty unknown to Corbett. "Gatty simply told us that he was supplying pilots to us from the RAAF. All we look for", wrote Fysh with asperity, "is your direction, and if you are not satisfied by the way in which the companies are attempting to finalise the agreement with Gatty, then it is hoped your Department will take the whole matter over and relieve us of a most difficult burden."[74] Corbett was unimpressed:

> Whatever arrangements Gatty made with you, he failed to let the RAAF know and you failed to let me know. The confusion occurred because at that time Qantas, Guinea Airways and Ansett Airways had all asked the RAAF to release pilots without reference to this Department. The Air Board issued instructions that no pilots were to be released unless this Department made the request. I am afraid I am not aware of any difficult burden imposed on the Companies in finalising agreement for US Transport. What difficulty have you experienced? The matter seems to be fairly simple and neither ANA nor Guinea Airways has found any difficulty. Why should you feel unduly burdened? You say you feel my remarks were unfair because I had not been shown the whole picture. Well, I was not shown the whole picture — neither was the RAAF. As you were one of the artists who painted it, you were credited with the results. However [Corbett concluded disdainfully] there are more important things to worry about at present.[75]

The task of the QEA aircraft in New Guinea was to help in the support and supply of Allied troops attacking the Japanese who, by now, had been driven back across the Owen Stanley Range to the areas where they had landed in July 1942. On the beachheads of Buna, Sanananda, and Gona, they were offering unexpectedly fierce resistance and draining Allied manpower and resources. The supply line from Port Moresby to the crude landing strips on the north coast of Papua was vital, but greatly extended, and Australian civil aviation (Qantas, Australian National Airways, and Guinea Airways) was called in to supplement the military transport fleet. When the emergency strips at Dobodura and Poppendetta (the main strips in use for the beachhead area) were closed by rain, supplies were kicked through the aircraft doors and dropped from low altitude. Both the DH86 aircraft were damaged in a Japanese bombing attack on Ward's Strip, Moresby, on 13 December but were repaired in time to resume operations the following day. Though Japanese fighters attacked the transport aircraft operating into the north coast, Qantas aircraft operated 146 flights in all without interception. (Operations with two Lodestars, VHCAK and VHCAA, to carry food, ammunition, troops, and equipment to the Buna front were carried out between 22 November and 3 December under Captain Denny.

89

Capt. Orme Denny who commanded the Mount Hagen evacuation operation in May 1942 demonstrates typical packages that were dropped from treetop level by QEA crews to Australian troops fighting near Buna in December 1942.

On 9 December, instructions were received from the Department of Civil Aviation for the two Lodestars, two DH86s, and the Lockheed 10A to proceed to Moresby.[76] Intensive operations to the forward areas commenced on 10 December and finished on 12 December. In all eleven civil aircraft were stationed at Moresby: five QEA, four ANA, and two Guinea Airways.) The company's flying boats, *Camilla* and *Coriolanus,* had, in addition, operated over one hundred round trips to Port Moresby since 20 September, as well as fortnightly flights to Darwin and flights to Milne Bay. (Hudson Fysh visited New Guinea in December to see the Qantas operations, and flew in a QEA Lodestar to the Buna area.)

At the end of January, Fysh summarized QEA operations as totally noncommercial, with the exception of the small Cloncurry–Normanton sector in northern Queensland. The company was operating flying boat services between the mainland and New Guinea; landplane services in Queensland and North Australia; aircraft were on charter to the US Transport services and Allied Works Council; flying boats were on charter to the RAAF; and the company operated the Flying Doctor Service. Total company staff was over nine hundred and growing. At the company's engineering workshops, work was undertaken through the Department of Aircraft Production for the RAAF, the US Army Air Force, the US Navy Air Force and for the

Royal Australian Navy. At the QEA instrument shop at Double Bay, Sydney, two hundred instruments a month were processed. In all, about 80,000 manhours monthly were being worked for the DAP, involving an annual turnover of £210,000 for labour and overhead costs.[77]

There were many individual flights that characterized the Qantas front-line involvement. On 1 January 1943, Captain Crowther in *Camilla* flew north from Milne Bay to the Trobriand Group to pick up the crew of a US Fortress which had been forced down. On 5 January Crowther, again in *Camilla*, operated another trip to the Trobriands to pick up the crew of a Liberator bomber that had crashed. A party of nine, including one dead and three seriously injured, was flown back to Milne Bay. On 6 and 7 January, Captain Hussey, under instructions from General Kenney, flew *Coriolanus* to Wamea Island to search for the crew of a B17. Fighter cover of three aircraft was provided because of the Japanese air presence. This crew was not found, but Hussey sighted and brought back another party of stranded airmen from Goodenough Island. In one strange interlude, the two flying boats at Townsville were hurriedly instructed to proceed to Cairns for an indefinite period as intelligence had reported a landing of between forty and fifty Japanese from a submarine at the mouth of the Nassau River, ninety miles north of Karumba. Captain Tapp in *Camilla* was sent to Karumba on 13 April with a party of troops and their equipment and a reconnaissance was carried out next day. The troops were landed in the Staaten River for some hours, but no contact with Japanese forces was made. The two flying boats subsequently returned to Townsville. Some months later, in July, the *Clifton* was sent to Horne Island to carry out transport operations to Tanahmerah in New Guinea, about a hundred miles north of Merauke, on the Digoel River. It operated under the direction of Torres Force on troop and equipment movement that had previously been undertaken by 41 Squadron RAAF. (The *Clifton* was handed back to QEA from the RAAF on 26 June 1943, and the *Coolangatta* on 29 July.)[78]

Though these demanding and dangerous operations made their modest contribution to the massive task of supplying the fighting troops and search and rescue operations, they were emergency and temporary activities for an organization that had been founded and structured for the regular operation of long-range, over-water passenger routes. McMaster continued his

91

pressure on government ministers for recognition of the value to the war effort and the national interest of a direct air transport service to link Australia with Britain. He wrote to the deputy prime minister and the army minister, F. M. Forde, on 5 November 1942 saying that neither the prime minister nor Drakeford had indicated whether proposals for the Indian Ocean service were being considered.

> I am somewhat disturbed in that we have had a cable from London to the effect that the Air Ministry is considering the operation of this air link, purely as a military operation. I submit that there is a danger to postwar Australian Empire aviation should the Government lose its interest and equity in the operation of the Indian Ocean section which, although of an immediate military nature, would actually again make operative the air link between Australia, India, the Middle East, Africa and Britain herself. Qantas has the air crews and the engineering staff experienced in the operation of heavy, four-engined aircraft suitable for the . . . service. You know the records of these pilots and their work in Java, Singapore, Malaya and Darwin areas and their present operations to Port Moresby and other forward areas. It would seem only sound national policy to maintain what rights we have . . . [79]

To QEA director A. E. Rudder, McMaster reported a personal conversation with Forde's ministerial colleague, Drakeford. "It must be realised", Drakeford had told McMaster, "that your thoughts probably are not in line with those of my government, in that Labor policy regarding aviation will be towards nationalisation."[80]

The underlying uncertainty about QEA's continuity as an organization that had pervaded the thoughts of McMaster and Fysh throughout 1942 was now modified by what Fysh described as "the most cheering cable we have had from England since the Empire route was broken". The cable came from Clive Pearson at British Airways, Bristol, and said: "It is evident that both the Air Ministry and BOAC have in view the re-establishment of air services by the Empire route, also that although it is expected that the Indian Ocean service will be initiated 'by the military, it is hoped that some allocation of equipment will be made available in the near future to both BOAC and QEA which could have as its objective the re-opening of an Empire air connection."[81] The possibility that an air route to Britain might again be operated was one small indication of what Alan Watt in *The Evolution of Australian Foreign Policy, 1938–65* described as "the justifiable grounds for the swing from pessimism to guarded optimism following upon developments in Europe, the Middle East and the Pacific dur-

ing the period from the fall of Singapore on 15 February 1942
to the fall of Stalingrad on 31 January 1943".[82]

Closer to home, Australia had seen the Japanese navy beaten
back in the Coral Sea battle in May 1942, ending the Japanese
thrust southwards and the likelihood of any invasion of the
Australian mainland. A month later, on 5 June, had come the
decisive defeat of the Japanese navy by the United States at
Midway, the turning point of the war with Japan, and the
month when control of the sea and air began rapidly to pass to
the Americans. The war itself was far from over, but the tide
had turned. It was possible to contemplate the coming of a
postwar world, and to begin to shape policies and plans. For
Qantas, the direction of government policy and the airline's
constant pressure to reopen a regular overseas route remained
subjects for misunderstanding and controversy.

> Quite an ugly matter has arisen out of a letter you wrote to Mr
> Forde on 5 November, and your mention of nationalisation [Fysh
> told McMaster on 5 December]. Mr Corbett is very upset about
> the matter and blames you for raising [it]. Mr Corbett says it is
> not for him to advise us . . . but he would not like you to write
> again on the matter to the minister. [He] says that if the present
> Government stays in power he expects it to nationalise aviation.
> This is now dynamite, Fergus, and I would beg you not to take
> any quick action. One thing seems certain and that is that our let-
> ters to Ministers should cease, except for certain special cases.
> They all go straight to Mr Corbett and annoy him frightfully.[83]

McMaster, however, was not intimidated by Corbett's attitude
nor those of ministers for he wrote on 22 December to Drakeford, commenting on a letter that he had sent to F. M. Forde:

> There is, I greatly regret to note, more than a suggestion in that
> letter that you are of the opinion that I have been over persistent
> in the matter of the proposed Indian Ocean air connection. I am
> genuinely puzzled to know why I, as Chairman of Directors of
> Qantas Empire Airways, should have incurred the charge of being
> unduly assiduous in the representations made which, after all,
> were in response to direct requests following my talks with politi-
> cal leaders . . . The next and only other issue . . . is the suggestion
> in your letter that I have been anticipating the nationalisation of
> airline operations in the Commonwealth. This is a very grave
> misinterpretation of a paragraph . . . of my letter to Mr Forde,
> and in no way accords with my personal viewpoint that develop-
> ment by private enterprise with strong government backing is the
> most satisfactory plan of operations. I am still of the opinion that
> the Commonwealth should not delay in adopting measures which
> will protect its equity in the operation of an Indian Ocean Air Ser-
> vice, and joint and speedy action with the United Kingdom
> would appear the logical solution. American interests are very

93

ambitious and have powerful and wealthy private backing, together with the support of a Government that has shown that it is very much alive to the great future of air transport, taking action that might result in the Commonwealth and the United Kingdom being either pushed aside or placed at a great disadvantage insofar as the main ocean air routes are concerned.[84]

To Fysh, McMaster rejected the suggestion that he tread softly. On Christmas Eve he wrote: "I have determined that firmness is necessary, otherwise our position will deteriorate if we do not meet the Government official attitude with clear, straight out statements. No worthwhile Cabinet minister would treat the position lightly and no petty restricted outlook should be let go unchallenged. My personal wish would be to keep quiet, but that would be a lazy, selfish approach."[85]

McMaster's assessment of American ambitions was fully shared by Runciman. He wrote to Fysh:

What you rightly call the commercial imperialism of the USA obtrudes itself upon us in many parts of the world. It appears the present policy of the British Government to refrain from taking any active measures to counter it. We have, for example, been instructed to refrain from publicity on our own behalf . . . lest the Americans might think that we were operating with an eye to commercial advantage of the British Empire. It is natural they should be meticulously careful to avoid giving the Americans any ground for saying that Lend-Lease material is being used commercially . . . There is a good deal of public interest beginning to show itself in this country about air transport problems . . . There is also considerable alarm about the extent to which our American friends are still being encouraged to lay the foundations of their postwar commercial expansion in a great many other fields than that of air transport alone.[86]

McMaster cabled BOAC chairman Clive Pearson that the initiative and drive concerning Empire air services

must come from the British government and yourselves . . . [a] lead from your Government would obtain ready support from Australia. There is immediate and urgent need for some basis of agreement regarding all ocean air routes of mutual interest to the United Kingdom, Australia and New Zealand if the imminent danger of any one Government making arrangements embarrassing to the Empire interests as a whole is to be avoided. [I] very strongly urge the wisdom of early action on the part of the British government while the position is still free from complications.[87]

It had been a year of danger, loss, and near demise for Qantas. The *Corio, Circe,* and *Corinna* had been lost through enemy action and the *Corinthian* had been lost carrying a military load into Darwin. Three other flying boats, *Centaurus, Coogee,* and *Calypso,* had been lost while under charter to the RAAF. (The three RAAF boats had been owned by QEA and the four operated by Qantas had been owned by BOAC.) In addition, the DH86 *Sydney* had been lost in the crash near Brisbane. In total, thirty-five passengers and ten crew had lost their lives. McMaster paid tribute at the twenty-second annual general meeting of Q.A.N.T.A.S. to the pilots and crews who had flown unarmed and unprotected commerical aircraft wherever they had been required and said: "The appreciation and thanks of this Company and, I am justified in stating, the Commonwealth, are due to Mr Hudson Fysh for the able way in which he has handled a very difficult position, both for the Company and for the co-operation and help he has given in the war effort."[88]

As the year drew to a close, Hudson Fysh sent a memorandum to senior executives, urging awareness of coming competition and the need for continued effort.

> We can only earn the right to operate the [US] aircraft by keeping them in the air more than the USA Army Air Transport Section did themselves. We must also see to it that we make a better job of keeping our aircraft in the air than the other two companies do, despite any handicaps. Out of three Lodestars, a minimum of two should always be flying, and what should be firmly aimed at is the estimated eight hours per day per aircraft in the air. Qantas is again entering a competitive cycle . . . The year 1943 is going to be a hectic year for Qantas and if we are to survive we have got to show we are alive and virile.[89]

As if to emphasize the scale of future competitiveness, the *Sydney Morning Herald* carried a story from New York on the closing day of 1942 quoting a statement by the president of Pan American Airways: "America", said Juan Trippe, "must dominate the air routes of the world."[90]

The Indian Ocean Connection 1943

5   "If a British policy is not agreed soon, it seems to me it will take years to pick up the pieces, if ever", Fysh wrote to McMaster on 4 January 1943. He had received a letter from Walter Runciman at BOAC suggesting he visit "home" for talks and was eager to go.

> For at least two years I have been waiting to visit the USA and England . . . I now feel the time is opportune [and] you have got to take the plunge and send me across to make this vital contact. A preliminary would be a discussion with Mr Curtin and Mr Chifley in regard to Australian policy and I feel that in all probability something is formulating . . . I anticipate I can only get a priority seat across to the USA by Mr Curtin asking for it, and to get this Mr Corbett's blessing seems necessary.[1]

He was right. Corbett had drawn up an outline plan for postwar civil aviation in Australia for his minister, Arthur Drakeford, which envisaged twenty-two aviation distribution centres across the Australian continent. Each would have a radius of some three hundred miles, so that any place in inhabited Australia, including Tasmania, would have a minimum daily service (up to four or five times daily between the largest centres). Mails, under Corbett's proposals, would be flown from any centre to any other centre in less than a day, with night flying of mails an essential feature. Corbett pointed out that in 1940–41 Australia's regular air services, including those operated overseas, made 40,768 flights in 60,000 hours, flying eight million miles. Some 262,000 passengers were carried without a single fatal or serious accident.

96

In the introductory remarks to his report, Corbett wrote: "A nation which refuses to use flying in its national life must necessarily today be a backward and defenceless nation." A nation unused to air transport would have great difficulties in terms of defence and might, he said, "have similar difficulties in raising infantry brigades wearing boots if its natives habitually went barefoot". All the essential needs for air transport had arisen in a short time and capital expenditure for every civil aircraft, aerodrome, navigation facility, lighting, fencing, and building from the beginnings of civil aviation in Australia had, he wrote, to date been less than £5 million, assuming that half had been paid by private enterprise. The United States, on the other hand, had "spent far more on one single aerodrome".[2] Comparing railways with air transport, he commented: "Both are a great national asset. One goes on from year to year adding to its value, paying its way, increasing its services. The other does not."

Corbett pointed out that the Commonwealth would need a well-defined policy on the international aspects of civil aviation "to ensure participation on just terms in the international postwar agreements . . . and the means to implement such a policy". Internally, he stressed, there was matter for grave concern, both for the present and after cessation of hostilities, because of the lack of suitable transport aircraft. He proposed the formation of an Australian corporation to own and operate aircraft, with the main object to obtain ownership of aircraft acquired under Lend-Lease (despite the fact that Article V of the Mutual Air Agreements provided that they be returned to the United States at the war's end). The Corbett Report, as it became known, was referred to an interdepartmental committee under Corbett's chairmanship and including D. McVey, director-general of posts and telegraphs and secretary of the Department of Aircraft Production; H. C. Coombes, director-general of postwar reconstruction; and P. Hasluck of the Department of External Affairs.

Corbett's views were summarized in an article in the Sydney *Sun* newspaper and did not impress McMaster. He told Fysh:

Mr Corbett is not original and he has dismissed the international factor . . . Air services for seven million people within Australia are a very small development indeed. Australian National Airways no doubt would be willing to give first class service between all centres which would be self-supporting . . . I am convinced that even with present aircraft, large scale operations between England and Australia and the US would be possible without Government

On 9 January 1943, the proto-type Lockheed Constellation made its first flight from Burbank, California, landing at Muroc Field in the Mojave Desert. Muroc, now known as Edwards Air Force Base, was the site for the prototype's subsequent test programme. Hudson Fysh visited Burbank in March 1943, while he was travelling to London, for talks with BOAC management and he was briefed by Lockheed on their future plans for the Constellation.

financial support other than mail contracts. The danger is that Mr Corbett and the Minister for Air, and evidently the Government as a whole, have no conception of the possibilities of post-war air transport.[3]

Fysh received a full copy of the Corbett plan and was less damning. "I feel that some very good points have been raised and that the various basic factors are well put together", he replied. "If Mr Corbett's Department is to go ahead and plan the whole project as he asks to be allowed to do on the last page, and as his Department at present 'manages' the airlines under war conditions, I do not see much chance of our survival in internal air transport."[4]

Despite their ongoing battles with what McMaster regarded as an obstructionist Corbett, there were words of praise from an authority nearer the battle front. Lt.Gen. George C. Kenney, Commander, Allied Air Forces South-West Pacific Area, wrote to QEA on 15 January:

> I wish to take this opportunity to commend you for your extra-ordinary devotion to duty under very trying circumstances, and to acknowledge the important part played by you in the active combat zone during the period 16 November to 15 December 1942. These operations involved air transport for great quantities of supplies and personnel, which were taken from the base area to the front where active operations were in progress. Despite the possibility of enemy interception, bad weather and many other hazards you succeeded in accomplishing an important assignment. Your work in removing the wounded to a place where medical treatment was available is worthy of special praise.[5]

Qantas had been as stretched in the previous two years by extension of its engineering operations as by the uncertainties of wartime flying. The maintenance, repair, and overhaul of service aircraft and engines of many kinds was the responsibility of the maintenance division of the Department of Aircraft Production, with McMaster's friend Sen. Donald Cameron as minister. The great increase in combat and military transport aircraft and trainers had provided rapidly expanding work opportunities for the workshops of Australian airlines, with QEA and Australian National Airways the biggest competitors. In 1942, work increased as US Air Force Fortresses and Liberators went into large-scale operation in the islands. These, with Airacobras and Ansons, were handled at the Archerfield, Brisbane, repair depot, while Cheetah IX and Wright Cyclone engines went through the company's engine shops. It was, though, said Fysh, a feast or a famine, with either too little or too much work coming forward.[6] A new engine overhaul shop was erected for QEA use by the department at Moorooka and Lester Brain was sent to Brisbane to manage operations. (By August 1944 there were 690 people employed at Archerfield, and 928 QEA employees in total in Brisbane.) The rapid expansion of engineering work had, however, brought problems. As early as January 1943, Fysh admitted to McMaster that there had been mistakes and inefficiencies. He was critical of Arthur Baird who had, since the original founding of Qantas, been the untiring mainstay of its engineering work and almost

Archerfield 24 April 1943. Two B-24D Liberator bombers parked in front of the QEA hangars awaiting modification to their forward armament. The US Army Air Force found that their heavy bombers were vulnerable to attack from head on. The B-24D was fitted with a single half-inch calibre machine gun in the nose which projected through a port. The arc of fire from this weapon was smaller than the area covered by the tail turret and urgent steps were needed to improve the B-24D's defensive capability. Supplies of tail turrets were sent to Brisbane where QEA staff removed the original nose structure and adapted the area to take the heavier armament.

certainly the chief reason, in the early years of constant break-down, for its survival.

> I have very definitely informed you [he told McMaster] some years back that we had a definite weakness in the engineering side. I took steps to put this right and BOAC chose an assistant to Baird, but on Baird objecting to having an assistant appointed from England the matter was submitted to you and you decided to let things run on . . . As every executive knows, and as you have been repeatedly informed, practically everything new that has been accomplished from the Mascot workshop to extending Department of Aircraft Production work, and even to the appointment of Wright as his assistant, has been done in spite of Baird. On many things, however, I have been unable to move him, such as training of men, appointment of engineering seniors of higher educational standards, etc. How to mend the situation now? Well, I am at a dead end.[7]

Both Fysh and McMaster continued to face competitive pressures from within Australia and uncertainties about the future of international routes. Everyone, Fysh wrote to his old friend from Imperial Airways, Woods-Humphrey, was groping in the jungle and waiting on an international agreement. "QEA, of course, is thoroughly out to support Empire inter-

Qantas engineering staff at Archerfield working on a tail turret from an American B-24D Liberator bomber. Another turret which has already been fitted with twin half-inch machine guns and bullet proof glass can be seen to the left. These turrets were being fitted in the nose position of the B-24D to improve its firepower against Japanese fighters whose pilots knew that this early version of the Liberator was vulnerable to a "head-on" attack.

ests. You, of course, are entirely to blame for starting me off on this course in 1933, and no harm has come of it yet. QEA, of which you are so largely the author, has done a job it can look back on with some satisfaction."[8] Within Australia, press reports of the merger of Australian National Airways and Airlines of Australia worried McMaster.

> This final move places ANA in a very strong position [he wrote]. We cannot expect that operations will be confined to internal airlines. Australia will not offer sufficient scope for ANA, Ansetts and Guinea Airways and we can expect that any one or all of these three organisations will strive to have some part in the ocean air routes. The present and immediate future holds the destiny of Qantas. To survive we must free ourselves from too much reliance and wet-nursing from the Government and London . . . Qantas cannot rest on any possible prestige it might have had in its reputation as an honest pioneering concern. From now on it will be the survival of the fittest and of the virile.[9]

He believed that, postwar, airlines would move away from government subsidy, and urged "an alliance with big capital and influence". With uncharacteristic pessimism he concluded: "The Empire Service as we know it has gone, but we must retain the Indian Ocean connection." It had been impossible, he said, to get an understanding with British Airways or anything from the Commonwealth government.[10]

Fysh also reacted to the growing dominance of Ivan Holyman at ANA and wrote to him about his actions in the role of chairman of the Airline Operators Association. "I have been increasingly disturbed by certain decisions and actions on the part of yourself which are tending to usurp the normal functions of the management and directorate of QEA." He thought, he said, that Holyman's actions might have been taken with "the urgent desire to forestall the rise of Ansetts".[11] Holyman replied that to say he was surprised at Fysh's letter was to put it mildly.

> I have problems enough of my own [he wrote] without worrying myself about other organisations. It seems to me that in the rapid expansion of our organisation you have a feeling that the prestige of your own company is on the downgrade. I think you are wrong in taking this view. You have primacy in overseas operations . . . whereas this company has built up for itself establishments from Perth to Cairns which have been costly both in buildings and equipment — and it is only natural that full advantage should be taken of this by the Commonwealth Government.[12]

Fysh did not accept these reassuring words. "Under the ethical code which I feel is right and fair it is impossible for you to reconcile your position as Chairman of the Airline Operators Association, equally looking after the interests of all, and the action you took as managing director of ANA when, through some circumstances unknown to us, you secured a very large amount of DAP work, to the elimination of increased facilities already promised to QEA."[13] Fysh commented to McMaster: "With Holyman's ethics prevailing, the Airline Operators Association is an uncomfortable affair for QEA because neither myself nor any of the other executives are trained to do business that way."[14] Holyman, he said, was fast turning into the dictator of all Australian airlines while Qantas was going through a critical stage, with great problems to face and an unknown future. He was, he said, preaching the old combative spirit to executives. "The first essential . . . is a fighting spirit. The second [is] a continuance of the old principle laid down by you over twenty years ago — that is, full co-operation with the Administration in power. The right political contacts seem essential to success."[15] Qantas had to get closer to the director-general, the minister for air, and the prime minister. "Our position seems to be slipping. Corbett is, of course, very difficult and adopting a petty tripping up attitude on anything QEA — the blame for which falls on me."[16]

As QEA's major formal link with government, Corbett was seen as a grave impediment. "I hope you realise", Fysh reminded McMaster, "that he is still a very difficult man indeed to deal with and he has never, all the time he has been Director-General, been in the habit of giving me anything except the most sketchy and unsatisfactory information."[17] McMaster shared Fysh's views. "Mr Corbett . . . is not big enough for the position and naturally is jealous of yourself and others who have a firmer standing with the public in aviation. For the whole of his life he was confined to a Department, and his highest position was Deputy Manager, and not handling policy . . . His attempt in his Report on postwar organisation, and outlining a plan for civil aviation, was a weak attempt at a big problem, ending up dismissing overseas routes as an international problem and beyond his capacity for direction."[18] But McMaster was not unreservedly sympathetic towards his managing director's difficulties. "There should be the same drive and energy put into QEA policy and operations as Holyman is putting into ANA", he commented in a separate letter. "It is perhaps an inclination to feel that too much consideration is being given to difficulties which apparently Holyman

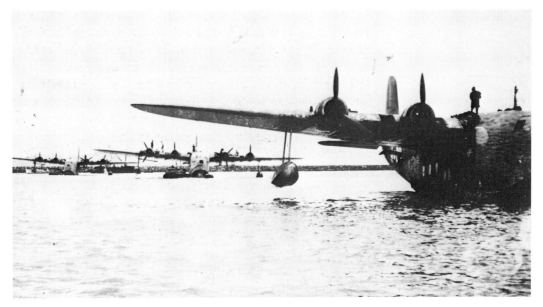

and Ansetts are overcoming more satisfactorily and effectively than Qantas Empire Airways."[19]

Despite uncertainties about future operations, the immediate financial returns for Qantas were good. Corbett had written on profit rates to be allowed for the two flying boats chartered to the RAAF and for the operation of QEA's civil aircraft. "Mr Turner's analysis is clear and shows that we are better off than expected, so long as the volume of flying can keep up", Fysh reported. "Department of Aircraft Production work, interest on investments and the very considerable work for the US Army Air Corps is extra, so it looks to me as if we are in a very favourable position."[20] Fysh pointed out that Turner had calculated total profit at about 8 per cent on invested capital, as against the company's aim for 7.5 per cent. On the operation of the Lodestars, Turner had estimated an annual profit of £10,000 to £12,000 per annum and, in addition, a contingency reserve of £9,000 per annum.[21]

There had been no intimation from Corbett of progress on plans for an Indian Ocean route, though Fysh had been aware from the beginning of the year that the matter was in the hands of the prime minister. "I should say that QEA comes in somewhere," he had told McMaster, "but I couldn't get anything definite."[22] All he could gather was that the Commonwealth had been in communication with the United Kingdom government about the supply of transport aircraft and about possible operation of the Indian Ocean route by Catalinas.

By early 1943, only four Empire flying boats were still flying in the Australian area. Ten Empire boats had been isolated on the eastern end of the "Horseshoe Route" when Singapore surrendered on 15 February 1942. This photograph was taken at Townsville in mid-March 1943. The aircraft in the foreground is *Coolangatta* which was then being operated by No. 41 Squadron, RAAF, as a transport. *Coriolanus* and *Camilla*, visible in the background, were carrying troops and freight from Townsville to Port Moresby; *Camilla* crashed off Port Moresby on 22 April 1943.

Fysh's plans to visit England, however, had firmed. Edgar
Johnston wrote to him on 9 March: "I sincerely hope you will
be successful in your efforts to see that British aviation (including our part in Australia) is not completely overshadowed and
jostled off the world's air routes after the war." (Edgar Johnston also said that he had been asked to raise the matter of an
account of £143 to Gen. Thomas Blamey, senior Australian
army commander in the Middle East, from BOAC for the
travel of the general's wife from Cairo to Durban. "It has been
suggested that it might be not inappropriate if some concession
on this charge could be made", said Johnston delicately. "You
will appreciate that the parties interested desire the request to
be kept absolutely confidential.")[23] Fysh left on 16 March 1943
for England via the United States from Amberley, near Brisbane, on a US Air Transport Liberator. He was to be away
until August and, with McMaster still far from well, George
Harman was appointed acting general manager of Qantas.

On 22 April, Qantas lost the flying boat *Camilla* off Port
Moresby and eleven passengers and two crew members were
drowned. The aircraft, commanded by Captain Koch, had left
from Townsville just after midday on a regular service with
twenty-two RAAF personnel and five Americans, with weather
conditions reported as normal. By the time it approached Basi-
lisk Light, outside Port Moresby harbour, it was early evening
and light rain was falling. But over the harbour itself, dark
cyclonic cloud had formed and visibility was nil. *Camilla* was
asked to hold off while a flare path was laid and Koch circled
the light. Lester Brain, in a formal report, wrote: "Thick
weather intensified and spread. Koch was circling at low altitude on instruments [which was] unsafe and perhaps impossible. [He] turned and flew away over the water on a straight
course on instruments, undoubtedly the correct action to
take." There was, said Brain, unusually protracted and heavy
weather and repeated radio reports of nil visibility. "He had
no option, and his final decision to land when his fuel was
nearly exhausted was the only competent decision to make.
[He] displayed sure, cool judgement and a very high standard
of endurance and morale [two hours flying under extremely
onerous conditions]." The later stages of his emergency descent were made in darkness and Koch used auto-pilot — a
sound decision, wrote Brain, as it was "more capable of accurately maintaining a slow rate of descent than any human
pilot". First Officer Peak sighted water with the aid of the

main landing light and advised the moment to hold off for a "pancake alighting". He misjudged the height (which Brain thought understandable) and engine power was applied, but the flying boat stalled in from a height of thirty to forty feet.[24] The time was about 7.45 p.m. Koch and Peak were picked up next day after swimming for eighteen hours. (It was, of course, Koch's second such experience; he had swum ashore to Timor Island after being shot down by Japanese fighters in *Corio*.) Some survivors were rescued by a small steamer, some by native lugger, and some by a service crash boat.

On the same day that *Camilla* crashed, Hudson Fysh in London received word from England's director-general of civil aviation, William Hildred, that policy had been settled by the United Kingdom for the operation of an Indian Ocean service by Catalinas. They had notifed the Commonwealth that four aircraft would be operated as a civil air transport service, with Qantas as the operating agent.[25] Captain Taylor had made the first flight across the Indian Ocean in June 1939 (in the Catalina *Guba*). His route had taken him from Sydney to Port Hedland in Western Australia and then, after a diversion to Batavia, through the Cocos Islands to Diego Garcia and on to Mombasa in Africa. The longest leg in that pioneering flight

This aerial photograph shows the Nedlands area on the Swan River. The QEA Catalina base can be seen on the far side of the point, directly above the top left corner of the sports field. The water beyond the point is Matilda Bay and one of the Qantas Catalinas is moored off-shore. Crawley Bay, in the foreground, was occupied by the US navy from early 1942 until mid 1944.

had actually been between Sydney and Port Hedland, across the Australian continent, covering a distance of 2,600 miles in nineteen hours and thirty-five minutes. The first nonstop crossing between Australia and Ceylon was made in June 1942 by two Dutch Catalinas that had escaped from Java during the Japanese advance. (They flew from Exmouth Gulf to China Bay, near Trincomalee.) Three further flights by Dutch crews, now serving as No.321 (Dutch) Squadron RAF, were made from Ceylon to Australia between December 1942 and May 1943, the last one flying nonstop the return journey of 3,634 miles between Perth and China Bay in twenty-eight and a half hours.

On 3 May 1943, the first of seven survey flights by the RAF (using the first two Catalinas delivered to Ceylon for use in the Qantas service) left Koggala, near Galle in southern Ceylon, for the nonstop flight to Perth. The last of these survey flights to Perth, landing on 25 June, was the delivery flight of the first Qantas Catalina. (Exmouth Gulf, though five hundred miles closer than Perth, was rejected as a landing place for regular services because the perfect water conditions needed for greatly loaded aircraft were not available.) While these surveys had been under way, Capt. W. H. Crowther had been appointed by Qantas to head their Western Operations Division, with responsibility for the new service. In charge of engineering — though without facilities for handling, servicing, fuelling, or despatching aircraft — was N. W. Roberts.[26] Their only spare parts were fifty spark-plugs and they had no servicing equipment or tools.[27] Qantas crews had undergone their basic type-conversion on the Catalina at RAAF Rathmines in new South Wales and the initial crews accompanied the RAF survey flights. All were members of the RAAF Reserve and were formally sworn in for service and issued with RAAF flying kits (though they wore Qantas uniforms).[28] It was their task to initiate the longest nonstop regular passenger air service ever attempted in the world. For Qantas, it was the company's re-instatement as an overseas operator and the renewal of the Australia–England air link that had been severed by the Japanese.

The distance from the QEA base at Nedlands, on the Swan River, Perth, to Koggala, in Ceylon, was 3,513 miles. The Catalinas had an average speed of 127 miles an hour and an accepted payload of 1,000 pounds. Their peacetime all-up weight was 29,000 pounds but both the British and Australian civil authorities authorized a wartime all-up weight of 35,000

pounds. All the Catalinas had been supplied under Lend-Lease to Britain from the United States from the military production line in San Diego but were modified for civil use by BOAC. (The last three aircraft were given final modifications by Qantas at Rose Bay.) They retained their RAF camouflage, serials, and roundels but had British civil registration numbers painted on the after fuselages (and sometimes on the tops of the wings). At the bow, on each side under the cockpit, "Qantas Empire Airways" was painted in black and, later, each was given the name of a southern star. On the sides of the fin, in white, was painted their fleet number.

The first flight from Perth to Ceylon with a Qantas crew under Senior Route Capt. Russell Tapp left Perth at 4.30 a.m. on 29 June 1943 and carried the returning RAF crew. The first officially recognized scheduled flight of the Qantas service, 1Q-1, left Koggala Lake ten days later for Perth on 10 July, again with Tapp in command. Their payload was miniscule — fifty-two pounds of diplomatic and armed forces mail. It was in no way an auspicious or encouraging beginning because there had, in fact, been an embarrassing false start three days previously. On 7 July, the aircraft had taken off from Koggala and three hours had passed before it was discovered that the two sextants necessary for navigation had been left behind. Tapp had been forced to return to Koggala. In spite of the small payload carried on 10 July, unfavourable winds so reduced their ground speed that a diversion to the coast of

QEA Catalina *Altair Star* flying along the coast of Ceylon in late 1943. The tail number 2 can be clearly seen.

Western Australia was contemplated. To add immeasurably to
the pressure on Tapp (and on Capt. Bill Crowther, who was
acting as navigator), all the crew went down with severe food
poisoning and were out of action. Tapp and Crowther, with
the Catalina on automatic pilot, operated all the crew positions.
They climbed the aircraft, found more favourable winds, and
continued on to land at Perth after a flight of twenty-eight
hours nine minutes. On 22 July, Tapp commanded the first
scheduled service westbound from Perth to Ceylon, and so
began what now became a weekly service in each direction
flown over enemy-patrolled sea areas in complete radio
silence.[29]

Though of central importance to the future of Qantas, the
Indian Ocean operations from Perth were far from the company's headquarters in Sydney. Visits by Fysh, and even by
Lester Brain, were few. The two main areas of activity were,
in fact, Brisbane (under Brain) and Perth (under Crowther).
QEA was, according to R. J. Ritchie (who flew as captain on
the Indian Ocean service and later rose to the position of chief
executive of Qantas), almost two airlines.[30] Crowther was the
dominant and controlling figure at Perth for the crews and
ground organization who now kept the new air link open.
N. W. (Norm) Roberts — with ingenuity, industry, and diplomacy — kept the aircraft flying. (Each Catalina — four to
begin with, with a fifth added later — was progressively modified by Qantas at Rose Bay; the position of the extra fuel tanks
was changed to improve the centre of gravity and aircraft flying attitude and fuel dump valves were installed.) In the air,
there was complete reliance on dead reckoning and astronavi-
gation, coupled with the most careful engine handling to opti-
mize range as heights changed and the massive take-off fuel
load of about seven tons was burnt off. The Qantas engine
operation plan that evolved gave the Catalinas a duration of
thirty-six hours and an extreme range at cruising speed of
4,650 miles.[31] Crowther noted in September 1943 that no other
regular air service in the world approached the distances flown
on the QEA Indian Ocean route. Those closest to it were San
Francisco–Honolulu (2,400 miles) and Montreal–Scotland
(2,870 miles and flown direct only with a following wind).[32]

Financially, all capital costs and operating expenditure of
the new service were recoverable by QEA from BOAC (who
in turn had an agreement with the Air Ministry). The service
was operated by QEA on behalf of BOAC with QEA receiving
a nominal £100 per year as profit. The United Kingdom gov-

ernment had, wrote Fysh, an agreement with the Australian government under which they would supply the aircraft and bear the estimated cost of operation (£A104,900 for a weekly service), while the Australian government agreed to provide up to £52,000 sterling per annum plus payment for mails and provision of some ground facilities.[33]

Hudson Fysh left England in August and flew eastbound across the Mediterranean, the Middle East, and India to join the eighth service by QEA from Lake Koggala in Ceylon for Perth on 30 August. It took, according to Captain Crowther's log, thirty-one hours forty-five minutes, and proved to be the longest trip of the entire Indian Ocean service operation. (Qantas Western Command report to head office recorded thirty-two hours nine minutes for the trip.)[34]

Fysh had found civil aviation in England in a mess and BOAC getting weaker and weaker.[35] The chairman (Pearson) and chief executive (Runciman) had both resigned and their places were taken by Lord Knollys and A. C. Critchley on 26 May. (His own name, he wrote, had been freely canvassed for the job as BOAC chief executive but was finally not forward because it might have caused trouble with other dominions.)[36] He returned to an Australia where the postwar prospects for civil aviation, summarized by Corbett for his minister in July, were even bleaker. "On present prospects," Corbett wrote, "[Australia] may have twelve obsolete and over-age transport aircraft with no organisation capable of national expansion to meet immediate postwar needs and no accepted plans for either national or international expansion. Civil aviation in Australia is expiring month by month." He estimated that by the end of 1943 there would probably be operating in Australia (apart from army transport aircraft operated by the RAAF): 130 aircraft mostly of the DC3 type, in the New Guinea area, of the 5th United States Air Force; 312 aircraft of the 5th USAF in the Australian area (52 DC4 types; 208 DC3 types; 52 Curtis Commando types); and 10 US Transport Command DC3 types — in all, 452 aircraft. "The probable relationship of air transport aircraft in Australia will be of the order of: US military-owned aircraft, 452; Australian-owned civil aircraft, 12." Corbett added: "I invite the Government's attention to what is happening and what will happen if nothing is done about it . . . This is no minor matter too persistently stressed by a civil servant to urge some importance to his own job. I have no personal interest because of my age. The

Government should soon make a choice of a new Director-General of Civil Aviation."[37]

The minister for air and civil aviation, Arthur Drakeford, sent a copy of Corbett's minute to the prime minister, John Curtin, on 17 July with the comment: "Immediately after the elections the Government should take definite steps to ensure that this country will be in a position to compete." The minute, he said, contained proposals worthy of serious and prompt consideration. (Elections for both the Senate and House of Representatives were held on 31 August and the Curtin government was returned.)

The prime minister evidently agreed as he placed Corbett's memorandum before the War Cabinet on 23 September. He commented, however: "As the Minister for Air and Civil Aviation has made no comments on the Director-General's proposals I am confining my own observations at this stage to certain broad aspects of Civil Aviation policy as a basis for discussion by War Cabinet."[38] Curtin recalled that in a policy speech on 26 July he had stated:

> In the postwar period, the Government is determined that Civil Aviation will be highly developed. Owing to demand for transport aircraft for military purposes, they are difficult to obtain for operation under civil control, and General MacArthur has not replied to representations which I made to him some time ago for his support in obtaining additional aircraft for civil aviation purposes. I now propose to press him strongly on this point in view of the extent to which civil aircraft are used for military purposes ... Australia must seek to organise its war effort in the air to obtain the greatest residual value that is possible in the postwar

Two of the aircraft proposed for postwar operations by BOAC and QEA on the UK–Australia service were the Avro York and the Handley Page 64. The York, shown here in BOAC markings about 1947, used the wings, engines and empennage of the Lancaster bomber.

period . . . There is also the vital question of participation in over-seas routes. In the pre-war period, the Empire services were being developed but they had not encircled the globe. The Pacific, how-ever, was crossed by US airlines and critical questions of reciprocal landing rights at intermediate and terminal points were arising.[39]

Fysh reported on his visit to England to the Commonwealth government on 25 September and described four British air transport types. The Avro York was, he wrote, a transport version of the Lancaster bomber, involving design of a com-pletely new fuselage and the result was "an excellent long-range transport . . . expected to fulfil a useful function until such time as the new postwar types make their appearance" and was now in production. The Handley Page 64, a version of the Halifax, was a useful medium- to long-range aircraft, the cabin of which had a greater cubic capacity than that of the York. The Bristol Buckingham was a transport version of the Buckingham bomber. The Short Shetland flying boat was "a most interesting type and by far the largest aircraft yet to be attempted in England". In the United States, Fysh reported, were "the best air transport types in the world in the DC4, Curtis Commando, Liberator etc — and the Constellation, when it is ready".[40]

Australia's first serious attempt to grapple with the likely postwar world of civil aviation began with the initial meeting of the interdepartmental committee under Corbetts chairman-ship in October. Corbett outlined the existing situation in Australia:

Handley Page did not proceed with the HP.64. Their first postwar airliner was a modified version of their Halifax bomber, based on the HP.70C Mark 8 transport built for the Royal Air Force. BOAC bought twelve for their UK–West Africa services in 1946.

111

> We have available . . . for operation of regular airline routes total-
> ling 22,003 miles only thirty-three aircraft with a total seating
> capacity of 358 passengers, and a total payload of 87,300 pounds.
> Of these thirty-three aircraft only seventeen (including one on
> loan from the RAAF) can be considered as large transport aircraft.
> The remainder are mostly small and practically obsolete machines.
> With these aircraft, 137,250 passengers were carried over
> 65,453,000 passenger-miles, together with 2,840,000 pounds of
> mails (representing 1,381,000 ton-miles) and some 2,256,000
> pounds of freight (representing 771,000 ton-miles) during the
> past financial year. Of the passengers approximately 68 per cent
> were Government priority.
>
> Before the commencement of the war in 1939, the Australian
> airline companies operated fifty-three aircraft over 25,721 route
> miles. . . . The aircraft now available for Civil Air Transport are
> insufficient to carry the load offering . . . No spare aircraft are
> available to meet emergencies.

Corbett told the committee that General Blamey on 20 July
1942 had drawn the prime minister's attention to the increasing need for aircraft and had asked that the Department of
Civil Aviation be supplied with fifty. The ministers for army
and air had supported the request, as had General MacArthur.

> A requisition was prepared and subsequently reduced from fifty
> to eighteen the number of aircraft at the request of the US
> Authorities. The requisition for eighteen aircraft was, in due
> course, presented to the Munitions Assignment Committee [in
> Washington] in January 1943 . . . It was rejected on 2 April. In
> the meantime, Canada obtained seven Lockheed Lodestar aircraft
> during 1943, New Zealand obtained two and Mexico obtained six
> through Pan American from the Munitions Assignment Commit-
> tee [in August 1943].

Australia, said Corbett, had not obtained from any source any
new aircraft for civil aviation since 1939.

> The Airline Companies, in addition to their regular services, are
> at present operating twelve transport aircraft owned by the USAF,
> for military transport for the Allied Forces. The cost of operation
> is paid for by this Department on behalf of the Commonwealth
> Government, and the amount credited to Reciprocal Lease-Lend
> [sic]. The aircraft, however, operate under direct orders of the
> Director Allied Air Transport Command. They serve no civil
> need; they do not carry PMG mails and they are not owned by the
> Commonwealth; they will therefore not be available after the war.
> It is important to note this.[41]

In information put before the committee, three of Australia's
twelve airline companies were shown as profitable. Australian
National Airways, with eleven aircraft, had an estimated profit
of £500,000; Qantas Empire Airways, with seven aircraft, an

estimated profit of £30,000; and Guinea Airways, with six air-craft, an estimated profit of £15,000. Neither ANA nor Guinea Airways received any subsidy. "The lesson of these figures", commented Corbett, " . . . is that well developed routes with population [centres] at each end, sufficient aircraft of suitable type operating at 65 per cent or more capacity and flying at least nine hours a day can make a profit." The Commonwealth, the committee was told, had provided from 1920 to 1940 £1,719,186 in capital expenditure for ground organization — an average of £86,000 per annum. The first controller of civil aviation had been appointed in 1920 to advise the minister for defence on aviation matters; in 1936 a Civil Aviation Board, under the Department of Defence, was appointed; and in 1939 the Department of Civil Aviation was created. Between 1934 and 1939 there had been eight aircraft accidents with thirty-nine deaths for nearly 93 million passenger-miles — or, one passenger had been killed for each 2,300,000 passenger-miles.

The submission said that Qantas

> may resume their overseas service after the war, depending on the international postwar arrangements, QEA have an agreement under the Empire Air Service Act No. 13-1939. Their internal service is not profitable and depends on subsidy. At present they operate two flying boats over ANA's Sydney–Townsville route in co-operation with that company, which pays QEA, through the Department of Civil Aviation, approximately £600 per trip each way. A third flying boat operates to Darwin for the Department which incurs a loss on the service.

The airline companies were invited to put their views before the interdepartmental committee. Ivan Holyman, as managing director of Australian National Airways, revealed a board plan to turn ANA (a private company) into a public company with £10 million capital. It would use £3.5 million to develop internal routes and proposed development of six overseas routes including Australia–England; the United States; New Zealand; East Indies; China; and Russia. Provided his company had all the services — internal and overseas — Holyman said he could operate without subsidy. The general basis for passenger fares would be three pence per mile, internal and overseas. He considered it would be impracticable to operate external services commercially without subsidy unless they had the backing of internal services. Private enterprise, he said, should operate all services.

Hudson Fysh, for QEA, urged retention of the existing sys-

After arriving in Perth from his visit to Britain, Hudson Fysh flew on to Sydney aboard one of the Catalinas under the command of Captain Crowther. This photograph was taken at Rose Bay after arrival. Arthur Baird is second from the left between Captain Crowther and Fysh's son John. Dudley Wright, one of QEA's senior ground engineers and deputy to Baird at Rose Bay is first on the right. Cedric Turner is second from right, behind QEA vice-chairman A. E. Rudder. George Harman is fourth from right.

tem by which various routes were allotted to different companies. For overseas routes he favoured a "chosen instrument". He was not, he said, opposed to more than one "chosen instrument". Some form of subsidy would, he thought, be necessary for overseas routes. Although he did not object to joint government and private ownership, he did not favour it; nor did he favour any merging of existing companies but if such was the government's policy, QEA would co-operate.

Ansett, in his submission, was wholly in favour of private companies and believed in competition over the same routes. (The interdepartmental committee report noted: "Mr Ansett withdrew his first printed statement and substituted another after the Committee had pointed out certain inaccuracies. He also submitted a third statement explaining certain remarks in his printed submission to which the Committee had taken exception. The Committee feels obliged to explain that there were many aspects of Mr Ansett's submission which were unsatisfactory.")[42]

Fysh wrote to McMaster on 18 October 1943, after a trip to Melbourne. "I found the attitude of Capt. Johnston one of hostility to QEA", he said. "I am sure this is all connected with Mr Corbett. Outside the Department I was well received and found Mr Drakeford anxious to assist and sympathetic." Fysh had lunched with both Curtin and Chifley and found the prime minister "very favourable to Empire interests. I was surprised at his knowledge. However, like everyone else, he and the Government have no firm policy yet." On nationalization, wrote Fysh, "Mr Curtin in answer to a direct question by me was non-committal but I thought decidedly not leaning towards Government participation".[43]

At much the same time, on 15 October, the leader of the Opposition, R. G. Menzies, sent a copy of a talk he had given on postwar civil aviation to McMaster. "You would never get a greater increase in the number of those regularly travelling

Prime Minister John Curtin. Picture taken in 1943.

115

by air after the war'', said Menzies, ''if you had to pack them into re-modelled military planes . . . Civil aircraft must offer a high degree of comfort and safety if they are to attract people away from the older methods of travel . . . You will have noticed that certain American senators who were here recently are reported to have ambitions for American flying in the South-West Pacific.'' Menzies said he believed heartily in Anglo-American co-operation, including Australian–American co-operation. ''But this does not mean that Australia, New Zealand and Great Britain have not their own proper and vital flying interests in the South-West Pacific and in the Pacific generally. We shall not lightly abandon these interests. We shall at times be prepared to make, with our great ally across the Pacific, arrangements of a reciprocal kind. But when we come into partnership, as I hope we shall, we want to come in as strong and well-equipped members and not as weak ones.''[44]

Fysh followed up his meeting with the prime minister by sending him a submission on 19 October to operate a postwar service to China. ''The unanimous view was taken'', he wrote, ''in discussions abroad with the Royal Air Force and with officials who know China, and in Australia with officials and businessmen, as to the growing contact and trade which must inevitably take place between the two countries.''[45] McMaster wrote at length to Lord Knollys, the chairman of BOAC, urging closer communications.

> It seems to me that our first move should be . . . in formulating a policy in which we can be in full agreement in regard to the operation of the Empire Service [England to Australia] which war conditions suspended. Then, with an agreed policy concerning aircraft and general modus operandi, to become effective as soon as war conditions permit, we would be in a position to urge its adoption by our respective Governments . . . [This] would also help to prevent those harmful cross currents on the issue of how and by whom this Empire service will be operated. To a certain extent, the dangers that were apparent have been temporarily countered by the opening of the Perth–Karachi service [The Indian Ocean service was increased to a frequency of three a fortnight from 3 November 1943 and was extended to Karachi.] . . . But the very inadequacy of the service in itself is a source of considerable danger.

McMaster then listed the services that Fysh had proposed to the Australian government — a Pacific service and a Tasman service, and services to China and the Philippines. He also put forward a Sydney–Salamaua (New Guinea) service, commenting: ''Carpenters may be willing to come into association with

QEA or Q.A.N.T.A.S. to develop services in and out and around New Guinea and other South Pacific Islands." He proposed the formation of a committee to be permanently based in London, comprising BOAC, QEA, Tasman Empire Airways, and Trans Canada Airlines and he asked Knollys to visit Australia. Stressing the need for British transport aircraft in the area, McMaster wrote:

> At the present time, with the exception of a few small de Havilland machines, the only British transport planes in Australia are two obsolete DH86s which QEA are using on its inland services, and three Empire flying boats operated by QEA on the Sydney–Townsville and Sydney–Darwin services. With these exceptions, the whole of the enormous air transport work in the Commonwealth of Australia and adjoining islands, for both military and civil requirements, is being carried out with American aircraft, among which are a number of the most modern types. The British Air Ministry could not be too strongly urged to divert a number of British machines to this and the New Zealand areas . . . [It] is a most dangerous and unfortunate position for British aircraft and Empire postwar operations here and in New Zealand . . . conditions must inevitably arise under which American interests will so tie up airline operations in these areas immediately following the

As 1943 drew to a close, the Indian Ocean Service was operating three times each fortnight. Four Catalinas had been delivered by December; this photograph shows a billy can of soup being heated by a crew member on the electric hotplate in the blister compartment.

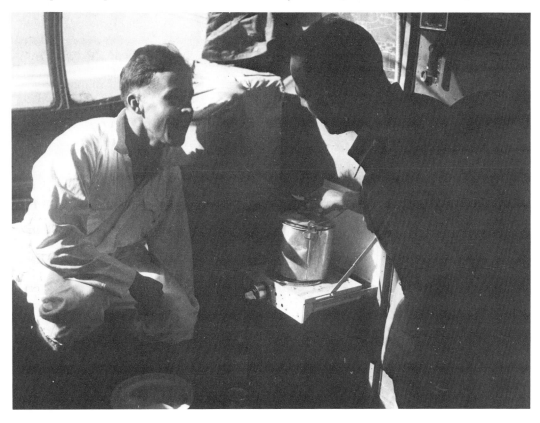

war as to have disastrous effect upon British aircraft manufacturers, making it extremely difficult if not impossible for them to regain their rightful position in the industry.

In regard to the British York aircraft, he said, Fysh had fully investigated this and other passenger types in England and was satisfied that, although not a full postwar development, they had possibilities as postwar types for use on Empire routes.[46] McMaster sent extracts from this letter to R. G. Menzies, who replied: "It is encouraging to the layman to know that men such as yourself are at hand to help direct us in the way of wisdom."[47]

On 28 December, as 1943 ended, Corbett wrote to McMaster that the report of the interdepartmental committee had been presented the previous Friday. He commented:

The Committee, which has just finished a most searching discussion on Civil Aviation, was a particularly strong one. There were many different views very strongly held. They sat for over sixty-six hours and had before them information and views from many eminent sources throughout the world — information not available to the man in the street. In the end, a unanimous report and unanimous recommendations were presented. I think this was an achievement where eight different Departments were represented, each by a specialist . . . There was nothing easy or slipshod in handling the wide range of subjects . . . The Report, of course, goes to Cabinet.

In Search of Postwar Policy
1944

On 5 January 1944 Fysh commented with some acidity on Corbett's closing letter of 1943: "Evidently he is basking in the after effects of a job he feels well done." His own conclusion was that it was a serious defect that no member of the interdepartmental committee had had any long experience of air transport.

Under the heading *Civil Aviation Policy Organisation During the War and Post-War Period,* the committee's report went to War Cabinet, and it summarized Commonwealth policy. Civil aviation was subject to those principles of international collaboration "which we also hope to see applied to the related problems of a world system of security and postwar economic reorganisation". There should be general inclusion of all air transport services within the terms of a convention which would supersede and take over the powers of the International Convention on Aerial Navigation, with powers revised and extended to control all international air transport. The actual operation of certain services (main international routes) should be by an International Air Transport Authority, with a system of devolution to national authorities for management of routes, either within their region or on particular services. The conclusion of an international agreement to create the International Air Transport Authority was envisaged. "In laying down these principles," said the report, "the Commonwealth Government has shown its preference for an initial attempt to obtain international collaboration before proceeding to discussions designed to produce an agreed Empire plan." The committee "assumed that the Commonwealth Government view is that the International Authority should both own and operate the aircraft on its services".

The committee drew attention to United Kingdom views on internationalization, including the Barlow committee's conclusion that "any of the systems of internationalisation with which we have dealt would probably be preferable to the system of cut-throat competition which prevailed before the war".[1] If reverted to, the United Kingdom would inevitably be severely handicapped, particularly having to compete with the United States in providing services on a lavish and world-wide scale. "We should be compelled", said the committee, "heavily to subsidise our services in the interests of national prestige." If internationalization were accepted, competition in civil aviation would be eliminated and it was felt "in unscrupulous hands, aviation can become a very powerful weapon whereby any one country could dominate weaker and poorer countries".[2] The committee realized that the future relationship between the United States and the British Commonwealth was vital.

> There appear to be dangers of a most serious rivalry between them . . . The present position is that the United States owns and operates most of the transport aircraft in the world . . . The British Commonwealth of Nations has no immediate means of producing transport aircraft capable of competing in the near future . . . There are undoubtedly strong interests in the US which favour the use of these present advantages to the maximum possible extent, regardless of future consequences. The Commonwealth and Empire possess an immediate advantage in territories held by them along the main trade routes of the world.

The committee was aware that a case could be made for setting up an all-British organization to operate all-British services between its own territories and extend such a service to foreign countries by reciprocal agreement. "There [are] influences in Britain that would favour outright and immediate competition with America on this basis." It observed that the proposed International Authority "to prevent affronts to prestige and to exclude even the appearance of national rivalry . . . should in word and deed operate as a world authority under its own name and flag and uniform". This idealistic vision was tempered by close attention to the necessity for plans to meet the possible failure of internationalization.

Proposals for the organization of Australian civil aviation made dismal reading for Qantas. The committee proposed that a joint company "be designed with a financial and managerial structure which will enable it to operate efficiently all internal airline services and such regular airline services to adjacent territories as may be permitted by international agreement". For operation of external air routes the question of a "chosen instrument" was best answered, they thought, by an extension of this joint company. They refrained from making a final recommendation on details of the joint company because of "the difficulties of the position of Qantas Empire Airways, which under the Australia–England agreement has a contract for that service for fifteen years expiring in 1953". QEA, they reported, is "an Australian company with half the shares held by BOAC which, in turn, is controlled by the United Kingdom Government . . . There are, therefore, very real difficulties in providing for Qantas Empire Airways in the future." They recommended that the Commonwealth government try to acquire the BOAC interest in QEA.

The report stated that executive of several US airline companies were serving as senior officers in the US Air Corps.

> They have established first class organisations to provide air transport for military needs for the South-West Pacific Area and have at their disposal a large fleet of the most modern American transport aircraft. After the war, Australian Air Services may have at their disposal a large fleet of the most modern American transport aircraft. After the war, Australian Air Services may have few if any suitable transport aircraft available. The possibility of pressure from US interests that they should be permitted to use [their] aircraft to develop operations in Australia cannot be ignored. This . . . emphasises the necessity for obtaining more aircraft for Civil Aviation use and for the Commonwealth having full power to control the operation of civil airlines throughout Australia.

The committee said it knew of no other means of obtaining transport aircraft than from the Munitions Assignment Committee in Washington.

Commenting on British aircraft, the committee thought that the York, essentially a long-range type, was restricted by its small fuselage and by its take-off needs and would be very uneconomic compared with the DC3. The Tudor (like the York a civil derivative of the Lancaster bomber) was not, according to the chief aeronautical engineer of the Department of Civil Aviation, suitable for Australian airlines. He did not know whether the Handley Page 64, developed from the Halifax bomber, was yet in production and said that the British Buckingham had twice the horsepower of the DC3 but carried only thirty-two passengers, making it hopelessly uneconomic for Australian airlines. "It seems", the report concluded, "that there are no immediate prospects of obtaining from England any transport aircraft which could be operated commercially in this country." With some vision it then recommended that £15,000 be made available for building in Australia a proto-type of a twin-engined civil aircraft for operation on the main trunk routes and said that the Department of Civil Aviation had already prepared a specification for such an aircraft, which could be ready for flight trials by July 1945. The committee unanimously recommended that "continuance of the present system [of airline operations] should be rejected". It was unprofitable and inefficient when compared with more integrated operations.

On the concept of a joint company it proposed voluntary amalgamation of existing companies but considered that the Commonwealth had no powers to force any amalgamation, though it did have the power to withdraw any airline licence and "undoubtedly had the power to refuse to continue pay-ment of a subsidy or to provide for the carriage of mails by air". On Qantas Empire Airways, the committee said: "QEA . . . would have two alternatives. They may amalgamate as to their inland route and continue on a charter basis to operate their flying boats for the amalgamated company, or they may risk staying out of the amalgamation in the hope of obtaining an Empire service, and abandon their inland route . . . The acquisition by the Commonwealth of the shareholding of BOAC in QEA would facilitate . . . amalgamation."

The committee went even further, proposing that the director-general of civil aviation be the special governing director of the joint company, with powers of veto to include any proposal to alter the company's financial structure or dis-posal of assets, or any alteration of routes, time-tables, fares, or freight charges. It recommended that the headquarters of the Civil Aviation Department and the new company be loca-ted at Essendon aerodrome, Melbourne. "There is", said its report, "almost an exact counterpart of interests between the Department and the Company in many respects . . . the De-partment administering and supervising regulations govern-ing flying operations, safety, radio, traffic etc, while the Com-pany executes these operations in the field . . . "

Corbett, in an appendix, commented on the wartime link between the Department of Civil Aviation and the Department of Air. "Since the Department of Air was separated from the

Department of Defence, the portfolios of Civil Aviation and
Air have been held by the same Minister . . . In my experience,
the Department of Civil Aviation has not in any way benefited
by this arrangement during the war years." He saw a greater
community of interests between his department and that of
the Postmaster-General's Department.[3]

The thrust of government policy and the report of the interdepartmental committee towards internationalization of air
transport under a world organization in no way accorded with
Fergus McMaster's convictions about Empire co-operation.
Early in January he wrote to Menzies asking him to continue
his series of radio broadcasts and deal with questions of Empire
aviation. He pressed, too, for the organization of a group of
"Empire speakers in Australia to deal with Empire questions
generally".[4] Menzies replied that he had reached the stage
where he doubted whether the broadcasts were worthwhile, a
view shared by Hudson Fysh. He wrote to McMaster: "Personally, my honest reaction to Mr Menzies is to turn to another
channel as soon as he starts speaking because of his uninspir-
ing style. I think the majority feel like myself amongst our
own class. Amongst the other class what he says may actually
do harm."[5]
   Fysh referred to a letter from McMaster and items in it

> which don't read very happily and seem to reflect lack of push
> and initiative on my part. Firstly, what further can I do in trying
> to hang on to the Queensland services for QEA? Secondly, you
> say: "Perhaps the Sunderland negotiations [for flying boats from
> England] are just one of the activities which require that bit of
> push and initiative that seems to be lacking in some of our work of
> late years." Third, you say: "A lot of trouble is evidently due to
> weak management." I would like an opportunity to reply at length
> to what amounts to an indictment of the management, in particu-
> lar, reference to myself as the Managing Director . . . an accusa-
> tion of want of initiative, weakness and looseness of
> management.[6]

McMaster replied promptly but less emotionally, regretting
that Fysh had taken the criticism personally. "The organisation involves all of us in some way or other," he wrote, "and
the slackness or bad management of one executive or even of
one foreman reflects on all members of the organisation. That
there has been slackness and weak management in several in-
stances is beyond question . . . My view is that there is need
for more direct control by you yourself. It is difficult to avoid
the impression that the organisation is top heavy." He referred

Clifton was holed by floating debris during a night landing on 18 January 1944. The crew ran the sinking flying boat into shallow water near the Rose Bay slipway but the tide was low. Before it could be recovered, the incoming tide submerged the fuselage and the salt water damaged the internal structure beyond economic repair.

Clifton is seen here some days after it was ashore. Engineers are removing the propellers and any other undamaged parts which could be used on the two surviving Empire boats, Coriolanus and Coolangatta. Note the Dornier Do24 flying boat in the right background; several of these German built aircraft were flown to Australia by their Dutch crews after the Japanese occupation of the NEI and were taken over by the RAAF.

to the *Civil Aviation Journal* for December 1943. "The figures show that the miles flown by ANA for the term given exceeds QEA by over 700,000 miles . . . and Guinea Airways even lead ourselves in hours flown . . . It is difficult to understand why QEA should always have such difficulties regarding staff and engineers and key men."[7]

On 18 January they were jolted by the loss of the flying boat, *Clifton* (one of the boats returned from the RAAF). In a night landing at Rose Bay, with a captain under instruction, the touchdown resulted in a high bounce from the water and a stall. The boat dropped heavily, was severely damaged, and began to take on water. The crew tried to save it by running it ashore but it was low tide. The incoming tide flooded the hull, damaging it beyond repair. To compound the effect on QEA operations, there was continuing trouble with the Lodestars. "In view of the loss of the *Clifton*, which has considerably reduced our airline operations, there is some excess personnel", McMaster wrote to Fysh on 1 February. "Also . . . it seems impossible to keep the three Lodestars fully operational as a result of recurring accidents. I suggest you go into the question with Civil Aviation and try to get agreement to operate at least an additional Lodestar pending possible relief in the flying boat position."[8] Fysh thought that only another Empire flying boat would be helpful, or possibly a Sunderland. He drew McMaster's attention to "the excellent flying results being obtained by QEA . . . we are far ahead of all operators except ANA, and even beating ANA in freight ton-miles and

124

route mileage".[9] He told his chairman that he had not received
any advice

> as to how to proceed further in the present difficult times which
> Qantas Empire Airways and Q.A.N.T.A.S. are in. I presume that
> you wish to leave matters until Lord Knollys comes out. How-
> ever, in regard to . . . the local Queensland services . . . I feel that
> representations could and should be made at once through suitable
> Queensland Federal Members, much in the same way as we have
> done in the past . . . I could be pointed out that if one big mono-
> poly organisation is formed, either along the lines of Amalgamated
> Wireless Australasia or a purely Government show, the future of
> aviation in Queensland will be dominated and run from Mel-
> bourne or Canberra.[10]

The implication in Fysh's letter that McMaster himself was
not above criticism and could do more brought a letter from
McMaster on 7 February which Fysh described as "rather
overwhelming". McMaster referred to a memorandum submitted to the interdepartmental committee by Ansett and
commented: "If Ansett is responsible for the memo he is a very
able man and has submitted a very well balanced and striking
paper. [It should] be studied by you and followed up for if
taken up seriously by the Prime Minister and members of Parliament there are certain submissions involving British Airways directly and QEA indirectly which should be cleared up."
Fysh told McMaster: "In regard to the twenty-seven separate
memoranda in the attachment to your letter I can only do the
best I can." Harman was away, he said, "with a virtual breakdown owing to overwork, and as a result of the heavy amount
of detail now being undertaken by me, and which is your wish,
I am unable to cope with some of the matters which I felt more
important . . . Paradoxically, the creation of the position of
Assistant General Manager seems to have increased the amount
of detail work falling on me, not lessened it as I had planned."[11]
Fysh thought that "Ansetts is only a wartime bubble, but a
bubble which is desperately trying to become something more
solid, with American backing. I believe Menzies is responsible
for much of the [Ansett] stuff."

He was sorry, he told McMaster, that apparently he did not
feel enough was being done in obtaining additional aircraft.

> I really do not know what further to do that is not already in train
> to meet your wishes. We are all disturbed at losing an Empire fly-
> ing boat but [our] advancement from the dark days following
> Japan coming in is far greater than any other company in Austra-
> lia. We have had more planes given us, we have opened up more
> new lines, we have done more war work, and [the number of]

pilots we have received from the Government has been greater. Our losses in war service have been greater.[12]

He said he had discussed extra aircraft fully with Corbett and Johnston who told him that the position was worse than ever from all points of view. The Australian government had, he said, refused requests from the USA that Australian companies operate more aircraft for them. "I have tried every channel I can think of, except approaching BOAC. No doubt [this] will be done during the forthcoming [Knollys] visit."[13] Management had, he said, had a bad run "with Harman away in a near breakdown, Turner very off colour with lumbago and Arthur Baird in bed very poorly with his old trouble, influenza".[14]

C. O. Turner, as chief accountant, had obviously not slackened his pace of work for on 22 February, Fysh sent a Turner memorandum to McMaster. "I feel", he wrote, "[that it] dramatically ands clearly shows (i) the great increase in the Company's business during wartime (ii) a considerable decrease in the percentage of administration to turnover and to labour [costs], which is the BOAC method of comparison (iii) a balanced net profit." Turner had also prepared a long, detailed, and complex report on the financial basis agreed between BOAC and QEA from the outbreak of war to the break of the Empire route on 19 February 1942. (It was, in essence, a cost-plus arrangement for QEA.)

Though Turner's report answered some of McMaster's criticisms on the operations of QEA, Fysh also faced complaints from Corbett of lack of co-operation between Qantas and Australian National Airways. In a memorandum to McMaster on 9 March, he wrote that ANA might make an issue of it.

> The story is really one of business rivalry. [We] cannot allow ANA to encroach on our interests in an undermining fashion. Any infringement and encroaching has definitely come from ANA. QEA is interested in overseas services and would not cross the path of ANA regarding internal services in Australia where it is pre-eminent ... The first estrangement of the two interests commenced when it became known that in addition to the ANA wish to dominate internal air transport in Australia, they also entertained ambitions and were proceeding with plans to operate overseas.

Fysh outlined the conflict of interests of Holyman as chairman of the Airline Operators Association and with "favouring ANA in its plans". QEA, he said, objected. ANA was also, he said, unfairly encroaching on QEA's Brisbane interests and war work.

> After strenuous and rather drastic protests at an unfair allocation of DAP work and new buildings as between ANA and QEA we secured a revised allocation, giving Qantas a good deal of the excess work allocated to ANA. The charter of Empire flying boats by QEA to ANA through the Civil Aviation Department is now the latest source of trouble. QEA has been in the unfortunate position of repeatedly having Mr Corbett oppose its wartime projects, but in favour of ANA projects. This has culminated in the receipt of the astonishing letter from Mr Corbett on 29 February which seems to condemn QEA on non-co-operation with ANA on the Sydney–Townsville flying boat route without having mentioned an actual complaint.[15]

(There was now a prospect that their problems with Corbett would end. Corbett's tenure as director-general ceased on 16 February when he was officially succeeded by Daniel McVey. He continued on as acting director-general, however, until 5 August 1944.)

Lord Knollys paid a brief visit to Australia in March and had preliminary talks with McMaster and Fysh on the future of QEA and BOAC.[16] A possible way of adding to the QEA fleet while outflanking Corbett emerged in a letter he wrote to

The QEA board gave a luncheon at Sydney's Hotel Australia on 3 March 1944 for BOAC chairman, Viscount Knollys, who had made the first of several visit to Australia via the Indian Ocean route. Left to right: Sir George Julius, Mr A. E. Rudder, Mr F. E. Loxton, Mr A. C. Campbell Orde, Mr H. Harman, Mr F. J. Smith, Mr W. A. Watt. Backs to camera: Sir Fergus McMaster, Viscount Knollys.

them on his return, which suggested that the Air Ministry was lending support to the opening of a London–Sydney service with Liberator aircraft, in which QEA would operate the Columbo–Sydney section. A special effort was being made to keep it entirely secret, Fysh told McMaster on 22 March. "The plan would revive the old system of working with through aircraft [London to Sydney], but I am wondering if this would attract great local opposition as being un-Australian. Should we ask for our own aircraft based in Australia?"[17] McMaster approved the secrecy and urged

QEA hangar, Archerfield, 21 March 1944. Viscount Knollys and Mr Campbell Orde with QEA staff members stand in the doorway of the Igloo hangar built to service heavy bombers. Behind them is a US Army Air Force B-24D Liberator which has been modified by QEA with a power operated gun turret in the nose. Note the new darker paint at the rear edge of the turret which was originally designed for installation in the Liberator's tail. Several hundred of these turrets were fitted to Liberators at modification centres in Hawaii and Australia, at least forty of them by Qantas at Archerfield.

that you do not mention it in any way in Canberra. The first objective is to secure the aircraft and agreement between BOAC and QEA, then operation of the Indian Ocean section satisfactorily . . . then put pressure to have the service continued to Sydney as the proper terminal and connection with Tasman Empire Airways. If the proposal is discussed with the Minister or others it will only get known in quarters capable of frustrating it at this early stage.[18]

(This correspondence with Lord Knollys was lightened by a request from Knollys for the recipe for baking an Australian damper. Fysh instructed him: "The actual dampers which are made by the people of the outback far inland, who can't get

bread when camping out, are somewhat more crude and do not
contain milk or sugar. They are also baked in the hot coals of a
wood fire and then cooked and dug out with a shovel or a stick
and the ashes scraped off them before being eaten.")[19]

The possibility of operating a Liberator service seemed to
hearten both McMaster and Fysh. McMaster wrote a personal
note to their friend of long standing from the Imperial Airways
days, Dismore. "The war has to be won and cleaned up before
much else can be done other than look out that British Empire
Aviation, which includes our Dominions, is not left on the
doorstep while other more virile and perhaps less scrupulous
[organizations] get a flying start . . . Keep the flag flying, old
friend."[20] Fysh set to and prepared a paper which he called
"Postwar Overseas Air Transport as Affecting Australia".
The first great requisite, he began, was for the Empire to
reach agreement, and after that to collaborate with the United
States. He recounted prewar moves for a Pacific service.

> Surveys by ship and from the air have been made of many islands
> between Honolulu and Fiji . . . and a government administration
> officer was placed as resident at Christmas Island . . . One of
> these islands was Canton, which had been visited . . . by a party
> of US astronomers, who left a large plinth recording the visit and
> bearing the American flag in stainless steel. The British flag was
> raised [there] in renewal of British sovereignty by HMS *Achilles*
> . . . and a British Assistant Commissioner arrived soon after . . .
> The status of the island in relation to the United Kingdom and
> United States Governments from the point of view of its use as an
> air base is now the subject of negotiations.

In 1938, HMS *Leander* carried out island survey work and
Imperial Airways despatched a member of the technical staff
with depth-sounding gear.

He wrote that it was essential to formulate a plan to function
immediately from termination of hostilities "to provide machinery for commencement of Civil Air Transport . . . Internationalisation has already been seriously and officially suggested
in England and by the Australian and New Zealand Governments . . . It should definitely be held as an alternative objective but [is] impracticable at this stage." Fysh referred to the
1919 Paris Convention (which the United States signed but
did not ratify) in which the right of Innocent Passage was
described as the right of one signatory country to fly over the
territory of another signatory. Nonratifying countries withheld this right. It was a right that would have to be universally
accorded in new postwar regulations, he wrote.

Australia, said Fysh, cannot stand alone, but "comes in as a unit of the Empire with Canada, New Zealand, South Africa and India . . . to collectively negotiate with the great powers of the world". There should then be Empire–US agreement, or "English-speaking agreement".[21] (QEA later prepared a summary of proposals for air services to New Guinea, China, Japan, and the Pacific islands as one co-ordinated operation in aircraft, personnel, and plant with the principal interest of QEA put as the operation — as the Commonwealth instrument — of the Australian section or sections of the Empire Service, or any duplication of that service.)[22]

Fergus McMaster now pressed Arthur Drakeford for recognition of war operations by QEA flying crews. In a letter on 28 April 1944 referring to press announcements of a special issue of medals, he recounted QEA's special work in delivering from America the nineteen Catalina flying boats in 1941; the operations during the opening phases of the war with Japan on 7 December 1941 to the suspension of the Empire service early in 1942; the operation of the Broome–Tjilatjap shuttle in Feb-

Rose Bay April 1944. The QEA staff at the Sydney flying boat base performed routine maintenance on many military aircraft flying through Sydney. This photograph of women workers from the fabric section is one of the few examples surviving in Qantas's records to show military censorship. The aircraft was one of a small number of Short Sunderlands flown from the UK in early 1944 by RAAF aircrews returning to Australia at the conclusion of their operational tours with the RAF Coastal Command. Before this photograph could be published, the radar aerials and the serial numbers would have to be touched out.

ruary 1942; and general operations in the forward area to Darwin and other centres from February to September 1942, until the start of the Townsville–Port Moresby operations. During the latter, said McMaster, practically the whole of the route from Townsville to the Gulf and Darwin was subject to enemy interception. He referred to the Mount Hagen evacuation, the service to Noumea, to Merauke in Dutch New Guinea, and to Vila in the New Hebrides. "In all, twelve members of the QEA flying personnel are included in the list of killed, injured or missing. Special recognition should be given to those who had done outstanding work", he wrote. He named captains Brain, Crowther, Hussey, Denny, and Tapp. Surprisingly, and certainly by accident, he omitted Captain Koch, who had been shot down by Japanese fighter aircraft.[23] (McMaster's representations were not successful.)

Lord Knollys's visit had set the scene for a return visit to England by either McMaster or Fysh. Fysh thought he should be the one to go and wrote to McMaster on 26 April: "I feel that it will not be easy to get a hearing in London until things settle down and, to be quite frank, if someone has to go I feel I should, because operations are so closely linked in the considerations . . . The mention of yourself as a possible starter to go to England is a surprise."[24] McMaster did not appreciate the tone of this letter, and responded that "the matter of handling the London negotiations must be [for] the best possible interests of the Company and not for any personal ambition. The inference possible in your letter is unfortunate, and could even suggest that personal interests and ambitions are involved. I do not feel that the time is opportune for either you or myself to go to London for the position there is still desperate."[25] Fysh agreed that some delay was necessary. "I think we . . . realise how difficult it would be to settle many of the questions now. It is not possible to settle them in a proper manner until such time as we know what link and relation there is going to be between the postwar operations to come and our pre-Japanese war contracts for Sydney–Singapore operations."[26]

The future role of Qantas on internal routes and across the Pacific was as unsettled as that for the Empire route. McMaster thought there was a threat that Pan American would operate exclusively on the Pacific.

> There would not seem to be room with modern aircraft for duplication [of operators] unless by payment of heavy subsidies. [However], I feel . . . there are sound reasons for more optimism in that

highly placed executives, businessmen and others will make personal visits to Australia rather than use correspondence and agents if by air the total travel time will be from two to four days, whereas in the past the total time by shipping has been anything from five to six weeks. The matter of a daily schedule as against a shipping service on a monthly schedule also will be a great factor in inducing travel.[27]

On internal operations, the future was clouded. "It is not easy to hit on any line of action which would have any real effect", Fysh wrote, "because anything virile enough to give any prospects of . . . success would cut across the overseas interests which all agree should have number one consideration."[28] One outstanding necessity, he said, was securing for the Brisbane–Darwin route aircraft more adequate than the existing fleet of two DH86s and one Lockheed 10A.[29]

A QEA operated Douglas C-47 transport at Archerfield, mid-1944. These aircraft replaced the Lodestars which QEA had operated since late 1942, primarily on the Australia–New Guinea route.

McMaster set down his thoughts about the future in a letter to Lord Knollys on 1 May.

It is felt here that matters will be decided in London which must have a very great bearing on the future of Qantas Empire Airways — both for the immediate future, for the balance of the war and for the period after the war. It has been realised that the Indian Ocean Service and its possible growth and improvement are matters of war service only, and that the problems are largely operational . . . But what happens in the course of this year may have a considerable effect on our prestige and future. We have made it abundantly clear that . . . we could not for long continue to operate Catalina aircraft alongside the more modern types . . . which would make [it] a wasteful and dangerous joke against the former magnificence of the Empire link . . . We want to see Sydney the natural and most important Empire Air route depot in Australasia and in the Antipodes.[30]

In a second letter, he urged again the extension of the Liberator service to Sydney "before any possible arrangement between the Australian Government and internal air services can militate against such extension and require overseas passengers to disembark at Perth and continue their journey by these inland services". He also raised at some length the possibility that BOAC might operate an Empire service from London to China and Japan that might link with QEA's proposed Australia–China–Japan service.[31]

McMaster was correct about the significance of impending decisions in London, made as the European war entered its final phases with the Allied invasion of Normandy on D-Day, 6 June 1944. Though initially only two new aircraft for QEA were to be involved, their operation was to lead to the gradual emergence of a modernized, postwar Qantas. Lord Knollys's letter to them on Air Ministry support for the opening of a Sydney–London service was followed by the release of two converted Liberator four-engined transports for use on the Indian Ocean route. The first arrived early on 3 June at Guildford aerodrome, Perth, ferried out by BOAC's senior commander, Capt. O. P. Jones, who provided QEA with technical advice for the new service. The Liberator service began on 17 June 1944, almost a year after the introduction of the Catalinas. As the new aircraft were land planes it was now possible to cut the length of the sea crossing from 3,513 to 3,077 miles by operating from Exmouth Gulf, and their higher cruising speed reduced flying time by about ten hours. Qantas crews, unaccustomed to nose-wheels and retractable undercarriages, carried out brief conversion courses with both the RAAF at Tocumwal in New South Wales and the RAF at Karachi. Separate engineering facilities were set up for the Liberators at Guildford aerodrome. (The aircraft had a longer nose than the Liberator bomber, for carrying freight, and a passenger compartment with seven windows down each side. There were no gun positions.)[32]

The new service was called the "Kangaroo Service", and BOAC's Captain Jones commanded the first flight from Perth, with captains Ambrose and Crowther and engineer Roberts on board as supernumerary crew. The flight to Learmonth, Exmouth Gulf, took three hours and forty minutes and the aircraft was refuelled. From Learmonth to Ratmalana aerodrome, Colombo, the ocean crossing took sixteen hours thirteen minutes. (On the return trip, on 21 June, Captain Ritchie took Crowther's place in the crew. Ritchie had joined Qantas

The crew of the first scheduled Ceylon–Australia Liberator service at Perth, 22 June 1944. From left: First Officer Wright of BOAC, Capt. Ambrose of QEA, Capt. O. P. Jones of BOAC, First Officer Ross of QEA, Capt. Ritchie, Radio Officer Mumford and Navigation Officer Bartsch, all three from QEA.

in October 1943 at Lester Brain's suggestion, converted to Catalinas at Rathmines, and flown as a captain on the Indian Ocean service.) This lone Liberator operated the new service until a second aircraft arrived on 14 August. Ten days later, the airmail service between England and Australia was resumed. (A further sixteen months elapsed before the third Liberator arrived on 7 December 1945, and the fourth and final Liberator was not delivered until 7 March 1946. All the QEA Liberators were further modified at QEA's Archerfield workshops to provide extra space for passengers and mail in what had been the bomb-bay. They then carried fifteen passengers and a crew of five, giving them a payload of 5,500 pounds — five times that of the Catalinas.)

Lord Knollys summarized BOAC's problems as the tide of war turned and made it possible once more to think of international operations by civil airlines.

> In spite of the constant pressure which we keep up to get some definite plans discussed and settled [he wrote to Fysh], I do not feel that there is much likelihood of that happening for the moment. The international conference which is to take place after the bilateral talks with the Americans, Russians etc. have been completed is unlikely, in my opinion, to occur before the end of this

QEA's second Liberator after
the nosewheel collapsed on
landing from a training flight at
Perth, 16 October 1944. It was
returned to service on 13
November. G-AGKU had been
delivered to QEA on 30 August
1944 and was flown to Brisbane
for modifications to increase its
payload. Fuel tanks were
removed from the bomb bay,
rubber fuel cells in the main-
plane restored the fuel capacity
and seven seats were installed
in the bomb bay. The portholes
for the passengers in this area
can be seen in the side between
the landing gear and the entry
door.

The seven seats installed in the
bomb bay of G-AGKU during
its pre-service modifications at
the QEA Archerfield workshops
in September 1944. The entry
door was behind the last seat on
the right. The modification
increased passenger capacity to
fifteen. The first Liberator,
G-AGKT, was modified to a
similar standard in October
1944.

year. That means that the general principles within which plans for particular routes can only be made will not be settled for some time, and you will have seen that there is considerable difference of opinion as to the form which international regulation and control should take between the Canadian, American and indeed the British Government viewpoints. I should have hoped that it would be possible to come to some limited agreement for services within the Commonwealth but I do not see much sign of this happening in the near future . . . I myself feel that we could be satisfied with reciprocal services in an agreed proportion between this country and Australia. This would mean that if we were both the selected airlines of our Governments, we should run our services right through to Australia and back with our own crews, the service to be based on this country, and that you would do the same based in Australia . . . As regards aircraft, the position is, I am afraid, little better than it was. The Tudor is bound to be delayed [because] of the natural and continuous demands for Lancasters, but in the meantime we are watching carefully the progress — not very rapid, I'm afraid — of the Handley Page transport version of the Halifax, which will at any rate have much greater capacity than the York.[33]

The QEA perspective for postwar alternatives in the operation of civil aviation was set down by Fysh in June. He told McMaster:

I believe that we are not out of the woods yet, though the outlook is not so doubtful as it was. The clearest vision and astute political handling and judgement will be necessary if Qantas is to come out of the delicate and all-deciding stage which is now almost right in front of us . . . The greatest question that has to be settled is that of possible Government intervention. This very question of who is to run civil aviation is being considered and debated in all parts of the world.

Fysh argued that if "controlled private enterprise" was allowed to continue on the domestic services in Australia, then Qantas should fight hard to stay constituted as it was; but if "an A.W.A. of the air be formed [a government-owned organization] to handle Australia's internal and home waters services, then it may be necessary for Qantas in its own defence to secure some suitable and sufficient Government [financial] participation, in order to secure a proper measure of Government support for Qantas during the years which lie ahead."

Among the alternatives he listed the final one was that the Australian government buy Qantas out. On this he commented: "I feel, however, that this extreme eventuality will not have to be faced, and it should be fought all along the line." In a separate letter, Fysh told McMaster that he had met the minister for external affairs, Dr Evatt, at a cocktail party and

they had had "a very brief but to the point talk". Evatt, said
Fysh, told him that "big changes will have to be faced" but
that Qantas was respected and had earned its place in any reorganization.[34] McMaster replied calling for Qantas initiatives.

> My own conviction is that if we ourselves cannot work out a solu-
> tion, we will be in a very weak position. Qantas with its long ex-
> perience and its reputation for efficiency and honesty of perform-
> ance surely should not remain silent or wait until the Government
> has made a decision. Government capital participation and repre-
> sentation on the Board is quite a practicable possibility. Before we
> can do anything worthwhile we want to know what we want to do
> . . . the services we would recommend. It all comes back to what
> has been urged before — that is, to get out estimates, not in
> elaborate detail but sufficiently to give capital and operating costs
> of any air line worth proposing.[35]

In another letter he assured Fysh that he was giving all the
time that he possibly could to setting out the broad principles
of the possible moves for QEA and Q.A.N.T.A.S., both with
and without government participation. "I do not look with
great anxiety to the future. The position, to say the least, is
very interesting and perhaps will be more interesting now than
at any time in the history of Qantas."[36]

Turner's growing importance in policy matters affecting the
financial relationships with BOAC was evident in a memorandum he wrote to Fysh on 13 June as he prepared the balance
sheet for the year to 31 March.

> In regard to the surplus of £116,000 held to the credit of BOAC,
> it is my definite view that agreement in principle that this sum can
> be used (within limits) to offset possible losses in the Empire Mail
> Scheme assets should be obtained before we close the accounts.
> There is no reason that I can see why a decision in principle on
> this matter should be left for postwar discussion . . . The simple
> fact is that we now have a credit of £116,000 built up mainly out
> of the RAAF charter and all we are asking BOAC to agree in prin-
> ciple *now* is that part of this can be allocated to writing off losses
> in respect of assets used in connection with the charter. There is a
> further point . . . that is perhaps not clearly understood . . . in
> regard to the method of arriving at the surplus of £116,000 in our
> accounts. Because of our complicated financial arrangements with
> BOAC and the impossibility of detailed consultation, I have been
> forced to place my own interpretation on accounts, and this invol-
> ved many unorthodox entries as at 19 February 1942 [when the
> Empire service was cut]. I consider therefore that it would be un-
> wise to attempt to close off this year's accounts without hearing
> the views of BOAC's accountants on the details.[37]

On 1 July, Fysh lodged a submission with Corbett (who continued as acting director-general of civil aviation while his successor, Dan McVey, was overseas) with the object of influencing the allocation among ANA, Guinea Airways, and QEA of twelve C47 Douglas aircraft obtained from the Americans. QEA proposed a Brisbane–Finschafen (New Guinea) service using two Douglases, linking with a Brisbane–Darwin service revised to operate two Douglases in place of the existing two DH86s (and leaving QEA's Lockheed 10A available for other purposes). He also proposed postwar operations linking these services with a trunk route between Sydney and Rabaul, with feeder services to the northeastern Pacific islands. Corbett, in what Fysh described as a full-scale row about the allocation of the C47s, pressed QEA for agreement on amalgamation with ANA and Guinea Airways in their future plans, with nationalization threatened as the alternative.[38] McMaster, however, put the QEA position and plans to the treasurer, Chifley, and Fysh followed up by sending notes of this meeting direct to Drakeford. The notes commented on QEA's submissions for the operation of Australia–New Guinea–China–Japan–Pacific islands services as a co-ordinated whole but stressed "that the principal interest of Qantas Empire Airways is in the operation as the Commonwealth instrument of the Australian section or sections of the Empire service, or any duplication of that service". The position in regard to the Empire service, McMaster had told Chifley, was still obscure, though it was obvious that Australian operations should be co-ordinated with BOAC's and that aircraft should be able to circulate from terminal to terminal (Sydney–London). "It is felt", McMaster urged, "that the Commonwealth could assist Qantas Empire Airways at this stage by a fuller and greater measure of confidence in regard to the immediate future." He also made direct suggestions for Commonwealth participation. "Proposals could be submitted", he told Chifley, "for Commonwealth consideration for the formation of a Company having as its foundation Q.A.N.T.A.S., and which could be on the basis of Amalgamated Wireless (Australasia) Limited, in which the Commonwealth hold a majority in number and value of shares; or on the lines of Tasman Empire Airways Limited, in which the New Zealand Government hold 19 per cent of the capital with representation on the Board of Directors."[39] It was, as Fysh wrote to McMaster, a very critical stage of air service developments and "not far short of the last round. I think that an interview with Mr Curtin in the very near future is essential [for] . . . what should be one of the most important interviews in our history." McVey, Curtin, and Chifley would, wrote Fysh, among them settle the future.[40]

To QEA director, W. A. Watt, McMaster wrote:

> I mentioned to Mr Chifley the question of the possibility of the Commonwealth establishing a Government instrument for air development on the lines of Amalgamated Wireless (Australasia). Mr Chifley said he favoured the idea but the matter as yet had not received Cabinet consideration. This question is of vital importance to Q.A.N.T.A.S. and QEA and I advised Mr Chifley that we would submit complete proposals for such an organisation . . . We wish to make it clear also that QEA and Carpenters could come together in regard to the operation of the Australia–New Guinea service, the contract for which is held by Carpenters. At the present time the Company [QEA] has over 1,800 employees, a large number of whom will be dependent upon the future success of the Company.[41]

QEA still had to deal, on more immediate matters, with Corbett and a Department of Civil Aviation that Fysh described as chaotic.[42] Corbett told them on 3 August that the C47 aircraft made available to Qantas (QEA finally received three) should be used to maintain a frequent landplane service between Brisbane and Darwin. It seemed unlikely, he said, that

Nedlands, Perth, 31 July 1944. Despite the introduction of the Liberators with their larger capacity for passengers and freight in June 1944, the Catalina flying boat service across the Indian Ocean continued to operate until July 1945. Two members of a British Parliamentary delegation, Col. Wickham and F/Lt. Perkins stand with Capt. Tapp on the boarding jetty before departure of Service 2074, the seventy-fourth scheduled westbound crossing.

ANA would want to continue the existing arrangements for joint operations between Sydney and Townsville on which the QEA flying boats were engaged. The most satisfactory use for the flying boats was a regular Sydney–Darwin service through Townsville. These arrangements were in accord with McMaster's views. "It is essential that we continue on the Sydney–Townsville section if at all possible", he told Fysh on 9 August. "The matter of whether the service continues to Darwin or Port Moresby . . . is not of so much importance provided we hold the inland service Brisbane–Darwin with the Douglas aircraft. We want to hold our flying boat connection both in Sydney and Brisbane and it is worth a considerable amount to do so. We should not, at this stage, ask for a heavy subsidy. It would be dangerous politically . . ."[43]

They still faced opposition from the retiring director-general of civil aviation and his advocacy of an all-embracing joint authority. Fysh wrote to Lord Knollys on 4 August: "The theme of one chosen instrument to operate both internally and externally, and which is designed around Australian National Airways (which in effect is the shipping companies) is one which has been solidly plugged by Mr Corbett for some time, and he has been trying to convert Mr McVey . . . but with, I believe, little success."[44] Corbett, however, was at the end of his career. "This week in Melbourne", wrote Fysh, " . . . was rather peculiar in that although Mr Corbett has been farewelled, he has been asked to stay on for another week pending finalisation of the position affecting Mr McVey, who did not seem at all certain as to whether he would be willing and able to take the job on or not." McVey did assume the position of director-general, but he did not share Corbett's views, W. A. Watt had talks with him almost at once and wrote to Fysh on 10 August: "Mr McVey . . . talked very freely to me. I don't think any trouble will come to QEA from his quarter. He seems entirely favourable, and hasn't any time for intruders or intriguers. I think that puts Holyman's pot on, as far as overseas operations are concerned."[45] To McMaster, Watt observed that "from what McVey tells me, the Government has had very little time for the Empire air project and has not yet made up its mind".[46]

England, too, had not made up its mind. McMaster told Knollys on 25 August that the report released by the British independent committee on future Empire aviation

> rightly states that if the Dominions through lack of a lead in policy by the United Kingdom Government make their own arrange-

140

ments for the international air services, the results for the Empire
could be serious. We are fully cognisant that high policy concerning Empire and international aviation is not yet determined . . .
Absence of knowledge of London policy or intentions, and particularly BOAC intentions regarding aircraft policy, are placing
QEA at a great disadvantage in its representations to the Commonwealth Government.[47]

To Fysh, McMaster wrote: "It should be pressed [to Knollys]
that it will be worse than futile for BOAC–QEA–TEA to attempt to operate with obsolete, inadequate flying boats against
certain competition by American and Dutch interests, probably combining in ANA, who have the most modern American
aircraft available. War planes will not be worth considering
for immediate postwar competition on world air routes."[48]

In that same week Qantas was advised by the Department of
Civil Aviation that the United Kingdom government had
offered the Australian government three York aircraft.
"McVey feels we should give serious consideration to acquir-
ing these aircraft and so be ready to commence overseas",
Fysh advised McMaster. "McVey feels that we will not obtain
American aircraft for some years perhaps . . . Brain says that
the idea of Qantas operating right to England is still in
McVey's mind . . . and that BOAC would like this. The cost
of the York delivered to Australia is now reckoned at £60,000
Australian. It is undoubtedly the York for us if the Skymaster
cannot be obtained."[49]

At long last the confusion and inertia appeared to be giving
way to firmer possibilities, though the options in aircraft were
dismal. "A cable has just come through from London dealing
with policy matters", McMaster advised Fysh. "The London
position seems more satisfactory [with] a really clear statement
of the position by London. The question of securing Yorks
can be left over until we more clearly study this position. In
the meantime you could advise the director-general that BOAC
is really moving."[50]

Fysh wrote to Lord Knollys that the impending England–
Australia airmail across the Indian Ocean Kangaroo Service
was taking its first step towards a civilian operation. "The
position in regard to the two Liberators which we operate for
BOAC across the Indian Ocean is that we are taking urgent
measures to install wing instead of fuselage tanks to allow
them to carry the originally intended payload of 5,500 pounds,
and making other necessary alterations including the fitting of
extra seats; . . . the extra tanks in the fuselage so blocked up

the area available as to prevent stowage." He hoped to double the weekly frequency of the service. "It appears that Transport Command has the idea that they can very quickly hand over services to civil operators after the war, just as the USA services can hand over. But we maintain that the USA services are in a far superior position because they are not only to an extent operating aircraft suitable for civil postwar transports but such military services are now largely crewed, and often ground-staffed, by actual members of USA civil airlines."[51] Fysh was certain that, with McVey as director-general and Johnston as his second in command, there would be a different and more helpful atmosphere in the Department of Civil Aviation, despite the lack of clear government policy in both Australia and London.[52]

Qantas, which had been negotiating with Carpenters, were now able to report to Lord Knollys that agreement had been reached for the acquisition of the whole of their assets connected with their Sydney–New Guinea airline. They consisted of one Lockheed 14 aircraft, with spares, a hangar and contracts with the Commonwealth, ANA, and other operators. (This Commonwealth contract had, in fact, been abrogated with the outbreak of war, leaving Carpenters an expectation only of re-instatement.) "The purchase price", McMaster told Knollys, "is approximately £42,000 Australian payable to Carpenters by issue to them of fully paid shares in Q.A.N.T.A.S. at present day market values. The Carpenters assets ... will be available to Qantas Empire Airways at cost."[53] Qantas immediately followed up this acquisition with an application to McVey to operate from Sydney to New Guinea on the Carpenter licence.[54] It was not granted. The director-general advised them that the Department of the Army had been told that the commander-in-chief considered that operational necessities prohibited the activities of civil airlines into New Guinea.[55] While these Carpenter matters were being settled, Qantas also approached Arthur Butler, offering to acquire his airline operations on the same basis. Butler preferred to stay independent. Fysh described him to McMaster as absolutely an individualist. "Straight, to a fault. He holds very definite and unshakeable views. He would not be an easy man to fit into any organisation unless he was running it, and we would not consider him suitable to run an important division of our business."[56]

Qantas now thought it timely to set down their views for the

immediate future for the benefit of the new director-general.
In a letter on 16 September, Fysh reminded McVey that

> this company in 1938 commenced operations between Sydney and
> Singapore under a Commonwealth–QEA contract with a fifteen-
> year tenancy, and under a QEA–BOAC agreement. We consider
> that these agreements are in cold storage pending a recommence-
> ment of operations on the cessation of hostilities, but the Com-
> pany, of course, is willing to discuss any alterations or modifica-
> tions . . . This Company, considerably by its own efforts in sug-
> gesting and pressing for a re-opening of Empire air communica-
> tions . . . succeeded in opening and successfully maintaining an
> Indian Ocean route from Perth to Ceylon, and in an extension to
> Karachi. This service is still operating after over a year of success-
> ful work, and has recently been supplemented by a Liberator ser-
> vice styled the "Kangaroo Service", operating between Perth and
> Colombo. These services carry civilian airgraph and air letter
> mail, in addition to their military and war loadings. You are also
> aware of the plan to extend this service to Sydney and inaugurate
> a London–Sydney service when further Liberator aircraft are
> available.
>
> It is now desired to advise that communications have taken place
> between ourselves and BOAC . . . As your Chosen Instrument,
> however, we realise that before a complete organised and settled
> system of Empire Services are possible, a good deal of discussions
> will have to take place in which we offer you our assistance as
> overseas operators.

Fysh then submitted a plan for the immediate postwar period
favouring a parallel operation of a Sydney–London express
service, and also a slower service making more frequent stops.
BOAC, he advised, planned a daily London–Sydney service
operating converted Lancaters. He suggested that QEA take
over all crewing and responsibility for operation of the proposed Lancaster service with BOAC east of Karachi or, if this was
unacceptable, Ceylon.

> It is recognised that the converted Lancaster is not economical,
> but it has the virtue of high cruising speed and should be suitable
> as a stop gap. Brief specifications of the converted Lancaster for
> use on a London–Sydney service are: all-up weight, 65,000
> pounds; load, 4,250 pounds including eight passengers by day;
> range, 4,400 miles in still air; cruising speed, 220 miles per hour.

The elapsed time between London and Sydney would be sixty
hours.

> It is only intended that civil Lancasters be operated for a strictly
> limited period and . . . supplemented by the York or by new
> British types. By the end of 1945 it is expected that the Avro
> Tudor One will be ready and that this aircraft will compare satis-
> factorily with the American and Canadian DC4 in performance

and capacity. BOAC also advise that certain Brabazon types, the specifications for which are now being reviewed, are expected to be well ahead of anything then flying when delivered in the future.[57]

It was all, necessarily, a mixture of unsatisfactory opportunism (with the Lancasters) and nebulous hope (for future British aircraft). McMaster told director F.J. Smith that he had instructed Fysh to secure aircraft "as such action appears to be a condition precedent to completion of discussions with the Commonwealth Government". Smith said he was entirely in accord with McMaster's view that the York could only be considered as a stopgap with a life of two years at the most.[58] QEA director W.A. Watt thought the BOAC board too weak and offered special action by himself through Prime Minister Curtin and McVey to shake up the Australian government.[59] McMaster held back. "There does not seem any need to worry you", he told Watt. "Everything would appear, at the moment, to be going on satisfactorily both with regard to London negotiations and with the Commonwealth. The BOAC board is doing good work . . ."[60]

Lester Brain had been sent to London as decisions on aircraft loomed. The editor of *The Aeroplane* magazine, C.G. Grey, wrote to Fysh:

> What a grand chap he is . . . Lester is one of the half dozen men in the world with whom I would rather spend a day with than with any of the rest. He is always full of information. Wherever he goes he sees things and he observes things and absorbs knowledge; and he has an extraordinarily good way of imparting it verbally. Whenever I have had a yarn with him I always feel as if I have been going places and seeing things. He is like you in that respect. I wish that both of you had time to sit down and collaborate in writing a book. You could teach the world something.[61]

The good news that the British government had decided to allot Lancasters to Qantas for conversion was received on 27 September, with the intention that when hostilities ceased in Europe, further Lancasters would be allotted to provide a fleet for a daily service to Sydney and Auckland.[62] But headquarters Transport Command RAF in a secret letter warned BOAC "and anyone else who ought to be warned that there must on no account be any publicity about the release of the Lancasters to BOAC at this stage. The details of the re-equipment of BOAC in new and additional types of aircraft is on no account to be divulged."[63] One of those new types was the Tudor I that BOAC, in an internal memorandum on 10 October, de-

scribed as an interim aircraft designed to replace Liberator, Lancaster, and similar conversions on the trans-North Atlantic service.

Australian Minister for Air, A. S. Drakeford — second from left — arriving for talks with NZ Government. Accompanying him are left to right Mr D. McVey (Director General of Civil Aviation), Lt.Col. W. R. Hodgson, OBE and Mr R. Gullick (secretary to the minister for air).

> In effect it may be said to provide Liberator or Lancaster loads at higher speeds with a greater reserve of range, but with a considerably higher standard of comfort. To ease production of the aircraft, it is designed to incorporate as many as possible of the major components of the Lancaster MK IV or Lincoln and it should therefore be regarded as a Lincoln bomber with a civil transport fuselage substituted for the military fuselage. The first aircraft [is] due to fly about the end of January 1945 and . . . the total order for fourteen aircraft will be completed and the aircraft in service by autumn 1945.

BOAC then compared the Tudor II with the Tudor I. It was similar, but with a maximum fuselage diameter of eleven feet as against the ten feet of the Tudor I and a length of ninety-five feet compared with the Tudor I's seventy-four feet. Power plant and operating weights were the same but the 4,600-mile range of the Tudor I was reduced to 4,100 miles for the Tudor II. The first Tudor II was expected to fly about March 1945 and fully equipped versions were expected to be in service by December 1945. BOAC described the Lancaster Mail Plane as the simplest possible conversion of a standard MK III Lancaster for the carriage of mail and a limited number of passengers. The nose of the standard Lancaster had been removed as far back as the pilot's dashboard and replaced by a streamlined nose. The bomb bay doors have been removed . . . The tail turret has been replaced by a good form tail cone. Fairly comfortable bench type seating is provided down the length of the interior on the port side. This seating is rather similar to that of the London Underground . . .

The power plants were to be Rolls-Royce Merlin XXIV single stage, two speed, permitting operations to 65,000 pounds at heights up to 23,000 feet. The future of the York, said the BOAC memorandum, was still under discussion.[64]

On 27 October Hudson Fysh left for London on the new QEA Liberator service across the Indian Ocean. In London he found BOAC unclear about the future, with only second-rate aircraft available and questions about how the airline units of the Dominions were to operate far from answered.[65] It was hardly surprising for agreement had not yet been reached internationally on the structure of the postwar regulatory apparatus for civil aviation. The British Labor Party, like the Labor government of Australia, supported the concept of internationalization of air transport, with an international authority owning and operating the aircraft used. In January 1944, this concept became official Australian policy when the governments of Australia and New Zealand issued their joint declaration known as the "Canberra Agreement", favouring an international authority operating aircraft for the United Nations. (Australia reserved the right to conduct internal and short local overseas services, maintain an aircraft industry, and use Australian personnel in overseas services by the authority to and from Australia.)[66] By September 1944, however, Drakeford had acknowledged to the Parliament that "certain nations are not in favour of international ownership and operation" and that the principle was unlikely to be accepted at the forthcoming United Nations conference. Australian would nevertheless, he said, urge the need for international co-operation in air transport and continue to advocate the appointment of an international air transport authority to have executive as well as regulatory powers. It was necessary, said Drakeford, in the interests of world security and to obviate the disastrous effects of unregulated competition.[67]

In November 1944, at the Chicago conference of the United Nations, the Australian concept proved unacceptable, but it was readily agreed that technical and navigational regulations should be governed by international agreement and that certain commercial air rights should be conceded. From this conference emerged the provisional International Civil Aviation Organisation and, after a meeting of operators in Chicago in December, the draft articles for the International Air Transport Association. The five freedoms — the basis for the conduct of future international air transport — were also agreed: (1) the right of the aircraft of one state to fly across the territory of another state without landing; (2) the right of an aircraft of one state to land in the territory of another state for nontraffic purposes (e.g. refuelling or maintenance); (3) the right of an aircraft of one state to set down in the territory of another state traffic (passengers, cargo, and mail) that originated in the country of nationality of the aircraft; (4) the right of an aircraft of one state to pick up in the territory of another state traffic destined for the country of nationality of the aircraft; and (5) the right of an aircraft of one state to pick up and set down in the territory of another state traffic that neither originated in nor destined for the country of nationality of the aircraft. These five freedoms did not, of course, address the problems of commercial competition, fare rates, or conditions of carriage.

The Australian alternative to complete internationalization was joint ownership and operation by British countries of inter-Commonwealth services, able to compete with Pan American Airways and others. Qantas, however, continued to favour the prewar system of sectional operation of part of the Australia–England route by Australia, and doubted QEA's ability to raise the capital necessary to conduct an operation in parallel with BOAC right through to London.[68] In London, in exploratory talks with BOAC on future operations with Lancastrians (the modified Lancasters), it was agreed that BOAC would operate from London to Karachi, and Qantas from Karachi across the Indian Ocean to Learmonth and Sydney. At a conference at Airways House, London, on 8 November, Fysh agreed to straight-through day and night flying of the route, but with a stop of approximately two hours at each landing place.[69] It was agreed that the trip for some passengers would be extremely fatiguing.

The Lancaster as a potential passenger aircraft, however, was unsatisfactory. Harman, Brain, Denny, and A. E. Rudder inspected one closely. "It would seem", Rudder wrote to McMaster, "just as hopeless to try and turn this machine into

a satisfactory operational craft as it would to convert a destroy-
er into a passenger or freight ship. The Lancaster is just a
fighting machine, with much less space than the Liberator. It
is narrow with little headroom. If this is the best that can be
done, the outlook is not very cheerful . . . At the best she would
appear to be merely a makeshift craft, and not particularly
attractive at that."[70]

Hudson Fysh cabled McMaster from London on 24 November on personal matters, following an announcement by the
deputy Australian prime minister, Forde, on 22 November
that the Labor government intended to nationalize interstate
Australian airlines. "The press here", Fysh said, "name me as
probable Director of the new Australian airways set up, but I
have not been approached and have no knowledge of this . . . I
should have thought the proposed Commonwealth set up contrary to the declared wishes of the people and, in view of State
rights, unsound in law. Glad if you would watch my personal
interests for me."[71] A little later, he commented: "Unless
something occurs to change my mind, I am much more interested in continuing in QEA than running internal airlines, but
if the Government decides to amalgamate both spheres then
would naturally be interested in the main position."[72]

In this atmosphere of uncertainty and possible change,
Harman had been looking closely at the constitution of
Q.A.N.T.A.S. as it affected ownership of shares.

> I have found that there is nothing whatever in the Q.A.N.T.A.S.
> Articles to prevent shares being acquired by anyone of any nation-
> ality [he told McMaster]. The point was brought home by the re-
> cent purchase of 101 shares by an American subject. In the Artic-
> les of Qantas Empire Airways it is made clear that it is regarded as
> a cardinal principle of the Company that the Company is to be
> and to remain under British control . . . As I see it, therefore, if
> Q.A.N.T.A.S. came under foreign control by the acquisition of
> the majority of its shares by other than British subjects, then
> Q.A.N.T.A.S. itself could no longer remain a member of Qantas
> Empire Airways. This risk might never be very real but should, I
> consider, be guarded against.[73]

On 9 November 1944 Harman's advice was taken. At an extraordinary general meeting in Brisbane a special resolution was
passed that the articles of association be amended to provide
that "no person shall become or remain a member of the Company who is not a British subject and no member shall hold
any share on behalf of or as a trustee for any foreigner". On
that same day, Q.A.N.T.A.S. held its twenty-fourth annual

meeting. McMaster reported a net trading profit for the operating company, Qantas Empire Airways, of £63,789 for the year to 31 March and confirmed the purchase of W. R. Carpenter Limited Air Lines and the agreement of Sir Walter Carpenter to join the Q.A.N.T.A.S. board. He said the company had ordered a number of Avro York aircraft, a four-engined machine with a commercial cruising speed of 220 miles per hour and a commercial version of the Lancaster bomber, to be fitted for Empire service to carry thirty to thirty-two passengers seated or twenty passengers with sleeping accommodation.

The two DH.86s, VH-USC and VH-USF, continued operations on the Brisbane–Darwin service until late 1944. Shown during unloading of baggage and mail at Archerfield, VH-USF retains the camouflage paint of the early war period but the registration letters are more prominent and it carries the new logotype adopted in 1944. Painted on both the aircraft and the baggage trolley, the logo features the Speedbird emblem as used by BOAC but painted in red on a blue disc.

> Whether air services of the future are to be operated by free enterprise by public companies or by Government Corporations or by some combination of both is a matter of Government policy which would seem as yet undecided [said McMaster]. But it should be a policy that the maximum Australian operation of services within an Empire plan, and direct to neighbouring countries, should be pushed to the utmost, and those services should be owned and based on, and fully controlled by, Australia. For Australia this means taking her proper place within a strong Empire air plan, and also the establishment of direct Australian services when the time is opportune to India, Java, China, Japan, Ceylon, Africa and the Pacific area.[74]

McMaster had had what he thought were helpful interviews with both the treasurer, Chifley, and the acting prime minister and acting minister for air, Forde, and he cabled Fysh:

We asked the Treasurer is it the intention of the Government to include overseas services within the ambit of the proposed Statutory Authority for Government operation of interstate services [and] if not, would QEA continue as the instrument of the Government for the operation of overseas services. The Treasurer stated that Government policy in regard to overseas services will not be determined until advice and recommendations are received from Mr Drakeford on the outcome of the conferences at Montreal, Chicago and London. Drakeford and probably McVey are proceeding to London. It now rests with you to further these important negotiations in London with our Minister for Air, our Director-General and BOAC. It is a recommendation of the Treasurer that pending finalisation of Government policy, QEA continue its present services . . . but we should not, repeat not, proceed further regarding our projected interstate services.

McMaster then urged that the United Kingdom and the dominions "should combine in Empire services and not enter into competition by parallel services".[75] In a second cable he had bad news. "Definite advice just received that our Department of Aircraft Production work in the Brisbane area terminates within two weeks. [Also] profit Brisbane–Darwin operations doubtful. Army authorities not yet prepared to allow civil operations to New Guinea. Major shrinkage QEA revenue seems inevitable until Empire Service re-established."[76]

McMaster had strong views on how the new Empire service should be operated. "We urge as a Board", he cabled Fysh on 15 December, "co-ordination and combined effort, and that the United Kingdom Government through BOAC should have a capital and directing interest in all Empire Services linking the United Kingdom with the Dominions . . . [it is] obvious that parallel services must be competitive and uneconomic."[77] These were views, however, that the Australian government and BOAC did not now share. On 22 December, Fysh advised him that BOAC, Drakeford, and McVey all favoured the operation of parallel frequencies on the England–Australia route through India, saying that the only other practical solution of an Empire operating organization was politically unacceptable at this stage.[78] A concerned McMaster asked how QEA at such short notice (of the Lancastrian services) would provide its capital. Fysh could not give details but replied that the possibility of a joint operating company was being kept in view, which could also include the Pacific, and he was in favour of this. There was comforting news. "It is not practical to operate parallel frequencies in the early stages," Fysh advised, "and it is now expected that QEA will operate Sydney-

Karachi. Regarding Pacific services, expect these will operate by development of an alternative form of Tasman Empire Airways except that Canada would operate her own parallel frequency right through the route."[79] For the proposed Lancastrian service, Fysh advised, QEA would not be asked to outlay any capital.[80]

That Qantas would continue and expand their operations with the coming of peace seemed assured as 1944 ended. It was not clear, however, who would be their owners or what would be the structure. What was most obvious was that only stopgap services could be operated with uncompetitive and utterly unsuitable aircraft.

Peace — and Problems 1945

7 Hudson Fysh returned from England in January 1945, travelling through Canada and the United States, where he flew in the prototype Lockheed Constellation; the year was to end with a recommendation to the board to buy these modern, long-range, pressurized airliners. In the intervening months, however, the British government would press hard for acceptance of the unsatisfactory Tudor II and the Australian government would intervene massively in internal airline matters and determine the future for Qantas and Australia's overseas airline operations. The defeat of Germany and Japan was to bring the challenges and problems of peace.

The government's intention to nationalize all Australian interstate airline operations threatened Qantas's aspirations to operate to New Guinea (following the acquisition of Carpenters). Drakeford, in a telephone conversation with Fysh, warned him that New Guinea might have to be considered as an Australian state, rather than warranting a service that could be styled as an overseas operation. "From this," Fysh commented to McMaster, "I deduce that some strong propaganda has been going in from the local operators."[1] Fysh prepared a Qantas paper for Drakeford on 19 February, advising that the company believed interstate and overseas services were two distinct operations and should develop under two separate constitutions or organizations. Overseas services, wrote Fysh, would be to a great extent a national prestige development in high performance aircraft, and he believed that the Common-

wealth government should participate financially and directionally in overseas services and that Qantas Empire Airways should be the Commonwealth instrument.[2]

McMaster did not like the government indecision on New Guinea and telegraphed Fysh on 26 February:

> Am astounded that the Minister is undecided regarding the New Guinea service. It was a definite understanding on behalf of the Government that the service was essentially a Carpenter operation and the Government agreed through its high officers to its transfer to Qantas. If such Government understanding and that of McVey is not honoured, all confidence in such negotiations would end. Please remember me to the Minister and the Treasurer.[3]

On that same day Cabinet approved government policy for Australia's postwar participation in international air transport. It abandoned the internationalization that it had urged at the Chicago conference and now adopted a policy that: (i) Australia should have a representative on the Commonwealth Air Transport Council (CATC); (ii) for the United Kingdom–Australia service via India, the Australian government would stand firm in the decision that the service not be operated by a joint operating corporation representing the United Kingdom, India, Australia, and New Zealand, but should be on the basis of parallel operation by selected UK and Australian operators,

On 17 January 1945, Hudson Fysh made his first flight on a Lockheed Constellation. He was returning from Britain via the United States and at the time of his visit to Burbank, six Constellations had been completed. The aircraft shown here was the sixth to fly — serial number 1966. All of the aircraft built during the war were delivered to the Air Force as the C-69.

153

each operating through services between the United Kingdom and Australia. On this basis the route would be operated by fully reciprocated services, with mutual assistance through the joint use of ground facilities for handling aircraft and passengers and with the pooling of revenue and resources, thus avoiding unnecessary duplication; (iii) the Australian government would form, with the New Zealand and United Kingdom governments, a joint organization to operate services across the Pacific, such services being in parallel partnership with services operated by a Canadian organization with provision of pooling of resources, sharing of revenue etc. as in the case of the Australia–United Kingdom service; and (iv) the standard clauses on the lines of those agreed at the Commonwealth discussions should be adopted for any bilateral agreements negotiated by Australia.

The Qantas prospects for a New Guinea service were not promising. The minister for external territories, Eddie Ward, and some other cabinet ministers thought that New Guinea, as a territory, should be considered an Australian service and fall under the government plan to take over interstate operations. The minister for civil aviation was not encouraging. "Drakeford thought our chances of operating the service were not very good", Fysh reported. "I told him that you yourself and the Board of QEA would take very badly any going back on the previous arrangements and that . . . we just could not contemplate not operating [to New Guinea]."[4] The course of the Labor government, set clearly on nationalization, was evident. McMaster, who had never opposed the concept of government involvement in aviation, told Fysh: "I feel that we have a possible chance if we drive quietly for an AWA basis in which the Government would have a majority in [QEA] capital and equal representation on the Board, to be adjusted as between Qantas and BOAC on a basis to be agreed."[5]

The uncertainty on New Guinea ended quickly, following the Cabinet policy meeting on aviation. On 7 March, Fysh advised McMaster by telegram: "Wish to confirm good news in today's papers . . . that Minister has advised QEA are to re-open and operate overseas services and the New Guinea run on behalf of the Australian Government."[6] Formal confirmation came in a letter from Drakeford to Fysh on 13 March. "The Commonwealth Government has now approved of your Company re-opening the civil air service from Sydney to Lae or such other centre in New Guinea as may be agreed. I take this opportunity of also confirming the advice contained in my

154

telegram of 10 March that the Government has approved a continuation of arrangements under which your Company operates conjointly with BOAC the service between London and Sydney."[7] Qantas Empire Airways was to retain its pre-war role as Australia's overseas airline.

The New Guinea service started on 2 April with DC3 air-craft. A few days later, on 9 April, Tapp left England in the first QEA Lancastrian. Fysh confirmed to McMaster that the Lancastrian service would start from England on 31 May and from Sydney on 2 June. The second Lancastrian delivery flight under Capt. O.F.Y. Thomas left England on 24 April and Thomas commented: "Knowing something of the contro-versy in respect of the passenger cabin I can say this — that it is more comfortable than at first they [the passengers] and I thought . . . The heating and air control are excellent. There is plenty of heat for the crew to remain in shorts and outside temperature at zero. The pantry, though small, worked satis-factorily, the urn and refrigerator proving very useful. Tea can be made from the former."[8]

Sadly, in all these excitements, McMaster's health declined. Fysh wrote to Lord Knollys on 26 April: "It is now three months since I returned from London [and] there is now the Chairman's unfortunate illness. Sir Fergus has now been in bed here in Sydney for some five weeks. I expect it will be some months before he is back to any real active participation." Once again, the full load of responsibility in an uncertain and demanding period was to fall on Fysh.

Dan McVey wrote critically to Fysh on 4 May.

QEA's first Australia–New Guinea service on 9 April 1945 was operated by this aircraft, VH-AFA, a former US Army Air Force C-47 converted to DC-3 specifications.

155

At the moment, beyond the establishment of the Lancastrian service, the re-opening of the Sydney–New Guinea service and the contemplated Fijian and inter-island services in the Pacific which are being discussed shortly with the Governor of Fiji, there are no additional services of immediate moment. As you know, the details of the trans-Pacific service remain to be discussed at a high government level . . . There are two matters which concern the Department of Civil Aviation directly. The first is the serious delay that has occurred in the establishment of the Lancastrian service. No really satisfactory reason has been given the department. The second is allied to the first. At the Commonwelth talks in London in December last it was agreed in respect of any proposal to extend the Lancastrian service from Sydney to Auckland that the three companies concerned — BOAC, QEA and TEA — would submit proposals for consideration by the three Governments. The United Kingdom and New Zealand Governments . . . have been kept well informed . . . but to date no proposals whatsoever have been received by the Department of Civil Aviation.

Crew and passengers on the first Lancastrian to arrive at Mascot, 17 April 1945. From left N/O Sander, J. Aldous and G. Williams (both QEA senior ground engineers), Captain Howard, R/O Clarke and Captain Tapp.

(The Lancastrian service had been scheduled to begin on 12 April. Qantas had been advised by Critchley at BOAC in a cable on 8 March that there had been a delay in the delivery of the Lancastrians because of war priorities and the need for further modifications.)

In April 1945, the Australian delegation attended the con-

ference at San Francisco to complete the charter of the United Nations. In that same month, at Havana, representatives of airlines of thirty-one nations met and brought into effect the articles of association of the International Air Transport Association (IATA). On 8 May, Germany surrendered and the war in Europe was over.

Less than one month later, on 2 June 1945, an Avro 691 Lancastrian left Sydney with high priority documents and air letters on the opening Sydney–London service through Learmonth (Western Australia), Ratmalana (Ceylon), Karachi (Pakistan), and Lydda (Palestine) to Hurn, in southern England. Qantas Empire Airways flew the service to Karachi, where BOAC took over. It arrived at Hurn on the morning of 5 June. (The Lancastrian had four 1,635-horsepower Rolls-Royce Merlin M500 or RAF T24-2 engines, a cruising speed of 230 miles per hour, and could carry up to nine passengers. Besides operating these fast Australia–England services, Lancastrians were later flown between Australia–Japan and Australia–Norfolk Island.)

Hudson Fysh left for England on 23 June by Lancastrian to attend a meeting of a committee of Commonwealth air transport operators and to assist Dan McVey at a meeting of the Commonwealth Air Transport Council. (Turner left on 19 June for a six-week visit, both to assist Fysh and confer on BOAC accountancy matters. G. U. (Scottie) Allan was already stationed in London as QEA technical expert.) Fysh was also scheduled to attend an executive meeting of IATA in Paris on 30 July. Before his departure Fergus McMaster, though his health was further deteriorating, summarized QEA policy.

Prior to the commencement of the Lancastrian services on 2 June 1945, the two aircraft flown out to Australia were used to train additional pilots and technical crews. On 29 April 1945, this one visited Archerfield, Brisbane, and drew a crowd of visitors to marvel at its size.

157

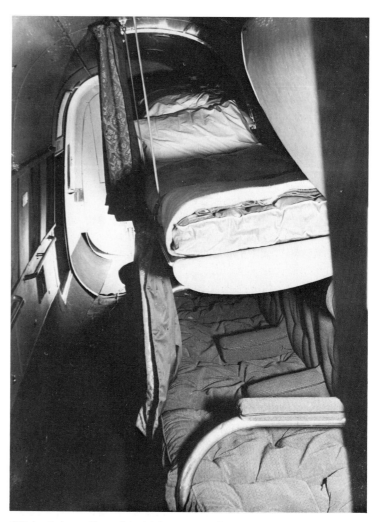

The cramped passenger compartment of the Lancastrian, looking toward the tail. Three couches were positioned along the left side giving seating for nine passengers by day. Three bunks could be lowered from above the couches allowing six to sleep in reasonable comfort.

"Principle policy should be not to isolate the small group of Qantas capital but make it fit in to any large Empire policy. Two principal factors will be agreement and finance for a new postwar England–Australia service and provision of capital for the purchase of aircraft, plant and general operations, [as well as] the financial return on capital to QEA under the above conditions."[9] Fysh, in a last message to McMaster before leaving, wrote: "You can set your mind quite at rest reference the possibility of my accepting any offers over there."[10]

On 6 July, the prime minister, John Curtin, died in office and was succeeded by Joseph Benedict Chifley. On that same day, Harman, who was acting general manager, wrote to Fysh about McMaster's health. "Personally I am very worried about the condition of our Chairman. He apparently has got pleurisy and in his weakened condition it is hard to throw off

— although apparently his heart is standing up well."[11] McMaster's doctor, however, thought there was no reason why he should not fully recover.[12] Harman advised Fysh that under the new prime minister Cabinet remained unchanged and that QEA were to begin thrice-weekly services with the DC3s to New Guinea from 16 July.

On his first trip by Lancastrian, Fysh found the catering from Sydney very good but the metal trays unsatisfactory. "Curry overflowed onto my lap instead of off the plate on to the tray", he wrote in his notes. He found that the majority of the long distance through passengers suffered from stomach trouble "brought on by eastern foods, eastern heat and lack of exercise aboard", and thought catering for this trip warranted a special study. He considered the long (sixteen-hour) wait at Karachi unnecessary and the lack of windows on the port side very noticeable. The starboard side windows were badly placed. "Neither when sitting down nor standing up can a passenger see the ground out of them. The passenger seats and the leg room are good. The bottom bunk is adequate. Passengers go to bed and read in real comfort before finally turning off their lights. In no circumstances", wrote Fysh, "can more than six passengers be carried [with five crew]."

Fysh continued his notes in England, reporting that Captain Allan "our Technical Representative in London, is installed in BOAC at Airways House . . . and is overworked. Office space . . . for Mr Turner and myself is desperate. The only solution is our own offices. What with normal work plus Empire and International Conferences I have been overwhelmed, and consequently inefficient, many important papers not having been read yet."[13] Turner, he noted, was in particular working on the future financial set-up in detail, and studying the various BOAC accounting departments. Fysh himself inspected British aircraft and saw the Tudor I, the Tudor II mock-up, Short's Shetland flying boat, the de Havilland Dove prototype, and visited Bristol to see progress on the Brabazon I and Bristol freighter.

The introduction of the fast Lancastrian service made the Indian Ocean service of the Catalina flying boats redundant. A QEA memorandum on 12 July advised all concerned that the service, between Perth and Karachi, would be withdrawn with the final service from Perth, No. 2Q132, leaving on 12 July, and the final service from Karachi, No. 18134, leaving on 15 July. Fysh wrote to Lord Knollys: "Now that the Catalina service across the Indian Ocean is ceasing after two years of

A little known aspect of life in Australia during the war was the use of coal gas as a substitute for petrol on civilian vehicles. This QEA van unloading the first Lancastrian at Mascot airport, Sydney, has been fitted with a frame on top to carry a rubberized bag filled with gas.

operations it is an appropriate time to draw attention to the fact of this rather unique service and its record of some one million miles flown without loss or accident on the world's longest ocean hop. As you know, this service was put in on the insistence of QEA and by QEA, and not only operated by its crews but managed and maintained from Australia . . . ''[14]

Harman sent final statistics on the Catalina service to Russell Tapp, now manager at Perth. There had been 271 crossings; total passenger count was 648; total freight carried was 14,383 pounds; total mails carried was 113,760 pounds; total miles flown was 956,630.[15] It had been an impressive and sustained operation in every way, but had had little impact on the head office structure and strength of QEA in wartime. Harman commented to Fysh on 20 July:

> I quite agree with you that we are becoming an international organisation; there is certainly no future for us internally, particularly if the Nationalisation Bill goes through, — and we have many weaknesses, not the least that [we] require strengthening of our executive side, particularly with your own absences at International Conferences etc, which is so vitally necessary to us. It is going to be an absolute necessity to have a Traffic Manager in Sydney. There is no one here fitted to take the job other than Neilsen, and I personally think he can handle it well. Brisbane is not of the importance that it was.[16]

On 14 August 1945, Japan surrendered and World War II ended. The momentum for radical change in Australian civil

160

aviation was, however, already well established. Two days after the Japanese surrender, the Australian National Airlines Act No. 31 of 1945 received Royal Assent, creating the Australian National Airlines Commission and conferring on it the power to operate between states and territories or within any territory of the Commonwealth. It also, in line with the Labor government policy on nationalization, provided that licences to private operators should cease to be operative as long as adequate services were provided by the commision. It was an act that set out to create a monopoly air service between states (and within territories) operated by a public corporation.[17] The act was challenged at once by Australian National Airways, Guinea Airways, and MacRobertson Miller Aviation with the High Court finding, under section 92 of the Australian Constitution, that providing an interstate air service was interstate trade and could not be prevented. The newly established Australian National Airlines Commission, though it could itself operate services, was not to be a monopoly.

Though this act in no way impinged on Qantas, and was solely concerned with domestic aviation, it was clear that change lay ahead for the operation of Australia's international services. Lord Knollys wrote to McMaster:

> There seems no doubt that we must face the likelihood of the Australian Government intending not only to take a share in [QEA] but to make it completely Australian by acquiring the interest of BOAC. Such a step is one which is clearly a matter for the Australian Government to decide, and our attitude is always that it is obviously the right of any Government to settle what form its national airlines should take. Much as I would regret the disappearance of our interest in QEA after so many successful years of partnership, we shall naturally be bound to accept the Australian decision if it is in that sense. We can in any case look forward to close association through the parallel services of QEA and BOAC between Australia and this country.[18]

Hudson Fysh, however, just returned from England, was apprehensive about the intentions of the government and the possible ambitions of the newly created commission. "It seems that matters concerning QEA and Q.A.N.T.A.S. . . . are now coming to a head. It would seem wrong just to let QEA drift on in a position where it could be lopped off at any desired moment by a Government Commission, which presumably will be shortly fully set up with a Chairman, Board and Director-General — and which would eliminate QEA well and truly." He thou·· ·t they should obtain the views of Chifley and Drakeford as soon as possible.[19] To Knollys, Fysh wrote:

"It is proposed that I should go ahead with the Australian Government and make every endeavour to effect the best compromise possible to prevent complete nationalisation, which none of us here feel would be a good thing."[20] Fysh saw Drakeford and wrote formally to Edgar Johnston, acting director-general of the civil aviation, on 27 August: "the Board of Qantas Empire Airways at its meeting in Sydney on Friday last considered the question of the BOAC interest in QEA being bought out by the Australian Government. The Board decided that if this was the wish of the Australian Government it would offer no objections, and it was also noted that BOAC would have no objections. It seems urgent to obtain Cabinet consideration of this matter right away . . . "[21]

With McMaster ill, Fysh was under pressure. His chairman praised him for his actions in a letter on 12 September: "I wish to congratulate you on the submissions you have made to the Government and on the way you have handled the business right through", wrote McMaster. "I have had a series of setbacks but now have been on constant normal temperature for over two weeks. The doctor seems assured, and I am satisfied, that the chest is clear." Fysh, in fact, carried the whole brunt of negotiations with the government. Prime Minister Chifley saw him in Canberra and told him that a memorandum was being prepared for submission to Cabinet for the Australian government to acquire BOAC's shares and that he, Chifley, would support this. Fysh wrote to Drakeford:

> My interview with Mr Chifley . . . was very satisfactory . . . I do feel, however, that care has got to be taken to avoid any unacceptable strings being put on the deal by Cabinet, and that it has got to be a straight out buy, which will leave QEA a working, living organisation. It is also a first essential that no conditions be imposed which would render it impracticable for Qantas to obtain its share of the new capital required. For instance, I honestly do not see how we could approach our shareholders and the public if the Commonwealth had the right to take over QEA or the operations of QEA at any time.[22]

By 26 September their main doubts were put at rest and Fysh was able to advise McMaster: "Drakeford rang last evening stating Cabinet had agreed to proposals along the mutually beneficial lines anticipated, and he and the Treasurer are finalising [them]. He stated no publicity desirable. Expect [it will be] some months before finalised."[23]

On 26 September, Fysh set out with Neilson by RAF Transport Command Liberator for the United States and Canada to

attend the first annual general meeting of the International Air Transport Association, then to continue on to England to discuss an agreement with BOAC and the Air Ministry for the operation of a provisional BOAC–QEA partnership (and for the postwar services with Lancastrians and Hythe flying boats until better aircraft became available).[24] Two days after his departure, McMaster was able to issue a statement on the purchase by the Australian government of BOAC's shareholding in QEA.

Sydney airport on the shore of Botany Bay about September 1945. QEA was using the two large hangars facing the camera to overhaul the Lancastrians and DC-3s operating from Sydney. The Royal Air Force Transport Command was flying Liberators from the UK to Australia via the USA until late November 1945. Four of these RAF aircraft can be seen parked wingtip to wingtip to the right of the control tower.

> The transaction was effected with the full concurrence of the directorates of Qantas and BOAC. In the opinion of Qantas directors it is a thoroughly sound move . . . as it now establishes Qantas Empire Airways as a wholly Australian national organisation in regard to both capital and direction. With the highly trained organisation which it possesses, together with its special and very valuable experience, QEA is well equipped to play a prominent and successful part in the intensive postwar development of overseas services.[25]

Though the QEA organization and experience were not wanting, the aircraft available were. "I am leading up to a talk with Lord Knollys and the Air Ministry over the whole matter of aircraft for the Empire routes." Fysh wrote to Harman, "but as usual not one wants to talk about it at all . . . It may be we will have Yorks out after all for a spell. It is a bit of a mess

163

but we have always been facing this sort of thing and must not get worried.''[26]

McVey was strongly critical of Fysh's comments to him on traffic rights and on the Qantas–BOAC planning for the Australia–England service. He cabled Fysh on 19 November stating bluntly:

> Your view that traffic between Honolulu and San Francisco constitutes fifth freedom traffic is erroneous. Such traffic is cabotage. This misconception on your part and views you consequently propound indicate some confusion in your mind on agreements for the trans-Pacific service. It is fervently hoped you did not express those views to . . . others in Canada. As you know, arrangements for landing and traffic rights are matters for Governments and not for operators. In view of your statements am compelled to inform you that at the moment we are in the process of formulating a reciprocal agreement with the USA in which fifth freedom traffic is a contentious and delicate subject. We have no intention whatever of seeking traffic rights between Honolulu and San Francisco for the simple reason that this is cabotage and reserved for American operators.[27]

Fysh replied with contrition that his comment had not been discussed with anyone else.

The director-general criticized BOAC and QEA plans for the Empire route to McMaster on 27 November and drew his attention to uncertainties that QEA faced on the Pacific.

> We are deeply concerned [wrote McVey] over the lack of finality of BOAC–QEA plans for the Empire service. Frankly, we view with no little dismay the suggestion that it may be necessary to conduct the Empire service with flying boats for a few years . . . The Dutch either have acquired or are in process of acquiring Constellation and DC4 aircraft and it is impossible to view with equanimity their operating a service which will take less than half the elapsed time of a flying boat service . . . Discussions on the Empire routes, as you know, have all been directed to the use of land-based aircraft in the postwar period.
>
> We know that the explanation is the prospective late deliveries of Tudor II aircraft but, even so, we hoped that the York would have proved acceptable as a reasonably suitable interim machine. Unfortunately, however, we are told in somewhat general terms that the York has proved a troublesome aircraft and, in any case, that they are not available. I personally find it difficult to accept this general statement. The York has been used for military transport for over three years . . . Lord Louis Mountbatten uses a York and will use no other aircraft. Lord Allanbrooke, now in Australia, is making his journey around the world in a York. Messrs A. V. Roe and Company deny most vehemently that the York is an unsatisfactory aircraft.
>
> The position is even more acute insofar as the Pacific Service is

concerned. If QEA cannot find satisfactory aircraft for their authorised services, it would appear we cannot expect help from them for an interim Pacific Service. Your most formidable rival, however, is likely to have four DC4 aircraft here in this country within a very short time and he is not likely to remain quiet when he knows there is a demand for services which he can meet and QEA cannot. [McVey was referring to Australian National Airways].

On the Government level, all that could be done has been done. We agreed on partnership arrangements at Montreal just twelve months ago and we chose as the operators BOAC and QEA. There has been practically no progress. Explanations will satisfy neither our public nor our Government when our competitors are in a position to provide a modern, fast service and our own chosen operator cannot. We must have a British plane to fill the gap until the Tudor II aircraft is available. We must press for more details of the arguments against using the York.[28]

McVey's frustration was fully shared by Qantas. Fysh wrote to Lord Knollys on 3 December, stressing the critical position of both BOAC and QEA without adequate aircraft. Action was vital, he said,

to turn aside the danger of a break-up of United Kingdom–Australian civil air transport co-operation on the Empire routes . . . which I am convinced would come if Australia makes the decision to operate with American aircraft while the United Kingdom remains with British aircraft. Even if the full-steam-ahead signal is given immediately, it would take at least three years, possibly five or more, before British manufacturers are turning out air transports equal to the Lockheed Constellation. However, some of us in Australia still feel that when the present depressing period has passed, fully comparable British air transports will be provided. The problem is — how are we to tide over the period? . . . Australia feels let down over this question of British aircraft. She has been let down in past years, and I consider she has been so in the present period, particularly in regard to the Tudor II. We have also been let down in regard to the York . . . QEA put a lot of time and thought into this project and prepared plans and drawings showing [how] this aircraft would have been able to carry twenty sleeping passengers. What has been the result? By all reports the York is still quite unsatisfactory for commerical use. It is problematical whether advances can be made by the United Kingdom to Australia for the use of British aircraft in 1946, on which depends a continuation of the old United Kingdom–Australia co-operation in air transport.[29]

These pressing issues were discussed in London on 6 December at a meeting of BOAC representatives, led by Lord Knollys; QEA representatives, led by Fysh; and the Ministry of Civil Aviation. Sir William Hildred chaired the meeting which agreed "for practical and commercial reasons" that the concept of parallel operations by the two airlines on the Empire route should be abandoned during the Lancastrian period. It was also agreed that in addition to the existing thrice-weekly Lancastrian service, the Sunderland III flying boat operation (soon to be extended from Rangoon to Singapore) would be further extended to Sydney, with QEA to have the operational responsibilty for the section Singapore–Sydney. It was pointed out by Fysh that McVey had asked him to explore the possibility of using Yorks on the service to Australia, though QEA felt strongly that flying boats were a better proposition. Convincing reasons would have to be given to the Australian government for not adopting Yorks at government-to-government level, Fysh stressed.

Hildred referred to the withdrawal of the Royal Air Force from the Pacific service and the urgent need for a civil service to fill the gap. It was, Fysh responded, a concern shared by the Australian government and people. Liberators could do the job and QEA was ready to undertake the task using the Liberator IIs presently employed on the Indian Ocean service — for temporary operation until replacement aircraft were available. There was, the meeting agreed, declining interest in the Indian Ocean service but for the time being it was necessary to maintain the twice-weekly frequency. There was emphasis on the importance of the method of approach to Australia and New Zealand in view of the intention that the Pacific service would eventually be operated by a new tripartite company. New Zealand would not easily take to a QEA operation even as a temporary measure.[30]

Fysh left London on 12 December. It had become quite clear that the commitment of British aircraft manufacturers to military aircraft production throughout World War II had left them incapable of providing competitive civil aircraft in at least the first few years of peace. Fysh set out his thoughts in a report to the chairman and board on his return to Australia. His recommendation — to buy American aircraft — was a drastic break with the past and a rejection of the problem-ridden British Tudor II.

The prototype Tudor II, wrote Fysh, should have been tested in the previous October but the test was now expected in January 1946; it was also expected to be overweight. It would, he said, be foolish to expect deliveries for the operation of an England–Australia service before January 1947, giving it "no competitive life against current United States types". Because of the weight problems the Merlin engine might not prove as satisfactory as the Hercules 130, and it was only expected to cruise at under 200 miles per hour. There were plans for a "tide-over" service (on the Empire route) during 1946 until more acceptable aircraft arrived — a continuation of three Lancastrian services a week plus three Sunderland III flying boat frequencies a week. These, thought Fysh, should give excellent temporary service.

> The great problem will be what aircraft are to replace the temporary aircraft . . . The only possible British alternative to the Tudor II (with the remote chance of the Hermes) is the Short Seaford Sunderland IV. But the Air Ministry has never even given orders for the Sunderland and prefer to leave the one egg lying in the one rickety basket. If it is accepted that there would be little point in putting in Tudor IIs or Seafords in as late as 1947, then the only alternative would be to consider United States aircraft . . . There is a black outlook for British aircraft over a vital period of three to four years. The United Kingdom could lead in five to ten years if energetic action can be induced on a political level.

Fysh found the same basic problem faced them for the Pacific service.

> After careful consideration and discussion in London it was the unanimous opinion that either the DC4E or the Constellation should be purchased and put on the Pacific service. Whether to buy the almost obsolete DC4E at $400,000 or the modern Constellation at $700,000 is the difficulty, but after careful consideration I incline to the Constellation as the best competitive proposition, — but subject to a final check on costs and whether to wait for the sleeper version or accept delivery of the Type 69. On the England–Australia service via India I also favour the same aircraft . . . England is in a sad state for want of suitable aircraft both for herself and for her friends.

Fysh reported that he had been impressed with the work of Captain Allan on technical matters; he had obviously relied heavily on Allan's evaluation of equipment alternatives for Qantas.[31] Two days later, Fysh made more specific recommendations to the board:

> In my cable to the Chairman of 6 December 1945 [he wrote], owing to the critical position then disclosed . . . I agreed and urged that three DC4E aircraft should be ordered by QEA for the Pacific service in conjunction with the Australian Government. There has been further time for consideration. I now recommend (i) that every effort be made to get into operation the suggested temporary Liberator service (ii) that we recommend to the Civil Aviation Department that with their OK we order the following aircraft for operation on the Pacific service by whatever body is

167

settled on at the Pacific Conference — three Lockheed 49s for delivery early in 1946; or three Lockheed 649s for delivery in the second half of 1946 (whichever is the most acceptable to the Department); or failing [these] order three DC4E types.

For the Australia–England service via India Fysh recommended for discussion and finalization with the Department of Civil Aviation that the proposed Lancastrian and Sunderland III services be installed and continued during 1946 until four Lockheed Constellation 649s could be introduced for a twice-weekly service, in conjunction with a similar number of services by BOAC (and with BOAC using the same type of aircraft). "The Lockheed Constellation is the only reasonably competitive type that I know of to tide us over the intensely competitive years we are entering on", wrote Fysh. "The alternative is to stick to British aircraft and carry on with the double service (express service by Lancastrian; slow luxury service by flying boat) until such time as the Tudor II or Seaford flying boat comes out at the end of 1946."[32] Meanwhile, in England, the Air Ministry had decided on the allocation of aircraft for civil use. In a letter to BOAC on 12 December, the ministry referred to Lord Knollys's note in September (to Hildred) stating that BOAC required 55 Lancastrians — 34 for the United Kingdom–Australia–New Zealand service and 21 for the North Atlantic. A decision had been reached, BOAC was told, that a firm allocation could be made of only 32 Lancastrians for the present. Knollys had asked for 58 Yorks but of these only 36 were definitely promised. The allocation of 32 Lancastrians and 36 Yorks, said the Air Ministry, had been made on the assumption that these aircraft would be used on services on which most of the traffic would be noncommercial, instancing the services to Australia and New Zealand involving Lancastrians. The 32 Lancastrian Mark III aircraft for BOAC were to be converted by A. V. Roe's to a standard agreed with BOAC.[33]

The twenty-fifth annual report of Q.A.N.T.A.S. dated 21 December 1945 summed up the year and the war period. Principal operations, it said, had been directed mainly to wartime needs. During the year "a fast mail and high priority passenger service had been commenced in co-operation with BOAC between Sydney and London with Lancastrian aircraft" and, in April, the company had reopened the service between Sydney and New Guinea previously operated by W. R. Carpenters. "Now that the European and Japanese wars are over, plans are being implemented with Government authorities in line with the Company's aim for the operation of peacetime international services." The year had seen W. A. Watt resign from the QEA board and be replaced by Sir Keith Smith. In the top management, Harman had been appointed general manager and Brain assistant general manager. "Brain has been a most outstanding officer of rare ability and judgement and loyalty to the Company", Fysh wrote to Rudder. "Although I agree with the Board that he has not had the recent financial training that some others have had, I do not feel that this should be a bar to his holding high office in QEA . . . "[34]

Two days before the end of the year that had brought peace, McMaster wrote a simple note to his friend Alan Campbell, who had taken on the honorary task of secretary to the newly conceived Queensland and Northern Territory Aerial Services Limited twenty-five years earlier. McMaster recalled the ebullient young pilot whose enthusiasm had started it all, but whose unrestrainable individualism had driven him to leave the airline just as it began its first regular services. "Paul McGinness", McMaster reminisced, "did more than any other single person in the establishment of Qantas."

Part 2
1946 to 1954

A British Diplomatic Blitz
1946

"We know of no suitable British [aircraft] types to competitively bridge over the vital gap of the next four, five or more years until competitive British aircraft again make their appearance", Fysh wrote to the director-general of civil aviation, Dan McVey, as the new year began. "We feel, however, that the Lancastrians and the proposed Sunderland III operations will hold the fort on the via-India route for six months or more, but could not possibly be considered in 1947."[1]

He described the current British aircraft types. The Avro Lancastrian was a wartime stopgap carrying six passengers in bunks plus 1,400 pounds of mail and freight between Hurn (England) and Mascot on a 63-hour service. Its cruise speed

The Hythe flying boats operated by BOAC had been built as military Sunderlands during the war. The airline was allocated twenty-four between December 1942 and August 1944; they were first used on UK–West Africa services and later UK–Karachi. After the war BOAC refurnished their Sunderlands to full airliner standard, G-AGJM being the first to be completed.

173

The Short Seaford entered service as the Solent but it was not used on the UK–Australia route.

was 235 miles an hour. The Sunderland III was very suitable in combination with the Lancastrian for operating a temporary service between Poole (England) and Rose Bay. It could carry sixteen passengers and 2,900 pounds of freight and mail over 1,200-mile stages at a cruise speed of 165 miles an hour. As for the Avro York, wrote Fysh, BOAC and South African Airways advised against it. At best it could only be considered as stopgap for immediate use. They were noisy and their bad construction rendered them a "one-year aircraft". The Short Seaford (Sunderland IV civil version) would carry 36 passengers and 5,340 pounds of freight and mail over a range of 1,200 miles at a cruise speed of 195 miles an hour. It was extremely comfortable, he said, but "we could not contemplate enough aircraft [from Shorts] to start a service until the end of 1946 or early 1947". The Tudor II landplane was too slow at 205 miles an hour for commercial use, was unpressurized, and was not a nose-wheel type. Its Merlin engine had not yet been fully proved for commercial use. The Handley Page Hermes first prototype had crashed on test. Its value for commercial use was doubtful and it would not allow carriage of a competitive load. Finally, the Brabazon III was only at the drawing-board stage and would not be ready for four or five years.

"As an operator with the strongest Empire leanings we have always backed up British industrial effort by using British aircraft", wrote Fysh, but, he concluded, "our general recommendation must be for the Lockheed Constellation".

Fysh tempered what was a bold QEA proposal for the use of American aircraft with an underlying commitment to Britain.

In regard to long range aircraft policy, it is the express recommendation of the Chairman of the Board . . . that the fewest possible USA aircraft, spares and special equipment be purchased, and that the object of changing back to British aircraft at the end of the life of the expected order of USA aircraft be kept firmly in view. If it is the wish of the Government that British aircraft be continued with on the England–Australia route via India, then our recommendation must be the Short Seaford, which should be a better proposition than the Tudor II.[2]

Lord Knollys urged the case for British aircraft, writing to Fysh on 16 January 1946. The proposal to use Constellations was, he said, a new one.

In considering the use of Constellations instead of the aircraft we have proposed, we must here appreciate the effect on the development of the next type of Empire aircraft, e.g. the Brabazon III. One of the greatest assets which the American manufacturers have had is the experience and knowledge gained in the actual operation of their aircraft . . . That experience is not at present available to the British manufacturer, and it is in our own interests if we are to get the best aircraft in the next generation to give the manufacturer every opportunity of obtaining it. If the next available aircraft . . . is entirely unsuitable then the price would be too

Taken early in 1946, this aerial photograph of the Lockheed Aircraft Company's factory at Burbank shows twenty-nine Constellations. The aircraft in the foreground are Model 049s being readied for delivery to Trans World Airlines and Pan American Airways. In the background are many of the fifteen C-69s built before VJ-Day for the USAF; now surplus to the military's requirements, they were made available to civil operators. BOAC bought six of them, five in 1946 and one in 1947.

great to pay, but we have no reason to assume that that will be the case with the Tudor II . . . If, after careful consideration, we feel that it will be in our best interests to operate our Australian service with Tudor IIs and/or Solents, and QEA, because public and competitive pressure in Australia forces them to do so, decide to use Constellations, it must be realised that the basis or full parallel operation with pooling of revenue and general allocation of expenses would disappear . . . for true parallel operation requires the use of the same type of aircraft. We would not for a moment wish to hold an Australian overseas airline back in the use of aircraft which they think are for the time being more up to date, but I hope the future will always be kept in mind, realising that these present advantages afforded by American aircraft are not likely always to continue. We feel that in the Brabazon III we are going to have an aircraft which will jump ahead of other aircraft then available . . . I am not trying to defend the use of inferior aircraft just because they have to be British — you know my views about that — but we are trying to look ahead . . . [3]

To McMaster, Fysh expressed his concern about the possibility of being saddled with British aircraft. Pan American would be using Constellations on the Pacific service, and Fysh felt they were more and more the obvious choice. But, he said, if most of the world trunk routes used Constellations and the Australia–England route via India Tudor IIs (equal to DC4s) or Short Seafords, they were in for a bad time.[4] Fysh thought that Knollys was supporting British aircraft in the face of these realities but his chairman firmly disagreed.

I am not . . . in agreement with your statement that Lord Knollys in his letter has made a desperate effort to evade the facts. I look upon his letter as a helpful contribution . . . It is for the Governments, not the operators, to make the final decision regarding aircraft. I further wish to stress that the matter of replying to Mr McVey and Lord Knollys in regard to those high policy questions should not be a matter for you or myself personally but for an official reply on behalf of QEA after the fullest consideration by us both as Chairman and Managing Director, together with the proper drafting of replies and the fullest consultation with the Board.[5]

Despite this severe admonition to Fysh, McMaster wrote a personal letter to McVey almost immediately precisely on these high policy matters.

The interim arrangements — in accord with BOAC and an examination of the aircraft position in Great Britain — appear the only solution, and there is no other suitable alternative with British aircraft or, immediately, with foreign aircraft. The interim arrangements proposed, although costly, will however provide the only service immediately available comparable for the time being with competitive services. The Lancastrian is operating the fastest service in the world and the Sunderland III will provide a standard of passenger accommodation and comfort superior to that of the DC4.

McMaster pointed out that the early end to the Japanese war and the fact that the Tudor II, which the manufacturers had assured BOAC would be ready in June 1946, would not be available until considerably later, had left no other British aircraft as an immediate substitute. As for future British aircraft, he wrote,

> the only possible aircraft to be anticipated later in 1946 or early in 1947 are the (a) Tudor II or (b) the Seaford (now referred to as the Solent) flying boat. Beyond this there is nothing of an advanced nature which can be looked for until the Brabazon III in four or five years time. The Tudor II is only comparable with the DC4, a type already proven and in operation shortly to be superseded by Constellations and other advanced aircraft. In recommending the Constellation we were taking a long range view to bridge the gap until reversion to a British aircraft could be considered.
>
> If the policy of the Australian Government is to be in cooperation and support of Great Britain and to operate only British aircraft on this route, then it appears that forward plans must be based on the Tudor II or the Solent flying boat. If on the other hand you consider that more effective competition is necessary for the next few years, then the only alternative is American aircraft . . . We all know why Great Britain has not competitive postwar civil aircraft immediately available and why America has, but admittedly that knowledge does not help.[6]

McMaster's personal letter went further than he anticipated and profoundly affected the director-general's view on choice of aircraft. McVey replied to McMaster:

> You have set out in very clear language the situation in respect to the United Kingdom–Australia service and I hope you will not mind if I pass a copy of your letter to the Minister, even though the letter is marked "Personal". I may say, on behalf of the Department of Civil Aviation, that the thought of using other than British aircraft on the United Kingdom–Australia service was never contemplated until Qantas Empire Airways advised that, in their opinion, Tudor II aircraft, even when they become available, would be unsuitable — and recommended authority be given for the purchase of Constellations. The information tendered regarding the Tudor II has proved very disquieting . . . [7]

McMaster now took the unusual step of distancing himself from his managing director's views, as expressed to both McVey and Lord Knollys, that the interim Lancastrian and Sunderland services would be adequate as temporary measures. On 11 February he wrote to Lord Knollys:

I cannot say I am entirely in accord with Mr Fysh's views, as I am strongly of the opinion that we have reached a stage when it is of vital importance for you to come over to this side and spend sufficient time to enable full and frank discussion with Mr Drakeford and Mr McVey. I am fully cognisant of the fact that the whole issue is one of inter-Government policy . . . Frankly, Australia looks upon the proposed introduction of the Lancastrian and Sunderland III on the via-India route as retrogressive and derogatory to the prestige of Empire aviation. In the face of . . . estimated costs, and having regard to the class of service proposed, political and press criticism might easily become so severe that no Australian government could succeed in withstanding it . . . There is, I feel quite sure, no need for me to stress that Q.A.N.T.A.S. and QEA always have been, and still are, strongly pro-British. This is borne out by the fact that over the twenty-five years of operations there have only been two non-British aircraft in the fleet. I wish to stress that we want to stay British, but at the same time we recognise that it would be foolish not to face the present position . . . Australian National Airways, as you know, has offered to operate the Sydney–San Francisco route entirely without subsidy . . . Pan American and QEA have both estimated that the Pacific route would be costly to operate. A conclusion could be that the offer of ANA is really a bid to run at a loss for a time solely for the purpose of establishing its organisation, and later on exercising the powers that could develop . . . The ANA organisation is completely American in its aircraft.

McMaster pointed out that a Pacific service operated with modern, fast landplanes could quite possibly secure the bulk of the Australia–United Kingdom mails. "We consider that the via-India route is faced with the same problem as the BOAC North Atlantic route, where emergency action has had to be taken to meet American competition and standards. For this service a small number of Constellations have evidently been ordered." He asked for Lord Knollys's support, with the Wellington Pacific conference to take place before the end of the month in New Zealand, for QEA to be the operating organization for the Pacific service.[8]

The selection of aircraft for the Empire route and the choice of both operator and aircraft for the Pacific route brought Lord Knollys to Australia where talks began on 23 February with McMaster, Rudder, Fysh, Sir Keith Smith, Brain, and Turner. It was agreed that the meeting "was only for general discussion so both could place before our respective Governments clear and concise recommendations". They began with the question of the Pacific which, said Knollys, it had already been decided to operate as a joint government organization though their meeting "was to have regard to the entity that may operate such a service on behalf of the Governments and particularly as to whom the Australian Government might nominate in this respect". He had, he said, no indication of the attitude Canada might take, though the principle of parallel operations had already been laid down. Lord Knollys said BOAC had advised their government that Liberators should be used and be based at Sydney. It was his view that the Pacific service should be controlled by a joint organization similar to Tasman Empire Airways. Their discussions then concentrated on the divisive issue of aircraft types.

Australian National Airways, said Fysh, had taken the greatest possible advantage of publicity to stress that QEA had nothing to compete with the new DC4s available to ANA. McMaster read a letter from McVey stating that the proposed use of Liberators was not attractive compared with Pan American's DC4s and, later, Constellations, and that the department "could not overlook the new DC4s available to ANA". McMaster said he could not see any British aircraft suitable for the Pacific "but it should be the ultimate aim to run the service by British aircraft". Lord Knollys persisted with the British view, saying the Tudor IIs would be competitive with the DC4, though they would not be available for two or three months and BOAC would not be ready to use them on the Atlantic until they were sufficiently debugged — probably towards the end of the year. He proposed a new design of the Lancastrian with thirteen seats which, he said, could possible be a stopgap for QEA on the Pacific run. BOAC advised that QEA operate the Pacific service as this would be more economical and efficient than an entirely new operating unit.

Turning to the England–Australia Empire route, Lord Knollys was adamant that there was a bright future for British aircraft. The Brabazon III was already on order and was going ahead smoothly. In his view, he said, the British were now leap-frogging the Americans with the Brabazon and indications were that the British would more than catch up with American designs. He admitted that the Constellation was a faster aircraft than the Tudor II but said he was unaware of its exact advantage. Pointing out the much higher capital cost of the Constellation he argued that the Tudor II would "go a long way in enabling the British aircraft to reach parity with the Constellation's ability to provide a lower fare".

Fysh said that the Tudor II's speed of 215 miles an hour could not compare with the Constellation's 260 miles an hour, Knollys countered that "both aircraft had comparative speeds

179

at the same heights". They could not immediately resolve their differences on this basic comparison. Fysh, however, insisted that the Constellation was altogether superior. He had no doubt, he said, that the Australian government would not agree to the use of flying boats because of costs. As with the facts on relative speeds, McMaster drew attention to the "very great divergence of estimates as between ourselves and BOAC" on flying boat costs. Knollys pointed out that BOAC had ordered three new very large flying boats and that the British government felt it would be unwise to neglect this type. BOAC, Knollys emphasized, was committed to British aircraft and pointed out that if it was not possible to use similar types of aircraft over the England–Australia route, then the whole basis of parallel operations would disappear. This first meeting concluded with agreement to recommend, for a period of from nine to twelve months, the use of the new thirteen-seat Lancastrian for the Pacific if Liberators were unacceptable. It would, said Lord Knollys "provide a fast, regular service comparable to that which could be given by American aircraft". It would be followed by either the DC4M (a Canadian version of the DC4 powered with the Rolls-Royce Merlin engine) or some other aircraft.

They met again, after the weekend, on 25 February to discuss the second phase of Pacific operations, from 1947. Lord Knollys pointed out that the Pacific service should be viewed as one of government policy concerning four countries — Great Britain, Australia, New Zealand, and Canada — and that in the final analysis it was not really a question of which country or operator would handle the service, but essentially one for joint governments to decide.

Once again, Lord Knollys argued the case for British aircraft, while McMaster urged that Constellations should follow the interim Lancastrian operations. A new version of the Tudor I with eighteen seats or twelve bunks could, said Knollys, be submitted. He pointed out that BOAC had ordered eighty Tudor IIs, with the first due off the production line in October 1946 for operations in the first quarter of 1947. Questioned about BOAC satisfaction with the Tudor, Knollys was hardly forthright. "No one could be perfectly satisfied with them as these aircraft have not yet flown", he said. "Insofar as increased weight is concerned, this would not make a great deal of difference as it did not affect the payload of the aircraft but it would affect the range that could be flown in any one hop

... We must always be in a position of doubt when ordering future aircraft and such a risk will always obtain."

The earlier disagreement over the relative speeds of the Tudor II and Constellation was cleared up. C. O. Turner gave BOAC's own figure on the average block speed of the Tudor II as 189 miles an hour and Lockheed's for the Constellation as 245 miles an hour. Lord Knollys volunteered a different comparison: At 10,000 feet and fifty-one per cent rated power the Tudor speed was 236 miles an hour (and 256 at 20,000 feet) while the Constellation (at fifty per cent rated power) had a speed at 10,000 feet of 263 miles an hour (and 256 miles an hour at 20,000 feet). Fysh commented that A. V. Roe's should guarantee their figures as the aircraft was not yet in existence.

As the meeting drew to its close, Fysh put the QEA view that because of the superiority of the Constellation for the Empire route they had no alternative but to advise the Australian government that, as operators, QEA recommended them. However, said Fysh, if the respective governments agreed on the use of the Tudor IIs and flying boats, QEA would accept such a decision. Lord Knollys acknowledged that the Solent flying boats could not be considered the answer to the Constellation and that the Constellation was better than any single aircraft available from British manufacturers. But, he concluded, it was his view that the Tudor II plus the Solents would be comparable to the Constellations. At a final meeting next morning it was agreed that joint submissions could be made to their respective governments.

Qantas Empire Airways was not to achieve its ambition to operate the projected British service across the Pacific. Two days after the Sydney meetings ended, a conference of ministers and officials from the United Kingdom, New Zealand, and Australia met in Wellington, New Zealand. Drakeford, was minister, and McVey, as director-general, represented Australia; the United Kingdom was represented by its minister for civil aviation, Lord Winster, and its director-general, George (later Sir George) Cribbett; New Zealand's representatives were Frederick Jones, minister for air, and T. A. Barrow, his departmental head. Lord Knollys was present as adviser, with Sir Leonard Isitt (Tasman Empire Airways), Fysh, and A. E. Rudder (both QEA) in attendance. Canada was not represented and had reserved the right to operate its own parallel Pacific service. It was the decision of this high level conference that a new company, British Commonwealth Pacific Airlines, be formed to operate from headquarters in Sydney air services across the Pacific linking Australia, New Zealand, Canada (Vancouver), and the United States (San Francisco). (In Wellington at the time, on business for the Commonwealth Treasury, was G. P. N. Watt, who was added to the Australian team. He later became chairman of the new BCPA.) The creation of British Commonwealth Pacific Airlines meant that QEA were now challenged as an international operator from Australia; there would in future be competition for the traffic to England, which could choose to fly westward on the Empire route or eastward with BCPA. (Ironically, Australia was to hold fifty per cent of BCPA's capital and would therefore be in competition with itself.) The new airline, like QEA, now had the problem of choosing the right aircraft for its operations.

Back in Australia in early March, Lord Knollys gave McMaster a considered BOAC view of the aircraft problem. In a memorandum he set down two phases for the United Kingdom–Australia route. Phase 1 covered the period immediately ahead; phase 2 the period from early 1947 to 1950. For the first period, the alternatives for providing greater capacity on the route were more Lancastrians, Yorks, Hythe flying boats, or C54E aircraft. BOAC and QEA had agreed, he wrote, that Yorks were unsuitable because of limited passenger accommodation and generally unsatisfactory passenger features; additional Lancastrians were uneconomical; and the C54E could not be considered because it required uneconomical conversion work. The only practicable aircraft to extend the service in phase 1 was the Hythe, which could offer a comfortable supplementary service to the Lancastrian. He acknowledged that the Australian government preferred not to use flying boats, but it appeared the only practicable way of increasing capacity on the route.

For phase 2, Lord Knollys accepted the strong demand, particularly in Australia, for the fastest and most economic aircraft; the prospective use by the Dutch of Constellations on the Amsterdam–Batavia–Australia service; the effect of Constellation services on the Pacific, with the real risk of passengers from Australia to the UK being diverted to a service across the Pacific, USA and North Atlantic; and the alleged offers of ANA to run an unsubsidized service to the UK with DC4s and DC6s. BOAC, he said, admitted that the Constellation, now a tried aircraft, could give a service between the UK and Sydney ten hours faster than the Tudor II, with the advan-

tages of a pressurized cabin and tricycle undercarriage. However he said that even if Constellations were used by Australia,
BOAC could not, "on its present information regarding the
Tudor II, advise His Majesty's Government that the Constellation should be used by it on this particular route". If the
Australian government were to decide on the Constellation,
wrote Knollys, parallel operations would become impossible.[9]

McMaster answered with QEA's firm views:

> QEA fully supports a long term policy which will allow 100 per
> cent British aircraft to be used when such aircraft are competitive
> with other contemporary aircraft . . . QEA's main anxiety is in
> regard to the long interim period 1946–1950 and we feel that it
> would be difficult to support BOAC proposals to use only British
> aircraft until the Brabazon III is available. Our conclusions are
> that (i) there is no better alternative to the use of Lancastrians and
> Hythes [flying boats] for the immediate interim period on the ser-
> vices via India (ii) that eight Lockheed Constellation 649 aircraft
> should be ordered immediately for use on the Australia–England
> route via India, [with] QEA and BOAC using the same equipment
> . . .

McMaster said that QEA did not agree that the Lancastrians
and Hythes should be followed by the British Tudor IIs and
Solent flying boats, adding that no Australian government
could withstand political and press criticism of a service using
Tudor II/Solent aircraft for four or five years. He proposed
that, until parallel services were practicable, the present operational arrangements should continue, with QEA being responsible for the Sydney–Singapore or Sydney–Karachi section
and QEA crews changing over with BOAC crews at an agreed
point. "If such a basis can be agreed it will avoid the possibility
of Australia operating a through service with American aircraft in competition with BOAC."

McMaster thought that the United States dollar shortage
could be overcome. "We do not anticipate difficulty with the
Australian Government. Lockheed Aircraft Corporation has
intimated that they would be prepared to accept dollar payments on a deferred basis of 25 per cent down and the balance
over, say, a three year period supported by a Government
guarantee." Capital outlay for eight aircraft at £224,000 each
plus spares and plant would total £2,800,000. (The Short
Hythe-class flying boat was a postwar conversion of the Sunderland III. BOAC had operated Sunderlands since March
1943. From November 1943, they had connected with the
QEA Catalinas at Karachi carrying passengers and mail on to

Britain. It had a wingspan of 112 feet 10 inches, four 1,086-horsepower Bristol Pegasus XXXVIII engines, a cruising speed of 175 miles an hour and could carry sixteen to twenty-two passengers.)

In a submission to the Department of Civil Aviation for phase 2, QEA at the same time pointed out that the Tudor II had not yet been tested and would be heavier than originally anticipated, with a consequent loss of payload. Apart from the Tudor II, no suitable British aircraft was likely to be available for four or five years. The submission said

> that serious consideration must be given to the employment of an American type of aircraft . . . with the intention to revert in due course to British aircraft. We therefore wish to recommend . . . the acquisition of the Lockheed Constellation 649 model for use on the England–Australia route via India, with QEA and BOAC using the same equipment . . . Fitted with long range wings, this aircraft has a cruising speed of 255 miles an hour at 10,000 feet and a payload of 15,800 pounds on stages up to 2,500 miles, after allowing for safety margins. It is fitted with 48 seats by day, convertible to 22 bunks plus four seats by night. The aircraft will be pressurized . . .

This clear disagreement between QEA and BOAC came to a head at a conference in Canberra on 8 March 1946 with Lord Knollys and Hudson Fysh representing their airlines and McVey and Cribbett the respective government. The deadlock was temporarily resolved by a compromise which stated: "A decision on the type of aircraft to be operated in the second stage (the first stage being the . . . Lancastrians and Hythes) should be postponed until a date not later than September 1946." For the British it was, in fact, a tactical defeat for it imposed a definite time limit by which they had to come up with an acceptable aircraft. For QEA, on the other hand, British government pressure to force acceptance of the Tudor II had been deflected.

With·the agreement of the Australian and United Kingdom governments, QEA and BOAC signed agreements to renew their partnership operation of the Australia–England route. It provided for pooled aircraft, with Qantas operating Lancastrians between Mascot and Karachi and Hythe flying boats between Rose Bay and Singapore. Described as phase 1 for the service, the agreement covered the twelve months from 12 May 1946 and provided that the cost of the service should be shared between the two countries (with Australia's share estimated at £A712,812).[10] On one of the last flights by the old route, between Ratmalana, in Ceylon, and Perth, a QEA Lancastrian with five passengers and a crew of five was lost on the leg between Ceylon and Cocos Island. The aircraft, under Capt. Frank Thomas, reported by radio when it was 690 miles northwest of Cocos but was never seen again. A theory that lightning, combined with a fuel leak, was responsible could not be substantiated.

On 7 April, QEA began operations between Sydney and Singapore with Liberator aircraft, pending the May arrival of the Hythe flying boats. Two days later the thrice-weekly service between Sydney and London by Lancastrians began, with QEA crews taking the aircraft to Karachi where they were taken over and flown through to England by BOAC crews. (The Hythe flying boat services replaced the Liberators on 16 May. From that date Sydney and London were connected by the express Lancastrian service in sixty-seven hours and the more comfortable flying boat service, taking five and a half days.)

Various staff problems preceded these new services and involved some argument between McMaster and Fysh. On 3 April, McMaster wrote to his managing director that every member of the board, rightly or wrongly, had the impression that the company could be overstaffed.

> After a full discussion, which unfortunately was unnecessarily heated at times, and in which none of us was free of blame, a resolution was adopted requesting you as managing director to intensify investigations into the economic working of the company. You have a very responsible position to the Board and over the last twelve months you have not been able to give the personal supervision which is necessary. . . We all realise the position and why it has been such. You were not asked to reorganise or act in such a way — as stated in your letter — "which would most probably precipitate a debacle in the staff". You do not do justice to yourself or the Board in stating that "the Board is out after a pence saving hunt when our competitors are out on a spending campaign and the Board is not planning and securing the future of the Company". As managing director it is your duty to place proposals before the Board, both as regards expenditure and on securing the future of the Company. I cannot help but feel you are taking a too personal attitude towards the whole question . . . instead of taking it as a question of management.

There was a postscript saying: "Please do not treat this letter as unfriendly, or other than as appreciation of your work."[11] Fysh responded that staff numbers had not been neglected but had been known and kept firmly under control all along.[12]

More serious staff problems at senior levels were threatening the company as a result of the formation by the government, under its December 1945 Australian National Airlines bill, of the government-owned Trans-Australia Airlines (the operating name of the Australian National Airlines Commission). In February 1946, A. W. Coles (later Sir Arthur, and one of the two independent members of Parliament who had voted against the previous coalition government and helped bring Labor to power) was appointed as first chairman of the new commission with W. C. (Bill) Taylor, a close friend and able adviser of the prime minister, Ben Chifley, appointed as vice chairman. Both began vigorous preparations for the inauguration of TAA's interstate operations, beginning with the recruitment of senior staff. QEA was an obvious source of able and experienced airline executives.

On 3 April, Fysh wrote to McMaster:

> I have fairly good reason to believe that Turner has applied to the Commission for one of the new jobs, and one has every reason to expect him to have done this considering all the circumstances [including] that of his underpayment here, and other matters about which he is not satisfied. I would also expect Brain and others to apply, and for all I know we may be left denuded of seniors unless we can prevent the Commission taking them . . . The Commission is advertising for an Operations Manager at a minimum salary of £2,250 per annum, about £1,000 per year more than we give.[13]

Lester Brain, one of the enduring pillars of strength in all operational matters, saw that advertisement. On 10 April he wrote to Fysh:

> I should like to apply for this position and feel that I should have a good chance of selection. I have given practically the whole of my life since leaving school to flying and Australian air transport, twenty-two years of that time with Qantas. I have served the Company conscientiously and loyally through much of its history in peace and war . . . I would not apply without first advising you and I should like to feel that if I secured the position I would leave Qantas with the goodwill of yourself and the other directors.

Brain, more than any other individual, had been responsible for the operational excellence of the airline. On 15 April, McMaster wrote to him regretting his move but completely understanding it. "The salary offered by the Commission is a salary far in excess of what can be paid you by QEA." Fysh told Brain that his application for the position of operations supervisor (*sic*) with the commission was his own affair, and that there would be no illwill.[14] On 3 May Fysh telegraphed Brain: "After discussion with the chairman yesterday I can now officially say QEA will release you. My congratulations on the new job and good wishes in it." Brain, in fact, was more successful in his application than he had initially expected. He was appointed as the first general manager of Trans-Australia Airlines (and took up his post on 3 June).

The creation of both Trans-Australia Airlines and the new British Commonwealth Pacific Airlines was greatly unsettling for Qantas. Fysh wrote to Scottie Allan, in London as the company's liaison officer.

> I have notified Captain Brain that, if satisfactory to him, 31 May will be the date for his leaving QEA to join the Commission. It will also be necessary at the next Board meeting to consider Turner for the post of Assistant General Manager, to assist Harman and understudy him — and try him out away from Accounts. I recommend this . . . Only for Board refusal to give favourable consideration to my recommendation and pleadings, Brain would be Assistant General Manager now, and still with us. The right step now in the best interests of the Company, as the only one we can take in a forced position, is to appoint Turner as Assistant General Manager.[16]

It was clear that Fysh did not relish the chief accountant's promotion but just as clear that he saw it as his duty to recommend it. He told McMaster that he still felt unable to reduce staff appreciably. "This is a most critical time for us re staff loyalty and satisfaction and any drastically hard action now would be preposterous."

On the same day that he wrote to his chairman, Fysh advised Lord Knollys: "This will serve to confirm . . . that Capt. Brain has got the position of Director General [*sic*] of the Australian National Airlines Commission. The salary is £3,000 to start, with ample expenses and a five year contract. Brain leaves with mutual goodwill, and he could hardly be denied his chance seeing the greatly advanced salary and status to that which my Board felt able to extend to him." The board, however, did not remain entirely insensitive. Fysh was able to write to McMaster: "I thank you and the Board for the raise [*sic*] in salary which was accorded me . . . and which I thought a generous gesture at a difficult time in QEA's history."[17]

In the QEA reorganization that followed, Turner became assistant general manager, the experienced Capt. Bill Crowther (who had managed the inauguration of the Catalina service across the Indian Ocean) was appointed operations manager.

Ian Esplin became secretary, Fred Derham chief accountant, Verdun Sommerlad staff superintendent, and E. Bennett-Bremner publicity manager. Nielsen continued as head of the traffic and commercial section.[18] At the Department of Civil Aviation, Dan McVey resigned his position as director-general (and director-general of postal services) to become managing director of Standard Telephones and Cables Pty Ltd. His place was taken by Air Marshal Richard (Dicky) Williams, under whom Fysh and McGinness had served in World War I. Williams, responding to a congratulatory letter from McMaster, wrote: "I often think back to those days when you encouraged McGinness and Fysh in their original attempts to set up what has proved to be very worthy of our support . . . I saw both McGinness and Fysh here in Melbourne last week. The former now has ideas of developing a part of the Northern Territory."[19]

Closely following these senior management changes, and as both TAA and BCPA geared up to commence operations, Qantas received bad news about the aircraft they had chosen as preferred equipment for the coming years of competition. On 1 July 1946 all Constellations were grounded, following a series of fires in flight. Trans World Airlines had pioneered the operation of Constellations from January 1946 on the North Atlantic with the early Type 49, followed by BOAC and both KLM and Air France had ordered them. Qantas's

Due to delays with the Tudor airliner that BOAC had intended to use on their Atlantic service, the British company was obliged to buy American aircraft. The order for five Model 049 Constellations was announced on 24 January 1946 and regular services commenced on 1 July between London and New York. The third aircraft, *Bangor 2*, is shown here flying over the Canadian border en route to New York during crew training.

confidence in the aircraft was not shaken, however, and Fysh, only five days after the grounding, repeated to Robert Gross of Lockheed his suggestion that Qantas order the aircraft with the right of cancellation which, he said, "would mean that we give you a definite order for aircraft which we would be prepared to publicise but we would privately retain the right of cancellation should our government eventually not agree our use [of Constellations] on the Australia–England route . . . We must take the initiative now, although this is most difficult owing to the QEA situation which is only half way in change-over to full Australian control."[20]

Fysh met with Chifley and Drakeford in Canberra and reported to McMaster on the two main issues of aircraft and the government purchase of BOAC shares in QEA. He would, he said, be most surprised if the price of thirty shillings per share were agreed to by the Australian government, "especially owing to the weak position of QEA without a long term contract and without any aircraft . . . to speak . . . Unless some unforeseen turn takes place it will be into 1947 until QEA settles down." It would be bad, he said, to await events before tackling the major decisions on the doorstep. On aircraft, Fysh wore, there was

> an expression of confidence by both Mr Chifley and Mr Drake-ford on the Constellation and that QEA should order, and that a cable should be despatched to the United Kingdom Government . . . Mr Chifley expressed himself as greatly opposed to flying boats . . . Without being alarmist, I feel that QEA is still in an ex-tremely delicate and vulnerable position and that unless we have the proper aircraft on order at an early date our chance of survival against the competition we have will be small indeed.[21]

McMaster replied immediately. "We have stressed time after time to Lord Knollys our lack of confidence in the Lancastrian–Hythe set up and the very great danger that the Australian Government must eventually meet in political and press criticism regarding the excessive fares and heavy subsidy required." Nevertheless, McMaster cautioned against premature direct action by QEA in opposition to BOAC. "We must secure full agreement and co-operation with BOAC if at all possible. I feel that this will be very difficult in view of the fact that BOAC apparently are determined on using British aircraft on the Empire route . . . The Lancastrian–Hythe operation is impossible and also dangerous, not only to QEA but also to the Commonwealth and UK Governments. I am also convinced that the Tudor II should not be further considered . . . "[22]

The proposed Lancastrian–Hythe service was described in a QEA board memorandum on 24 July as uneconomical.

> The present Sydney–London passenger fare is £A325. It is expected, as a result of the IATA Regional Traffic Conferences to come, that Australia will virtually be forced to agree to a fare as low as £A200, to become effective during 1947. It is also a fare which the public and press will demand, but which the Australian Government cannot reasonably give effect to unless forced, until QEA is enabled to purchase economic aircraft . . . The fact of operating two services, the landplanes and the flying boats . . . is proving wasteful. It is essential to supersede them by 12 May 1947 by one service of an economic nature.

The memorandum then compared available aircraft, noting that the Constellation cost $US750,000 and the Boeing Stratocruiser (the commerical version of the Super Fortress) $US1,250,000. Permission had been obtained from the director-general and Australian Treasury to buy two American army DC4 aircraft for conversion to civil DC4 Skymasters at a total cost around $US600,000, with the two aircraft intended for use on QEA's proposed Sydney–China–Japan service. Minutes of this board meeting record

> the serious position in which QEA will be placed without competitive aircraft such as the Constellation in readiness for overseas operations not later than May 1947, following Phase 1 of the England–Australia service, and whereas it is adjudged that if QEA do not have aircraft approved by the Commonwealth Government other organisations will, in order to ensure the future of QEA the Board hereby resolves that four Constellation aircraft be ordered.[23]

"How futile so far have been our efforts to get realistic thinking in the United Kingdom", Fysh wrote to McMaster on 29 July. He advised acceptance of the terms of payment to Lockheed of the deposit for the Constellation order — "twenty-five per cent down payment within thirty days from execution of the contract or 15 September whichever is the later". He wrote that everything was under control, "the great objective being to have the Constellation order confirmed — which is going to be a job, and which is further complicated by the election recess of Parliament".[24] He did not, he said, foresee any great difficulties in the negotiations with Lockheed. "What is difficult, however, is to get the consent of the Australian Government, and to stay the steady inroads of the Australian National Airlines Commission [TAA] into our experienced staff and, later, into our business. Here we are certainly faced with great difficulties."[25]

190

There was some disagreement on the amount required by Lockheed as deposit on the Constellation order, with McMaster and the board inclined to think it excessive. On 5 August McMaster admonished Fysh.

> It is unfortunate that you should imply that you know the right thing to do and that the Board did not and that the Board did something which would not inspire confidence in QEA as a business concern . . . Experienced big businessmen such as Mr Rudder, Loxton, F. J. Smith and Sir Keith Smith are not men who would leave themselves open to attack such as you infer. They are all men of keen business instincts, and very much more so than you or myself. It is most unfortunate that you should make such criticism of the Board for you are not only a member of the Board but also the Chief Executive of the Company. The Board looks to you to put into effect its policy to which you are a party, and I know that you will be loyal to this trust . . . After fully debating the terms incorporated in the cable to Lockheeds [the Board] were unanimously agreed [on a lower deposit]. I personally feel strongly that once the Board makes a decision that decision should be respected irrespective of any personal view.[26]

Fysh responded: "As I explained to the Board, I am familiar with the basis of this sort of contract . . . and when a deposit with order is necessary." McMaster, testily, regretted this implied assertion of superiority and replied: "When all is said and done, who cares much what you or I think of ourselves?"[27]

QEA cabled BOAC pressing that Constellations should be ordered by both airlines. "The Board of QEA recognises that under the Canberra agreement a decision as to the type of aircraft to be used in parallel frequency in Phase 2 on the England–Australian route is to be decided between the Australian and United Kingdom governments not later than September 1946", cabled Qantas. In principle the Canberra agreement envisaged the use of British aircraft based on hoped-for success of the Tudor II.

> The reports on the Tudor II are unpromising and indicate that there can be little hope of it being operationally and economically competitive . . . The Board therefore, and knowing the views of the Australian Government, is unanimously of the opinion that the decision should be made on this matter before September . . . we consider that the Constellation for use commencing 1947 is the only aircraft which can be recommended, subject to the present trouble being overcome. Lockheeds have made us a firm offer expiring 27 July of deliveries of Constellation 749s (developed versions), two for May 1947, two for June 1947 . . . In event QEA placing an order for Constellations [it] shall have the right to cancel without compensation if the Australian Government fails

to authorise use of Constellations on the England–Australia route, provided that such cancellation is notified by us by 16 September 1946. In order to protect the position the Board has ordered four Constellations . . . My Board would deeply appreciate BOAC urging the United Kingdom Government to give immediate consideration to making similar arrangements.[28]

From Lockheed Aircraft Corporation's vice president Courtlandt S. Gross came a cable on 30 July accepting the Qantas order. There was reassuring news from the new director-general of civil aviation, Air Marshal Williams. "I have taken the attitude", he wrote to Fysh on 8 August, "that the troubles with the Constellation are undoubtedly technical ones that can be remedied. They may indeed call for quite small modifications."[29]

McMaster told Fysh on 9 August that before he could "get beyond spade work with Mr Askew" [of Lockheeds], QEA would have to obtain Government approval and secure from the government in some way at least a provisional guarantee of a contract of reasonable terms and tenure. The position was difficult and was made more so by the approach of the elections.[30] Fysh told his chairman that same day that Drakeford had advised him that at the last minute it was decided not to put the bill through the House enabling the Australian Government to acquire the BOAC share in QEA, for fear of criticism in the House and in the press of rushing it through at the end of the session.[31] McMaster appreciated the political forces at work but saw the central problem as one of aircraft choice.

Unless the Commonwealth Government takes decisive action . . . when the Bill does come before Parliament, and it becomes known that in addition to the excessive passenger fare the taxpayers will be called upon to meet an also excessive subsidy of well on to £1 million, and for what is an obsolete service, there will be such an outcry from both Government and Opposition sides of Parliament that the Government will find itself thrashed right and left. The position is made more dangerous by the broadcasting of the debates and questions from Canberra. QEA will also get kicked but the Government will get such a mauling it will be impossible for it to go on with the present arrangements, which are economically impossible to defend. The sooner the Government can come out and support QEA in the provision of suitable aircraft the better . . .[32]

The economics of the Australia–England service were, besides being in McMaster's view indefensible, also complex and murky. Turner prepared an internal memorandum on 19

August to explain them headed "Notes on Methods of Operating the Australia–United Kingdom Service". Although, he said, the Lancastrian–Hythe services had been operated on a sectional basis, QEA and BOAC had endeavoured to get

> as near as possible to parallel operations in framing agreements and accounting. The Commonwealth Government asked that we approach the problem in this way so that the change to proper parallel operations in Phase 2 would be facilitated. Phase 1 operations are cost-plus operations, wherein the Governments agree to share nett costs in accordance with frequencies operated, with no limit to their expenditure to be fixed, while in Phase 2 each company will have to quote a mail rate to the Governments and will . . . bear its own costs. In my view, this type of cost-plus arrangement imposes a very serious responsibility on both companies to see that operations are carried out as economically as possible. Unfortunately BOAC is suffering very seriously by reason of being forced to virtually scrap all costing work during the war, and it will be many months before they will be in a position to adequately control expenditure, or in fact tell us what the actual costs of the Hythe–Lancastrian operations are at their end. Also at present, there is absolutely no evidence to show that they think services should be operated "economically", nor is anyone in their organisation worrying about profit or loss in their operations. As evidence of this, no one has made any effort to estimate revenue or compare it with costs four months after the services commenced.

It was a damning indictment of BOAC lack of organization. Turner continued:

> BOAC claim most emphatically that their costs have nothing to do with us or the Australian Government, but are a matter as between themselves and the Ministry of Civil Aviation. In other words, if Australia thinks costs excessive, they can protest through Government circles. All this emphasises the point that cost-plus arrangements are unworkable and should be avoided if possible.

Turner then proposed that QEA should "insist on certain principles being observed" in the phase 2 proper parallel operations so that each company could budget for its own expenditure and "if savings are effected in its organisation, the full benefit of such savings would be retained by it or go back to its own Government". Turner summarized the previous plans for Tudor II operation and the revised proposals to use Constellations. On the basis of forty seats in each Constellation and four frequencies each week there would, he said, be 160 seats a week available each way. QEA should work on the basis of sixty per cent loadings and on the basis of revenue, not passenger seats. This, he said, would provide 96 seats per week "and we are already selling 66 seats per week at impossibly high fares". He believed, he said, "that the machine must go right through flying day and night. Passengers should be given 'stop-off' privileges at definite points and in order for this scheme to work we must be working to a fairly low percentage load factor. However, under no circumstances is it considered that mail or the machines should have to stop overnight at any place between Australia and the United Kingdom."

There was also a need, he said, for a short-range stopping service in addition to this long-range through service, to be operated by Tudor IIs, DC4s, or further Constellations. He did not think that the importance of the mail loadings could be overemphasized, with the growing trend for all mail to go by air. "From figures estimated for the Hythe–Lancastrian service," he wrote, "it appears that the mail revenue to be received will more than cover net cost of the Hythe–Lancastrian operations [despite] the uneconomic nature of the services." Turner noted the value of frequency in operating the Australia–UK service, and that the aim should be an eventual daily service.

The question whether parallel operations as such, with the contemplated pooling of traffic revenue, would continue was, he said, yet to be decided.

> If BOAC and the UK Government oppose Constellations and the principle of parallel operations is scrapped, then I believe we could operate very successfully on our own in competition with British services . . . In considering capital requirements of the Company, I suggest that we should plan to get at least two DC4s for the China service and either three Tudor IIs or three more DC4s for the short-range stopping service to the UK. We should also have in mind that a fleet of four Constellations is not an economic unit and if we had, say, two more Constellations we could operate Pacific services if called upon to do so . . . I believe that our total capital requirements will be in the vicinity of £11,500,000 and that we should have no difficulty in getting this sum.[33]

Fysh wrote to Lord Knollys on 14 August setting out forcefully the QEA argument on aircraft and stressing that there was a deadline with Lockheeds of 16 September. The Constellation, he said, was the best tried, tested, and operational international type available for use from 1947. It was fifteen to thirty per cent faster than competitive types, it was pressurized, it had up to one ton greater payload, it was a proved type, its still air range at 5,000 miles was 1,500 miles greater than its nearest rival, and its two-engined performance was unrivalled. The Tudor II, by contrast, had an excessive take-off run, payload was small, and range not comparable. It was slow and it had not yet passed its tests. Both the DC4 and DC4M were well below the general performance of the Constellation.[34] (In fact, though Fysh did not then know it, the Qantas view had already prevailed. In a note from BOAC's "Morning Meeting Case Book" dated 9 August 1946, held in the archives of the Royal Air Force Museum at Hendon. Lord Knollys is reported as saying: "It was agreed by the Ministry that we cannot refute QEA's argument in favour of the purchase of Constellation aircraft. Our [BOAC] proposal to operate a fast Constellation service in conjunction with a slow stopping Tudor II service was generally accepted by the Ministry.")[35]

Lord Knollys did not make these British views entirely plain when he replied to the 27 July Qantas cable on August 16. Despite the attitude of the Air Ministry, the United Kingdom's Labour government firmly believed Australia should favour British aircraft. His Majesty's government, said Lord Knollys, would have to consider carefully the implication of any proposal to introduce Constellations on the Empire route; BOAC was studying how a parallel service with night stops could be operated with Tudor IIs. Then came a surprising request from QEA's senior partner. "It would help our consideration, particularly in view of the very real dollar problem, if you could say whether [it is] possible [that] Qantas Empire Airways could obtain two or three additional Constellation 749s if BOAC decided it necessary to use them ... "[36] (McMaster cabled Knollys on 21 August that he did not anticipate any difficulty in obtaining the extra Constellations for BOAC but six days later was forced to advise that he was unable to obtain Australian government approval.)

On 20 August Lord Knollys cabled McMaster that His Majesty's government had received a cable from the Australian government officially proposing Constellations. "Minister here views proposals with grave concern", said Knollys.[37] On 22 August, McMaster advised Drakeford that he had sent a telegram to the prime minister urging a decision by cabinet at its last pre-election meeting. On 30 August Fysh told Air Marshal Williams: "I saw the prime minister at Mascot yesterday which helped, though I realise the dollar difficulty and the diplomatic blitz which is being put out from the United Kingdom in an effort to prevent the order. QEA must, however, refuse to be victimised . . . the cable from the Air Ministry could only be classed as blatantly misleading."

Fysh went public on 31 August with an article in the *Sydney Morning Herald* stating that suitable British airliners for long-range operations on the Australia–England route were not available.[38] The tempo and pressures were mounting but a decision from Australia's Labor government had still to be taken. Early in September, at Victoria Barracks in Melbourne, the minister for civil aviation managed to secure for Fysh an interview with Chifley. "Smoking his pipe . . . " wrote Fysh, "Chifley invited me to sit down. In front of him on his pad lay the leaves of an urgent telegram. He did not waste words. He and Drakeford had made up their minds." Chifley showed Fysh the telegram which was from the British prime minister, Clement Attlee, "begging us", said Chifley, "not to go on

In early September 1946, Australian Prime Minister J.B. Chifley announced that QEA had been given authority to purchase four Lockheed Constellations.

with those Constellations you want". Chifley, wrote Fysh, paused and smiled and then said: "Well, anyhow, I have decided. We'll give it a go."[39]

In a telegram to the Dominions Office in London on 10 September, Chifley advised the British government:

All my experts and Qantas Empire Airways are satisfied that, notwithstanding the favourable figures anticipated for Tudor II operation, the Constellation remains a superior and more economic aircraft from the airline operator's point of view . . . We had agreed at the March Canberra conference to await trials with the prototype Tudor II, which was expected to fly in June, but that in any case a decision must be taken not later than September. Your telegram indicates that there are likely to be further delays . . . We feel, if we delay a decision any longer, that there is a grave risk of Qantas Empire Airways losing an opportunity to acquire Constellation aircraft under favourable conditions . . . Not without regret we have therefore decided to authorise Qantas Empire Airways to proceed with the purchase of four Constellation aircraft and we hope that, in order to preserve the principles of parallel partnership operation, the United Kingdom will see its way clear to agree also to the purchase of Constellations by BOAC for the London–Sydney service.[40]

(The Tudor suffered a sad end. One vanished on 30 January 1948 with twenty-five passengers and six crew aboard. A second was lost early in 1949 with its thirteen passengers and four crew. Both were operated by British South American Airways (BSAA), the only airline ever to use them. They were withdrawn from service).

This decision by the prime minister of an Australian Labor government was made with Qantas Empire Airways still a private enterprise organization — its shares still held half by Q.A.N.T.A.S. and BOAC. The BOAC shareholding was yet to be acquired by the Australian government. Formal approval for the Constellation purchase came from Drakeford on 10 September 1946. "I am glad to be able to advise you that although the provision of dollars for their purchase presents very serious difficulties, in order that the offer of the Lockheed Corporation can be availed of and that Phase 2 of the proposal to operate the Sydney–London service may be effected with as little delay as possible, authority has now been given by the Treasurer to purchase the four aircraft."[41]

Fysh took the opportunity to score a deserved point against BOAC in a note to the prime minister attaching a cable from BOAC dated 1 September advising the order of six United States Stratocruisers by the Ministry of Civil Aviation "costing some $US1,500,000 each ... while at the same time urgent representations are being made to Australia to confine that country's main overseas operations to non-competitive and unacceptable British aircraft."[42] On 25 September he celebrated the QEA victory with a cable to Drakeford: "Contract for supply of four Constellations signed today."[43] The financial terms, QEA advised Air Marshal Williams, provided for a deposit of fifteen per cent on order, a further ten per cent on delivery, and the balance of the purchase price being spread over thirty-six equal monthly instalments, commencing one year after the delivery of each aircraft. "Initially the Lockheed Aircraft Corporation was requiring a bank guarantee to cover payment of the instalments but by reason of the fact that the Commonwealth Government is acquiring the 50 per cent share interest held by BOAC in QEA, Lockheeds agreed to dispense with such guarantee, provided that such acquisition by the Commonwealth Government is completed by 1 March 1947."[44]

On the same day that the Constellation contract was signed, McMaster's doctor, W.J. Arnold, sent a telegram to Fysh from Brisbane about McMaster's poor health: "Sir Fergus is making satisfactory progress and [his] indisposition probably probably only of short duration. My opinion is he should be relieved of all business and other worries until you hear from me further."[45] His message sparked an initiative from Hudson Fysh that was logical but hardly sensitive.

McMaster telegraphed Fysh on 17 October: "I have fully consulted my doctor who assured me I will be fit and strong enough to carry on as chairman. However, he wishes me to take things easy if possible for a few weeks."[46] There was, of course, implicit in the two words "if possible" a plea to Fysh. On the following day, however, Fysh wrote to QEA director F.E. Loxton: "I cannot help feeling honestly and truly that Sir Fergus will be unable to measure up in health to the job ahead and should retire. However, for old friendship and association's sake I cannot actually state to him it is my opinion he should retire, especially because I am an interested party."[47] Despite this declaration of reluctance, on that same day Fysh wrote bluntly to McMaster:

> For a year or more now your frequent absences have become more and more disturbing and some changes for a better working Board were indicated. Now, however, we are obviously faced with Board changes which demand the position be cleared up and the situation

undoubtedly demands a strong chairman who can attend every meeting. To put the matter frankly it has come to a matter of your making up your mind with the support of your doctor that you will be fit and able to take on the Chairmanship under the new conditions.

If you are able to take it on then the new QEA Board would start off with yourself as Chairman, myself as Managing Director and a Government-nominated director as Vice-Chairman. The problem is this. If you at any time are unable to turn up to a meeting the Vice-Chairman would automatically take the Chair, and if you later should retire, then the Vice-Chairman would probably become Chairman and Qantas, firstly, would have lost control and, secondly, I would obliged to work under the new Chairman.

Can you measure up to the health requirements? Messrs Loxton and Templeton are impressed with the interviews with you and your enthusiasm to continue, and I agree too that you should continue so long as you can attend the meetings ahead regularly. If you decide to go on with the job, Mr Loxton and Mr Templeton suggest you should come to Sydney to live. The whole question has gone far beyond personalities and it would be wrong to drag them in, and I think we have all got to look at the future of QEA, a national concern, and do the right thing.

That the future of QEA was a sincere concern of Hudson Fysh was in no doubt. But that his immediate concern was also strongly personal was evident in a postscript to his letter to McMaster.

I have now come to the conclusion that the solution lies in your explaining your position in regard to your health to Mr Drakeford and that an assurance in writing be obtained from him that should your health at any time not allow you to carry on, I am to succeed you as Chairman, combining the position of Managing Director as is common practice. This . . . would secure for Q.A.N.T.A.S. the Chairman's position during the working lifetimes of yourself and myself.[48]

Without waiting for a response from McMaster, Fysh wrote an unofficial "personal" letter to Drakeford.

Dear Arthur [it began]. We have just had a QEA Board meeting here . . . and had discussions reference Sir Fergus McMaster and [the] continuing chairmanship of QEA. Sir Fergus is considerably better but can take little on for some weeks yet. However, he is most anxious to continue the Chairmanship of QEA, though there is grave doubt in the minds of Mr Loxton and myself that he can carry it on and attend meetings as a Chairman should. After all Sir Fergus has done in the past and his sterling character, none of us would go against his wishes but unless he can turn over a completely new leaf medically things will be difficult ahead. The only solution I can see, short of his retirement, is for him to undertake the Chairmanship for start with a proviso from you as Minister that if he cannot stand up to it, I take his place as Chairman, combining the jobs of Chairman and Managing Director as Arthur Coles does . . . [49]

Fysh now left for an IATA conference in Cairo and talks with BOAC and United Kingdom officials. The year had been an exhausting one for both himself and McMaster and had certainly taken its toll on McMaster's health. Fysh had undoubtedly borne an increasing burden both in matters of policy and administration. Just as clearly, he had recognized that with the coming purchase by the Australian government of the BOAC interest in QEA and the inevitable appointment of directors by the government to look after this interest, his own future prospects for one day assuming the chairmanship were at risk. He had worked hard, loyally, and ably for over a quarter of a century under McMaster's leadership. Ambition and anxiety, however, now made his efforts to secure the prize of the chairmanship (without doubt his due) at best clumsy and at worst verging on callousness. His parting letter hurt McMaster deeply, who responded:

> I have your letter, which, although stating many cold facts, was not a happy letter to receive from you after such a long and close association in building up Q.A.N.T.A.S. and QEA. I quite realise the position as stated . . . although in fairness to me you might have stated that, during the twelve months of broken health you mention, I attended in Sydney the whole of the five weeks that Lord Knollys was out here, and later I stayed practically two weeks down there assisting in placing the position before BOAC in regard to the dangerous position for the Empire Service if the Hythe–Lancastrian operations were unduly prolonged . . . Later, I again spent nearly two weeks in Sydney during our negotiations with Mr Askew and Lockheeds. It was while in Sydney that I contracted the present illness, which has nothing to do with the heart, but the recovery of physical strength is slow and depressing.
>
> In asking for a complete rest I . . . had in mind that all the vital negotiations were well in hand. I felt that you would be the first to agree to my request: "Sir Fergus . . . can safely rest easily and for the time being forget all about airways problems." What a difference it would have made to me had I received such a goodwill message from you after our long and close association in Qantas.
>
> In my letter to Mr Drakeford I have asked that should my health fail, you should be appointed Chairman in my place. I naturally would like the Government to give me a chance to carry on as Chairman . . . I do not think we should assume that Mr Drakeford will be hostile. Neither do I think we should contemplate a hostile Board, no matter who the Government appoints. You appear afraid of hostility. I feel the new Board will be

honourable and as easy to get on with as that of the original QEA Board.[50]

McMaster's letter to Drakeford, written that same day, referred to the reconstruction of the QEA board when the acquisition by the government of the BOAC shares was finalized.

> When QEA was formed in 1934 [he wrote], it was agreed with Imperial Airways that the Chairman be a Q.A.N.T.A.S. representative and the Vice Chairman a representative of Imperial Airways. This arrangement continued when BOAC took over from Imperial Airways and we feel that [it] should continue when the Commonwealth takes over from BOAC if possible. In regard to the personal aspect, it has been made clear to me by Mr Fysh and all the other Qantas directors that it is their desire that I should continue as Chairman if this is possible . . . I do not wish to disguise the fact that my health is not good and also, if appointed, a considerable amount of the detail work for a time would have to be undertaken by the Vice Chairman . . . I was appointed Chairman of Q.A.N.T.A.S. in 1920 and that of QEA in 1934 and have taken my part in the many developments over that long period. Naturally, with the big developments ahead, it is my desire to continue with that organisation. However, I think it perhaps desirable to leave it to you and Mr Fysh to fully discuss the whole question . . . I would like to make a recommendation for your serious consideration that if I am appointed Chairman and should my health later prove unsatisfactory . . . Mr Fysh be appointed Chairman . . . I am sending Mr Fysh a copy of this letter . . . May I congratulate you on your splendid majority and I feel we are all happy that you are again in your old position as Minister for Air. [The Labor government under Ben Chifley had romped home in the 1946 election.]

Rudder wrote to McMaster with more grace than Fysh had shown on 13 November.

> Sickness has evidently not made any difference to the clarity of your thought and power of expression. I have very little fear regarding the men the Government may appoint to the Board. In any event they will have to serve a long apprenticeship before they will know a great deal . . . The greater their ability and the stronger their personality, the better you should be pleased. I don't think either you or I suffer fools gladly. Don't forget you and Fysh have between you almost a lifetime of experience in practical air operations.[51]

McMaster's health was, as Fysh had observed, now more than a matter of personalities. McMaster was forced to telegram QEA's general manager, George Harman, on 20 November: "I will be unable attend Sydney and doubtful if could attend effectively any meeting held in Brisbane . . . I am feeling the effect of this special treatment and the extremely hot weather. Please avoid if possible referring details to me for I feel sure everything will be done that is required but I do not wish to be cut off altogether."[52]

Five days later, Rudder wrote to him with tact and gentleness:

By reason of the fact that I represent interests which are about to pass to the Commonwealth . . . I must, I think, be looked on largely as a sympathetic onlooker, rather than one in authority. On Friday morning, Loxton, Fysh and I had a meeting . . . We came to the conclusion that it would be best for a little while to relieve you of all worries and anxieties regarding the immediate affairs of the Company and thus provide better prospects of your being restored to health. To accomplish this it was recommended and later approved at the Board meeting to offer you six months leave of absence . . . In appointing Fysh as Acting Chairman we had in mind that at this stage it is most desirable to give him as much authority and freedom of action as possible . . . We are all in agreement that everything that is possible should be done to ensure that the Company is not dominated by Government interests, which would be the case if the Government were to pass over Qantas claims to the Chairmanship. There is no question whatever but that you are entitled to the Chairmanship, but if you are unable to act then everything that is possible should be done to secure the position for Fysh. In any event I think Qantas will have a hard fight to retain the lead against political opportunists . . . [53]

On the same day that Rudder wrote to McMaster, Fysh wrote promptly to Drakeford.

On present indications it certainly does look as if Sir Fergus will not be able to continue the active Chairmanship, but he has made extraordinary recoveries before and may do so again. My loyalty to him is unimpaired but facts must be looked in the face and I must confess that we are not too hopeful. As you can see from my letter I have been made Acting Chairman in his place, and I wish to reaffirm that if Sir Fergus is unable to take the Chairman's job on in the new year, I am desirous of holding the position. There is no need to point out my association with Q.A.N.T.A.S. and QEA over twenty-six years and my qualifications, and as my political views do not swing either to the right or the left, and this is well known, I feel I am acceptable for the position, and I do not see how anything else in all fairness could be contemplated.[54]

As in his letter to McMaster, the facts were all in place to support him, as Fysh set them down; only the manner of their expression detracted from the merits of his case.

Arthur Drakeford continued as minister in the newly re-elected Labor government and on 4 December, in his second reading speech on the Qantas Empire Airways agreement bill in the House of Representatives, stated: "The Government has considered Qantas Empire Airways as the appropriate organisation for the operation of external air services out of Darwin and it is logical to make the purchase now [of the BOAC shareholding] in order that it shall be a wholly Australian company. This aspect has, in fact, no little importance in the completion of agreements with other nations for international services." It was proposed, said Drakeford, that in 1947 the Australian service would extend to London and operate in parallel with BOAC's service along the same route. Two days later, Fysh cabled Lord Knollys: "Bill to acquire BOAC shares passed both Houses today and expect early agreement on price and transfer shares allowing new Board to sit on conclusion old Board meeting scheduled 24 January 1947."[55]

Following a meeting with Chifley and Drakeford, Fysh wrote to QEA director F. E. Loxton: "Mr Chifley thought . . . W. C. Taylor would be suitable as Vice Chairman but that he would not desire him to be Chairman, and that Sir Fergus should continue in this position, and if he could not measure up later owing to ill health, then I should succeed him. He did not wish to disturb those who knew the business and had made a success of it."[56] To Air Marshal Williams, Fysh summarized the new position:

> In regard to the chairmanship, the position is that at present Sir Fergus is Chairman. I am Managing Director and Harman is General Manager, while Turner is the Assistant General Manager. However, owing to the illness of Sir Fergus for some years I have greatly been doing the work of the Chairman . . . Should Sir Fergus not be able to continue, the logical and most suitable arrangement would be for me to become whole time Chairman on my present salary and eliminate the position of Managing Director, leaving the top set up as it is in Trans-Australia Airlines, with Coles and Brain, and as it is in BOAC . . . Harman is a top ranking man indeed in Civil Air Transport administration and I know of no better man in this country.[57]

Arthur Baird, of course, remained as works manager; Captain Crowther was operations manager.

As the bill for the government acquisition of BOAC's interest in QEA went through Parliament, British Commonwealth Pacific Airlines held its first annual general meeting in Sydney, following its incorporation on 24 June. Its directors were A. W. Coles (also chairman of TAA), New Zealander Sir Leonard Isitt, and Viscount Knollys. Its nominal share capital was £1 million but only £10,000 had been called up. Its imme-diate duty, said the first annual report, was to contract for an interim trans-Pacific service. Australian National Airways had provided a temporary service from Australia from 15 Septem-ber. On outward trips there had been capacity passenger load-ings, but on return trips loads had been below expectations. As Australian National Airways was the only company in a position to operate the service, it was proposed to enter into a short-term contract with them (with DC4 aircraft). On com-pletion of bilateral landing rights agreement with the United States, it was proposed to run three trips per fortnight from Sydney and one from Auckland to San Francisco. As yet, said the report, no right existed to pick up or set down passengers or freight in US territory and passengers and freight would meantime be carried on to Vancouver.[58] The QEA competitor for traffic between Australia and the United Kingdom — under its able, thrusting, and ambitious chairman Arthur Coles — was as 1946 ended, now in business.

With the Profoundest Regret
1947

A confidential QEA management memorandum dated 7 January 1947 summarized the airline's position as phase 2 of the Australia–England service came closer. Since introduction of the Empire flying boat service in 1938, it said, QEA had been virtually operating on a cost-plus basis in one form or another. Although this did not allow for the possibility of a good financial return or the building of reserves against time of financial stress, it did ensure financial stability of operation. For operation of phase 2, expected later that year, the trend would be towards operating on a mail payment per pound per mile basis, and careful safeguards would be necessary. Aircraft operation, said the memorandum, was still distinctly a hazardous business. QEA had no reserves adequate to see it over a really bad period. When the large amount of new capital (to buy Constellations) was called, QEA would have practically no reserves. Financial catastrophe might come from grounding of QEA aircraft for a considerable period, the loss of one or more aircraft, or the strike hazard. The danger from strikes came mainly from air crews and engineers and was now a real one. "QEA would not admit", said the memorandum, "that her lines would ever be held up owing to a strike, but the hazard is there."[1]

Lockheed Aircraft Corporation, on whom QEA had now staked its future, was itself under financial pressures with the Constellation programme. Courtlandt S. Gross, its vice-president, wrote to Fysh on 17 January that he was very disturbed that Qantas might feel that their original quotation of

$25,000 for interior modifications to Qantas aircraft, since reduced to $10,000, "reflected a desire on our part to make a large profit on this work after we had, so to speak, gotten you committed on the basic airplane". A long letter followed explaining "that the Constellation is proving to be a very unprofitable operation for this Company, and one the losses on which may very possibly extend to $15 million or more . . . First, we originally planned the amortization write-offs over a considerably larger number of machines than it now appears probable we will sell . . . Second, the cost of complete redesign of the airplane, as between Model 49 and Models 649 and 749, has proven to be much greater than originally planned." They had costed the Qantas modifications "to make each job stand on its own feet", said Gross. "I certainly do not mean to parade before you our troubles and problems as such, but I am most anxious to have you realise that our original quotation (in which I believe no profit was included) did not represent an attempt on our part to do $10,000 of work with $15,000 or $20,000 profit added . . . Uppermost in our mind was the motive of having you feel that we have dealt equitably with you."[2]

Fysh informed McMaster on 20 January that steady progress was being made in preparing to operate the Constellations, as well as to prepare financially for them. Correspondence with BOAC in London was, he said, almost nil as they waited for agreement between the Australian and United Kingdom governments on methods of operating phase 2. There was also "an expected lull, awaiting the appointment of Government directors".[3] McMaster told Fysh that although he was making some progress and was better than he had been for a considerable time, "I have a lot to pick up before I can do more than attend to a limited amount of correspondence and will not be able to attend meetings for a considerable time yet".[4]

On 6 February 1947 Fysh advised McMaster that the Australian government had nominated as directors on the QEA board W. C. Taylor, G. P. N. Watt, and Sir Keith Smith. Taylor, a Sydney solicitor and son of a shearer and staunch unionist, was a specialist in industrial law and a close and respected friend of the prime minister. G. P. N. Watt (not to be confused with W. A. Watt, who had resigned as a BOAC representative on the QEA board in 1946) was deputy secretary of the Treasury and a director of Trans-Australia Airlines. Sir Keith Smith, who had made the first flight from England to Australia with his brother Ross in the Vickers Vimy in 1919, was the Australian representative of the British Vickers group of companies. Fysh wrote: "We have come out of the matter very well indeed . . . We have a very heavy programme ahead this year, especially with overseas talks and conferences. I will have to try and limit my overseas trips and get Harman and Turner on to the job as they both have a splendid grip of the business."[5]

The anticipated heavy programme relied for its implementation on important decisions of policy by BOAC, but there were frustrating delays in England. Fysh told Lord Knollys: "As time goes on and no arrangements have yet been made for the proposed Phase 2 operations . . . we are becoming increasingly anxious that the new BOAC–QEA operations, which it is assumed will commence following the delivery of the QEA Constellations scheduled for August of this year, should be agreed so that ordering and effective planning can take place." Knollys, in the hands of the Air Ministry, was apologetic.

> I have been waiting for the last few months for a decision as to the type of aircraft which we shall operate on the Kangaroo route . . . I can do no better than tell you the alternatives for which we are planning. There is still a possibility that we might be allowed to buy Constellation 749 aircraft. It is, however, more likely that we shall not . . . in which case we propose to operate two or three services weekly with flying boats and two or three with Lancastrians. I do realise how irritating to you the delay . . . must be. I can assure you it is equally so to us, but major questions of Government policy are involved.

QEA's main operations, as 1947 began, were from Sydney to Karachi with Lancastrians; Sydney–Singapore with Hythe flying boats; Sydney–Rabaul with DC3s; Sydney–Fiji with one Empire flying boat; Brisbane–Darwin and Queensland internal services with DC3 and Dragon aircraft; plus operation of the Flying Doctor Service from Cloncurry and Charleville in Queensland with Dragons, and inland charter services in New Guinea, also with Dragons. The company's fleet was seven DC3s, one Lockheed 10A, one C-class Empire flying boat, four DH84 Dragons, two Liberators, two Fox Moths, and one Dragonfly. On hire from BOAC were five Lancastrians, six Hythe flying boats (owned by BOAC and hired through the Department of Civil Aviation), with one DC3 on order for delivery in August, and four Constellation 749s on order. It was a hotchpotch of a fleet and route pattern and little more than the unplanned residue of war and the transition to peace.

Fysh told McMaster on 24 February that the first board meeting with the new government-appointed directors in attendance "went off without a hitch in an amicable and generally helpful way. There is", he said, "every indication of a good, workable Board and close co-operation between QEA, TAA and also TEA." Australian National Airways was, said Fysh, "still proving difficult generally but they represent private enterprise and I realise we must be careful we do not come to a point where we would be thought by the press and public as too much in the pocket of the Government. We still have firmly in mind that we are still non-political servants of the Government of the day."[6] That McMaster yearned to be more involved in all the new developments is evident in a letter to Drakeford. "I do not wish any misunderstanding on the part of yourself and Mr Chifley, especially regarding my health, which I admit is unsatisfactory", he wrote. "But at the same time I do not wish to be thrown out of aviation at this important period."

Fysh advised McMaster on 10 March that the articles of association of QEA would be altered, following a special general meeting, "to enable BOAC constitutionally to sell its shares to the Commonwealth". He thought they should not

> decide on the actual amount of capital required [for the Constellation purchase] until it is known just how the England–Australia route will operate, and what combination of aircraft is used. It is hoped that there will not be a delay of more than two or three months and meanwhile the Government will have the Commonwealth Bank carry us on, and such overdraft loan will be at 4 per cent or lower, we hope, which will be less than the 6 per cent we would be paying on Qantas shares.[7]

McMaster thought Fysh should try for 3.5 per cent. Two weeks later, on 24 March, Fysh wrote that the old QEA board had met at noon when the BOAC shares were transferred to the Commonwealth government. "Then at 2.30, we had the first meeting of the new Board. Mr Taylor was appointed Vice Chairman."[8]

As the new board took over, Pan American Airways had begun, on 17 March, scheduled weekly services to Sydney. The DC4 Clipper *Kit Carson*, left San Francisco on 17 March and arrived in Sydney on 21 March. (Pan American had begun operating special flights each week from San Francisco to Sydney and return on a trip basis on 21 January 1947. Airmail was inaugurated from San Francisco to Sydney on 22 Febru-

ary, arrived on 26 February. Pan American considered, however, that the airline's official inaugural date into Australia
was 21 March.)

At the first meeting of the new QEA board, the new directors
had been asked to agree immediately to an issue of private
shares through the Melbourne broker, J. B. Were, to provide
cash for the purchase of the Constellation 749. Both W. C.
Taylor and deputy secretary of the Treasury, G. P. N. Watt,
asked for time to consider this proposal which was, wrote
Norman Watt, "grudgingly given". Watt submitted a recommendation to the treasurer that the share issue be not approved "but that Civil Aviation should purchase the aircraft and
charter them to Qantas".[9] Fysh was quick to learn of this attitude and told F. E. Loxton on 28 March that the Treasury was
not at all happy about the proposed Qantas share issue.

> My summing up is that they will try to stop it going through and,
> in fact, have no doubt already advised that it not go through . . .
> One view was that the Government and not QEA should own the
> Constellations. The other main view is that Qantas shareholders
> "might get something out of it" in the proposed issue and in
> other issues to follow and that this is against Government policy.
> (You will realise they have just ended the Government–Private
> Enterprise partnership in A.W.A.) I feel that now the Government
> are realising for the first time what sort of a partnership they have
> gotten themselves into with Qantas and are fearful of criticism
> from their own people. They also visualise difficulties . . . in deal-
> ing with QEA which will not exist in TAA and which mainly
> concern finance, profit, rates of interest and the like. You will
> realise the present position, of course, in that the Government has
> got our Qantas share issue deferred on grounds we could hardly
> object to, and that we are being completely financed by the Com-
> monwealth Bank, and this is an arrangement under which no
> doubt we could carry on fairly indefinitely . . . As we have always
> realised, the Government has the whip hand should it care to use
> it through its control of contracts to be let to us . . . At present
> QEA has no contract for its Constellation operations and it is
> quite impossible to do anything about getting one until such time
> as the UK Government come out of their dream and decide what
> type of aircraft they will use . . . [10]

Norman Watt had discussions with the secretary of the
Treasury (McFarlane), who favoured the outright purchase of
the fifty per cent Q.A.N.T.A.S. private shareholding.[11] (It was
subsequent to these deliberations that the prime minister
approved this course and Watt was commissioned to negotiate
the purchase with Fysh. The decision was closely in accord
with the Labor government's plans for nationalization of the

private banks and its general philosophy favouring government ownership of major national enterprises. It was also a recognition that a capital issue to private shareholders in a company with the unlimited security of the Commonwealth government behind it would have presented those shareholders with a valuable risk-free investment.)

The old QEA directors and management had expected that, with the government acquisition of the BOAC shares, there might also come complete government ownership and purchase of the privately held Australian shares in the old holding company, Q.A.N.T.A.S. When this did not happen, wrote Fysh, "we fully expected that the new Commonwealth–Qantas partnership would be a lasting one, at any rate for a few years".[12] However, on 23 April a surprised Fysh returned from a meeting in Canberra with Chifley and Drakeford. Chifley had decided that QEA should be fully government-owned. "I regret I found the Prime Minister's mind firmly made up on the question," Fysh wrote to Loxton, "making it quite useless to pursue any further argument to the contrary . . . What has caused the Government to change its mind now is mainly the question of finance concerning provision of new capital . . . The present position is regrettable indeed, especially for myself, but I am afraid that it is the penalty, if it can be put that way, of growing too big." Once again Fysh saw his position as chairman threatened.

At this unsettling moment, affecting the very basis of the control of the company, McMaster's declining health forced him to recognize that he could continue no longer as chairman. The news did not come directly to Fysh from McMaster but in a letter from Loxton on 8 April 1947.

> It is with the profoundest regret [wrote Loxton] that I advise you, in consequence of our Chairman's health not having recovered to the full extent anticipated, I have today been requested by Sir Fergus McMaster to officially tender for and on his behalf his resignation from the position of Chairman of the Company, effective from 23 May next . . . Sir Fergus has asked me to explain that he has only arrived at this decision after long and careful consideration, and in the realisation that the state of his health does not permit him to devote the necessary energy, concentration and attention to detail inseparable from the position of Chairman, more particularly in this present stage of the Company's development. The hand of Fergus McMaster has guided the destiny of this Company, one might say unerringly, ever since its inception, and his ability and the high esteem in which he is held in Government circles, both in Australia and overseas, as well as in very

many other quarters, have been tremendous factors in the sound progress that the Company has recorded. Sir Fergus is desirous . . . that the announcement be kept strictly private and confidential until the next meeting of the Directors on the 18th inst.[13]

(Loxton also wrote to Edna, Lady McMaster, to "save her undue worry about Sir Fergus's remuneration". He advised: "Fergus gets £1,250 per annum as Chairman and on retirement to the position of ordinary director this could go back to £200 per annum. However, I do not anticipate any difficulty at the next meeting in the Board agreeing to his old rate to continue and so I do not feel you or Fergus should worry on this score.")

Fysh expressed his reaction to McMaster's decision in a letter to Loxton dealing with the Commonwealth government's reservations on proposed methods of financing the Constellation purchase and the possible acquisition of the Q.A.N.T.A.S. shareholding, adding: "I must with reluctance and regret point out that the present discussions and decisions which must follow are 'Charman's' decisions, yet we are in the unhappy position that Sir Fergus McMaster is apparently not in a fit state of health to discuss or transact business of this nature. I would like your advice on this matter." He asked Loxton to see McMaster "as he may improve", to get the benefit of McMaster's advice. Formal notification of the government's intentions came in a letter from Drakeford. The minister referred to Fysh's discussions with the prime minister and himself on the additional capital required and said that the government was considering the question of acquisition of the existing private shareholding in Qantas Empire Airways and hoped to reach a decision at an early date.

Uncertainty about the very structure of the company was compounded by continuing doubt about BOAC's plans. BOAC's technical director, Sir Victor Tait, wrote on 14 April: "I am afraid we are still in the position of not knowing definitely how we are going to operate the Australian route as there is still a possibility that we may get Constellations. We find ourselves in the awkward position of not being able to go ahead with any definite plan."[14] Almost at once, however, and just as unsettling, there was a cable from Knollys to Fysh: "Final government decision that BOAC cannot repeat not operate Constellations Kangaroo route. Therefore we must now take alternative . . . Do not expect Solents to be available to replace Hythes till sometime first half 1948."

There were immediate practical problems of finance and

cash flow for QEA. Turner advised Fysh on 1 May: "I have had a further examination made of the current cash position and as far as we can see now we should be able to definitely carry on without an overdraft during the month of May. It is possible that by delaying payments to BOAC for petrol and oil and such items that we may be able to extend this position further . . . "[15] Fysh at once advised QEA vice chairman Taylor: "In regard to the question of bank overdraft . . . without mortgaging the company's assets, I feel it would be best to defer consideration of the matter of security for the overdraft if possible till something more concrete is disclosed in regard to the Government's intentions . . . The letter from Mr Drakeford leaves QEA in a state of suspension and uncertainty at a time when arrangements for the new capital and interim financial accommodation were on the point of being arranged."

They had two weeks to wait before the situation was clarified. On 15 May the acting minister for civil aviation, H. C. Barnard, wrote: "I have to inform you that the Government, after full consideration of the developmental programme and greatly increased capital expenditure requirements for expansion of the Empire air service conducted by Qantas Empire Airways Ltd has decided that it is desirable that the operating company be entirely Government owned."[16] Now began a period of negotiations, through the Treasury, for the purchase of the Q.A.N.T.A.S. shares in QEA. Fysh had written to the prime minister on 6 May: "I am heavily personally involved, and a good deal depends on my attitude . . . You mentioned in Canberra that, should QEA become a wholly Government concern, it would be the wish for me to carry on but, as you will realise, consideration of this would depend in the first place on the deal accorded to the organisation in the future."[17]

Loxton had discussions with McMaster and told Fysh: "Sir Fergus agrees with my viewpoint that the directors should avoid being placed in a position where it could be claimed that the approach had been made to the Government by Qantas, whereas it is the Government that has opened the issue . . . In such a case our bargaining powers would be greatly weakened." Loxton urged that the government make an offer in writing. He also chided Fysh for plans to leave for the United Kingdom in the midst of these activities. Fysh replied: "Unable postpone visit London as arrangements already made meet BOAC and Australian and Air Ministry officials there for conference on operating Constellations."

At the board meeting of 26 May 1947, Hudson Fysh succeeded
Fergus McMaster as chairman of Qantas, retaining his position
as managing director. A press release was issued the following
day:

> The decision of the Commonwealth Government to purchase the
> private shareholding in QEA has come as a result of greatly in-
> creased expansion and capital requirements for the latter organi-
> sation, and is in line with Government policy and with previous
> action by all other main Empire units where we see British Over-
> seas Airways Corporation, British South American Airways,
> British European Airways Corporation, Trans Canada Airlines,
> South African Airways, New Zealand National Airways Corpora-
> tion, Tasman Empire Airways Limited, British Commonwealth
> Pacific Airlines all owned by their respective Governments or
> groups of Governments. The taking over of principle airlines in
> the various British communities is not confined to Labour
> Governments only, but follows a common trend of political
> thought and represents the will of the people, which must prevail
> in democratic countries . . . Qantas, originally founded by
> Queensland enterprise and shareholders, is the oldest name in air
> transport in the Empire . . . [18]

Shareholders were advised on the same day that the government had decided that the operating company should be entirely government-owned and that "your Directors have agreed
to enter into discussions with the Government with a view to
reaching some mutually just and satisfactory basis for the
transfer which we can recommend to our shareholders for
acceptance. During the period of negotiations, effective forth-
with and until further notified, the transfer books and share
register of the Company will remain closed." From Norman
Watt, at the Treasury, came formal advice to Fysh that the
matter of a retiring gratuity to Sir Fergus McMaster had been
referred to the prime minister "who is in agreement with the
proposal to pay to Sir Fergus an amount of £1,250, representing one year's salary".

Fysh left for London on 29 May to join Turner and Edgar
Johnston for talks with BOAC and the Air Ministry. He found
that Turner had been of considerable assistance to Johnston
and BOAC and that preliminary agreement had already been
reached. Each airline would, initially, fly entirely different
types of aircraft; QEA would use Constellations and BOAC
Lancastrians and Hythes. Each airline would operate its own
services, but revenue would be pooled and shared each year on
the basis of actual capacity ton-miles flown. There would,
therefore, be no competition. Rates and conditions and other

details were agreed and it was envisaged that mail would be carried at a surcharge on the basis of gold francs per ton-kilo-metre. "The death knell of that great and ambitious venture of 1938, the Empire All Up Mail Scheme [to carry mail throughout the Empire without surcharge] was", wrote Fysh, "thus finally sounded."[19] QEA was to operate two Constellation services weekly and BOAC two Solent flying boat services and one Lancastrian service weekly. Pending the introduction of the Solents, BOAC would operate three Hythe flying boat services and one Lancastrian service each week. The Lancastrians were to carry mail and freight only. The basic passenger fare was to be £220 single. Fysh returned from London by BOAC Lancastrian on 17 June.

Back in Australia, Fysh found much criticism of the government decision to purchase the private Q.A.N.T.A.S. share-holding. In Parliament, R. G. Menzies declared: "Commonwealth control of Qantas Empire Airways would not mean a better running of the services. Nobody could suggest that Qantas was not one of the best run airlines in the world, and that its shareholders were not responsible for a marvellous pioneer work. They [the government] come in later and reap the benefits of the pioneers."[20] The Sydney *Daily Telegraph* thought QEA profits might be used to offset the government-owned TAA's losses. The *Sydney Morning Herald* was fearful for Qantas efficiency.[21]

Fysh was still abroad, however, when QEA advised its share-holders on 11 June that agreement had been reached on terms of the share purchase with the Commonwealth government. A circular stated

> that the Commonwealth government had agreed to purchase the 261,500 shares held by the Queensland and Northern Territory Aerial Services Limited in Qantas Empire Airways Limited for the sum of £455,000, approximately equivalent to £1.14.0 per share. The purchase is to be effective as at 30 June 1947 ... QEA will declare and pay a dividend before June 30 1947 in respect of the financial year ending 31 March at the rate of 6 per cent, and a further bonus dividend at the rate of 1 per cent ... Your [Q.A.N.T.A.S.] directors unanimously recommended ratification of the sale to the Commonwealth on the above basis.[22]

A meeting of directors to consider formally the take-over terms was arranged for 27 June but on 18 June McMaster told Fysh he felt it would be better if he stayed away and left the whole of the final meetings to Fysh and Loxton. "I feel I would be risking a breakdown," he said, "for there is bound to

be a good lot of speaking which, when you are not fit, could be upsetting, especially under the circumstances where it means the winding up of an organisation such as Q.A.N.T.A.S. and the severance of old and valued associations." In his accustomed practical vein, McMaster said there should be no loose ends. "Q.A.N.T.A.S. should completely sever all connections with QEA and nothing be left to doubt with the financial adjustments. International aviation has become too involved for private capital. Again," McMaster concluded generously, "I congratulate you."[23]

The 27 June meeting agreed formally to the take-over terms and these were endorsed at an extraordinary general meeting of shareholders in Brisbane on 5 July. The agreed price was based on the current stock exchange figure as representing true value. No allowance was made for goodwill, though McMaster had recognized more than a year before that the company had a case for such an allowance. On 10 May 1946 he had written to Lord Knollys in relation to the purcahse of the BOAC shareholding:

> Although BOAC evidently are not claiming goodwill . . . regarding the sale of BOAC shareholding in QEA [I] would greatly appreciate your emphasising . . . that considerable goodwill value nevertheless exists, particularly in relation to Q.A.N.T.A.S.

27 June 1947. The last meeting of the Qantas Empire Airways Board of Directors in which Q.A.N.T.A.S. Ltd participated. From left: R. E. Fulford (secretary), H. H. Harman (general manager), W. C. Taylor (vice-chairman), Hudson Fysh (chairman and managing director), G. P. N. Watt, F. E. Loxton, and Sir Keith Smith.

Limited carrying over twenty-five years outstanding reputation Empire and worldwide for integrity and efficiency ... There should be recognition of the principle of goodwill value ... in case Q.A.N.T.A.S. Limited at some future date should decide to dispose of its shareholding.[24]

Norman Watt, the government appointee to the new QEA board, wrote that despite the denial of this goodwill consideration in the sale price, "Hudson Fysh was secretly happy; it assured his continuance as Managing Director and removed the threat — very real at the time — that shipping interests would have provided the money to subscribe to the proposed share issue, and that Captain Holyman would thus have become a strong influence in Qantas affairs".[25] On 3 July, Fysh's future was formally assured when Drakeford wrote to him: "With regard to your own position, which was considered by Cabinet yesterday, I can now, in confirmation of our telephone conversation tonight, offer you the position of Chairman and Managing Director in the new set up. The appointment will be for a period of five years from 1 July 1947 at salary of £3,500 per annum."[26] Fysh wrote accepting the appointment.

Neither Fysh nor McMaster, nor any of the founder shareholders of Q.A.N.T.A.S., received anything like adequate financial reward for their pioneering investment and continuing support of the early airline, perhaps least of all Fergus McMaster who, wrote Fysh, "led the company along lines of extraordinarily high and patriotic principles and was extremely hard on himself". There were moves to recognize McMaster's long contribution. On 8 July, Alan Campbell (who was pro-tem honorary secretary of the early Q.A.N.T.A.S. during its formative period in 1920) wrote to the directors

that before the company is finally wound up, provision be made to fittingly recognise the services of Sir Fergus McMaster, and the extent to which those services were responsible first of all for the survival of the Company and for its later prospering ... I am aware that early liquidation was avoided only because a precarious financial position was bolstered by Sir Fergus and Mr Templeton using their private resources. In the case particularly of Sir Fergus, the out of pocket expenses incurred by him on the business of the Company were very considerable ... and never charged up.[27]

Sir William Glasgow, former minister of defence in the twenties, also urged the directors "to show recognition in a tangible way of the great service Sir Fergus McMaster has rendered not

216

only the shareholders of Qantas, but civil aviation generally and the Commonwealth".

Hudson Fysh was sensitive to the suggestion, in Alan Campbell's letter to the directors, that Ainslie Templeton's support for the infant Q.A.N.T.A.S. should merit special mention, and about his own part in those endeavours. He wrote to Campbell on 14 July:

> In an effort to do all possible towards assisting the worthy case of Sir Fergus, events in regard to the history of Qantas, and who did this and that, are getting out of line with the facts. This is a pity because we have got to see that we end up the great history of Qantas in the same spirit that it was born in and carried on. It was McGinness who supplied the main drive and push which caused the formation of Qantas and, in Darwin in 1919, I was writing articles and talking on the coming service before McGinness met Fergus. McGinness always wanted to start a service and I was his partner. We worked together. Then we had the meeting of McGinness and Fergus and the great work the two of them put in. Then Ainslie was brought in and the historic meeting in Brisbane of the four of us took place in 1920. McGinness put in £1,350 and myself £500, every penny we had in the entire world. Two wealthy squatters with great public spirit put in £1,500 — this was Ainslie (£1,000) and Fergus (£500). When the pinch came, Ainslie increased his holding and Fergus stood ready to do so . . .
>
> I see that you bring Mr Templeton into consideration for some recognition . . . Mr Templeton is a wealthy man and in these days of high taxation a man's position is measured by his capital standing, and not so much by his salaried income, and I for one have given twenty-seven years of my life to Q.A.N.T.A.S. and QEA without recognition for the work which has been put in on a far too low salary and ridiculously low director's fees over a period of some seventeen years . . .
>
> Owing to the way in which Fergus has led the Company morally, owing to his great initial work, and to the out of pocket expenses he refused to claim for so long, and his reported present poor financial condition, I realise he is the one who should receive the main recognition, but if it is desired to bring in any others, then you must inevitably bring in Mr Loxton and others who shared in not only the foundation but carrying on of the work of Q.A.N.T.A.S. and QEA . . . [28]

If there were to be rewards for individuals for their contribution to Q.A.N.T.A.S. following the government's share purchase and sparked by events following McMaster's resignation as chairman, Hudson Fysh clearly saw himself as worthy of consideration. There was full justification in this assessment but Fysh soon realized that questions of recompense for those early years were difficult ones. He wrote again to Campbell:

Mr Loxton and myself talked over the whole matter of recognition for Fergus and any possible other Qantas pioneers . . . with the result that we decided that the only practical way is to go ahead with something for Fergus alone . . . Once we start bringing in others in addition to Sir Fergus, we are in a hopeless tangle. For instance, McGinness has been here at the weekend and feels that he should be in it, and if anyone in addition to Fergus is to be in it, then he should definitely participate as he was the first true spark that lit Qantas . . .

Ten QEA captains and six first officers had left progressively since June for the United States for training on the new Constellation aircraft and technical courses at Lockheed in Burbank, California. Four captains, including R. J. Ritchie (a future chief executive) did additional courses in the use of ILS (Instrument Landing System) at Pan American's flying school at La Guardia airport. D. B. Hudson became the first Qantas

Air Marshal George Jones, RAAF Chief of Air Staff, visited the Lockheed plant at Burbank while Qantas crews were training on the newly built L-749 Constellations prior to their delivery flights to Australia. Air Marshal Jones is speaking with Capt. Howse of Qantas beside the second L-749 of the Qantas order. The number 65 on the nose is a Lockheed designation which identified serial no. 2565. This aircraft became VH-EAB *Lawrence Hargrave* before delivery. Note the first use of the flying kangaroo symbol.

technical representative at Burbank. In the meantime, worried about loss of staff to both TAA and BCPA, Fysh had written to Arthur Coles (chairman of both airlines) about the necessity for Qantas to retain its key men in view of the considerable losses over the past year:

> The following is a list of names . . . whom we particularly could not afford to lose: H. H. Harman, general manager; C. O. Turner, assistant general manager; Capt. W. H. Crowther, operations manager; Capt. G. U. Allan, official in charge of Constellation project; Capt. O. D. Denny, assistant operations manager; C. W. Neilsen, traffic manager; J. N. Wright, assistant traffic manager; D. H. Wright, assistant works manager; F. C. Derham, chief accountant; Capt. R. J. Ritchie, flight captain, Lancastrians; Capt. R. O. Mant, inspector of air accidents and safety.

All these staff, said Fysh, were engaged on the specialized Constellation project. "I see", he added meaningfully, "that BCPA is calling for a manager." (In fact, Alec Barlow, from ANA, became general manager of BCPA throughout its existence.)

Fysh wrote to McMaster that the new ownership and contacts of the new board members had greatly facilitated QEA's general business

> and this specially applies to new services and contracts [and] all financial matters and obtaining of new plant and equipment. We still have the same freedom of management and in dealing with staff but we are having to pay much more top attention to industrial matters than in the past. When the House meets in Canberra in September I am expecting a Bill to go through turning QEA into a Commission. This I think will be shown necessary as under our present set up we are subject to State laws controlling public companies. This can hardly fit in with full state control . . .

(No such bill was passed; Qantas retained its public company structure.) On 8 September Fysh advised McMaster on the final constitution of the QEA board.

> As you know we already have W. C. Taylor as Vice Chairman, Norman Watt and Sir Keith Smith. Mr D. McVey has now been agreed by Cabinet, and Mr A. R. McComb from the Civil Aviation Department . . . It is now a particularly strong Board . . . Personally, I can see a big red light ahead for us in industrial troubles and the infiltration of Communist elements, principally in regard to the Ironworkers Union, who are giving us a great deal of trouble . . . The first Constellation should be here in six weeks.[29]

The board of the old Q.A.N.T.A.S., with the completion of the government purchase of the company's shares in QEA, now recommended liquidation of the company to shareholders. The twenty-seventh and last annual meeting was set for 2 October, at the Wool Exchange building, Brisbane. On 29 September, Fergus McMaster sent a telegram to Fysh: "Regret but doctor definitely against my attending meeting."[30] Hudson Fysh was elected to chair this final meeting at which sixty-one shareolders were present. A special retiring allowance of £2,500 was voted to McMaster and a retiring allowance of £250 to H. H. Harman. The meeting voted £500 for directors' fees. At an extraordinary general meeting that followed immediately a special resolution was passed "that this Company be wound up voluntarily". Fysh wrote that it was "an historical and harrowing occasion".[31]

The directors met at the conclusion of the meeting to consider the distribution of the £500 voted them as fees. It was agreed that McMaster should receive his usual £200 but there was then disagreement.

> I felt [wrote Fysh] that as vice chairman and the one who had led in the difficult negotiations connected with the wind up, I should receive more than last year's equal split of £75 for Loxton, Templeton and myself. This was opposed; I stuck to my guns, claiming that as acting chairman I had a casting vote . . . They walked out and this meeting was never recorded. Anyhow, how could we hold the usual post-annual general meeting directors' meeting when, meanwhile, the company had been wound up?[32]

Notes on this meeting, described as "informal", record: "Mr Loxton suggested to Mr Templeton, who agreed, that in the circumstances they should yield any share and vote the whole amount to Mr Fysh. Mr Fysh said that under no circumstances would he accept such a proposal. All he advocated was a fair and equitable distribution." (The issue was later resolved when Fysh met with the liquidator and agreed that the fees should, as in the previous year, be split equally.)

Hudson Fysh was now the only founder or director of Queensland and Northern Territory Aerial Services Limited to make the transition to the new government-owned Qantas Empire Airways (though Arthur Baird remained in charge of engineering).

> Our stalwart Board members, Fergus McMaster, F. E. Loxton and A. N. Templeton, not to mention the shareholders, many of whom were of twenty-six years standing, deeply felt the passing of the old Qantas. There must have been quite a bit of feeling [wrote Fysh], that, with only myself as a founder and director to go with the new set up. I had landed a good job for myself. It was natural that I should feel more than a little unhappy about this.[33]

There had been changes at the top in BOAC too. Lord Knollys had resigned and been succeeded as chairman by Sir Harold Hartley (the airline's seventh chairman); BOAC's chief executive, General Critchley, was replaced by Whitney Straight. Fysh had worked closely with them all and spent much time abroad. In a handwritten note he set down a list of his overseas trips since QEA's formation in 1934; there had been seventeen, a total of twenty-one months absence, plus eleven board meetings of Tasman Empire Airways in New Zealand. In thirteen years he had spent twenty-five months away from Australia.[34]

Hudson Fysh was now, after twenty-six years, the leader of the enterprise that he had helped to found. He was no longer in the shadow of the personality and reputation of his former chairman, Fergus McMaster. He asserted this new freedom in an extraordinary letter to McMaster only five days after the meeting that saw the demise of the old Q.A.N.T.A.S. It set down what Fysh saw as grounds for gratitude from McMaster which wiped out any debts owed by Fysh. He wrote:

> I have been in the thick of the happenings as concerning Qantas over the past year and, owing to the strenuous new work which we have to face in Qantas Empire Airways, I have found it the most trying year I have encountered in the business so far. Personally, in regard to the two retiring grants to you totalling £3,750, one from QEA and the other from Q.A.N.T.A.S., I feel that owing to my part in this I have fully discharged my debt of gratitude to you for your support in the early days of the Company. In addition to this, I have been glad to deputise for you in Qantas as chairman, and also in regard to QEA . . . in a way which would relieve you of anxiety as far as possible . . . It seems that our positions have been reversed in that, in the early days of Qantas, you [did] the work without adequate financial remuneration whereas the same can be said of what I have done over the last few years.[35]

Though the Australian government had now assumed complete ownership of Qantas Empire Airways, their future corporate structure and constitution remained in doubt. Following discussions in the boardroom on 3 October, Fysh advised Drakeford of directors' attitudes to the adaption of the Australian National Airlines Commission act (under which TAA operated) to the creation of a new corporation to take over the business of QEA. There were, wrote Fysh, three points raised: whether the new body should be called a corporation or a commission; its exact name; and the use of the name Qantas Empire Airways in assisting in its trading activities. (The directors' meeting had considered the name "Australian Overseas Airlines Corporation", to carry on business under the QEA name.) Fysh advised Drakeford: "Perhaps provision should be inserted that the chairman is to be the Chief Executive . . . in view of the possibility that he will be expected to devote the whole of his time to the affairs of the Corporation." Fysh's memorandum discussed the financial provisions of the TAA act and BOAC's structure but suggested that the words "having regard to sound commercial practice" might be used for application to Qantas. "This", wrote Fysh, "has become quite a common feature of current English legislation creating public corporations." (The directors, in meetings in Sydney and Melbourne, had stressed that the new body "must possess the hallmarks of the public corporation — namely complete freedom from political interference, coupled with the fullest possible financial autonomy, but remaining accountable to the public through its obligation to furnish an annual report and balance sheet".)[36]

The year closed with the introduction of new services and new aircraft. On 14 October, a fortnightly Lancastrian service to the former Australian penal settlement of Norfolk Island, a thousand miles northeast of Sydney, was inaugurated. On 9 December, the first charter operation to Lord Howe Island, five hundred miles from Sydney, was carried out using the first of a number of reconditioned Catalina flying boats bought from the RAAF. Of far greater long-term significance, on 16 December, a weekly Lancastrian service via Darwin and Manila to Japan began, to serve the Australian forces that

Disembarking passengers from a Qantas Catalina at Lord Howe Island in December 1947. All Qantas Catalinas operating after the war were late model ex-RAAF aircraft, distinguished by their taller tails from the Catalinas used on the Indian Ocean services during World War II.

formed part of the British Commonwealth occupied area based on Bofu. (It replaced the RAAF courier service that operated to Bofu from November 1945, using Dakotas.)

On the same day that the Norfolk Island services started, the first Qantas Constellation, the *Ross Smith*, completed its delivery flight from Burbank to Sydney in the record elapsed time for a commercial flight of forty-three hours. (Actual flying time was thirty-three hours.) A beautiful aircraft, with its upswept triple tail, the Constellation was fast, capacious, comfortable, and pressurized. Much organization and activity had preceded its arrival. Pilots and engineers had been sent to the United States for training, while in Sydney practice in instrument flying procedures was under way on Link Trainers and in two Wackett trainer aircraft. Under Arthur Baird, as engineering manager, and D. H. Wright, as chief engineer, preparations were completed for the introduction of the 2,500-horsepower Curtiss Wright engines, together with requirements for ground and in-flight spares procurement. Jack Avery, in charge of the renovated engineering workshops and overhaul shop, was ready to tackle these complex and temperamental engines. George Roberts, after training in the United States, was put in charge of the new instruments and electrical systems. The site of the Rose Bay flying boat base was chosen for the first QEA frozen food factory, under Ron Edwards. There had been two thousand applications for nine initial vacancies for training as air hostesses for the new Constellation service; head steward J. Martin led a staff of fifty-four. Flight engineers, new additions to Qantas air crew, were trained and in readiness. Under Capt. Scottie Allan, Qantas representative at Burbank, the complex procurement programme and supervision of the installation of QEA interiors and equipment had gone smoothly. At QEA's Shell House headquarters in Sydney, activity in every department was at an unprecedented pitch of intensity.

Qantas showed off the Constellation to the prime minister in Canberra, flew it to Melbourne and, with Captain Ritchie in command, carried out a proving service from Sydney to London and back. On 1 December, after ceremonies at Mascot airport, the first service to London was inaugurated under the command of Capt. K. G. Jackson in the Constellation *Charles Kingsford Smith*, carrying twenty-nine passengers and 2,000 pounds of food parcels. It flew the 12,137 miles in fifty-five hours seven minutes flying time via Darwin, Tengah, Dum Dum, Karachi, Cairo, and Tripoli, arriving in London on 5 December. (At Karachi, Capt. D. F. McMaster took over command.) The fare (one class) was £A325 one way, or £A585

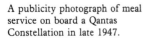

A publicity photograph of meal service on board a Qantas Constellation in late 1947.

return, and the airmail fee was one shilling and sixpence a
half-ounce. (The bunks were not used on this service; two
nights were spent in the air and two on the ground — one at
Singapore and one at Cairo, making the elapsed time a little
under four days. The initial frequency was weekly, increasing
to three times per fortnight.) BOAC had to be content with
parallel services operated, for passengers, with Hythe flying
boats; boath airlines operated cargo Lancastrians.

On 11 December, Fysh told Courtlandt Gross at Lockheed:
"Today we completed the first scheduled return trip between
Sydney and London on the longest air route in the world. The
Sydney–London leg was completed fifty minutes behind
schedule and the London–Sydney return leg fifteen minutes

A Qantas Lancastrian prepares
to depart from Norfolk Island
for Sydney in late 1947. The
RAAF style roundels on the
sides of the Lancastrians were
necessary when these aircraft
operated under RAAF charter
into Japan.

The veteran Empire flying boat
Coriolanus comes ashore for the
last time. It made its last flight
into Sydney just before Christmas 1947; *Coriolanus* was also
the last Empire boat to be
retired. Since its delivery to
Imperial Airways in June 1937,
Coriolanus had flown 18,500
hours.

ahead of schedule. This means that the four QEA Constellations are now in full operation." But only two weeks later, the Constellation's temperamental engines were posing problems. "Will operate three services fortnightly from 1 January with four Constellations," Fysh cabled Gross, "but now definitely anticipate lack spare engines will severely jeopardise successful operations. On spread out 12,000 miles route we have sixteen spare engines . . . and four more are urgently required."[37]

Fysh wrote to McMaster: "I and all your friends here feel very sorry that you are in one of your low periods and [hope] that there will be a turn and that you will be able to take more interest in affairs . . . So far there has been no [government] interference . . . into the affairs of QEA, though I realise it is going to be far from plain sailing when, economically, things get difficult."

Mandate for Expansion
1948

Though World War II saw undreamed-of expansion in all aspects of aviation technology and a great proliferation of airfields, radio aids, and air traffic control systems, it was within the United States that the basis for the future development of the civil airliner and commercial aviation was laid. Twin-engined Douglas airliners dominated the United States airline industry in the war years, achieving utilization rates in revenue flying that kept them airborne for almost one hour in two throughout each day and with average loads that kept nine out of ten of the available seats filled. Both the Douglas and Lockheed companies were close to the airlines and receptive to the specifications that the users put forward for purely civil operations. From this expert and professional environment emerged the two new postwar four-engined civil airliner types (designed from the beginning purely for civil use) that were to dominate the air routes — the Douglas DC4 and Constellation O49 and their descendants.

For Qantas, the acquisition of Constellations was by far the single most important postwar decisions for it was to become the central factor in growth and development of their operational and commercial expertise. From the chaos of the war years and the uncertainties and ad hoc operations that followed them, there now began the rapid emergence of a great world airline with route expansion across both the southern Indian Ocean to Africa and across the Pacific to America to make them, within a decade, the first airline ever to operate a scheduled service circling the entire world.

10

Growth and government ownership brought other changes. The departure of Sir Fergus McMaster ended a period of more than a quarter of a century in which he and Hudson Fysh had between them made all the major decisions and been the prime links with their British partner in Qantas Empire Airways and with the Australian government. McMaster was older, wiser, and wealthier than Fysh and respected by all who dealt with him for his integrity and selflessness. Fysh, from the very start of their joint enterprise with Paul McGinness, had had little but his own tenacity, industry, and loyalty on which to build his career. His childhood had been plagued with ill health, family difficulties, and constant changes of schools that left him for forty years always lacking in self assurance. McGinness had been his pilot in World War I, with a glamorous record and a strong personality, and had been the dominant force in the creation of the early Q.A.N.T.A.S. McMaster had been the father figure and powerful personality in the years that had followed. Honest, hard-working, dogged, and able, Fysh's feelings of inferiority in personal relationships never made him doubt his abilities on the job and never dimmed his ambition. Utterly different in make-up, McMaster and Fysh had been forced together by their common commitment and vision; and while Fysh, from the time of McMaster's heart attack in 1938, had had before him the tantalizing prospect of the chairmanship to at times influence his perspectives, both men had been loyal to each other and to the airline. Now that intimacy was to end as McMaster's health declined and Fysh as chairman of a strong board and chief executive of a government-owned expanding national airline began a new period in his life; but he would never again be able to share his concerns and anxieties with anyone as he had done for so long in his correspondence and talks with McMaster.

As QEA began services with the airliner that was to make them supreme on the Kangaroo Route until 1957 (when BOAC introduced Bristol Britannias), Fysh wrote consolingly to BOAC's new chairman, Sir Harold Hartley, "Particularly do I sympathise with BOAC in the failure of the Tudor II to come up to specifications which", he said, "threw not only BOAC but, to a lesser degree, QEA into disorganisation of plans for operations on the Empire main trunk routes."[1] The QEA board had a setback, however, to their plans for the Kangaroo Route frequency; the minister advised them that the prime minister could now allow purchase of a fifth Constellation because of the shortage of US dollars. Fysh wrote to BOAC's chief executive, Whitney Straight, on 2 January 1948 on the problems raised by their shortage of aircraft:

> It is obvious to us, as I know it is to your organisation, that it is not going to be possible for QEA to operate twice weekly in each direction between Sydney and London with only four Constellations. Even with four aircraft operating only three times fortnightly, we are going to be subject to delays and difficulties . . . We also have in mind that the strong depot which exists in Sydney to help out on Hythe and Lancastrian operations is not available to us in the United Kingdom . . . Having these and other points in mind, we must continue to solidly go for one or two more Constellations, and we feel that we will get them as soon as the dollar position eases or shows some loophole for us . . . If BOAC and QEA cannot secure the required aircraft and do a job on the England–Australia route, then someone else will . . . [2]

Concurrently with the new services to England, QEA on 2 January began operating (previously irregular) services to Noumea and Suva on a scheduled basis and, on 5 January, the first nine women accepted by QEA as air hostesses began their training under Marjorie de Tracy at the company's Double Bay training school, with six more joining them on 1 March. All met the strict requirements of the advertisement: age 22 to 27; British subject; Intermediate Certificate or higher; height 5 feet 3 inches to 5 feet 6 inches with weight in proportion to height; nursing certificate or St John's first aid certificate; good appearance and grooming, particularly skin and teeth; good eyesight; nice personality. They were to receive £5 a week basic pay plus £2 a week service pay. They had been chosen from the two thousand applicants by Bruce Hinchcliffe (staff department), Bill Nielson (traffic manager), George Harman (general manager), and Mrs Hudson Fysh. All had had previous experience as air hostesses with the domestic airlines except two, who came from QEA staff. The first QEA flight with air hostesses aboard left Sydney on 8 May.

In March, the board approved negotiations for the purchase from the RAAF of three Douglas C47 aircraft at £6,000 each but QEA's government-appointed vice chairman, Bill Taylor, warned Fysh on 22 April of possible competition on overseas routes from Australia by the domestic airline, Australian National Airways.[3] ANA had, from September 1946, proved its undoubted capacity to operate efficiently on long international services by flying under contract to British Commonwealth Pacific Airlines their route across the Pacific. With the signing on 3 December 1946 of an air transport agreement between the United States and Australia (and New Zealand), the previous interim service between Sydney and Vancouver had been converted into a regular scheduled weekly service, with traffic rights in United States territory from 21 February 1947. From 23 July 1947, the frequency was increased to three per fortnight, to compete with Pan American's newly introduced twice-weekly serice. The BCPA service from New Zealand began on 25 April 1947, following the issue of the relevant United States and Canadian permits. Under the terms of the contract considered by the South Pacific Air Transport Council at its first meeting in Canberra in December 1946, ANA was guaranteed a gross revenue of £12,000 per trip from Auckland to Vancouver and £10,520 per trip from Sydney to Vancouver. Unfortunately for BCPA, traffic on the service from Auckland proved low and that from Sydney declined when the frequency was increased so that although ANA maintained its revenue, BCPA had to provide money to meet their guarantee. BCPA, however, in April 1948, bought from ANA the two DC4 aircraft it had used to operate the route and at the same time purchased from TAA two additional DC4s, and on 25 April 1948 operated on its own account its first service from Sydney. (BCPA drew heavily on TAA for support, particularly in the engineering, financial, and stores areas.)[4] It seemed likely to Bill Taylor that Australian National Airways intended to continue operating overseas, though to the north. He told Fysh:

> Next Sunday, 25 April, BCPA commence to operate the Pacific service. ANA's association with China National Airlines and Cathay Pacific suggests to me that next week they may announce their plans for overseas operations . . . A submission has been made [by QEA] to the Minister for an Australia–Hong Kong service with flying boats . . . If the Board approves, ask the Minister to make an announcement immediately so as to forestall any possible announcement by ANA.[5]

ANA still had ambitions to fly to England via India and had begun negotiations that were to give them a holding in Air Ceylon and, later, Hong Kong's Cathay Pacific Airways. QEA had discussed operational links as early as January 1947 with China National Airlines at Shanghai and Philippine Airlines at Manila. Both had approached Qantas asking if they would carry out maintenance for them at Sydney in respect of proposed operations. Fysh had informed the director-general of civil aviation and said: "It seems important to know how many services are to be granted permission to enter Australia, what type of equipment they will use, and the frequency they will operate to. QEA must then apparently make up its mind and select one or more foreign services to operate in conjunction with . . . " This low-key request had been accompanied by the suggestion that QEA be given permission to operate through or to any Dutch territory, the Philippines, Hong Kong, China, and Japan. It was the hesitant beginning for more and far-reaching change in the roles of both Qantas and Australia; since its inception, QEA had flown mainly through areas where rights were controlled or influenced by the United Kingdom. (Qantas had no competition between Sydney and Singapore until December 1950, when Air France began their service. KLM followed a year later.)

Fysh tackled Chifley on the pressing need for extra Constellation capacity.

> We are having a difficult time on the Sydney–London route of some 12,000 miles with only four Constellations [he wrote]. The great thing is that the service is running but we must have supplementary aircraft soon. We must also have aircraft to operate extra Sydney–Singapore services and thus hold the growing Australian interest and connection with that area. We must also have aircraft to operate a direct civil service through to the Philippines, Hong Kong, China and Japan . . . These are our main interests and it is now clear indeed that unless we have aircraft shortly . . . it will be impossible to maintain the present status for the Government interests through QEA, and inevitably ANA, together with non-Australian airlines, will have to be admitted. In short, our aircraft position has now reached a really critical stage.[6]

The prime minister responded positively and on 23 April the board was told that approval had been given to negotiate for two additional Constellation 749s at a price not to exceed £1,000,000 sterling.

At that same board meeting the government's advice on the areas of responsibility of QEA and TAA were communicated. Trans-Australia Airlines was to operate services within the mainland, inclusive of Tasmania; Qantas Empire Airways would operate outside the mainland and Tasmania but including Lord Howe Island, Norfolk Island, Papua, and Mandated Territories.[7] Though BCPA was installed on the Pacific and ANA remained a potential threat, Qantas now had a broad mandate for expansion. The board moved to acquire land at the corner of Hunter and Elizabeth streets from Modern Hotels Limited at a price of £87,000 as a site for a future Qantas building. There was welcome news that BOAC was to buy five Constellations from the Irish airline, Aerlinte Eirann Teoranta (Aer Lingus). (QEA had wanted to buy one of these aircraft but, after some argument with BOAC, arrangements were made for QEA to lease one from July 1948 to April 1950.) There would, with these aircraft, be nine Constellations in the BOAC–QEA Kangaroo Route pool. The impetus for growth and change was reflected in an increase in QEA's nominal capital to £5,000,000. A further two million shares were issued to the Commonwealth to complete the financing of the Constellation purchase and provide for general development, bringing total paid-up capital to £2,523,000. Proposals were put to the board for a Hythe flying boat service to Hong Kong with BOAC and Fysh reported that a case should be submitted to the director-general for a QEA service to South Africa.[8]

BOAC's representative with Qantas in Australia, Phillip Hood, reported to London that Qantas was worried that a faster Constellation schedule now proposed would result in more fatigue and discomfort for passengers, with the possibility that they might then prefer to go via the Pacific where Pan American provided full sleeperettes and BCPA reclining chairs as "slumber seats".

"The latter tendency", wrote Hood, "is already being felt. We have the case of Mr Frank Packer (managing director of the influential *Daily Telegraph*), who has booked by Pan American. We tackled him and he said frankly he could not contemplate sitting up all night and did not care which service he travelled on or in which direction he went to the UK, as long as he could lie down." Hood said that he had pointed out to a worried Fysh that "one cannot expect the Constellation to combine all of the following: (i) a de luxe comfort aircraft with sleeping facilities (ii) a 38-seater with good comfort with, in this case, the large QEA composite crew slowly encroaching into the cabin on account of ICAO regulations calling for rest facilities (iii) on aircraft with plenty of volumetric capacity for mails and freight." QEA, he said, was examining the feasibility of providing some bunks. One solution was for "two of each sex [to] share the lower bunk, which is much wider than the upper, . . . but I very much doubt if the idea is really feasible". Fysh, he said, was very worried about the replacement of the promenade compartment by a baggage stowage, crew rest, and a bunk for sick passengers.

> In my opinion [said Hood], they will have to consider a reduction in crew strength and slip more often . . . the more one looks at the entire operation, the more I am convinced that sectionalised crew

operations are infinitely superior. There are, of course, those in QEA who entirely agree with this point of view and they contend that it is only a matter of time before this comes about. The question of the Constellation timetable is now very important indeed and somehow we must find a compromise on speed combined with comfort. Otherwise we shall lose business to the Pacific . . . not forgetting the Dutch . . . [9]

Hood was correct and from 4 September QEA introduced limited, experimental bunk facilities (two in the passenger lounge, one on either side of the aircraft).

The pressures for new aircraft and new routes continued through the year. The board considered it urgent in September to press the RAAF to release two Catalinas for operations in New Guinea as shortage of dollars made it impossible to acquire Skymasters. An application to the minister was made in October to acquire BCPA's four DC4 aircraft, following their acquisition of DC6s. The government was pressed to allow the start of a service to Hong Kong. By November, the board was so seriously concerned at what it saw as a serious shortage of aircraft and the unavailability of any US dollars that it considered the possibility of exchanging QEA's Constellation aircraft for Canadian Canadairs.[10]

Despite these considerable problems, on 14 November, a few minutes before midnight, a QEA Lancastrian under the command of Capt. L. R. Ambrose took off from Mascot to carry out a survey flight for a route cross the Indian Ocean linking Australia with South Africa. It was to fly via Perth, Cocos Island (where the Department of Civil Aviation, assisted by the RAAF, had established a base), and Mauritius to Johannesburg, passing over the Frence island of Reunion. QEA survey personnel on board were Captain Crowther, operations manager, and D. Maitland, traffic representative, with others from the Commonwealth Meteorological Service, the Shell company, and the Department of Civil Aviation. (Both Captain Ambrose and his navigator, J. L. B. Cowan, had flown the wartime Indian Ocean service between Perth and Colombo for Qantas.) The 8,644-mile flight was completed on 20 November in forty-one hours fifty-two minutes flying time. (The return trip took off on 27 November.[11] The service to South Africa, however, was not to be established until September 1952.)

In all these new initiatives, Qantas had carried on under their normal public company status with the shares owned by the Commonwealth. The QEA board and management, how-

233

Johannesburg, 20 November 1948. Qantas Lancastrian VH-EAS comes to a halt after completing the first direct flight between Australia and South Africa across the southern Indian Ocean.

Qantas executives at Mascot after the return of the survey flight to South Africa. From left: Capt. G. U. Allan, controller of technical development; W. A. Baird, engineering manager; Capt. Crowther, operations manager; and H. H. Harman, general manager.

ever, saw anomalies under these arrangements for an organization that was now under the authority of a federal minister. Fysh had outlined the problem to Dan McVey on 11 August.

Though we are established as a Limited Liability Company which is owned by the Government, the "book of rules" is not complete by any means regarding finance, and many matters vital to our future are not laid down, with the result that till a basis is agreed we are proceeding in a dangerous hand to mouth manner. Normally, in the past, these matters would be agreed with the Director-General of Civil Aviation and the Minister consulted, with the Treasury of course in the background, and a basis agreed. At the moment, however, the Treasury are being brought in more directly and the machinery as between the Minister, the Civil Aviation

Department and the Treasury does not seem to be as clear as it might be, and this does not make it any easier for us. I advised the Minister a good while back that either Civil Aviation would have to be really strengthened or some set up put at Canberra to advise the Minister.

However . . . it is felt essential to submit to the Board of QEA a memorandum covering QEA financial matters which can be considered and agreed after alteration or amendment if required, and then sent on to the Minister for his approval, as the basis under which QEA shall operate regarding financial matters. I have done a rough draft of the provisions which I feel should be included. Turner has also been working on the problem and has submitted his views. Before going any further, it would be of great benefit to have your views . . . The thing is that we now require a clear, not too lengthy statement in a form which is likely to prove acceptable to the Board and to the Minister . . . [12]

On 7 December 1948, Fysh wrote to Drakeford:

The decision to retain QEA as a limited liability company regulated under the Queensland Companies Act, has resulted in the Board working within the framework of a set of Articles of Association which are quite satisfactory for a normal public company, but which differ from the regulations normally adopted in Acts creating Commissions operating with Commonwealth funds, e.g. the Australian National Airlines Commission. To rectify this anomaly, the QEA Management and Board has prepared a carefully considered Directive on Financial Matters, a copy of which is attached. Its object is to define responsibilities in financial matters and to lay down, for the guidance of the Board, a Financial Policy approved by the Government, including matters requiring the specific approval of the Minister prior to action being taken. The Board considers that a financial directive substantially similar to the draft attached should be approved and issued by you to the Board as an official directive on behalf of the Commonwealth of Australia, as the owner of Qantas Empire Airways. When this is entered in the Board records, its provisions will have the same effect as if included in the Articles of Association. The Board does not consider it advisable to amend the Articles of Association, which are public property and require registration with the Company Registrars at the numerous places where companies are registered. [13]

This initiative from the QEA board was accepted by the government and a formal financial directive from the minister for civil aviation to the board of directors of Qantas Empire Airways Limited was issued on 1 May 1949 (see Appendix A). In its preamble, the directive included these two important clauses:

(i) in assuming full ownership of Qantas Empire Airways Limited, the Government is fully conscious of the value of taking over as a

235

going concern an efficient, established organisation with many years experience of international air transport, and it is the desire of the Government that there should be as little change as possible in the existing organisation and the managerial and operating practices in existence prior to Government ownership [and (ii)] within the framework of this Directive, the Board is authorised to direct the affairs of the Company as it thinks fit, with due regard to the practices in existence prior to Government ownership.

The directive then set down guidelines for provision of capital, borrowing powers, powers of investment, revenue and expenditure, reserves and provisions, profits and dividends, losses, audit, programmes and estimates, accounts and annual reports, and capital expenditure. It was to remain the guiding document from the government for the Qantas board, with only minor alterations, for thirty-five years (when the Hawke Labor government of 1984 revised it to allow greater freedom and flexibility).[14]

Under their new directive, QEA submitted the fifteenth annual report and financial accounts for the nine months ended 31 December 1948 to the minister for civil aviation. (This report complied with the May 1949 directive as it was not completed and submitted until 26 August 1949.) It listed, at the end of 1948, QEA's board of directors as Hudson Fysh (chairman), W. C. Taylor (vice chairman), G. P. N. Watt, Sir Keith Smith, and Dan McVey. The executive management was Hudson Fysh, managing director; H. H. Harman, general manager; C.O. Turner, assistant general manager; Capt. G.U. Allan, controller of technical development; W.A. Baird, engineering manager; C.W. Nielsen, traffic manager; Capt. W. H. Crowther, operations manager; and F. C. Derham, chief accountant.

The company's main operation was the Sydney–London service, the Kangaroo Route, using Constellations in parallel partnership wth BOAC. Traffic and mail revenue was pooled and shared, with each operator bearing its own costs.

A fast freighter service with Lancastrians was in operation in conjunction with BOAC. Other air services operated included: Sydney–Papua-New Guinea (and internal Papua-New Guinea services for the administration plus extensive freighting operations); Pacific Island Services to Noumea, Fiji, and the New Hebrides, plus services to Lord Howe Island and Norfolk Island; Sydney–Iawkuni–Tokyo courier services for the RAAF.

The aircraft fleet at 31 December 1948 was: five Constellation 749s (one leased from BOAC), used on the Australia–UK route; three Lancastrian 691 passenger aircraft, used to Japan and Norfolk Island; thirteen Douglas DC3s, used for New Guinea, Queensland, and charters; two Catalina PBY flying boats, on the Pacific Islands route; two Liberator LB30s, for training and relief flights; eleven DH84s, used internally in New Guinea and in Queensland; two DH83s, also used internally in New Guinea and in Queensland; two Wackett trainers; and five chartered DC3s, for use in New Guinea, Queensland, Singapore, and charter work. There were in all forty-four QEA aircraft, plus the Constellation leased from BOAC. (BOAC and QEA also shared in the operation of eight BOAC-owned Lancastrian 691 freighters on the UK route.) On order were four de Havilland Drovers for use within new Guinea. Five DC4 Skymasters had been bought in the previous year. Their BOAC partners had, during the year, begun replacing their Hythe flying boats with Constellations (Hythes ceased operations on 6 February 1949), and the BOAC Lancastrians were replaced as passenger aircraft in December 1948. While QEA had increased its Constellation frequencies from three a fortnight to the full twice-weekly schedule as initially planned, BOAC ended the year operating a once-weekly Constellation frequency (with a second planned).

QEA had accepted responsibility for all air transport services in Papua and New Guinea for the administration and had, during the year, undertaken a joint survey of needs. At the end of December, three Douglas DC3 freighters and four DH84s were being operated from Lae and arrangements were

Hangar 85 was originally erected at Rose Bay near the end of the war to supplement the Empire flying boat hangar completed in 1939. H85 was dismantled early in 1948 and transferred to Mascot. It is seen here nearing completion.

237

initiated to begin Catalina flying boat services from Port Moresby. The QEA operations within Q.A.N.T.A.S. now included a weekly Brisbane–Cunnamulla service and continuation of the Flying Doctor Service from Charleville and Cloncurry with DH84 Dragons.

The annual report noted that the government's plan to establish Kingsford Smith aerodrome at Mascot as the international airport for Sydney had entailed a general replanning of engineering facilities. The Department of Civil Aviation had, during the year, transferred the large flying boat hangar from Rose Bay to Mascot. A five-year plan had been agreed with the department and a considerable building programme was to be undertaken. Extreme shortage of office accommodation, said the report, had made it necessary to distribute administration and office staff over a number of city buildings. It listed "European" staff of the company at the end of 1948 as totalling 3,018, an increase of 507 from 1 April.

Financially, the introduction of the Constellations had increased profit during the nine-month period to an equivalent yearly rate after tax of £139,179 (compared with £79,900 for the year ended 31 March 1948). The £2,000,000 increase in capital, however, had lowered the return from 15.26 per cent in the previous year to 7.27 per cent. (Revenue earned on the UK service included payment for carriage of airmails at the rate of 3.50 gold francs per tonne-kilometre, equivalent to 0.0622 pence per pound weight per mile.)

Despite the success of the Constellations, the report said: "The Company's policy is to give preferences to British air-

To provide sufficient spare parts for their Catalina fleet, Qantas bought several ex-RAAF aircraft and dismantled them at Rose Bay. Two can be seen in this photo taken late in 1948, on the site formerly occupied by Hangar 85 which had been transferred to Mascot. Grass can be seen growing along the foundation line where one of Hangar 85's walls once stood near the two parked vehicles. *Island Warrior* in the foreground was owned by W. R. Carpenter but it was bought by Qantas the following year.

craft, and it is to be hoped that suitable British types will soon
be forthcoming, not only for existing services but for new services which the Company, with Government approval, plans
to operate." Meanwhile, because of dollar shortages, "the
Board and Management are compelled to plan their operations
and the development of new services in accordance with currency limitations".[15]

The Prestige of Australia 1949

11 "I believe that QEA is firmly established now as the Australia overseas operation", Hudson Fysh told BOAC chairman Sir Harold Hartley as the new year began. "Any alteration in BCPA's method of operation should entail QEA taking over the Pacific run." He said this had always been BOAC–QEA policy and was the logical one. Operation of the run was only lost because BOAC directors of QEA, at the initial tendering for the operation, were unwilling to allow QEA to purchase American aircraft, but said Fysh, "we look for BOAC support should this be necessary".

Fysh wrote that he could not see any chance of the merger of QEA and BCPA.

> Operation under more than one government is inefficient and ineffectual . . . The BOAC–QEA set up is as near the ideal as we can get. When you consider the closeness of Australia and New Zealand to the United Kingdom in comparison with Canada and South Africa, and when you consider the great flow of population and industry from the UK and Europe to Australia — and that the route via India is some 1,300 miles shorter than via America — I think it can be realised that the old traditional aerial highway between the two countries will remain the main highway. In regard to aircraft, QEA is in a lamentable position in that they only own four modern aircraft and have none on order.[1]

The QEA board, at its meeting on 14 January, agreed to seek approval to buy four additional Constellations.[2] On 21 January an "urgent application for permission to place orders for purchase of four Constellations for delivery in 1950" was put to the government by a board that believed QEA would be pushed off their routes by other operators without the extra aircraft. The submission outlined aircraft requirements for 1950: Eight Constellations were needed to operate three and a half services per week on the route to England; five other machines were required for two services a week to Hong Kong and Japan and a weekly service to South Africa. The submission continued:

> The eventual plan is to replace DC4s, which are out of date, with Constellations . . . We have not provided for increase in services in 1951, 1952 and later years but present indications are that expansion of services in these years will require further aircraft . . . The operation of three and a half services per week with eight Constellations provides for an annual utilisation of 2,300 hours per aircraft which is about the maximum we can obtain in operations over a 12,000 mile route. We doubt if any other International Operator gets any better utilisation . . .

The QEA submission pointed out that already traffic justified operation of seven services a week but that directors had carefully considered the effect of competition from shipping, air services via the Pacific, and other air services. "Shipping is, of course, coming back strongly into the Australia–United Kingdom trade . . . The Company feels that any competition from Shipping cannot have a very serious effect until we develop our traffic to an extent where we are directly competing for a very much larger volume of traffic than we are at present." QEA would not, said the company, ignore the recent development by Pan American in carrying traffic from the United Kingdom via America to Australia nor the fact that Canadian Pacific Airways was likely to operate a through service via Canada. Other competing air services on the United Kingdom route included KLM.

> The fact that a small nation like Holland with less direct interest in the traffic potential along the route is operating eight and a half services per week [between Amsterdam and Batavia] is surely a clear indication that BOAC and QEA are not even half doing their job . . . The fact is that large numbers of passengers are being pushed on to KLM aircraft because we cannot provide the accommodation. While the Dutch services have not yet been given permission to extend to Australia it is expected that meanwhile they will link with other airlines such as Philippines Airlines operating via Batavia and providing a through connection to compete for Australian traffic.

The document noted that Australia proposed to sign agreements with Pakistan, India, Ceylon, the Philippines, and France (Indo-China) who all wished to operate air services to

Australia. It stressed that the first year of Constellation operations ending 31 December 1948 would show a profit substantially in excess of budget estimates.

> The purchase of four Constellations will require a total additional outlay of £2,270,000 . . . There are various ways of financing this outlay but Lockheeds have indicated that it can be spread over a period of seven years by financing through the Import and Export Bank [*sic*] of America by requesting no payment for twelve months after order and the balance over six years . . . It is respectfully submitted that from the point of view of Defence, the securing by Australia of a further four Constellations would be of immense importance . . . QEA at present owns only four Constellations but has one [additional] on hire from BOAC until about the end of 1949.[3]

While Qantas recognized their basic responsibility to run and develop services on sound commercial lines, they also saw for themselves a national role in projecting the prestige of Australia, in the development of British Commonwealth and foreign trade relations, and in providing a valuable role in the country's defence infrastructure.[4] They set out, during 1949, to consolidate and extend the passenger and freight services to the United Kingdom, begin a service to Hong Kong, introduce a civil service in conjunction with the existing RAAF courier service to Japan, and develop services both to and within New Guinea and the Pacific Islands. They saw as their main responsibility the operation, on behalf of the Commonwealth, of their share of the Australia–United Kingdom air service under a parallel partnership arrangement with British Overseas Airways Corporation, representing the United Kingdom government.[5]

The search for suitable aircraft had, Fysh reported to the board after his visit to London in September and October of 1948, been a major quest. He found that the increase in operation of second-class air services and the mass carriage of immigrants had made Skymaster aircraft scarcer than ever. QEA had missed out on carriage of immigrants, he said, through lack of equipment with the result that they had let other operators in on the main QEA route. Amongst possible British aircraft, the Tudor IV remained unsuitable, the Hermes IV lacked range and flexibility, and the Hermes VI, though suitable in range and "the only possible bet amongst British aircraft coming forward" was still untried. The British Lancastrian freighter aircraft service was, in financial terms, disastrous but very little freight could be carried on the Constellation after mail was loaded. To take the uneconomic Lancastrians off would, Fysh pointed out, throw the valuable freight business built up on the Kangaroo Route into the hands of KLM and other operators. In the absence of further Constellations, said Fysh, the Canadair IV was recommended, having the two essential attributes of range and competitive economy of operation. It was also cheaper in first cost and part payable in sterling currency. "In all orders of aircraft now made," wrote Fysh, "the question of initial delivery [date] and future deliveries of spares is a factor which should be most carefully taken into consideration owing to the abnormally disturbed international state." (The cold war confrontation of the Berlin air lift did not end until 11 May 1949. In its ten months, British and American aircraft made almost 200,000 flights. The end of the blockade saw a great surplus of transport aircraft and crews.)

Availability of aircraft was not the only problem facing QEA, however. Difficulties were arising on the governmental level, Fysh commented, with Australia now negotiating her own bilateral air agreements on the route which were not in line with the agreements the United Kingdom had or was negotiating. Great traffic difficulties were caused in parallel operations when BOAC obtained rights that QEA did not have.[6]

The financial arrangements with QEA's BOAC partner were also made increasingly complex by the differing aircraft types and numbers that each airline was able to operate. QEA's Turner (with chief accountant F. C. Derham) met with BOAC in February 1949 to alter the financial arrangements that had been agreed in mid-1948. That earlier agreement had anticipated a joint pool of nine Constellation aircraft (five owned by BOAC and four by QEA) operating a twice-weekly service on the Kangaroo Route. In October 1948, however, BOAC had agreed to hire one Constellation to QEA for a period of twelve months and to eliminate planned arrangements for interchange of aircraft and crews. Some idea of the complexity of the financial arrangements that Turner had to clarify emerges from the bare outline of the four operational phases that both airlines agreed on. From 27 August 1948, BOAC were to operate three Hythe services weekly and one Lancastrian mail service weekly; QEA were to operate two Constellation services weekly. From 1 December 1948 BOAC were to introduce their first Constellation service and, until 6 February 1949, operate two Hythe flying boat services. From 7 February, BOAC were to operate one and a half Constellation services weekly and QEA two. The final phase agreed commenced with the introduction of two Constellation services weekly by each airline. Revenue from the parallel services was to be shared between operators at the end of each phase under agreed principles.[7] These talks took place as the House of Lords debated civil aviation and it was disclosed that Britain's three airline corporations (BOAC, British European Airways, and British South American Airways) were costing the nation £26 million yearly.[8] From Downing Street came news that Sir Harold Hartley, then seventy, would resign the chairmanship and be succeeded at the end of June by Sir Miles Thomas, with Whitney Straight as deputy chairman and chief executive.

The last Hythe flying boat service left Rose Bay, Sydney, on 6 February. Only three years before, BOAC had seen such a secure future for flying boat operation that water strips for landing had been included in the plans for the new Heathrow airport.[9] Landplanes were now recognized as faster and more economical, even if less sumptuous, with their operation no longer restricted by shortage of aerodromes and facilities. They were not, however, without their problems. Unexpected engine failures on QEA Constellations forced a doubling of spare engines along the route from an iniaial fifty per cent to a costly one hundred per cent. (During the worst period, fifty-two per cent of Constellation engines were removed before reaching their time-expired schedule of 800 hours.)[19] As QEA brought Constellation services to Australia, their rival for overseas traffic, BCPA, acquired that second great postwar American aircraft, the DC6. During October 1948, the Australian government bought four DC6s (which were in storage at Douglas Aircraft Company's Santa Monica plant in California) from Sweden at a cost of £A1,008,000. The first DC6 was delivered to Sydney on 24 November 1948 and the aircraft went into service with BCPA within a mere twelve weeks. The speed of the DC6 allowed a Sydney–San Francisco flight time of forty hours forty minutes. (Three of BCPA's then surplus DC4s were sold to QEA and one to Trans-Australia Airlines.)[11]

QEA director G. P. N. Watt (from the Treasury) was appointed to the board of BCPA at this time. Fysh had briefed Watt previously on what was now an increasing preoccupation of Qantas and other world airlines — the role and functions of the International Air Transport Association in the

Dubbo, NSW, 7 April 1949. Qantas Lancastrian VH-EAS which made the first direct flight across the Southern Indian Ocean from Australia to South Africa in November 1948, is destroyed by fire after a landing accident.

expanding international airline industry. The brief sets down the Qantas perception of IATA.

IATA [wrote Fysh] is an association of scheduled international operators. Its aims and objects are:

(i) To promote safe, regular and economic air transport for the benefit of the peoples of the world; to foster air transport and study the problems connected therewith.

(ii) To provide means of collaboration among air transport enterprises engaged directly or indirectly in international air transport services.

(iii) To co-operate with ICAO [the International Civil Aviation Organisation, which dealt with technical matters] and other international organisations.

The Director-General of IATA, Sir William Hildred [Fysh continued], expressed the aims and objects more pithily when he said:

"A single aircraft operates today over ten or fifteen countries in carrying out a one-way flight. For absolute safety of plane and passenger and of the public on the ground, there must be only one way to do things . . . The policy is elementary: simplify, unify, standardise. IATA's job on its own and working with ICAO is to make absolutely certain that a Venezuelan pilot, flying a British plane, can navigate the international routes and land safely, regularly and promptly at a Chinese airport with a Czechoslovakian traffic controller."

This policy applies equally to Government requirements (e.g. landing, health and immigration regulations) and airline requirements (e.g. engine maintenance, fuelling, other technical matters and traffic matters).

To some extent IATA duplicates ICAO. But neither can exist without the other. ICAO consists of regulators, who must consult the practical men — the operators ... IATA furnishes a means of putting the total view of the world's operators before the assembly of governments. In this way the importance of the operators' opinions is seen in true perspective. In addition, quite apart from ICAO functions, IATA enables operators to arrive at and adopt a common solution to purely business problems. Some of the basic matters with which IATA concerns itself are:

(i) the highest degree of safety for plane and passenger

(ii) the highest standard of service and courtesy

(iii) the uniformity and thus certainty of legal relations between operator and customer

(iv) the elimination of cut-throat competition by both fare cutting and variation of passenger privileges

(v) the fixing of fares at reasonable levels, rejecting the principle that operators shall charge what the traffic will bear ...

The benefits of membership are both intangible and real. On the technical side, this Company enjoys a real advantage from the presentation to ICAO of a total operator's view. ICAO's standards are thus rendered more practical. Moreover, advance information is received of ICAO's decisions and discussions and trends of policy. But the greatest advantage is in receiving operational information drawn from every airline in the world. As an example, this Company receives a full report of even minor engine faults in Constellations.

From the financial side, the benefits of the IATA Clearing House are obvious. Instead of separate cheques being sent and received for every interline transaction, one cheque suffices for the balance of payments on each month's transactions and this balance can be settled in sterling.

From the traffic point of view, the Company operates free from any necessity to counter the blandishments of other operators. Rates, services and passenger privileges are standard.

The intangible benefit is that enjoyed by a member of any trade association where competition is fierce, particularly where that competition is inspired by nationalism and can call in aid [from] Government discrimination.

Shortly — through IATA — this Company enjoys a measure of co-operation from its rivals instead of uninhibited competition.[12]

QEA's carefully argued case for doubling their fleet of Constellations to meet traffic growth and competition in 1950 was considered by the government and rejected. On 11 March the minister told Fysh that "it was decided that in view of the substantial dollar commitments of Australia in the next two years the proposition was not acceptable". It was felt, however, that Qantas had a case for additional aircraft and that "when the dollar budget is being examined against shortly consideration can be given to the possibility of setting aside an amount to meet indispensable requirements ... There would be no justification for assuming, in view of the non-likelihood of the overall dollar position easing, that dollars for further new aircraft can be made available in any subsequent year." Drakeford asked that the possibility of purchasing additional aircraft partly for dollars and partly for sterling or entirely for sterling be carefully examined.[13] Fysh responded bluntly. "The question must be squarely faced as to whether your National Australian Company is to retain its premier position, hard won over fifteen years of effort and support in money by the Australian Government, or whether it is to lose that position, which it surely will do if the equipment essential for the retention of that position is denied to it."

Fysh reaffirmed QEA's rejection of the Canadair IV aircraft (available in sterling) as an alternative to the Constellation.[14] To add to Qantas worries, Lockheed's export sales manager, R. H. Askew, applied courteous pressure in a letter to Fysh on 20 May 1949.

> For my part, I think I have done everything humanly possible to try and assist you in solving your equipment problems . . . I should like to point out that delivery dates have been set back on three different occasions as a result of purchases by Air France, Royal Dutch Airlines and South African Airways. I would like to tell you in confidence that at the present time Lockheed is negotiating a purchase to one operator which may be anything up to twenty aircraft. Should this order be placed before the Qantas order, delivery to Qantas may well be very far down the line. At

The eighteen cylinder Wright R-3350 Duplex Cyclone engine fitted to Qantas L-749 Constellations.

247

the present moment the best delivery that we can offer you is May of 1950 and I am empowered to offer this position only for the balance of this week . . . [15]

Eleven days later an irritated minister advised Fysh that after further consideration "authority has now been given for the purchase of one Constellation aircraft and spares which accompany it to the extent of $1,500,000". But the minister added that strong representations should be made to Lockheeds and Curtiss Wright Corporation to remedy defects in the Constellation engines that had been causing delays. "the Government is concerned at the economic loss in operations and the effect on the prestige of QEA due to these delays . . . "[16] The government, however, was soon to change its mind yet again on even this concession.

In a letter to Sir Harold Hartley on 8 April, Hudson Fysh indicated that QEA did not now consider the Canadair IV aircraft (purchased by BOAC) as a serious alternative for QEA.

> As you know, we have Constellations — only a small number of them, but based on an expensive set up. We also now have five Skymasters and . . . myself and my Board [feel] that it would be folly indeed to go into a third type, and that without even having enough Constellations to support that type as a group operation. It would be different, of course, if we could order, say eight Canadairs — which we can't. We are still continuing our efforts to obtain more Constellations and this is likely to be left now till our Prime Minister is in London. We would appreciate your support if you feel able to give it, as the question is likely to come up to your Minister and may be referred to BOAC. Our latest request is for two more Constellations.[17]

On 1 May 1949, Qantas formally received the "Financial Directive from the Minister for Civil Aviation to the Board of Directors of Qantas Empire Airways Ltd." Its preamble — "that the Government is fully conscious of the value of taking over as a going concern, an efficient established organisation with many years of international air transport" and the government's desire "that there should be as little change as possible in the existing organisation and the managerial and operating practices in existence prior to Government ownership" — was of central importance, coming as it did from a Labor government, and it reflected to the letter the wishes of Fysh and the QEA board. It was a unique and flexible arrangement when compared with the other main public enterprises founded by the Chifley government between 1944 and 1949. (These were the Australian Aluminium Production Commission, 1944; the Australian National Airlines Commission, 1945; the Overseas

Telecommunication Commission, 1946; the Joint Coal Board, 1946; the Stevedoring Industry Commission, 1947; the Australian Broadcasting control Board, 1948; the Australian Whaling Commission, 1949; and the Snowy Mountains Hydro-Electric Authority, 1949).

A few days after QEA received this directive, Fysh attended an informal dinner party at which senior members from a range of what Fysh described as "nationalised shows" attended. Among them were H. C. Coombes (later secretary of the Treasury), Richard Boyer (Australian Broadcasting Commission), Tom Molvey (Radio), and Arthur Coles (TAA and BCPA). He noted in his diary tantalizing but incomplete notes of their conversation. Coombes, he wrote, was

> interested in the whole problem of making a success of government shows. He spoke very seriously. Boyer generalised and evidently has problems which are not ours. Molvey [has] difficulty keeping interest and senior staff . . . These three all spoke of altruistic incentive. Working for the people. Coles and self said money, status and position all went together. Coles laid stress on personal contact with the Minister and Prime Minister, and [to] push for what is right. Then [it was] up to Government to state policy and decision. If [one] could not support policy then [one] should resign. Coles outlook realistic and business effective but obvious he laid greatest stress on his personal contacts in Canberra. He told us several times of how he got the DC-6 aircraft and stood up to tell us. He then told me all again about it in the street. Great weakness of this near boasting even to boredom. Personal ego.

Fysh summarized his own contribution as

> to clearly state that for survival of our shows we must be in a position to effectively compete with private enterprise. My concern was for the continuity of QEA into the years ahead as an effective competitive unit . . . QEA was old, successful. The Minister [was] slow. No chance of help from Government. My weakness is in articulating. Coles and self the only business people there with realistic ideas. Coles [is an] outstanding businessman but beset terribly with his own supreme importance.[18]

Fysh recounted a similar assessment of Coles made by Ivan Holyman after a cocktail party at the Royal Sydney Yacht Squadron in a later diary entry.

> Holyman accuses Coles of boasting, which is true, as he is a ghastly and boring boaster. But Holyman under a few drinks himself then launches out into terrible boasting. He says he is a director of thirty-two companies and chairman of all but two. That his word is law and unquestionable, and so on and so on. When Coles and Holyman talk this stuff I sit and listen and do not reply. I realise

Archerfield, Brisbane, 1 April 1949. The last domestic flight service by Qantas arrives in Brisbane from Mount Isa. From 2 April 1949, Trans-Australia Airlines took over the Queensland and Northern Territory services which Qantas had operated since the 1920s.

they both are very efficient people but both obviously are stark naked directors . . . [They] have done magnificent jobs but sabre rattling like dictators. They are the dictators. QEA is a democracy.[19]

The Labor government policy that Trans-Australia Airlines should operate services within Australia and Qantas confine itself to overseas routes now affected Qantas's traditional operations in Queensland and the Northern Territory. On 2 April 1949, Arthur Coles, as chairman of Trans-Australia Airlines, with TAA general manager Lester Brain, took over from Qantas in Brisbane the Queensland and Northern Territory services and the Flying Doctor operations. Forty-one Qantas staff transferred to TAA. Four de Havilland Dragon aircraft and some old hangars were acquired by TAA for £26,000 but there was no payment for goodwill. From now on, Qantas would operate solely as an overseas airline. Another link with the early Qantas was severed soon afterwards. Arthur Baird, who had made the operation of the infant airline's old and unreliable aircraft possible by his single-minded diligence, retired as head of Qantas engineering on 30 June 1949 after twenty-eight years of service. "I cannot think of anyone", wrote Fysh, "who has done more in laying the foundations of Australian air transport engineering, both in regard to the work he did himself and what he initiated . . . " [20] Baird was succeeded as chief engineer by D. H. Wright.

Hudson Fysh had already drawn attention to the negotiation by Australia of her own bilateral traffic agreements on the

Kangaroo Route, and the difficulties caused when these were not in line with BOAC agreements. The negotiation between countries of traffic rights for their international airlines was already a tough and complex form of horse-trading in which each country used the bargaining power of access to its territory and the traffic generated there to obtain for its designated international carrier (or "chosen instrument") as much commercial and operational advantage as it could from other countries. These negotiations were conducted within the framework of the five freedoms of the air (see p. 147) agreed on as the basis of the conduct of international air transport at the 1945 formation of the Provisional International Civil Aviation Organisation (which became ICAO).

Qantas director Dan McVey prepared notes for the board on bilateral agreements, with particular reference to India, in June 1949 and sent them to Turner. "I should be glad," he wrote, "in the light of your intimate and detailed knowledge of the subject. Kindly to go through the draft, correct any obvious inaccuracies and generally edit it to bring it into a form which may safely be presented to the Chairman and other member of the Board for their consideration as a statement of the views of the QEA Board on the Indian negotiations."[21] McVey's notes, though lengthy, give a clear and concise account of the scope and complexity of the negotiations (between governments) involving traffic rights that were to become a permanent and critical part of the Qantas expertise in future years (see Appendix B).[22]

Turner thought the McVey statement an excellent one and devoid of jargon. He replied to McVey on 1 July 1949, demonstrating his own clear grasp of the complex issues involved.

> Some progress has apparently been made by Johnston in India. You will recall that in Johnston's cable produced to the Board, it was suggested that we should deny India any right of operating a service between Sydney, New Zealand and Fiji and his "personal view" was that if necessary we should deny this even if it meant "no Agreement".
>
> Apparently, India is now agreeable to give what Johnston considers "generous" rights to QEA to share Fifth Freedom traffic between India and beyond, and in return Australia is agreeable to allow India to extend to Fiji via Townsville. (Difficulties regarding New Zealand have apparently been cleared with the Indians.) However, the Indians are insisting on traffic rights between Darwin, Sydney and Fiji and probably the Minister will allow this.
>
> India is very suspicious of the "sharing provisions" of the

BOAC–QEA services and these are to be dropped. The chief reason for dropping them is that the United Kingdom is apparently not making very much headway with their Agreement with India, the stumbling points being pre-determination and drastic restriction on Fifth Freedom rights being insisted on by India, and since these are the two main issues it seems doubtful if the United Kingdom would, in the final issue, be prepared to hold out for the sharing provision.

Australian right to Fifth Freedom traffic from India and beyond is to be restricted to "10 per cent of capacity" provided, and Johnston estimates that this will allow us sixty seats per month India–UK and the same number UK–India. I am unable to check how he arrives at this figure.

How we will pre-determine traffic and control booking of Fifth Freedom traffic is still to be worked out — also we have no indication as to what frequency India–Australia and India–Australia–Fiji will be demanded by India on basis of Third and Fourth Freedom rights on these services.

A point I am still concerned about is that KLM, PAA, TWA and Air France will have unrestricted Fifth Freedom rights in India. BOAC is fighting restriction and have a good case whereas Australia has, herself, proposed accepting restriction, thereby placing herself in a less competitive position. This, of course, has its origin in the Commonwealth Agreement formula which it appears India is now adopting herself.[23]

While these matters of high policy were being explored, operations more reminiscent of Qantas's pionerring past were being extended to and within Papua-New Guinea. In 1948, QEA had accepted the responsibility of operating all air transport services for the administration in Papua and New Guinea from centres at Lae, Madang, and Port Moresby. At the beginning of 1949, three Douglas DC3 freighters and four DH84 aircraft were being operated from Lae. During the course of the year, frequency of service between Australia and PNG was increased from three to five a week and DC4 Skymasters were introduced on the route. (There were no subsidies for these services.) Within Papua and New Guinea total route mileage grew during 1949 to 5,017 and the aircraft fleet involved in regular internal services to twenty, including six DC3s and twelve DH84s. Two Catalina flying boats were based on Port Moresby for operation to points where landing strips were not available. Mere figures, however, in no way indicate the unique nature of the operations carried out. A typical flight, in mid-1949, was described in a letter by Qantas captain, Hugh Birch:

We left Port Moresby at 0805 on 7 June 1949 in Qantas Catalina *Island Chieftain* VH EBC with myself in command . . . [and] flew direct to Lake Murray in Western Papua . . . probably one of the most remote places in the world. The natives [were] completely uncivilized and their mode of dress was a walnut shell. The flight itself was a special, non-scheduled charter to convey medical supplies to the Government Police Post at the northern end of Lake Murray. Lake Murray is very shallow and full of crocodiles and the Qantas aircraft was the first ever to have landed there.

We flew from Lake Murray to Kikori in the Papuan Gulf, an area which has one of the highest rainfalls in the world; 300 inches. We flew through low cloud and landed in the river at midday and moored at the buoy in this very fast-flowing river . . . The river was full of logs and crocodiles and not a very attractive place. The District Officer .was Clarry Healey, who loaded on the cargo, which consisted mainly of live mud crabs. We also had a consignment of mummified hands for a museum . . . The loading took place from canoes manned by about eight paddlers, who were most skilful in bringing what looked to us a large, hollowed-out log alongside the Catalina. We left there after about half an hour and flew to Yule Island headquarters of a Catholic mission, then back to Port Moresby, arriving there at 2.15 p.m. . . . This was typical of the many flights we operated into West Papua at that time,

Qantas Catalina *Island Chieftain* in New Guinea, mid-1949. Captain Hugh Birch leans from the cockpit window to speak to a crew member in the mooring compartment at the bow. Flt./E. Ken Smith watches from a hatch behind the flight deck.

253

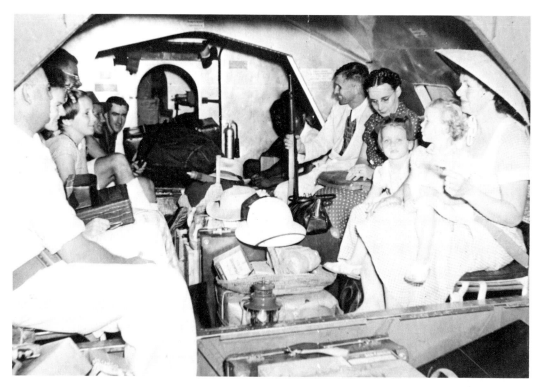

The passenger cabin of a
Qantas Catalina operating in
New Guinea, mid-1949.

although our normal itinerary was Port Moresby–Yule Island–
Kerema–Kikoru–Lake Kutubu (high in the Southern Highlands)–
Lake Murray–Daru–Kerema–Yule Island–Port Moresby. This
flight used to take us about ten hours with ten landings. Not a bad
day's work.

The other scheduled services which we operated on a regular
basis in the Catalina were: Eastern service; Port Moresby, Abau,
Milne Bay, Samarai, Esa'ala, Losuia (Trobriands), Woodlark
Island, Deboyne Lagoon (Misima), Samarai and return. Western
service; Port Moresby, Kandrian, Rabaul, Buka, Inua, Kieta,
Buin, Rabaul, Casmata, Jacquinot Bay.

I think it could be said that this unique flying boat operation
provided a great service to the people of New Guinea and to some
of the most remote and inaccessible places in the world.[24]

Both Qantas and BOAC continued to face the basic problem
of aircraft acquisition in a world desperately short of US
dollars. BOAC, with Sir Miles Thomas as the new chairman
from 1 July, were still hopeful of persuading Qantas to give up
their Constellation fleet and substitute Canadairs, though
their motives served the convenience and self-interest of
BOAC more than of Qantas. Under the impression that Qantas
had firm Australian government approval to buy a fifth Constellation, BOAC chief executive Whitney Straight wrote to
Phillip Hood.

254

This . . . raises various questions of policy. Having obtained the fifth Constellation, what view would the Australians take if we withdrew our Constellations from the [Kangaroo] route and operated them on the Atlantic, substituting Canadairs? Do you think the Australians would consider a proposition . . . [that] they give up their Constellations in exchange for a large number of Canadairs? I am proposing to take no action in this matter as obviously it is a tricky one . . . I hardly need ask you to be extremely circumspect and entirely unofficial in any approach you may feel it necessary to take.[25]

Straight had good reason to believe that QEA had finally won government approval for the fifth Constellation. He was not to know that there had been another change of mind and a telephone call from Arthur Drakeford to Fysh instructing QEA to cancel the order they had so recently placed. Drakeford wrote in a follow-up letter on 5 July that the decision "was arrived at after discussion with the Treasurer, the Rt. Hon. J. B. Chifley, respecting the dollar situation and it is a source of considerable regret to me as I realise it must be to your Board and yourself".[26] Chifley formally advised Drakeford that subsequent to the government's approval for the Constellation order "advice was received from the United Kingdom Government of a serious deterioration in the Sterling Area dollar out look, and of an unexpectedly large increase in the current drain on the gold and dollar reserves held by the United Kingdom Government".[27] The Lockheed company, however, showed its resourcefulness. Courtlandt Gross came back swiftly with a proposal that the Constellation contract with QEA be suspended for ninety days rather than cancelled. A pendulum that swung so freely could obviously swing back in QEA's favour. Fysh recommended the Lockheed initiative to Drakeford. "The way we look at the question is that at the end of the ninety day period neither the Government nor QEA will be in a worse position if a cancellation has to be negotiated with Lockheeds . . . cancellation of this contract amounts to repudiation of a firm contract entered into and such action is bound up in a consideration of Australian goodwill and National credit in the USA."[28]

Whitney Straight had, however, gently made his suggestion about Canadair aircraft on the Kangaroo Route to Hudson Fysh in a letter on 23 June, but without success. Fysh replied that he did not see any chance of QEA switching from their present Constellation operations. One day after this Fysh letter, however, BOAC's Sydney representative commented to Whitney Straight that "Hudson Fysh changes his views very

255

A BOAC Canadair C-4 and its crew. BOAC proposed that Qantas should consider replacing its Constellation fleet with Canadairs in 1949 following a deterioration in the Sterling Area dollar reserve. Built in Montreal, the Canadairs were based on a DC-4 airframe, powered by British built Rolls-Royce Merlin engines and incorporating features from the DC-6. These included pressurized cabins, large, square windows and long-range wing tanks. They were known as the Argonaut Class by BOAC and entered service in August 1949 on the UK–Hong Kong route.

regularly and I would therefore prefer to see the trend of thought in the executives". Fysh, wrote Hood, "will not move without consulting his Air Minister . . . Any suggestions to change the equipment on the Kangaroo Route should be put to him in writing without delay." He thought that Australia would hesitate to part with the Constellations on strategic grounds. QEA, he said, were now "hopeful of operating their Constellations as efficiently as we do. As they see the problem, the Constellation appears capable of steady development in weight carrying etc. . . . and have no information as to whether the BOAC Canadair could develop in the same way."[29] In another letter, Hood advised BOAC:

Mr Hudson Fysh has always been opposed to the Canadair IV because of its noise level and other factors . . . It is thought Mr Fysh is forced by political face-saving to defend and support Constellations in view of his previous slogan and policy "Nothing but Constellations for QEA" . . . Our last impression is that the QEA rank and file, especially the engineering staff, are not keen on obtaining more Constellations. In fact, they would prefer to get rid of all they have in exchange for a fleet of DC4s and Canadairs, in view of the trouble Constellations have given them, as well as adverse press reports.[30]

Fysh advised Whitney Straight on 8 July that owing to the dollar crisis, the Australian government had asked them to cancel the contract with Lockheeds to purchase one Constellation 749 that was ordered some weeks back, telling also of the suggested ninety-day postponement of QEA obligations under the contract. He said there still remained a chance to receive this "much needed" aircraft, but "we have lost our place in the delivery line".[31] Straight received additional details from Hood. "As soon as the dollar shortage became paramount," he wrote, "the Treasury [Mr Chifley himself] instructed QEA to find out what it would cost in dollars to cancel the contract, and Capt. Allan was sent to Burbank in a hurry . . . You will know that Australia is a partner in the Empire Dollar Pool . . . "[32]

While the US dollar crisis severely constrained Qantas and BOAC fleet expansion, Britain's challenge to American supremacy in aircraft manufacture was now dramatically demonstrated. On the evening of 27 July, test pilot John Cunningham took off on the first flight of the jet-powered de Havilland Comet, inaugurating a new age in commercial aviation. There was no immediate effect on the hard-pressed airlines, however, for BOAC were not to take delivery of the Comet until 1951 nor put it into airline service until 1952. Much more relevant to Qantas was the inauguration on 26 June of a regular Hong Kong service and the board's formal agreement, on 29 July, to the financial directive issued by the federal government in May. Capt. R. B. Tapp, from April, had been appointed line manager, Hong Kong and Japan services, from the position of Singapore manager and Capt. O. D. Denny manager, New Guinea and Island services, from June 1949. Denny, who had been assistant operations manager from 1946, had been suc-

Qantas inaugurated its Australia–Hong Kong service on 26 June 1949 using Douglas DC-4 aircraft. The fleet comprised three DC-4s, all former BCPA machines. The Qantas Empire Airways titles made a strange contrast with the BCPA pale blue fuselage band and the VH-BPA registration markings in this photograph taken at Mascot in early March 1949. This aircraft made a survey flight from Sydney to Hong Kong and return between 15 and 21 March 1949.

257

ceeded in that position by Capt. R. J. Ritchie. (Tapp had joined Q.A.N.T.A.S. in 1928 and Denny in 1930.)[33]

The first directors' report to the minister, under the terms of the financial directive was, though much delayed, now being prepared. Fysh wrote to Dan McVey on 5 August.:

> This first report is not an easy one and its importance is realised by us all. When the draft is ready I will be sending it on to you. I know it is imposing a lot on your time, but I feel that you are the one most calculated to produce something final which will be acceptable to all directors and be suitable for forwarding to the Minister . . . Perhaps the most important part of the report is contained under the heading "Conclusions" . . . I regret I am the author and as I feel you are rather a master of words in drafting a report, I do not mind how you chop it about, but I feel that the main ideas expressed below should be touched on . . . "[34]

Among those conclusions, Fysh wrote that the essentials for successful international operation were modern competitive aircraft, obtaining of traffic rights on chosen routes, and the correct operating organization. Qantas was entering an era of greater competition in which the public appeal of air transport was expected to increase, and Fysh wrote that "no progressive country with worldwide interests can afford to be without its modern air transport fleet to carry its flag, to assist in contacts and commerce, and as a means for defence". The board, wrote Fysh, wished to restate their previous policy of preference for British aircraft where such aircraft were competitive with types from other sources.[35]

There were, of course, no competitive British aircraft available and no dollars for American aircraft. Fysh nevertheless wrote to Lockheed's Askew on 4 August:

> The position is that we are still interested in obtaining one Constellation if an acceptable plan can be devised . . . As there is somewhat of a traffic recession on at the moment I do not feel that more than one aircraft would receive consideration . . . Can Lockheeds sell us a [Constellation] 749 for sterling? Have not Lockheeds and Curtiss Wright enough future stake in this country along with the USA to transfer a million and a half dollars to Australia where it would be earning interest, and which would cover the purchase?

Fysh told Askew that he was leaving for England on 29 August and he expected BOAC "to feel us out again reference exchanging our [Constellation] 749 aircraft for Canadair Fours [*sic*] on our Kangaroo Route and we could be forced into it through sheer lack of aircraft".[36]

On Saturday 27 August, in dramatic circumstances, Qantas lost their Catalina flying boat VH-EAW. At 2.22 a.m., a loud explosion rocked sleeping Rose Bay and the Catalina, three hundred yards from shore at its mooring, was soon to be on fire. QEA's head of security, Gordon Fraser, wrote that launches were unable to get close enough to extinguish the fire and the aircraft sank in about twenty minutes. The aircraft (valued at £24,000) had arrived from Noumea the day before and was due to leave for Lord Howe Island on the Monday. "Following salvage operations," said Fraser, "a piece of fruit case board was found under the seat of the flight engineer attached by string and fishing line, and there was an alarm clock, a six volt battery and a vibrator coil." (Gordon Fraser had been appointed security supervisor when a Qantas security department was formed on 1 November 1948.)

The rear fuselage of Qantas Catalina VH-EAW is brought to the surface by a salvage vessel. It was destroyed by sabotage while moored in Rose Bay on 27 August 1949.

Only two months before (on 23 June), QEA Catalina VH-EAX had been lost under suspicious circumstances in the lagoon at Lord Howe Island. In eighteen months of operation to Lord Howe, Qantas had seen traffic build up, despite competition from the small operator, Trans Oceanic Airways. In strong winds, the QEA Catalina had broken her moorings and had been wrecked. The aircraft had been secured with a three-inch manilla rope mooring pennant and a storm pennant of galvanized steel cable with a breaking strain of almost forty tons. The cable had been inspected and approved by a Civil Aviation Department officer on 7 April and 1 June, yet had parted on 23 June. (After official investigations it was found that "a red corrosion product had accumulated between the strands" of the steel cable.)[37]

No evidence for foul play was found in the Catalina loss at Lord Howe but after investigations by the Arson Squad following the Rose Bay explosion and evidence given in the City Coroner's Court, the managing director of Trans Oceanic Airways, Bryan Monkton, was tried before Judge Curlewis on the charge of causing malicious damage to the aircraft. Monkton, however, was able to supply (with the help of aviation pioneer, P. G. Taylor) the strongest of alibis and he was acquitted.

Fysh wrote to Sir Miles Thomas on 6 September asking for an extension of the lease of BOAC's Constellation G-ALAN. "The hire", he said, "relates back to the Irish Constellation deal . . . The Australian Government wished to purchase one of these aircraft and out of this desire a compromise was effected and the aircraft was hired to QEA and based in Sydney."[38] Fleet problems were compounded by problems on the ground at Mascot airport and at the board meeting of 14 October it was agreed to put pressure on the Civil Aviation Department to improve Mascot to international standards. (It was here that Turner, as assistant general manager, first attended a board meeting.)[39]

The Department of Civil Aviation announced, in 1949, a long-range plane under which it would own all buildings on Commonwealth airports. It was a sound concept, wrote QEA general services superintendent Hudson Shaw, but quite impracticable to execute. "It was to bedevil Qantas' development for the next few years; DCA never had the money necessary to put it into effect."[40] Only buildings directly required for aircraft operations could be erected on the airport, which "cut right across the efficiency of Qantas operations", wrote Hud-

son Shaw. "It was not possible to plan for all aircraft support facilities to be located in one area."[41] The department, in 1949, did however undertake to make land to the north of the airport available to Qantas. It was land that had been acquired to enable the lengthening of the first Mascot runway (established during the war) to the north, across the railway that served Bunnerong. Replanning was accelerated when an aircraft collided with a train, despite the installation of traffic lights. The new plan involved redirecting Cooks River and constructing a new and much longer east-west runway into the old river bed, with a new north-south runway crossing it to the edge of Botany Bay.[42] (These new runways did not come into operation until 1952 and 1954.) The 1949 departmental undertaking to reserve the land north of the airport for future QEA use now made rational forward planning possible.

Despite the considerable problems facing Qantas, Hudson Fysh was in high spirits. In his diary for 8 November 1949 he recorded:

The Qantas hangars at Mascot in late 1949. Constellation maintenance took place in Hangar 85 on the left, Lancastrians were serviced in Hangar 58, while Hangar 20 — third in line from the left — was used for work on the new DC-4 fleet.

261

QEA Board working together wonderfully in full accord. Dan McVey a wise and helpful man indeed; QEA owes a lot to him. Bill Taylor with great future ahead if he keeps his nose clean . . . a great help and asset to the Board. Keith Smith — a sound knowledge indeed of air affairs and always gives advice to help QEA first. Norman Watt an acute brain, gives great help to the Board. In fact, the Board of QEA that are there to help me are brilliant indeed and Qantas is blessed indeed. I feel humble, as humble as a man can feel, when I realise these people are supporting me in my job . . . [43]

On the same day he recorded:

The weird picture "Holiday" on my room table is to remind the staff as they come in that it is the future and the unsolved things that we are interested in. The past is immensely interesting and useful for experience. The present, if all goes well, is a comfort and, if things go ill, a discomfort to be endured. But it is the future that we are really interested in and we work for.[44]

QEA now operated to Hong Kong and Japan (with DC4 Skymasters); to New Caledonia, New Hebrides, and Fiji (with Catalinas); and to Lord Howe Island (Catalinas) and Norfolk Island (DC4s). It also operated to Lae (New Guinea) and Honiara (British Solomon Islands) with DC3s and provided internal services on behalf of the administrator within Papua and New Guinea (DC3s, DH84s, and Catalinas). Plans to extend the Hong Kong service to Shanghai had been shelved because of civil war in China. On the Kangaroo Route between Australia and the United Kingdom, their BOAC partner (which twelve months before had still been using wartime Hythe flying boats and Lancastrian passenger aircraft when QEA had changed to modern Constellations) now operated Constellations in parallel with Qantas on a combined frequency of four services a week. Although the pound sterling had been devalued in September 1949, QEA had carried out their Kangaroo Route operations at a profit during the year. The profit was earned despite one of the lowest mail rates received by any international trunk operator (two gold francs per tonne kilometre) and without increasing the passenger fare between England and the United Kingdom. (It was retained at £A325, or 6.8 pence per pasenger mile.) Calls at Djakarta had been introduced and air transport agreements concluded with the governments of India, Pakistan, and Ceylon (with QEA operating a Constellation service through Colombo each fortnight). In December 1949 a second-class mail facility was introduced between Australia and the United Kingdom. But the company was still tied to the loss-making Lancastrian air cargo services

on a twice-weekly basis in conjunction with BOAC. The QEA fleet had been greatly modernized, though the airline still had nine different types of aircraft. In addition to the four Constellation 749s, there were now thirteen DC3s and five DC4s to contrast with the remaining three Lancastrians, four Catalinas, eleven DH84s, two Liberators, one DH83, and one Wackett trainer. The company had flown 127 million passenger miles during the 1949 year without accident or death or injury to passengers or crew.

The Constellation and Skymaster aircraft of the fleet had three to four years of useful competitive life ahead of them but the company was carefully evaluating developing jet aircraft. "The directors believe that Australia should take an active part in the development of jet types for commercial use", concluded the annual report for the twelve months ending 31 December 1949. "As the British Comet is the first of these types actually flying, it provides an early opportunity of gaining experience of this type of operation and at the same time assisting the British aircraft industry."[45]

Six of the nine different types of aircraft in the Qantas fleet at the end of 1949 are included in this unique photo taken from inside Hangar 20 at Mascot. The nose of a Wackett Trainer points towards one of the two Liberators from the lower left. The nose of a DC-4 is visible from the right. Outside, a Lancastrian undergoes an engine run with a DC-3 parked to the right. Part of a Constellation can be seen at top right.

Ruthlessly Right
1950

12 Sir Miles Thomas, as chairman of QEA's partner BOAC on the Kangaroo Route, also faced the critical problem of aircraft choice. "There was", he wrote, "this nagging problem of what aeroplanes BOAC could mount to attract custom as against the other world airlines."[1] The American aircraft available were faster, more comfortable, and cheaper to operate. "With us," he commented, "it was always jam tomorrow. We were going to have the Comet quite soon; we were going to have the Bristol. In the meantime we had to make the best of it." He thought the attitude taken by Qantas "was not too helpful, either". Lying on a beach one day near Sydney, Hudson Fysh had told him that the Lockheed aircraft were far better than anything Britain had to offer. "Maybe they were ruthlessly right, but I could not help feeling that they were unco-operative with the Mother Country to which they pay so much homage."[2] BOAC's major aircraft choice was the hybrid DC4M (Canadair IV), a shortened version of the DC6 fitted with Rolls-Royce Merlin engines. By early 1950 it had taken delivery of a fleet of twenty-two of them. (The drawing board name of DC4B, built in Montreal by Canadair, became the Argonaut in BOAC service. BOAC also pinned their hopes on the turboprop Bristol, which they ordered in 1949 but did not receive until late 1956. (BOAC were also operating the American Stratocruiser, the York, the Lancastrian, the Hermes, the Constellation, and Short Sandringham flying boats. In accordance with government policy to back the diverse British aircraft manufacturing industry,

BOAC ordered three of the giant Saro SR45 Princess flying boats, first flown in August 1952. These huge boats had an all-up weight of 330,000 pounds and were powered by ten Bristol Proteus turboprop engines. They were all eventually scrapped before delivery to BOAC.)

Qantas, closely involved with BOAC on the single route between Australia and England, considered their major responsibility international airline operator for the Commonwealth. They were intimately affected by BOAC's management styles, equipment choices, and by the political pressures on BOAC by the British government to support Britain's aircraft manufacturing industry. Miles Thomas wrote scathingly of previous senior management attitudes in BOAC.

> There were the good solid executives of the Lord Reith days. They were men of dependability, with enough imagination to have a healthy and active forward look. Then there were the extroverts who had been brought in by Brigadier General Critchley, when he was chief executive under Lord Knollys' chairmanship. These were mostly large, ebullient gentlemen who were first class golfers. They were hail-fellow-well-met, husky types who could go through wine list and menu with facile deftness . . . In practice I found that their deliberations usually ended in a kind of relaxed compromise in which a programme for action was invariably missing.[3]

Of Sir Harold Hartley's predecessor as BOAC chairman, Lord Knollys, Miles Thomas wrote:

> Lord Knollys, who previously had been Governor and Commander-in-Chief, Bermuda, had quite naturally provided for his expectations of BOAC's great expansion by creating posts for executive assistants to himself, assistants to executive assistants, and what, in the light of later events, looked typically Parkinsonian figures.[4]

Thomas started sacking midlevel executives and their supporting staff. "When pruning in BOAC really got rolling we began to shed our fat at an almost visible rate." The new chairman had as his modestly stated aim for QEA's partner airline "re-shaping BOAC into some semblance of a commercial organisation".[5] This partner airline was, together with the dead hand of the bureaucracy of the Ministry of Supply and the political pressures through governments on behalf of British aircraft manufacturers, part of the working environment of the small but rapidly expanding Qantas. In the two years to March 1950, however, the measures taken to reshape the BOAC ground organization had almost doubled employee productivity (from 3,700 to 7,000 capacity ton miles per employee per year).

Within Australia, the domestic political environment had

On 19 December 1949, the Liberal–Country Party coalition led by Robert Gordon Menzies — pictured — defeated the Labor Party. Menzies was to remain Prime Minister of Australia until he retired in January 1966.

changed dramatically on 19 December 1949 when, after eight years in power, the Labor Party was defeated at the polls by the Liberal–Country Party coalition under R.G. Menzies. His government was to hold office for sixteen consecutive years and he was to exercise an unchallenged (though often criticized) personal dominance with his keen intellect, "fine presence, ease of manner, poise and style".[6] His deep reverence for Britain and its institutions, wrote Alan Watt (*Australian Foreign Policy 1938–1965*), "became part of his blood and bones, and substantially fashioned his mental outlook".[7] Australian historian Manning Clark described his stance as "almost superstitious respect . . . for British institutions".[8] Qantas were to feel the force of these attitudes when decisions had to be reached on new British aircraft. Menzies came to power in the same year that Mao Zedong won the civil war in mainland China and Stalin's unsuccessful blockade of Berlin ended. In the previous

266

year, Czechoslovakia had come under Stalin's control and there
had been Communist insurrections in Indonesia and Malaya.
Within Australia, Chifley's Labor government had been forced
to send troops into the coal mines to end a communist-domina-
ted strike that had held the nation to ransom. The new Menzies
government was fiercely anti-communist and just as fiercely in
favour of private enterprise.

Rapidly expanding passenger traffic was causing Qantas quite
new problems on the ground in 1950. Finding good hotel
accommodation for passengers in Sydney grew increasingly
difficult. The city had in total only about eight hundred rooms
in first-class hotels and Qantas alone needed, each day, ten per
cent of them.[9] Even these rooms had few private bathrooms.
Despite permanent bookings at the Hotel Australia, passengers
often had to be sent to second-rate hotels. On 10 January a submission was put to their new minister in the Menzies government. T. W. White (a World War I airman and author of *Guests
of the Unspeakable*), to buy the Wentworth Hotel, which had
normal accommodation for 161 guests. White was, however,
wrote Fysh, "a man with extreme views on the necessity to
limit government participation in industry . . . we were to have
a torrid time with him".[10] On 16 January White informed him
that the proposal for the purchase of the Wentworth was rejected by Cabinet.[11] It was clear that the new private enterprise
government was not sympathetic to such initiatives from a
government-owned airline. Determined to persevere, Qantas
began drawing up a scheme for the formation of a separate
company with private shareholding and Qantas participation.[12]
Fysh was quick to sense the new minister's attitude to the
airline that a Labor government had acquired for the Commonwealth. He warned Turner that "rightly or wrongly we
are going to be attacked on costs this year". He asked him to
pursue the special effort started the year before to reduce the
number of staff, increase the efficiency and simplicity of the
organization, and reduce costs where possible. They had for
some time, he said, been in the midst of expansion in new
routes and with new work, with costly equipment constantly
being needed. Many other organizations had been obliged to
retrench severely because of overexpansion. "In the case of
QEA . . . undoubtedly the past period of rapid expansion of
services will be temporarily slowed." He asked Turner to
institute a searching overhaul right through the organization,
including the number of aircraft. "Elimination of the Lancas-

trians", he wrote, "should enable reductions in staff right through from the Operations to the Accounts departments. I hope, for a start, that the Liberators can be disposed of immediately." He drew attention to heavy capital commitments that lay ahead, including the problem of expensive bases, especially Singapore. "There is nothing which brings greater criticism", he wrote, "than redundant staff, or staff unnecessary if the organisation has been right ... The building of little empires should be ruthlessly stopped."[13]

Turner had meanwhile been studying Allan's report on the Comet jet airliner.

> As requested I have had a look at the report by the Controller of Technical Development [he wrote]. To put it bluntly this report indicates that the Comet cannot be considered for the Australia–United Kingdom route at this stage of development. However, I would hesitate to make this view public in any way without a great deal more investigation of all the figures. Obviously de Havillands would not have gone ahead with their very large expenditure if they did not have something up their sleeve. Also, BOAC has ordered a large number of the machines but presumably they are protected if the actual performance does not come up to the guarantee (it does not at this stage).

Turner recommended that Qantas should have their own technical experts on the job consulting with de Havillands. "From a policy point of view the development of the Comet is of such importance that we cannot afford to be only partly informed on the position. If it is a failure then we may have to investigate the Bristol 175 Britannia or other types as a replacement for the Constellations."[14] It was a clear indication that Qantas, whatever its uncertainties about the Comet, genuinely desired to have the option of buying British aircraft.

On 22 February, at a metting in Fysh's office, the de Havilland representative admitted that the Comet could not be considered as an economical aircraft if it had to carry fuel reserves such as those carried on Constellations. The 5,000 pounds thrust of the Ghost engine would, though, he said, increase by 1954 to 6,000 pounds. More air turbulence had been experienced by the Comet at thirty to forty thousand feet than expected but at no time could it be called serious. However, with an indicated airspeed of 400 miles per hour at near sea level, bumps experienced were of such a nature that they could only be borne by passengers for a few minutes. British European Airways had, he said, conducted high altitude tests in a Mosquito in the European area for over four years and had not experien-

ced turbulence of a serious nature. "The dangers of de-pres-
surisation at great heights was raised", the minutes of this
meeting recorded, "and Lucas [the de Havilland representa-
tive] stated that the structure tests of the aeroplane had been
made and that de Havillands were fully confident of the
strength of the structure."

There were considerable discussions on fuel reserves, centr-
ing on whether the Comet could carry a reserve sufficient to
allow a descent at the destination and then a flight to an alternate airport if necessary. They were told that this would mean
an extra 5,000 pounds of fuel and that the Comet could not
bear this penalty. Qantas operations manager, Captain Crowther, pointed out that would have to be vast improvements in
weather-reporting systems for Comet operations which,
acccording to Australian meteorological authorities, would
take two years to introduce, and similar improvements in both
long-range and short-range position-fixing facilities. There
had been, said de Havillands, eighteen Comets ordered to date
— two by the Ministry of Supply, fourteen by BOAC, and two
by Canadian Pacific. The second Comet prototype was expected to be flying by August. A Qantas order could not be met
before 1953.[15]

Allan's report on the de Havilland Comet DH106 was sent,
after some amendment by Turner, to Fysh on 23 January. It
said that in recent flight tests the Comet's performance "falls
below both the Guaranteed and Specification figures at the
Specification engine powers. The engine cruising revolutions
per minute have increased to 92.7 per cent of maximum and
maximum cruising altitude has been increased to 44,000 feet,
and as a result the Guaranteed performance has been met",
though it was thought doubtful that the Air Registration
Board would accept the increases. The all-up weight, reported
Allan, had been increased from 100,000 to 105,000 pounds.
Flight test cruising speed was 490 miles per hour (specification was 505 miles per hour and guaranteed speed 460 miles
per hour). At standard conditions and 105,000 pounds, the
take-off distance was greater than both guaranteed and specification figures. "The reserves of fuel quoted in the de Havilland brochure are most unrealistic," wrote Allan, "even considering improvements which might be made to airport facilities in 1955–56." The use of rocket motors, he said, was not
considered practical (to assist take-off). His report pointed out
that the configuration of the aircraft being considered was the
36-passenger version, at an all-up weight of 105,000 pounds

269

and a landing weight of 75,000 pounds. "From the flight test results available the Comet is not capable of economic use on the Australia–UK route", wrote Allan. (Turner inserted the words "at present" into this remark.) "After taking developments already assumed into consideration," Allan continued, "a through service is not practicable owing mainly to lack of tankage and take-off restrictions. The flight tests have shown no major reason why the Comet would not eventually be developed to prove successful on the Empire Route . . . QEA should maintain interest in the Comet." (Turner added the qualification: "But at this stage it is difficult to see how we could justify placing definite orders.")[16]

At the Qantas board meeting on 27 January 1950 it was agreed that though interest would be retained in the Comet airliner, no definite order would be placed.[17] Thus began a long and difficult period in which genuine hope for the success of emerging new British aircraft would be tempered with cold fact and professional analysis from QEA's growing cadre of technical and performance engineers. (Two British Short S25 Sandringham flying boats did, however, join the QEA fleet in April 1950, and a further three in the following year; the first of four DHA3 de Havilland Drovers was also acquired in 1951. The aircraft dilemma was to be concerned with major items of fleet re-equipment.)[18]

Fysh now recorded in his diary observations that were at odds with his favourable comments on fellow board members in November. At a party at Elanora (a golf club north of Sydney) attended by Miles Thomas, who was visiting BOAC stations, Dan McVey's attitude annoyed Fish.

> Dan McVey [he wrote] always takes up whatever I say to him or anyone else and takes the opposite view, making out I am wrong. This is . . . at Board meetings and with anything I have said which unless it is one hundred per cent factual, unalterable and has got to be done, is criticised. This is (i) jealousy . . . for a man in a superior job with a less brilliant intellect (ii) my own shortcomings which, I suppose, rile him.[19]

A few days later, he wrote in stronger terms:

> Nothing but intrigue, intrigue, intrigue. When Labor tpok over QEA we had it from Watt and Bill Taylor. Then things settled down. QEA as an organisation was not injured. Now Labor is out we have it all again — this time from McVey and Keith Smith, but in a different sense. They know the names of the deadly opponents of QEA but will only hint at them so as to save their face,

should anything happen detrimental to QEA. Meanwhile the continual jealousy of Dan makes things interesting; but no one sees it but me, Dan being far too subtle and cunning. To keep me in my place is the aim.[20]

Despite these board tensions, Qantas were well served in terms of policy advice and operational standards. Sir Miles Thomas, in a letter to Whitney Straight that was clearly not intended to be seen by Qantas, praised the airline's Constellation cabin standards.

> . . . may I say that I have noticed a considerable difference in the operations between the Qantas 749 Constellations and the two BOAC 749 Constellations in which I travelled out. In the first place, the Qantas aircraft are properly air-conditioned and refrigerated, and they seem to handle the cabin pressure rather better than we do because at no time was the pressue inside the cabin greater than 4,000 feet altitude. My pocket altimeter told me on the way out that the BOAC aircraft were running at about 8,000 feet and, of course, that does have a considerable effect on the passengers' ears. Then again, in the Qantas Connies, they have hot and cold water in the toilets whereas the hot was conspicuously missing on the BOAC machine. Another point I noticed is that, whereas BOAC use thin trays for fixing to the seats in front of the passengers, Qantas have rather attractive wooden trays which make much less noise, and then Qantas serve their food on china plates which hold the heat and are much more attractive than are the plastic plates of BOAC . . . [21]

On matters of high policy, Turner drew Fysh's attention to possible changes and opportunities for QEA on the Australia–United States route, urging that Qantas should run this service in place of British Commonwealth Pacific Airlines. "It appears possible", wrote Turner in a "strictly confidential" memorandum, "that the [Pacific service] might come up for review as to method of operation and finance. Other operators such as Australian National Airways will dobtless make offers to run the service at lower costs than at present and I feel that QEA should anticipate the position and make an offer to run the service." Turner set down what he called strong reasons why QEA should run both the Pacific and Kangaroo routes. Most trunk operators were developing round-the-world services and Australia should do the same to stay in the field. "The eventual aim is an all-British service by joining Atlantic services with the Pacific . . . " Present competition for Sydney–London traffic by two Australian companies (QEA and BCPA) could not, he wrote, continue without trouble. "Our only competitor on the Pacific should be Pan American Airways." It was unreasonable, argued Turner, that BCPA should be subsidized to enable them to compete with QEA "but the fact is that if they cannot win traffic from QEA then their net loss (or subsidy) will be greater". Future operation should, he said, demand concentration on one aircraft type.

Turner recommended that QEA make an offer to run the service in conjunction with the Kangaroo Route on a mail payment basis. "This would result in the elimination of subsidy payments to BCPA by the three governments [Australia, the UK and New Zealand], which is estimated to be at the rate of about £379,000 per annum at the present time." QEA, he thought, could recover this loss.

> Figures for 1949 show that QEA made a gross proft of about £320,000 while the Department of Civil Aviation received about £150,000 benefit from the pooling of mail carriage fees with the United Kingdom — in other words, Australia benefited to the extent of about £470,000 out of the Australia–United Kingdom service. As against this, the United Kingdom operator, BOAC, sustained very heavy loses (something like £A7,500,000) in developing British services throughout the world, which presumably include a contribution to the loss on the Australia–United States service. Not all of the BOAC loss can be due to inefficient operation, as they carried out a considerable development programme in which Australia might eventually share the costs . . . As a matter of high policy, Australia might adopt full responsibility for the Pacific services as a means of relieving the United Kingdom of some of the burden. Also, since New Zealand does not share in the profits of the Australia–United Kingdom service and does not run a separate New Zealand–United Kingdom service, she might well be relieved of any payment to the Pacific beyond payment for the carriage of her mails on the service.

Turner suggested running the Pacific service using the existing BCPA DC6 equipment.[22]

On 20 April 1950, QEA proposed to the minister that they take over BCPA and that future Qantas expansion should include extending across Canada from Vancouver (to link with BOAC in New York); introducing a service from Sydney to Johannesburg (again linking with BOAC); and, at a future date, operating from Sydney to Valparaiso and concluding a third BOAC link.[23]

Others had their eyes on the Pacific. Ivan Holyman at various times pressed Hudson Fysh to aim at a Qantas takeover of Trans-Australia Airlines leaving Australian National Airways to run the Pacific route.[24] BCPA had, from the start, operated under severe handicaps and, directly as a result of the election of the Menzies government, now lost its able and diligent chairman, Arthur Coles. Coles had been one of the two independent Victorian members of Parliament who had in 1941 voted to bring down the short-lived coalition government under Fadden that had been sworn in following Menzies's resignation as prime minister. Coles resigned from the chairmanship of Trans-Australia Airlines on 10 May and of BCPA on 22 May 1950, with Norman Watt succeeding him in both positions. Sir Keith Smith became vice-chairman of BCPA.

From the start, wrote Norman Watt, the problems of operating a small international airline had not been realized by government. The appointment initially of Australian National Airways to run the service under charter for BCPA under contract had not helped. Their standard, wrote Watt, was not up to general international standards and they lacked international experience. BCPA had relied heavily on Trans-Australia Airlines, in particular on the engineering expertise of TAA's John Watkins and able director of finance, Dick Pope. There was, said Watt, no depth in the BCPA staff and great reliance was placed on the general manager, A. A. Barlow, and the secretary, I. O. lawson. Decision making, with three governments involved, was laborious and ineffective and there was a growing loss of enthusiasm for the airline by the United Kingdom as BOAC policy to operate both the Atlantic and South Pacific firmed. Finance was a basic problem as mail was sent by the Kangaroo Route and BCPA operations, as a consequence, had to be subsidized. There was, wrote Norman Watt, no hope of profitable operations without mail. Irregularity of service flowed from financial constraints. Four aircraft was the minimum number needed to ensure regular schedules but the airline could only sustain two in continuous operation. Continuing speculation about the airline's future had a bad effect on staff morale.[25] Shortage of dollars made travel by Australians to the United States on BCPA's route difficult and the airline could expand neither eastward nor westward. Almost from its beginnings it seemed that the airline had so few resources and so many handicaps that change had to come.

Turner, like Fysh, wanted Qantas to inherit the Pacific route when such change eventuated. They had begun to carry civilian passengers on their RAAF charter service to Japan as from 3 March and now sensed that the opportunity to operate the great Pacific route, denied them previously by ANA when Qantas could only propose Lancastrians, could at last be won. Qantas was fully confident of its true role. In a letter to Sir

Keith Smith, Fysh reminded him of the previous minister's speech on the Qantas Empire Airways bill 1948, when Drakeford told the House on 11 June:

> In brief, the bill provides for ratification of the Commonwealth's purchase of Qantas Empire Airways Limited and for the availability of funds to allow of its future development as Australia's international air transport operator. I am firmly convinced that this purchase has been in the best interests of Australia, and that in Qantas Empire Airways we possess an instrument which is serving, and will continue to serve, Australia in the maintenance of our rightful place in international air transport, with its consequent benefit to Australian trade and industry and the reduction of our geographical isolation . . . [26]

Change was in the air, for the new government had also asked QEA to consider the possibility of introducing private capital into the company. At the same time, Ivan Holyman, chairman of Australian National Airways, was publicly criticizing fare levels between Sydney and London. Fysh responded to Holyman's criticism with a press release pointing out:

> It is not altogether feasible to compare costs of overseas operations with those of interstate services . . . For example, a Skymaster on an internal run carries a crew of four who need little or no baggage; a Constellation on Sydney–London duty carries a crew of ten, all of whom need baggage with them. A navigator alone carries 60 pounds of maps, instruments and manuals, apart from his personal baggage. Then there is petrol. On the average sector of the Sydney–London route, a Constellation would carry probably four times the weight of petrol needed on the comparatively short interstate hopes.

Passengers on overseas flights carried more free baggage; three times the weight of food had to be carried for the longer overseas hops; and though the Sydney–London journey took only four days, it included nightstops at Singapore, Karachi, and Cairo where first-class hotel accommodation had to be provided. "On air services from England to Paris passengers pay ten .pence a mile and it costs them eight pence a mile to cross the Atlantic. Compared to these rates, the seven pence per mile charged on the Sydney–London air journey is most reasonable."[27]

Fysh sent the new minister for civil aviation a summary of QEA's plans and requirements on 18 April 1950.

> It may at first glance be thought a big programme [he began diplomatically], but it must be remembered that Air Transport is advancing very rapidly . . . QEA operations, as Australia's designated overseas operator, are fairly widespread. Many of our routes

274

are developmental lines without any great traffic density now, but on which a claim must be staked for Australia. They will develop later . . . QEA fleet and operations are not large compared with the reputable international operators and, in fact, our traffic and mileage flown is quite small compared with internal operators such as ANA, TAA, BEA or the internal operators of the USA . . . A very great deal of expansion must yet take place before the organisation undertakes what are its natural functions, and before it would be in danger of becoming unwieldy or inefficient. In fact . . . the balance of size is against QEA.

He outlined the development of the main QEA trunk routes. The Kangaroo Route

allows of individual national services and expansion by each partner, of individual control of costs but pooling of technical, aircraft and other resources on the Route, thus preventing wasteful overlapping of costs, yet eliminating competition for traffic on the route and allowing a combined front to be presented in competition with the strong Foreign operators . . .

To be in the picture in the future, large operators must operate round-the-world services . . . It is clear to us, therefore, that an essential part of planning for the future will be the operation of British round-the-world airlines, organised as round-the-world units.

Fysh described the growing competition with British Commonwealth Pacific Airlines on the Pacific as embarrassing and uneconomic. On aircraft requirements, he wrote that "dollar restrictions prevented additional [Constellation] purchases, except for one Constellation purchased for sterling from Air India. We are informed that Air India may have two more Constellations for disposal . . . [28]

On the same day that this brief went to the minister, a meeting of senior executives headed by Turner noted that recent QEA–BOAC talks had agreed on the joint operation of five Constellation services per week on the Kangaroo Route from June 1950 using the existing combined fleet of ten Constellations. Seat density was to be thirty-six on BOAC aircraft and thirty-eight on QEA's. One Lancastrian freight service between Sydney and Singapore would be eliminated from April and, if the Constellations were found capable of carrying the load, the elimination of the second Lancastrian service would be examined (BOAC then substituting a York aircraft once a week between London and Singapore to replace its two Lancastrian services). The meeting, however, was convinced that separate freight services should be maintained.[29]

Fysh prepared a memorandum for the board at the minister's

request on the possibility of introducing private capital into QEA. With Holyman in mind, he wrote:

> A point always considered most important by the old Qantas was the question of control of the Company, and in this respect large subscriptions from big, private transport interests were not welcomed and, in fact, excluded. In this way Qantas kept its independence of service to the Government on the one hand and to the shareholders on the other. In the event of calling for the large amount of capital required in this new issue [for private shares in QEA] it would seem that the intrusion of these big interests could not be prevented on the private side of the Board.

Fysh pointed out that QEA's paid-up capital was £3,623,000, with an additional million pounds possibly required within a year. "At least £2,000,000 would be required for public subscription if a set up was contemplated on the basis of 50–50 or 51–49 Government–Private capital." In going to the public, the position of QEA and its prospects would have to be clearly stated and decisions made by the government on (a) confirming QEA's position as the international operator; (b) who should operate the Pacific service; and (c) a term of contract for all QEA's main routes "with a provision for action in the event of war". Fysh suggested a term of ten years, with the contract guaranteeing mail rates.

> The introduction of private capital would again reintroduce as the paramount interests the interests of the shareholders and the payment of dividends . . . The change, unless unquestionably shown to be the correct course for the proper service of QEA to the Government into the future, should not take place because it would again disrupt the organisation without compensatory results . . . I recommend against change at the present juncture as being in the best interests of QEA in its continuing long range service to the Commonwealth . . . [30]

The essential difference between an airline owned by private shareholders and one wholly owned by government (a difference not confined to Australia) was felt by QEA in the continuing necessity to argue cogently for an increase in their aircraft fleet to meet competition and desirable route expansion. Qantas had not only to develop arguments internally and present them for approval by the board; they had then, after board approval and at the stage when a privately owned airline could have proceeded to implementation, to reargue and represent the case to obtain the approval of government (the shareholders). A reasonable parallel would be the requirement for a special general meeting of shareholders in a public limited company to ratify every major board decision. (There were, of course, evident advantages that came with government owner-ship; but the handicap of inevitable delay in implementation of major decisions was to become a normal part of the working environment of the airline.) On 4 April 1950, QEA once again argued their case to government for enlargement of the fleet in a memorandum "Justification of need of aircraft on Australia–United Kingdom route".

QEA, it said, needed a forward planning period of at least five years for new equipment. Comets would not be replacing Constellations before 1954–55 or even later, chiefly because of ground oranization restrictions but also because of difficult operational problems in flying the Comet at 40,000 feet, said the report. "Despite the fact that BOAC have ordered 17 Comets, they have also ordered 25 Bristol 175s (Britannias) for delivery in 1954 and for operation along the same routes. The Bristol 175 is virtually an enlarged Constellation type." Five Constellations would not cover operational requirements for the next five years and QEA did not want to introduce other types to operate alongside the Constellations, for economic reasons. Any QEA capital outlay on Constellations (including those already bought) would be fully recovered by 1955.[31] The company's persistence was rewarded in mid-June, six months after the original request for additional aircraft, when the acting minister for aviation, R. G. Casey, announced approval for the purchase for sterling of two Constellations from Air India International.[32]

QEA's partner on the Kangaroo Route, BOAC, had fleet plans for the route that differed dramatically from those of Qantas. BOAC expected to have Comets in operation on the route to Australia in 1952, after their earlier introduction from April 1951 on routes in the Near and Middle East. BOAC ex-pected to have all fourteen Comets before the end of 1952 and gradually to extend their use on the route to Australia. When they placed the Comets on the route, they planned to remove the Constellation 749s. The new turboprop Bristol 175 — considered a suitable aircraft for the Pacific route — was ex-pected to be in operation in 1954, for use as an all-purpose machine doing either long- or short-range work. At a meeting with QEA in London on 14 June, BOAC chief executive Whit-ney Straight said there were no plans for developing a Comet with a longer range and the existing Comet would not fly the Pacific route. He thought Qantas could take an early interest in the Comet operations by buying two or more Comets from BOAC. For Qantas, Turner explained that Captain Allan had been brought to England for a direct study of the Comet.[33] Current operations were discussed with BOAC during Turner's visit and BOAC chairman Miles Thomas advised Fysh that Turner

> has very clearly and explicitly stated the position from QEA's point of view and we now understand one another's problems in a way that will lead to optimum operation in the future. We both realise that our common anxiety is to get the utmost revenue earning capacity out of the Constellations, and while the freight picture from London to Singapore is different compared with . . . Singapore and Sydney, we are going to watch the traffic offering . . . and determine the point at which it is uneconomic to carry freight on Constellations . . . [34]

In Sydney, meanwhile, there was an unresolved and growing issue of contention between the partners concerning hotel accommodation. Phillip Hood wrote with far less good will than his chairman to Qantas on 13 June that "the inability of QEA to provide suitable hotel accommodation in Sydney for transit passengers and BOAC crews is not only a serious handicap to the furtherance of traffic but also a serious expense to our company . . . We look to our company to provide adequate, if not similar accommodation, to that set up by my company in the United Kingdom . . . The plight of the passengers transiting Sydney is really acute."[35]

Disagreements between the partners on an even more important issue was also surfacing as a result of Captain Allan's visit to England to study the Comet. On 23 June, as he prepared to leave for Australia, Allan referred to a request from Air India that he call en route and advise them about the Comet. Fysh had given permission for this call but Allan wrote to him:

> This may not prove advisable as much of the information I have received is given to me as confidential. In addition, inferences from information collected so far might lead to giving advice detrimental to de Havilland's sales policy. To be specific, it is evident that the Mark I Comet will be more costly to run than the Constellation; the Mark IA at 110,000 pounds gross weight would appear to break level. Tentative plans are being considered for a Mark II Comet at a higher gross weight, probably about 130,000 pounds and with bigger engines. This latter, BOAC and de Havilland wish to be kept secret on the score that American firms who have inspected the Comet Mark I are reported to be planning a competitive machine. Since the Mark II Comet will obviously be much more economic, I suspect that the probable reason for secrecy is that nobody will buy the Mark IA if they get to hear of the Mark II. I will therfore decide to by-pass Air India if I find

that I am not in a position to give advice favourable to other Comet interests.[36]

Hudson Fysh had (on behalf of the QEA-nominated directors on the board of Tasman Empire Airways Limited) suggested to the minister "that from Australia's point of view it would be advantageous for an Australian operator to operate across the Tasman in parallel to a New Zealand operator". TEAL, jointly owned by Australia, the United Kingdom, and New Zealand, now owned four Solent flying boats. Its agreement with the three governments extended to the end of 1951 but the Solents could not be written off until the end of 1954. For their economic utilization a monopoly of the air traffic between Australia and New Zealand had been relied on. (TEAL was operating between Auckland and Sydney with plans to extend during 1950 operations to Auckland–Fiji and Wellington–Sydney.) There were, wrote Fysh, possible complications "in TEAL maintaining her position of absolute monopoly over the Trans-Tasman from an international standpoint". There was also "pressure to allow operation of a landplane service between Christchurch and Melbourne which would have an adverse effect on the finances of TEAL if such service was allowed to commence on a competitive basis". It was difficult to see how Australia could operate a parallel service on the Tasman by itself while the Solents remained in use, said Fysh, "until such time as New Zealand possesses proper city aerodromes at Auckland, Wellington and Christchurch which would allow the country to procure some use between these cities for the type she would procure to operate . . . New Zealand Government spokesmen have stated she desired to look after her own Civil Aviation industry by organising all the ground facilities possible in the Dominion, but at the moment she is finding it difficult to finance a desirable programme . . . A decision on this matter is therefore political." Fysh concluded that the present TEAL organization should be supported for the life of the flying boats. QEA, he reminded the minister, held the £263,185 Australian interest in TEAL on behalf of the government and expected only an unsatisfactory five per cent return in 1950. In contrast, the United Kingdom government held the UK shares and the New Zealand government the New Zealand shares. He suggested that in the case of Australia, the government should own the shares.[37]

Turner, about to leave for meetings in London and Montreal, received a warning from his chairman on the limits of his responsibilities.

> A note to wish you success in London and Montreal . . . There is no need to give you any directive except to say that the question of responsibility should be watched and that no decisions or agreements should be made by you on behalf of QEA which should rightly come before myself and/or the Board. You well know our policy — the extension of the BOAC–QEA partnership to embrace round the world operations. You are free to push the submissions . . . to take over the Pacific operation.[38]

Despite the new Australian government's abrupt rejection of QEA's proposal to buy Sydney's Wentworth Hotel, the mounting need for secured accommodation (so forcibly emphasized by BOAC's Sydney representative) precipitated further action. There had been increasing passenger complaints both about the facilities provided for handling passenger arrivals and departures and the lack of guaranteed hotel rooms.[39] Increases in QEA frequencies on the Kangaroo Route to England, on the Far Eastern service, and from the TEAL Solent service had compounded the accommodation problem. A company analysis showed that an average of 82 passengers left from Sydney each day and 83 arrived from the combined QEA, BOAC, and TEAL flights. Some forty per cent of the outgoing passengers originated from points other than Sydney and QEA had to find rooms for them as well as for incoming passengers and all BCAC and TEAL crews. A conservative estimate of needs had risen now to between 120 and 140 persons per day, excluding BCPA passengers. In great part, Qantas had only been able to book second-class accommodation.

Despite the government's attitude, the QEA board decided to take out an option to purchase the Wentworth at a cost of £2,000 a month (to be deducted from the sale price if the hotel was bought), with the intention that Qantas should itself hold a controlling interest. Fysh advised R. G. Casey, acting minister for air, that the accommodation position for QEA in Sydney was now desperate and that they had taken an option on the Wentworth for three months from 29 May. So pressing was the problem that Fysh wrote directly to the prime minister on 23 June:

> I have wished to see you for some time but have fully realised the impracticability of this owing to the strenuous times which you have been having . . . However, there is one matter which now cannot wait . . . the re-submission of the Hotel Wentworth proposition under an entirely new plan. The new proposition, in place

of the plan for outright purchase at £275,000, is . . . a reconstruction of the Hotel Wentworth Limited . . . to provide for QEA to hold 160,000 £1 shares for controlling interest.

The plan, he said, approximately halved the amount of capital which QEA would need to put in. Fysh stressed that "it is us or our competitors, and securing the use of the property is going to possibly affect QEA balance sheets in the future".[40]

On 26 June an unpromising telegram was received from the minister for air: "Wentworth proposal was rejected by cabinet as you were advised and surprised to learn now of expensive options involved and prepared to see you sometime during Wednesday in Canberra to discuss your new submissions." Fysh saw White in Canberra and followed up on 3 July with an official letter.

The heart of the matter, as we see it, is that passenger accommodation to a successful airline is an essential part of its business, and that airlines are forced to own their own accommodation in cases where satisfactory first class accommodation is not catered for by others. Sydney is obviously one of these difficult spots, where the position is worsening all the time. Airlines are now beginning to advertise "accommodation arranged" and we believe that just these words describe what QEA must do . . . In such circumstances, to turn down an offer like the Wentworth would, in my opinion, be suicidal . . . There is no question in our minds but that the Wentworth will be a profitable undertaking . . . [41]

On 22 July 1950, Qantas took another pioneering initiative when the Catalina *Island Voyager* under the command of Capt. Hugh Birch left Sydney to survey, with Captain Crowther in charge, a possible new route from Sydney to Tahiti by way of Noumea, Suva, and Tonga. It was to prove a long-term investment of enterprise; Qantas did not fly through Tahiti until 1964, when they inaugurated their service to London through Mexico City. (Qantas made an unsuccessful offer to operate a local service for the Fijian government in 1950.) The Qantas survey did not proceed beyond Tahiti to QEA's ultimate goal of Valparaiso because a refuelling stop at Easter Island would have been necessary in the open sea. ("It was not a risk we should take in our business", wrote Fysh.)[42] Crowther's report on the survey concluded that "the only reason for QEA to consider any extension flights from Suva to Tahiti would be on the basis of further Australian communications in the South Pacific from a strategical point of view and to encourage better relationships with the French possessions in this sphere". Crowther said there was insufficient traffic from

Tahiti itself to support any air communication. Potential passengers were estimated at only six to eight per fortnight.[43] (Australian pioneer aviator P. G. Taylor made the crossing to Valparaiso the following year, but used Jato rockets to accomplish the tricky take-off at Easter Island.)

On 28 July Qantas submitted a report to the government on the introduction of private capital.

> The Board [it said] is of the opinion that various factors weigh against the introduction of private capital under existing circumstances. These are (a) on the basis of 49 per cent private capital, private investors would be called upon to provide over £2 million immediately, and large and frequent further issues may be expected over the next five to ten years . . . It is considered that such issues may not be attractive to private investors . . . (b) BOAC . . . is wholly Government-owned (c) Financial negotiations for the purchase of new aircraft frequently require strong Government support . . . Such support might be difficult to justify if the Company is wholly or partly representing private interests . . . The Board is of the opinion that . . . there should be no change in the ownership of Qantas Empire Airways Limited. On the other hand, if as a matter of high Government policy it is desired that a change should be made, no difficulty need be anticipated in having such a private issue underwritten . . . [44]

The problems of BCPA and future QEA expansion, of possible introduction of private capital into the company, and of the pressing requirement for guaranteed hotel accommodation in Sydney were compounded by difficulties with BOAC in the parallel partnership operation of QEA's main route from Sydney to London. Turner was sent to London for discussions with BOAC and Fysh summarized his detailed report when he returned in a letter to McVey on 13 July.

> The BOAC–QEA parallel partnership is one of some complexity. This has tended to increase of late as BOAC have been handed flying equipment by their Government without reference to our Government and ourselves, and QEDA have been obliged to take their own line. The partnership has, however, worked satisfactorily and is still working, but Mr Turner's notes . . . show up the difficulties which exist. . . The position exists of reconciling the equipment which BOAC have and will have in the immediate future with what QEA had and will have. . . The problem also exists of QEA particiption in BOAC experimental work on the Comet and jet aircraft in general — a matter which will prove expensive.[45]

Captain Allan's report on the Comet was not encouraging. There was, he wrote, a general ralization that reduced operating costs would result from an aircraft larger than the

Comet but no practical attempt to increase its dimensions had been made. Improvement in the overall Comet I and Comet IA performance was therefore dependent on improvements to the power unit, particularly as more than half of the direct operating costs were due to fuel costs. Allan noted that "the engine now in use is the de Havilland Ghost, remarkable for its extreme simplicity . . . It is, however, heavy on fuel [and] . . . is somewhat low in power for tropical take-offs." A future de Havilland engine, he said, would depart from the configuration of the Ghost and was expected to have a specific fuel consumption equal to the Rolls-Royce Avon engine. "Details of this engine are secret but the erection of rigs to test parts has started." Allan pointed out that the Ghost engine was a centrifugal jet engine, while the Avon was an axial engine. Axial engines had, he noted, approximately fifteen per cent better fuel consumption than centrifugal engines.[46]

He also provided a preliminary description of the Bristol 175 turboprop airliner (the Britannia), for delivery about 1953, but concluded that with the prototype still under construction and the engines still under development, he could only estimate performance figures.[47] The aircraft had a gross weight of 130,000 pounds, four Bristol Proteus turboprop engines, a maximum range of 4,550 miles, and a cruising speed between 320 and 340 miles per hour. It could carry from fifty to ninety passengers depending on route application.

Following Captain Allan's report on the Comet, Turner prepared a memorandum for the board, saying QEA must now consider what part, if any, they should take in Comet development. On the Australia–United Kingdom route, wrote Turner, it would be uneconomic in comparison with Constellations and would not do all the work required by Qantas. "The possible development of a Comet Mark II in 1957 or later is of great importance but it should be emphasised that a machine of this type has not yet been ordered by BOAC and, as far as we can find out, is not even at drawing board stage. However, sufficient is known of all-jet aeroplanes to state that it is possible to develop machines capable of economic operation on all our major routes — but this is not expected until 1957 or later." Management therefore felt that QEA and the Commonwealth "must take a direct interest in the present development flying of the Comet Mark I". A recommendation should be made to the Commonwealth, wrote Turner, that it purchase two Comet Mark Is and spares at a cost of approximately £A1 million "and that these should be handed to QEA to enable them to take part in a jet aircraft development programme with BOAC".[48]

Two weeks later, Hudson Fysh wrote to Air Marshal Williams but in much more tentative terms than those suggested by Turner. "The Directors of QEA feel that some Australian support should be given in the cost British development of jet and turboprop aircraft . . . if we do not share in the initial troubles and costs of these new types, it is difficult for us to come along later and want to share the benefits . . . Before we formulate a definite policy and make a submission to the Minister, it would greatly help to have your views as far as you feel able to advise us." QEA's chairman had decided, with caution, to first dip his toe in the sometimes chilly and turbulent bureaucratic ocean.

Future aircraft policy was not the only area where BOAC and QEA disagreed. On the Kangaroo Route, Fysh wrote to McVey, differences were difficult to simplify but included BOAC's operation — in virtual competition with the Kangaroo Route — of services between Britain and Egypt, Malaya, Tokyo, and India.

> To secure the maximum business, BOAC are now increasingly taking the line of wishing to limit the Kangaroo Service frequencies to cover end to end loadings only, and to fill up the Constellation service with freight, second class mails and parcels post without increasing frequencies, and therefore pushing off the sectional traffic on to BOAC competing services. BOAC say that the watershed of traffic on the route occurs at Singapore, BOAC being interested in all traffic to the West, outside the Kangaroo route agreement, and QEA being similarly interested to the South East on the route to Sydney. The QEA answer is that she is and always has been interested in all the sectional traffic she can obtain along the whole route, that this is international airline operation practice and that it is necessary from a payability [sic] point of view.[49]

On the same day that he wrote this letter, Fysh wrote in his diary:

> The trouble with me is that I expect the perfect all the time and make no allowances for human nature and imperfections which exist in all of us. [I have] lack of proper training in articulating. Since 27 February [the date Fysh made his diary entry about McVey and Sir Keith Smith and "intrigue, intrigue, intrigue"] . . . much has happened and it has been a particularly interesting period. It seems that . . . Cabinet is split in regard to whether our constitution should be altered [and] whether QEA should buy a hotel. Since last October the QEA Board has been solid on this. Tommy White has proved himself simply a psychotic. Bob Menzies, of course, as befits a truly big man, is all for it . . . A tragic

thing is that for a period in our existence we were cursed with a b. . . fool Director of Civil Aviation [Fysh was referring to Corbett] and when for some years we had to fight [for] everything . . . against ignorance and prejudice. Now, it is even worse. . . . How long will it last? What will be the outcome? What will come of the fight in Cabinet over this . . . ? What bloody damn fools we all are.

On 8 August 1950, Sir Fergus McMaster died. For twelve years, since a heart attack in 1938, the man who had gathered the support of local Queensland graziers in 1920 to launch the precarious enterprise of Queensland and Northern Territories Aerial Services Limited, had fought ill health with the same selflessness and courage as he had fought for development of Australian civil aviation. Though Paul McGinness had provided the initial spark, and Hudson Fysh the diligence and tenacity essential to the survival of the unlikely enterprise, it had from the start been McMaster who had, by his sagacity and integrity, persuaded the politicians, public servants, and his peers in Queensland that Q.A.N.T.A.S. was worth their support. Arthur Drakeford wrote to Fysh:

> I felt a high personal regard not only for the character but for the nature of Sir Fergus McMaster. His willingness to submerge strongly held views and his steadfastness in supporting decisions when reached, his complete freedom from prejudice or hostility towards, and respect for, opinions held by others, made him apart . . . [his] name, I feel, should be perpetuated as one of the early pioneers of the development of civil aviation in this country.[51]

(Fergus McMaster is, in fact, one of the forgotten names of Australian aviation three decades after his death.)

Fysh sent a detailed and final proposal for the purchase of the Wentworth Hotel to the minister, Thomas White, on 21 August 1950. "You will observe", he wrote, "that 31 August 1950 is the last day on which we can exercise our option and, as there is an amount of £4,000 involved, the Board of QEA would be grateful if a final decision could be received by that date."[52] Among the points made supporting this submission, the company said: "QEA must not be denied the taking of business opportunities allowing it to compete. The alternative would be for it to go out of business or lose heart and initiative . . . "[53] On 29 August, two days before the expiry date of the QEA option, Fysh sent a personal telegram to the prime minister:

> Firstly: apparent that real issue is broader one of capital construction of your national overseas operator, as our case for accommo-

The Wentworth Hotel opposite
Lang Park in Sydney.

dation is clearly proved and supported by Pan American Airways
and KLM activities. Secondly: it should be realised we already
lease hotel in Djakarta. We also own and operate accommodation
at Darwin and Lae; also St Mary's quick freeze [food] production,*
and what we now ask rounds off requirements [for] catering and
accommodation. Thirdly: submit Board should be granted authority [to] carry out all necessary functions incidental to the successful operation of its international air transport services and that
investigation of our constitution if desired is another matter and
one on which [the] Board will carry out the wishes of the Government.[54]

Qantas won their argument with the minister. Thomas
White wrote to Fysh: "This is to advise that Cabinet approved
the proposal of Qantas Empire Airways Ltd. to purchase the
Hotel Wentworth, Sydney, in terms of the proposal last submitted by you. This confirms the telegram to you to that effect
... "[56] A final paragraph in his letter asserted ministerial
authority on a second Qantas project: "The proposal for the

¢ In 1950, QEA's St Mary's Quick Frozen Foodd Centre was opened and a staff of
thirty produced up to two tons of frozen food daily.

286

building at Kingsford Smith Airport to be erected by Concrete Constructions Pty Ltd at a cost of £242,223 was not approved, it being decided that any decision on this subject be postponed for twelve months."[57]

There was a more encouraging note from the prime minister, who had been abroad. "I would like to pay tribute to the all round efficiency of Qantas as experienced by members of my party and myself on our recent overseas visit", he wrote to Fysh.[58]

While the problems of equipping the future QEA fleet for international operations were to intensify, Qantas took delivery on 13 September 1950 of the first production de Havilland Drover aircraft, designed and built in Australia by de Havilland Aircraft Pty Ltd. A light transport with three Gipsy Major 10 engines, it replaced a Dragon operating in New Guinea. The de Havilland *Gazette* reported: "The aircraft is fitted up as a freighter with collapsible seats and can accommodate up to twelve New Guinea passengers, who weigh less than their Australian neighbours. The cabin has a plywood lining and the passengers' luggage, consisting usually of a pig, or perhaps a dog and a bag of rice, is pushed under

Qantas General Manager George Harman accepts the first Australian built Drover aircraft from Maj. Murray Jones, Managing Director of De Havilland Aircraft Pty Ltd, Bankstown airport, Sydney, 13 September 1950.

the seat."[59] The QEA board agreed to order three additional Drovers.[60]

The proposal to approach the government to assist financially with QEA participation in the Comet project was considered by a special QEA-departmental Comet committee meeting in Melbourne on 16 November. Captain Allan reported to Fysh: "The committee was doubtful of advising an approach to the Government on the score that Australia and Australian sphere route facilities were quite unprepared for jet operations and that they were not sure that the Comet was representative of future jet aircraft . . . They were of the opinion that pure jets were still economically at least four years off."[61]

There were other important issues to resolve as 1950 came to a close. Turner informed Edgar Johnston that Qantas were examining with BOAC the possibility of operating a number of special services to bring migrants to Australia. "The company understands that some 25,000 migrants are to be brought from Holland and that KLM has already arranged to participate in the carriage of this traffic. It is understood that an Italian airline is seeking also the right to carry migrant traffic to Australia. No doubt these operators would seek back loading from Australia and the company desires to operate services if suitable aircraft can be obtained, in order to protect its interests." Turner also said that Qantas wanted to terminate the existing fortnightly service to Hong Kong and reroute one of two services proposed each week for Japan with DC4 aircraft through Hong Kong.[62]

Other subjects discussed at this meeting were mentioned by Fysh in a letter to the director-general on 9 November.

> Despite all our efforts through this year, QEA has not even yet been officially advised of its mail rate for the current financial year, though we have only some six weeks to run to complete the year . . . QEA has rather terrific extra costs to meet next year which have to be met by raising the air mail rate and/or fares . . . The QEA air mail rate at 3.5 gold francs per tonne kilometre is the lowest received by any long range international operator. Through favourable conditions and the combined efforts of your Department and QEA the QEA service in low cost to the Government is rather unique in the world.[63]

The carriage of mail, and the rate paid, had always been critical to the profitability of Qantas. In the postwar years on the Kangaroo Route, revenue from carriage of first-class mail sustained the airline through the recurrent economic crises of the period and their effects on passenger traffic. High mail revenue helped Qantas (unlike many other international airlines) survive without government subsidy. The rate for the carriage of this mail, it had been agreed, should be closely related to those adopted by the Universal Postal Union (UPU), a specialized agency of the United Nations. The UPU congress held in Paris in 1947 had agreed to a rate of six gold francs per tonne kilometre for first-class mails and one gold franc for other classes (the gold franc itself contained a specified amount of gold of a defined fineness). The revenue yield to both BOAC and QEA from the carriage of mail was considerably higher than that from the carriage of passengers and cargo and both airlines jealously guarded their rights to carry national mails (as well as seeking to maximize uplift of foreign mails at intermediate points). In 1950, the yield of some $4 million from mail constituted about one-quarter of QEA total revenue. High mail revenue was to help bridge the gap between income and expenditure until passenger traffic grew in relative terms. (By 1983 mail revenue had reached $17 million but constituted only 1.3 per cent of total Qantas revenue.)[64]

More immediate fleet requirements prompted Fysh to write to the chief of Air Staff, Air Marshal G. Jones, on 30 November.

We have two matters in hand which we feel are of considerable import to Australia's overseas air transport and at the same time to the RAAF. They are (i) preparation of Cocos Island as a refuelling base in the Indian Ocean (ii) order of a replacement Constellation in place of the crashed Air India Constellation which was to come to us. In regard to Cocos, for two years we have been battling for this facility. One can see that without Cocos our whole Australian air transport communications with Europe and Africa could be broken overnight. On (ii) we are desperately short of long range aircraft. Can we have your active and urgent support with the Minister?"[65]

Fysh also wrote directly to the prime minister enclosing a briefing on the Cocos proposal and the QEA fleet position. He said that Qantas had closely investigated other British and American aircraft, including the Comet, Bristol 175, and Douglas DC6B, and the QEA board had decided to build on the existing fleet of long-range Constellations.[66]

Yet another paper was put to the government, on 25 November, on the seriousness of the fleet position. Lockheed, said QEA, had a completely overhauled Constellation 749A ex-KLM available at the low price of $700,000. "The case for the purchase of two Constellations from Air India has already been established with the Government. We would only add that the Company's need for these aircraft is more urgent than it was . . . because of the development of the war situation in Korea and the necessity for the opening of an alternative route to South Africa and the United Kingdom via Cocos Island."[67]

A further memorandum was sent on 28 November pointing out that both the department and the RAAF were now ready to act in establishing the required base at Cocos. Chinese involvement in the Korean war made Fysh fear for the implications elsewhere. On 30 November he wrote to Air Marshal Williams on the fleet position and said: "In regard to our route being broken, I am personally most frightened in regard to Singapore, eighty per cent of the population of which is Chiense, and who have no love for the British."[68] Captain Crowther raised another issue of concern for the company — there was a general pilot shortage. "Since World War II," Crowther advised Scottie Allan, now assistant general manager, "air operators have been able to recruit discharged RAAF pilots . . . This source is now depleted and the Australian air operator must take immediate decisive stesp to meet this grave situation. Pilots are required not only to replace the normal 10 per cent turnover of Flight Staff of QEA but also to meet the constant expansion." For 1951 QEA required thirty pilots plus an additional reserve of fifteen in case of a national emergency. Some could be obtained from overseas and some could be trained from junior pilots holding commercial licences in Australia. Allan strongly recommended pressing "the DGCA to set up a National Training College or that we immediately implement a Company Cadet Pilot Training Scheme".[69]

Fysh wrote a year's-end secret memorandum to Turner, "On the Position and Development of QEA".

> QEA fleet and operations are not large in comparison to leading international operators . . . a very great deal of expansion must yet take place before the organisation undertakes what are its natural functions and before it would be in danger of becoming unwieldy or inefficient [he began, repeating his comments to White]. There is a current tendency for Australia and the United Kingdom to grow apart in the use of commercial aircraft. The UK uses its operator, BOAC, to support its aircraft industry, the two working together . . . In Australia we buy in a competitive open market, and this is an essential policy for the future. The easiest way to commit financial suicide in the air transport industry is to operate a lot of different types of aircraft . . . It is now generally recognised that the larger international operators must develop round the

world services . . . When fast jet aircraft become standard equipment it might become the only economic method of long distance operation. It is clear to us therefore that an essential part of planning for the future will be the operation of British Round the World airlines organised as round the world routes. At present the competition which is growing and must increase between QEA, BOAC and BCPA is becoming embarrassing, is uneconomic — with competition on two routes which should be economically one — and is considered not in keeping with the best progress of British World airlines. It is considered that the objective should be for both BOAC and QEA to operate round the world in parallel.

Ironically, Turner had written in much the same vein to Fysh in his memorandum of 20 January.[70]

As the year ended, Fysh received a note from one of Fergus McMaster's contemporaries about the estate of the late Qantas chairman. "I do not know the particulars of Fergus McMaster's will," it said, "except that Jean, Ken and Duncan got £1500 each and the balance [went] to Edna at a very rough guess round about £27,000 . . . I am sorry to disillusion you but one cannot become wealthy from selling wool."[71]

The British Network
1951

13 The critical issue for Qantas in 1951 was still fleet expansion and the pressing need to win government approval for the purchase of additional Constellations, either with dollars or by other means. But long-term fleet planning was further complicated during the year by increasing British pressure to buy the Comet and the need to appraise accurately when pure jet and turboprop aircraft would become necessary for long-range, competitive operations. These equipment choices were at the heart of the changing relationship between BOAC and Qantas, of the gradual distancing of Australia from British and Empire considerations in aviation policy, and the emergence of a far more moderate government policy on negotiation of traffic rights with foreign countries. The predominantly protectionist policy followed for the decade from the end of World War II was — as Qantas grew in competitive strength as a world carrier and as the traditional route to England was threatened by developments in the Middle East that led to the Suez crisis — modified greatly as Australia softened its negotiating stance and shifted policy to Bermuda type agreements.[1] Though interest in the Comet I quickly waned because its size, range, and economics did not match Qantas routes, an intense interest in the Rolls-Royce Avon-engined Comet 2 developed and, for a time Qantas believed that its future might lie with either the Bristol Britannia or the advanced Comet.[2] One of the first letters received by Fysh in 1951, from A. C. Campbell Orde at BOAC, provided initial BOAC calculations on the performance of the Avon-engined Comet.

Except for the Karachi–Cairo sector, which presents a special problem of range with most types of aircraft, the Avon Comet is weight restricted (due to runways only) on the Calcutta–Singapore sector, but this problem is likely to disappear by the time in question. In other words, the Avon Comet should fit the London–Sydney route very well and offer not only a much reduced schedule but a very attractive seat-mile cost. . . Now that we are assured of the necessary official support for the development of the Avon Comet it is clearly possible for us to put ourselves in a commanding position on the London–Sydney route by, say, 1953.[3]

Even though the advanced Comet clearly promised the possibility of dazzling results for the two airlines, Sir Miles Thomas was worried that Qantas appeared unenthusiastic. He wrote to F. E. N. St Barbe at de Havillands (copying his letter to Sir Geoffrey de Havilland):

From the point of view of de Havillands, BOAC and British Civil Aviation generally it is, you will agree, important that the Comet should be put into service by the Australian authorities. From what I learned when I was on the West Coast of America recently, and from reports I have received from our representative in Sydney, it seems as though the whole drift of Australian thought in connection with aircraft at the present time is in terms of long range, and although dollars are tight they are being drawn towards the DC6B and the 1049C Constellation. I do think it is important that the Prime Ministers of Australia and New Zealand, Mr Menzies and Mr Holland, when they are over here, should be indoctrinated with full information about the characteristics of the long range Comet which is now being developed. The matter has more importance than simply the immediate sale of aircraft built in England. It could undoubtedly have an impact on the manufacturing policy in Australia. I don't want the Australians making American-designed aircraft . . .

Miles Thomas offered to arrange a lunch or a dinner for the two prime ministers "under the umbrella of our associations with QEA and TEAL".[4] It was the beginning of moves to bring to bear ever-increasing British political pressures.

At much the same time, Fysh wrote to the minister for civil aviation telling him that Lockheeds had advised with regret that they could not accept sterling for Constellations. "Our urgent need is still unabated",[5] wrote Fysh. Turner, in a memorandum to Fysh on aircraft policy on 9 January, confirmed Miles Thomas's suspicions. "The main types being considered are the Constellation 1049C and the Douglas DC6B," he wrote, "but we are also including figures covering the Comet I with Ghost engines. There is insufficient information available to include the Avon Comet. On figures available, the

Constellation 1049C appears to be by far the best aircraft to follow on and work in with present Constellations in 1953." Turner was well aware of the political considerations. "Undoubtedly a considerable discussion will be raised immediately we make our submission to the Government on the Constellation 1049Cs and we will have opposition from the United Kingdom who have now brought forward the Comet I with Avon engines."[6]

Phillip Hood informed Sir Miles Thomas in a confidential memorandum on 19 January:

> I do not know what Mr Fysh has said to you since the Avon Comet news broke but from reliable sources it is known that dollars will not be made available in Australia or in New Zealand for any further purchases from America ... The existing QEA fleet numbers five Constellations and five DC4s — one more Constellation ex-Air India is due to be collected about May, and QEA would like more DC4s if they could be obtained. If, then, the decision on dollars is to persist, the Lockheed 1049C will be out of reach and QEA must look to the Comet or Bristol 175.

Hood said that Captain Allan

> rightly or wrongly, in his role of technical adviser, has consistently played down the Comet and, in fact, any kind of turbo-jet aircraft. His report to the Board on the Ghost Comet was sufficient for the Board to defer any decision. I should say, however, that although he may have been correct in his interpretation of the Ghost Comet, he seems to have failed to emphasise the obvious developments. Further, I believe him completely sold on American types and he shows his preference by underestimating British equipment.

Turner, wrote Hood, "tends to show a little interest now that the Comet is to have more range but he prefers the 175, particularly if this aircraft could be produced earlier. At the same time he is personally of the opinion that QEA needs more Constellations and DC4s." Two QEA directors, said Hood (not naming them), were undoubtedly anxious for a decision in favour of the Comet.[7] It was a good brief, though not fully accurate. Allan advised the board that the Avon-engined Comet should be able to operate on the England–Australia route with paying loads once necessary ground facilities were adquately developed.[8]

On 28 February, in a formal submission to the government for authority to order aircraft, Qantas advised the minister that the company's present aircraft fleet was already dangerously short of minimum requirements. The government, said Qantas, had refused permission to order a Constellation that would have been available by December 1951; now no Constellations were available before December 1952. Aircraft procurement from the United States was now even more difficult because of the US rearmament programme (and the Korean war). Lockheed and Douglas productive capacity was fully committed until the end of 1952 and, in the United Kingdom, the best delivery for new aircraft being developed was 1955. The problem was compounded by the recent loss of the Constellation that was on order from Air India. Qantas, therefore, now applied for an allocation of dollars to enable them to secure three Constellation 1049C aircraft plus spares and engines and two Douglas DC4 aircraft. They would, said the submission, bring the QEA fleet by early 1952 to nine Constellations and seven DC4s. Seven Constellations were required for the United Kingdom service, two for South Africa. The additional DC4s were required for QEA services to Japan and Hong Kong which were growing in importance. The company stressed not only the necessity to assure the operation of Australia's international air services on a competitive basis, but also the urgent defence needs of the Commonwealth for long-range transport aircraft.

The Constellation 1049C was recommended for its competitiveness, its compatibility with the existing fleet, and the fact that it was to be fitted with the Curtiss Wright compounded engine similar to that installed in the Lockheed Neptune bomber ordered by the RAAF. "The present model of the Comet . . . is not considered to be up to requirements in such vital factors as payload-range and competitive payability . . . Late efforts are being made by the United Kingdom to fit the aircraft with the Avon engine . . . However it is the view of our experts that the aircraft will remain experimental for a number of years . . . Delivery of Avon Comets to QEA would be 1955 at the earliest." On the Bristol 175 (Britannia) Qantas noted that the prototype would not be completed until 1952 and delivery could not be expected before 1955. "Providing the necessary dollars can be made available to it, the Company expects to be in a position to finance the purchase of the aircraft nominated [Constellation 1049Cs] without making further calls for capital from the Government, subject . . . to the continuation of the present overdraft facility up to the limit of £1 million as already arranged through the Commonwealth bank." The three Constellations with spares would cost $6,248,000. For the two DC4s, $500,000 should be set aside.[9]

Following Allan's advice to the board on the possible suita-

bility of the Avon Comet for the Kangaroo Route, Fysh wrote
to Sir Miles Thomas on 2 April asking his advice on "how
best QEA can become interested in the general programme of
development. If, for instance, QEA were to advise the Australian government to purchase, say, two Avon-engined Comets,
at what date could we expect to get the machines . . . Without
some knowledge of your plans it is difficult to formulate proposals . . . As you know, Australia is now electing a new
Government and we will not be able to discuss proposals to
finality before late in May."[10] (The Menzies government was
returned in the election and H. L. Anthony succeeded Thomas
White as minister for civil aviation.) As this letter was written,
Hood (now aware of a tentative decision by QEA for the purchase of two Comets by the government) wrote to Miles
Thomas: "It will be essential for somebody of high BOAC
seniority to come out here within the next two months and
talk facts. By this I appreciate that the mere selling of British
aircraft is somebody else's problem but the advantage of having
our associated companies using the same equipment as BOAC
must be enormous and of tremendous prestige value. I believe
it is a BOAC problem to attend to this matter because we are
not suspect."[11]

As Qantas firmed their choice in favour of the Constellation
1049C, BOAC's managing director, Whitney Straight, responded unhelpfully to Fysh's request for advice on how QEA
and the Australian government might assist in the Comet programme by the possible purchase of two Avon Comets. He
pressed Fysh for a firm QEA decision on the Comet.

> Our [BOAC] fleet will . . . amount to twenty Comets of which
> nine will be Ghost-equipped and the remainder Avon-equipped
> . . . Our plans provide for the full utilisation of the first nine
> Ghost Comets. With regard to the Avon Comet . . . we feel that if
> you are seriously contemplating the use of this aircraft, it is time
> for you to take the bull by the horns and place a definite order . . .
> We are extremely anxious that our partnership should be a true
> partnership in every sense of the word and I think we both agree
> that there is tremendous advantage and economy in using the
> same type of equipment.[12]

(The partnership arrangements were described succinctly in a
QEA draft of 19 March. "Each operator bears the expenses incurred in the operation of its own aircraft. Revenue earned
from traffic and mail, apart only from certain incidental
revenue, is credited to a pool account and these earnings are
divided between the two partners on a capacity basis at speci-

296

fied periods. Where both airlines use the same equipment, this is simplified... The routes followed and the frequency of operating are those as agreed from time to time ... subject to approval by their Governments ... Each has the right to operate an equal number of services." Between the partners there was collaboration on general commercial policy and consultation on international negotiations and bilateral agreements. Fares and rates were determined in accordance with resolutions of the International Air Transport Association subject to approval by governments.)

The Lockheed Aircraft Corporation did not remain inactive as British pressures on QEA to buy the Comet mounted. They communicated their own assessment of the Avon-engined Comet's poor potential on the Pacific between San Francisco and Honolulu to John Watkins, TAA's superintendent of organization and technical services and adviser to BCPA. Summer temperatures at Honolulu, said Lockheed, would restrict the Comet's take-off weight on the 7,000-foot Honolulu runway and give it an actual payload of only 4,772 pounds. Further, if reserve fuel allowance were carried for the most distant alternate airport (which Lockheed believed they should) the Comet payload would be further reduced to a mere 2,325 pounds.[13]

Despite these Lockheed criticisms, BCPA remained optimistic about the Avon Comet. A de Havilland representative, F. H. M. Lloyd, reported on 5 May after a visit to Australia: "Due almost entirely to Scottie Allan's influence, Qantas appear to be about as firmly against the Comet as BCPA are for it ... The main reason is his insistence on vast reserves for diversion and holding combined with the worst conditions of wind and temperature ... Of course, so long as you stand out obstinately for three hours holding, plus diversion, you can knock the Comet out of any long range operation and that is just what Scottie is trying to do." His reception by BCPA and John Watkins provoked a more cheerful response. "Thursday and Friday of last week in Melbourne I spent with John Watkins and his technical people pushing the slide rule over the new data I have brought out with me and they are quite satisfied now with the Comet 2 series abilities on the South Pacific run from San Francisco to Sydney with all the reserves they want ... There is a suspicious school of thought in BCPA that think their technical advisers at TAA are urging them into the Comet so that TAA can buy their DC6s cheap ..."[14] Lloyd was shown the letter from Lockheed's Heymanson to

John Watkins. "You will find it quite amusing", he wrote. "But it is amazing to me that a reputable company would stoop to these methods and lay themselves open to being proved wrong."[15]

Fysh wrote to Sir Miles Thomas that BOAC planning changes for the Kangaroo Route, altering their projections of progressively increasing traffic to no increases, were

> making it difficult for Qantas in getting new equipment and to hold its place against competition. You know, for instance, that KLM is to fly 5,000 immigrants in here this year. This means two services weekly, and KLM is increasing pressure all the time for back loading. Once a period comes where we are overloaded, we are gone to the clouds on this issue . . . The real competitors to the Kangaroo route are the shipping companies who are carrying enormous traffic between Europe and Australia. What we compete against is an air fare at £260 sterling against a berth in a two-berth cabin of £150.[16]

Fysh made private notes on the changing relationship with BOAC and the difficulties with British Commonwealth Pacific Airlines a few days later.

> The last talks of any consequence [between the UK and Australia] took place in London in June 1947 . . . Changing conditions now make it essential that a further conference should take place. In the past . . . a meeting of Empire units would have been called. Canada was always difficult in these meetings and never freely participated owing to her position in North America. It is doubtful if Canada would attend a meeting now and India, Pakistan and Ceylon make the matter doubly difficult. Therefore, perhaps, the thought of such meetings is obsolete and the units must carry on more as nations than Empire units. No more is the United Kingdom the Fairy Godmother . . . [we] must demand equal opportunity for all.

On more specific issues he noted that BOAC and QEA needed to discuss the Kangaroo Route; a plan embracing a correct development in the future of BOAC and QEA global airlines; and the method of operation of the British Pacific Ocean Service "as a lead in to the inevitable future globe circling service of BOAC and QEA". The first step, Fysh wrote, should be Qantas taking over the Australian interest in BCPA. "The greatest competitors with the Kangaroo route for the Sydney-London traffic are the three trans-Pacific operators. Yet BOAC has a share in BCPA which makes for an impossible position and one most embarrassing to them. QEA is also embarrassed in regard to the whole relationship. The longer it is looked at, the more certain it seems that change must take place."[17]

Phillip Hood, reported that QEA's continually deferred decision on the Comet now put them in danger of being at the end of the queue. "No doubt they hope to get the best of two worlds by hanging on to the last minute and then getting an allocation out of BOAC." More sympathetically he added:

It is fair to say, however, that there have been difficulties . . . QEA is a small company [about 3,700 employees] and is not suffi-ciently strong to go all out for a new type . . . Even partial failure of new equipment would be a disaster to QEA, particularly as ANA or BCPA would immediately jump in and claim the right to operate more overseas services. For the past fifteen months Aust-ralia has been saddled with an air minister anti-sympathetic to QEA. Because of the recent election there has been no minister at all for two months . . . Australia is few in population and small matters go to a minister here which would be settled as a matter of routine in the UK.

Hood also reported that a decision to purchase Series 2 Comets could not be ruled out. John Watkins, he wrote, wanted to re-equip BCPA with this aircraft but Scottie Allan did not agree with his analysis.

These two have now been told to get together and sort out the differences in their figuring. Obviously the chairmen of QEA and BCPA realise the absurdity of approaching Government with dif-fering views on technical subjects . . . I have no hesitation in re-commending that a strong BOAC team should come to Australia without delay — there is no prospect of Hudson Fysh or Turner appearing in London until the end of August . . . Our subsidiary companies BCPA and TEAL will unquestionably be influenced by the line taken by QEA . . . The next few months (if not too late already) will decide whether British network in this part of the world is to operate British aircraft . . . or whether Australia goes American for many years to come.[18]

Whitney Straight's reply to his briefing was succinct. He told Phillip Hood that BOAC were well acquainted with QEA's difficulties which, he said,

are not really very different from those which any other airline is faced at the present moment. Our experience with the Comet to date . . . rather indicates that airlines which have the courage of their convictions are likely to profit thereby. There is certainly no question of our sending a technical mission to Australia with the objective of convincing QEA to buy Comets. If QEA cannot make up its own mind on this matter, it is certainly not our business to try and make it up for them.[19]

Two days later, BOAC chairman Sir Miles Thomas received a short letter from St Barbe at de Havillands. He had, he said, reported Lloyd's comment from Australia to the Ministry of Supply because "they have a tremendous stake in the Comet". St Barbe said he told the ministry:

> Lockheed and Douglas, of course, are fully alive to the serious menace of the Comet. For the first time in history their completely dominatng position is seriously threatened and obviously they are going to fight tooth and nail to try and hold the position over the next five or six years when they will, no doubt, produce jet transports of their own. As you know, they are stocking up KLM, Air France, Sabena, SAA, Swiss Air etc and are fighting hard to do the same with Air India and other operators. We are quite confident that in due course this battle will sway in our favour, but in the meantime we do feel that we are entitled to unbiased and even sympathetic consideration from British operators in whom HM Government has a stake.

St Barbe concluded his letter to Miles Thomas:

> I believe that the Comet is extremely important nationally. It is, by and large, correct to say that every major airline operator in the world is equipped with American aircraft. If the Comet is not given every assistance to penetrate this situation I do not believe this country will ever get into the game. But if the Comet can break the American monopoly, then the way is wide open for the aircraft industry of this country to follow.[20]

The stakes were high and the pressures mounting for Qantas. The British Ministry of Supply wrote officially to Sir Miles Thomas on 31 May:

> De Havillands tell us that the major obstacle with which they are faced at the moment in selling the Comet in Australia arises from attitudes of Quantas [sic] who seem to be very powerfully influenced by the sales propaganda of Lockheeds. It appears that in particular an individual called Scotty [sic] Allan in the QEA organisation is very much against the Comet . . . De Havillands are most anxious to have a talk with you about the situation to see how far it would be possible for BOAC to use their good offices with Quantas [sic] at a high level to persuade them of the merits of the Comet. . . We here would be very grateful for any action you can take. George Cribbett, with whom I have discussed the matter, and I would be very happy to join in any meeting . . . [21]

Fysh wrote to Sir Miles Thomas on 1 June that QEA were continuing to consider the matter of the Comet. But, he said, "there is still no plan, or even the first nucleus of a plan, forthcoming as to how BOAC intend to operate . . . and how the gap can be bridged on the Kangaroo route between now and 1955 when, presumably, regular operations with the Mark 2

Comets could commence. I think I can say now that QEA would not be interested in the Comet Mark 1 as this appears to us an aircraft already rendered obsolete by the Avon-engined Comet . . . "[22] Five days later there was a meeting at the highest level in London at the Ministry of Supply. The deputy secretary of the department, F. C. Musgrave, was in the chair. Present were Sir Miles Thomas and Whitney Straight of BOAC, F. E. N. St Barbe and F. H. M. Lloyd of de Havillands, Sir George Cribbett from the Ministry of Civil Aviation, a representative from Commonwealth Relations, and others. The Ministry of Supply, said the chairman, was anxious to help de Havillands in their efforts to sell the Comet in Australia and the meeting had been called to consider what action could be taken either by BOAC or more directly by the government to overcome Australian opposition.

St Barbe said that Qantas were showing a strong preference for the Constellation 1049C; that Qantas alleged they had received no guidance from BOAC on the operation of the Comet on the London–Australia route; that they considered their requirements could only be met by a super long-range aircraft such as the 1049C to develop the route to Africa and meet wartime strategic requirements; and that they had become used to operating Lockheed-type aircraft and were prejudiced in favour of this manufacturer's products. The problem was not only that Qantas themselves were opposed to the Comet, said St Barbe, but that they were using their influence to persuade BCPA and TEAL to buy the Constellation as well. Sir Miles Thomas stated that there had been the fullest possible exchange of information among Qantas, BCPA, and TEAL but the Qantas view was that only the Comet 2 was suitable and as this would not be available to them for four years, it would be too late. The meeting then agreed that efforts should be concentrated on persuading Qantas to buy the Comet 2. St Barbe said it could be delivered to Qantas in time for operation in 1954. As no official representation had been received on the defence aspect from Australia, the chairman suggested that for the present BOAC and de Havillands should approach Qantas purely on the economic and commercial advantages of the Comet. Sir George Cribbett pointed out the great advantage to Qantas in the operation of a standard type of aircraft, with BOAC, Canadian Pacific, BCPA, and TEAL providing a round-the-world Comet service. Sir Miles Thomas thought it likely the Australians still regarded the Comet as something of an experiment and that this impression might be dispelled by

301

the flight of a Comet to Australia. The chairman then said that the Ministry of Supply might also consider asking the Treasury to make representations to the Australian Treasury regarding the undesirability of allocating dollars for the purchase of American aircraft when a superior British aircraft was available.[23]

Two days later, Sir Miles Thomas cabled Fysh: "Seriously suggest you defer commiting yourself to other aircraft before further consideration of latest information [on the] Bristol 175 and Comets. Both from Commonwealth aspect and as your partners on Kangaroo [Route] we consider long term collaboration of first importance."[24] He followed up with a letter saying: "Frankly, a number of us over here are becoming deeply concerned at the apparent resistance on the part of QEA to the Comet."[25] St Barbe told Miles Thomas: "I find their attitude to the Comet quite extraordinary. Anyone with an open mind can see that the Mark 2 is going to be a better airliner than the Constellation 1049C for the main world trunk routes . . . But apart from all the facts, Qantas seem to have lost all their old spirit of adventure."[26]

Phillip Hood was advised that a Comet demonstration flight to Australia would be made in the late (northern) summer, to "help the Australians realise that the Comet is in fact an aeroplane and not a pipe dream".[27] In that same week, Hudson Fysh told Norman Watt, chairman of BCPA: "I am more convinced every day that our decision in favour of the 1049C is the correct one."[28] Hood reported to BOAC that Lockheed was putting the pressure on Qantas to order.

> I have seen a letter written by Robert Askew dated 8 June to QEA which is clearly an attempt to force QEA into an immediate decision. The letter states (i) Lockheed has to date orders for various aircraft amounting to $850 million (ii) a further $250 million is almost finalised (iii) there are 135 L1049Cs on order (iv) a further thirty may be ordered during the month. QEA realises . . . that if their proposal to buy three L1049Cs does not receive approval quickly they will find themselves without any additions to the existing fleet possibly up to 1954.

Hood summarized what he thought were the views of QEA directors and wrote that Dan McVey, although backing the purchase of three 1049Cs, was determined that QEA should come in with BOAC, although he did not like the Ghost Comet; Keith Smith "apparently says nothing; Bill Taylor is clearly sold to Lockheed, while I think Norman Watt, knowing the dollar situation, is willing to take on Avon Comets for

BCPA as well". Hood said that the new minister, Anthony, "lives in the flat right alongside mine so I shall undoubtedly get opportunities to give him our views on overseas and international operations".[29]

On 1 July 1951, C. O. Turner succeeded H. H. Harman as general manager of QEA. Hudson Fysh continued as chairman and managing director. Qantas put to the government in July a final proposal for their operation to South Africa (and an opening date for this service was agreed to by the minister some six months later for 1 September 1952). But the BOAC–QEA re-equipment difference continued to dominate affairs. The minister, Fysh told McVey, confirmed the actions taken by "our friends in the UK", and he wrote that "what amounts to a protest was lodged and the form which this took plus the attitude of Sir Miles Thomas seems to indicate that a crisis in the history of the BOAC–QEA partnership is approaching".[30]

While this British versus American aircraft drama was being played out, BOAC met with Qantas in Sydney from 3 to 13 July to discuss Kangaroo Route planning. They found that the recently promoted Turner was difficult to deal with. A memorandum on the meetings began: "We never expected the talks to be easy and we were not wrong in this, the difficulties being mainly attributable to the odd character of QEA's new General Manager, C. O. Turner, whom we found often out of tune with his own staff and more intent on recording differences of opinion than on reaching agreement." There was, though, "in spite of much seemingly unnecessary argument, a considerable measure of agreement on immediate forward plans". A decision on the ordering of aircraft, said the memorandum, had become an urgent necessity for QEA.[31]

There were still differences of opinion between Qantas and BCPA's advisor, John Watkins, on the relative performance of the Comet 2 and the Bristol 175. Qantas believed there would be little difference in scheduled flight times between Australia and the United Kingdom using either type. John Watkins's analysis showed a flight time twenty per cent less for the Comet 2 (thirty-two hours for the Comet and forty for the 175). Watkins also calculated the cost per mile of the Comet 2 and the cost per passenger mile as twenty per cent less than that of the Bristol 175.

In provisional comparisons of the direct operating costs of the Constellation 1049C and the Avon Comet in still air conditions and on critical sectors of operations, Qantas calculated that on stage lengths up to 1,500 miles both aircraft had a cost per capacity ton mile of two shillings and onepence, and on stage lengths of 2,500 miles the Comet cost was twopence more than the Constellation. But on the critical sectors of over 2,500 miles the cost disparity widened appreciably. On the tough Karachi–Cairo route the Constellation capacity ton mile cost stayed down at two shillings and fourpence while the Comet rose to four shillings and fivepence. Cocos–Mauritius and San Francisco–Honolulu also showed the Comet to disadvantage. On these three critical sectors, Qantas calculated that though the Constellation 1049C speed was 124 miles an hour slower than the Comet, its payload was much more than double because of the fuel requirements of the Comet.

Norman Watt wrote to Fysh on the matter:

> I am very concerned that nothing should go out with my endorsement as a member of the Qantas Board in relation to the Comet 2 which won't stand up to the searchlight of criticism. I feel that the case in support of the Lockheed 1049C . . . is quite strong enough without taking anything away from the Comet 2. We must be particularly careful on this point. The Comet 2 is a proud achievement and the UK people are very sensitive and would not hesitate to expose any inaccuracy or wrong emphasis in any presentation from the Qantas Board.[32]

As the pressures for Qantas expansion, new equipment, and changing relationships grew, it was obvious that neither de Havillands, BOAC, nor the British government shared the view so tentatively expressed by Hudson Fysh in his notes that the Empire units should now perhaps carry on more as nations. The United Kingdom government wrote directly to the Australian minister, H. L. Anthony, and BOAC pressured Qantas. Fysh wrote to Anthony on 25 July 1951 plainly stating the Qantas position.

> From correspondence received in the last few days from the Chairman of BOAC it is apparent that BOAC are opposed to QEA ordering Constellation 1049C aircraft and my Board consider it advisable that this fact be made known to you. The opposition of BOAC, it would seem, arises primarily from a fear that if QEA increase their fleet of Constellation aircraft there is a possibility that QEA will be committed irrevocably to American aircraft and will be unable to participate in the Comet development on Empire routes. In the judgement of my Board, the attitude of BOAC is unjustified . . . QEA do not regard the Comet with Ghost engines as a practical proposition for operation on the Australia–United Kingdom route. The aircraft is under-powered, it has not sufficient range to ensure economic operation, and it lacks volumetric capacity essential for the handling of the traffic on the Kangaroo route.

BOAC had not supplied QEA, as their partners on the route, with detailed operational plans. BOAC, in QEA's view, were "more or less obliged to use the Ghost Comet because a number of them have been ordered by the British Ministry of Supply . . . The trouble is that British operators are not only obliged to use the aircraft so ordered, but they are expected also to become first line salesmen for them . . . We feel that we must be left free to exercise our own judgement." Fysh pointed out that Qantas were interested in the Avon-engined Comet but earliest possible deliveries would be 1955.

> My Directors desire that I should re-iterate and emphasise that it is the policy of the Company to buy British aircraft wherever possible . . . The proposed introduction of Comets on civil routes by BOAC is obviously only part of their future programme, because they have placed orders for the Bristol 175 type . . . which will not be in operation before 1955–56 if manufacture is proceeded with. . . BOAC are not immediately dependent upon the successful operation of the Comets because they already have five types of large transport aircraft in operation, including the United States Boeing Stratocruisers and Constellation 749As. QEA . . . is not in such a favourable position.[33]

In yet another strongly argued application to order three Constellation 1049Cs on 11 July, QEA emphasized that the Comet was an experimental aircraft, was inefficient, and lacked range, and would as a jet aircraft require special ground facilities that could take years to develop. Ordering Constellation 1049Cs would not, said the submission, rule out the possibility of later ordering the Comet Mark 2 or other jet types.[34] Fysh told Air Marshal Williams: "QEA are going to be truly in a mess unless this now urgent order can be agreed very shortly, and that is not overstating the case."[35]

The day after this QEA submission to buy Constellations, Anthony received a long letter from James Marjoribanks, acting high commissioner in Canberra for the United Kingdom government. That letter gave up the British fight to sell the Comet 1 to Australia, but pressed the Australian government to delay any QEA order for more Constellations and argued strongly for the Avon-engined Comet 2.

> It has been decided . . . to concentrate upon the Comet 2 series which have not only greater speed but also range to make it greatly superior to the Super Constellations . . . You will recall that what was the immediate concern of the High Commissioner when he saw you about this question was the apprehension which was felt in the United Kingdom about the possibility of BOAC and Qantas flying different types of aircraft . . . I understand that you expressed a preference for sterling purchases over dollar expenditure.

305

He gave the initial cost of the Comet 2 as £515,000 sterling with delivery dates commencing in 1954. Air speed was 500 miles an hour and number of passengers forty to forty-eight by day. Direct operating cost was, he said, nineteen shillings and sixpence sterling per capacity ton mile as compared with twenty-three shillings for the existing Constellation 749 for the Kangaroo Route.

Marjoribanks continued:

> Analysis has shown that the Comet 2 series will . . . be superior to the Constellation 1049C in every respect except perhaps as regards overall range, payload and volumetric capacity. These considerations are, however, largely offset by the Comet's superior speed in that it can do the same work in considerably less time than any other transport aircraft and thus permit a greater number of frequencies per aircraft. It has also been confirmed that the Comet 2 series will be capable of operating over both the Indian Ocean, including the routes both to South Africa and Ceylon via Cocos, and the Pacific routes, with the necessary fuel reserves . . . The first Comet 2 is confidentaly expected to be flying in England towards the end of this year and . . . deliveries to BOAC will start in 1953. . . It is of interest to note that Canadian Pacific Airlines have placed an order for both Series 1 and Series 2 Comets for Pacific routes.
>
> The United Kingdom authorities are confident that the Comet . . . is an aircraft of revolutionary type which will be infinitely superior to any other contemporary transport aircraft . . . I therefore venture to suggest for your consideration that a decision [on the Constellation order] might be deferred until Mr Hudson Fysh has had the opportunity of further discussions during his visit to the United Kingdom next month.[36]

Pressure was increased only five days later with another letter from the United Kingdom High Commission to Anthony. BOAC, it said, were deeply concerned at the consequences to the Kangaroo Route partnership if the partners were to operate different ways. BOAC were convinced that the Comet was so superior in speed and passenger appeal that operation of differing types would unbalance the distribution of traffic, which was also the official view of the Ministry of Civil Aviation. BOAC, said the letter, had five Comet Series 2 on order and were about to exercise an option for the next six to be delivered; their concern for the future of the partnership was so strong that they were prepared to postpone other plans to allow Qantas Empire Airways to share two, or possibly three, of the six Comets on option. "IF QEA are prepared to take an early decision," continued the letter, "de Havillands are prepared to negotiate a contract for Comet Series 2s on the following basis. The price will be £515,000 sterling for each completed aircraft excluding radio . . . Delivery would commence in July 1954. During the negotiations this date may be advanced by up to three months." The matter, said the closing sentence, was receiving "the most serious consideration by the United Kingdom government."[37]

These formidable pressures were immediately and bluntly rejected by Qantas. The minister sent copies of the British letters to Fysh who replied on behalf of the QEA board on 3 August:

> It would seem, from the action of the High Commisioner for the United Kingdom in Australia, that the United Kingdom Government has assumed the right to intervene in the consideration by the Commonwealth Government of the appropriate policy to be pursued in respect of the types of aircraft to be used by QEA. The justification of such intervention is seriously questioned; and, but for the fact that my Board are anxious to continue friendly relationships with BOAC and the Mother Country, we would suggest that exception be taken to what appears to be an unwarranted action.

The United Kingdom, wrote Fysh, had overlooked the fact that Qantas were a successful airline operator and not by mere accident. Nor had it made reference to QEA's close study of the Comet. Information give in the high commissioner's letter was inaccurate and misleading on payload, costs, deliveries, and passenger appeal. "The effect of representations such as those made . . . has been to delay QEA being granted authority to order Constellation 1049C aircraft", Fysh said.[38]

On the same day as this Qantas response went to the minister, Fysh wrote to Air Marshal Jones, attaching notes on the Qantas case for three Constellation 1049Cs. "The order has unfortunately been delayed as to final Cabinet consideration by delaying tactics on the part of the UK and BOAC . . . The matter will probably come up to Cabinet within the next ten days or so and if you still feel that QEA should order the 1049Cs as preferable to other types from a RAAF angle then I would be grateful if you felt able to lend urgent assistance to the matter."[39]

While the Comet conflict was intensifying, Qantas were further appraising the British Bristol 175 turboprop airliner, Bristol quoted a price for the equipped aircraft of £525,000 (much the same as for the Comet 2) and delivery in early 1955 unless BOAC made available for earlier delivery some of the fifteen aircraft it had contracted for.[40] (The first prototype

Bristol 175 was scheduled to fly in October 1952 with the first BOAC delivery in March 1954.) Capt. Scottie Allan reported that assessed improvement in the performance of the Bristol 175 "is entirely due to changes in the engine, which is now the Proteus III". It was not scheduled to be run until the end of 1951 and full data on it was restricted "so that a criticism of the possibilities of meeting proposed performance is not possible". The Proteus engine had not been successful to date, he wrote. The American Allison engine was more efficient, and "chances are that when the Bristol 175 is fully developed and fitted with an engine as efficient as the Allison, it will be a more economic aircraft overall than the Constellation 1049E".[41] Because the prototype had now flown and the Proteus III engine was undeveloped, Fysh noted that the type "cannot be considered for order at this stage".[42]

Despite Qantas anger at the intervention of the British government, at the instigation of BOAC, talks held in London with BOAC by Fysh were, he wrote, "held in an attitude of mutual help and the desire to keep the partnership working as smoothly as possible". QEA's judgment that traffic would increase was born out. But the meeting, far from allaying Qantas's doubts about the Comet, confirmed them. "In my opinion," wrote Fysh, "the Comet 2 falls short in several vital respects for operation on the Kangaroo route and must be regarded as a jet experimental project." He also felt that the economics of the Comet 2 were suspect; its mail, baggage, and freight space extremely inadequate; and its practical range under the route conditions available was not yet established. BOAC, said Fysh, also wanted Qantas to order Bristol 175s. "Our close consideration was promised for the placing of an order for three aircraft, should we be satisfied with prototype trials." His overall summary was not promising for the British aircraft industry: "The general impression gained on British international type aircraft is that the present policy can only result in US-produced aircraft maintaining, if not increasing, their present leadership."[43]

Phillip Hood swiftly realized that both BOAC and the United Kingdom government had gone too far. He advised Whitney Straight on 18 July that Norman Watt had told him privately "that the official intervention of the British High Commissioner is regarded in a very poor light . . . Although QEA feels badly at the High Commissioner's intervention, there is no doubt of the Civil Aviation minister's interest in our side of the picture, and his inquiring mind might well defer the ordering of the 1049Cs, and quite surely insist on Mr Fysh's going into the matter of Comet 2s with you and the chairman in September." A nasty reference to Lockheed was included. "Continued pressure by Lockheeds is too obvious and overstressed . . . the Australian representative of Lockheeds is a Jew and although a pleasant fellow, his incessant persistence has resulted in QEA asking Bob Askew to 'call off his dog'."[44] Hood wrote to Sir Miles Thomas that "the most forthright and British-thinking of the QEA directors told me plainly that our intervention had done nothing but harm . . . any further attempt at this stage to deflect QEA away from the 1049 would be prejudicial to our case. [Hood was referring to McVey.] Interest in the Comet 2 and Bristol 175 is very real . . . "[45] He recommended that no further action be taken until Hudson Fysh visited London. "Lockheeds themselves have overplayed their hand . . . "

In England, the deputy secretary of the Ministry for Civil Aviation, Sir George Cribbett, wrote to Sir Miles Thomas saying: "We would like if possible to dispel the Australian resentment of what they seem to consider has been high handed behavior on the part of BOAC . . . Recent announcements in the Australian press . . . cannot but convey to the Australian public the impression that there is sharp controversy between the partners . . . We are naturally anxious at all times to avoid any ill feeling that may lead to divergencies of views between the partners being aired in public."[46] Miles Thomas replied: "I do not think there is any need for too much excitement at high level over this QEA–BOAC equipment situation. As partners we have frank talks; we understand each others prob-

The first production model L.1049A Super Constellation began flight testing in August 1951. The L.1049 was 18 feet (5.5 m) longer than the L.749 Constellations then flying with Qantas. When this photograph was taken, N6201C was fitted with water ballast tanks in the cabin for load testing and the propeller blades were strain-gauged to measure vibration. Twenty-four L.1049As were built, fourteen for Eastern Airlines and ten for TWA.

lems. It would be unfortunate if any impression in Government circles, either here or in Australia, was created that there was any real friction between the two partners." He acknowledged that there was a great deal of resistance in Australia to purchase of the Comet, much of it emanating from Scottie Allan, supported by Turner.[47] It was evident that both BOAC and the ministry now understood that it would be counterproductive to lean too heavily on either Qantas or the Australian government.

Fysh was at last able to report to his minister, on 5 October, that following discussions in London with Sir Miles Thomas and BOAC executives, BOAC had withdrawn their objections to a Qantas order for Constellation 1049Cs. Minutes of the London meeting recorded that BOAC "welcomed QEA's proposed acquisition of Constellation 1049Cs as providing a valuable addition to the partnership's aircraft resources, particularly during the interim period before Comet 2s and Bristol 175s are available on the Kangaroo route". Qantas had won the battle, if not the war. Qantas went ahead with the preparation of a submission for the government on the possible purchase of two Comet 2s for use in the Comet development programme, though there remained a dearth of accurate information. Turner asked Whitney Straight for specific delivery dates and a copy of the aircraft's specification but was told that BOAC itself had not yet received one from de Havillands and that it was unlikely to be available until the northern spring of 1952.[48]

On 18 October Fysh wrote to the minister: "On 30 May last this Company applied for permission . . . to place an order for three Constellation 1049C aircraft involving dollar expenditure for aircraft, spare engines and spares of £6.5 million spread over three years . . . Approval was given for the purchase of only one of these aircraft and a contract has been signed . . . You have requested that we should detail further points in support of the proposal [for the remaining two aircraft]." All the major airlines of the world, said Fysh, had ordered replacements for the existing Constellation type 749 except QEA. BOAC and the British Ministry of Civil Aviation were concerned with the threat from KLM, which had ordered ten Constellation 1049Cs, giving them at least a year's start in deliveries. The partners were seriously short of competitive aircraft to cover the service in 1954, 1955, and 1956.[49] In a further letter on 3 December (following a Qantas board meeting attended by the minister), Fysh gave details of the way in which the United Kingdom government had continuously made available to BOAC dollars for the purchase of aircraft.[50]

Government approval for the extra two Constellations was given. Phillip Hood reported promptly to Sir Miles Thomas that

> Mr Anthony confirmed this [decision] to Mr Granville [BOAC] and myself at a lunch in Canberra and he gave us a brief resume of the cabinet decision. As a result, Hudson's main worry is behind him and you will find he no longer bears any resentment at BOAC's early thoughts on this matter. Another Solent arrived yesterday and he now feels he has his immedaite fleet position in hand — with a little time ahead to consider the complete re-equipment problem. . . I detect an almost marked lack of enthusiasm for the Comet 2. I should say that Hudson Fysh is resigned to the [Comet] proposition but from C. O. Turner I believe we must expect opposition . . . I firmly believe Turner will do his utmost to acquire more Constellations and block the Comet deal if he can use his power to do so . . . [51]

Turner and Fysh, with the Constellation battle won, turned their attention briefly to QEA operations in New Guinea. Turner wrote to the director-general of civil aviation on 6 December about the renewal of their contract, pointing out that QEA were experience heavy losses in New Guinea. He asked for a new basis for the contract for the operation of specific services for a period of at least five years.[52] Hudson Fysh wrote to the administrator, Col. J. K. Murray on 18 December that QEA operations in New Guinea now involved very considerable capital investment.

> It seems to me that QEA so far has achieved what the Government and yourself set for us to do in taking our place in your development plans . . . We entered Papua and New Guinea under the policy of one Government and are now faced with carrying on under a different policy which has developed under the present Government, and it is not for me to say which policy is correct. Though we recognise competition is a very good thing in all undertakings where sufficient business exists to enable such competition to produce good results and not bad ones, I doubt if business and air traffic is developed in your Territories to a sufficient degree to warrant competition in operation . . . After all the pioneering work we have done for you in Papua and New Guinea, I can assure you we are facing a difficult prospect indeed . . . it does look as if QEA will have to retrench in New Guinea in some directions . . . Owing to the usual political influences which always cloud the true issues and objectives in these matters, whether a proper rationalisation of the position is possible or not I am not sure.[53]

Colonel Murray responded promptly. "I appreciate very much indeed what Qantas has done for the Territory but I am aware that what is wanted is conditions under which your Company can carry on so that your services will pay . . . You may depend on it that, in any representations made, the invaluable services which your Company has given will not be forgotten."[54]

On the last day of the year, de Havillands issued a release stating that British Commonwealth Pacific Airlines, jointly owned by the governments of Great Britain, Australia, and New Zealand, had announced in Sydney that all government approvals had now been secured for its proposal to purchase six de Havilland Comet 2 jet airliners for its main trans-Pacific services. It was not, of course, an actual order for Comets but it sounded very like it. (John Watkins states that no firm orders were placed for Comets by BCPA. Towards the end of 1952, BCPA was still only "looking hard" at the Comet 2.) British pressure on Australia to buy the Comet had not weakened and QEA's poor opinion of the Comet as a commercially competitive aircraft had not changed.

One Wreath, No Bugle Call
1952

Phillip Hood wrote from Sydney in early January to Sir Miles Thomas that there was even less enthusiasm at Qantas for the Comet than previously reported. The lack of a specification might, he said, have delayed a Qantas order but "this does not seem to have deterred BCPA who have now publicly announced the intended puchase of six Comet 2s". Hood added:

> Confidentially to you, I am somewhat sceptical of QEA sincerity in the Comet 2 participation scheme and I have gone so far as to say that Turner will do all he can to block the deal. His influence (good or bad) with Hudson Fysh is more than considerable but, fortunately, one of the Directors [McVey] is much too strong for them, both in personality and in breadth of vision. That he will eventually force Management into the right decision is reasonably assured . . . BCPA, having its Chairman [Norman Watt] also on the Board of QEA must surely be aware of QEA's cautious approach.[1]

A few days later Hood reported that Turner had criticized the Comet "on almost every possible count, maintained that there would be innumerable modifications and said that it was impossible to put up a case to the management without the serial numbers of the aeroplanes and delivery dates. . . Turner is required to produce a plan for his Board in the next few weeks, therefore it might put him on the spot if it were possible to let him know the number of aeroplanes allocated to QEA and estimated delivery dates."[2]

Turner wrote to Whitney Straight on 11 January that he was preparing a board submission on the case to the Australian government for participation by QEA in the Comet Series 2 development on the Kangaroo Route.

> The delivery dates of aircraft which we can secure will be of great importance. It is disturbing to note that aircraft Nos 38 and 39 have now been allocated to British Commonwealth Pacific Airways, particularly in view of the statement by your Chairman . . . that these arcraft have been earmarked for QEA. QEA are not entirely free agents to order aircraft and we must prove our needs before the Department of Civil Aviation and the Cabinet because it involves Government moneys in the form of capital advances. The fact that BCPA has recently ordered six Comets colours the position because this meant that the Australian Government will be committed for at least 50 per cent of the capital cost of these aircraft, which on our reckoning will be a considerable sum of money. It is therefore essential that we put forward a really good case . . . Undoubtedly our submission will be weakened if we are obliged to state that Comet 2s will be introduced in other parts of the world in preference to what is regarded in Australia as the Main Empire trunk route . . . The order by us of, say, three Comets plus spare engines and spare parts will involve a capital outlay of about £A3 million and request for funds to this extent to our Government will not be very popular just now, particularly since BCPA has ordered six Comets.

Turner himself asked Straight for possible delivery dates and any available information on financing or terms.[3] A few days later, on 22 January, at Hatfield, England, the British minister for civil aviation signed and delivered to de Havillands the formal certificate of airworthiness of the Comet, making British the first country in the world to issue such a certificate for a jet airliner.

Fysh now began to suspect that Turner was ignoring him in some matters of high policy and wrote a terse memo to the general manager. "In regard to 'Participation in Comet 2 Project' as mentioned in your action sheet arising out of the Board meeting last week: this is down for dealing with by the General Manager but, as the subject is a top line one, it should be dealt with by myself." Fysh was also wary of possible moves by the free enterprise federal government, canvassed in the press, to reorganise the government-owned Trans-Australia Airlines and the privately owned Australian National Airways in a way that might threaten QEA. He wrote to the director-general of civil aviation on this and on the threat from BCPA, saying that it seemed essential for Qantas's position to be closely watched and protected for the overseas operation. A combination of internal and external aviation would, said Fysh, create an un-

wieldy monopoly. "QEA competition is with foreign operators
and this is so alive that it keeps us efficient. The attitude we
take up is that QEA is your Australian overseas operator carrying the flag of Australia abroad and that, as such, must be fully
supported by Australia . . . We are not satisfied with our position in this respect and see British Commonwealth Pacific Airlines expanding independently, and millions of money being
expended without any consideration of economic objectives as
between the two . . . The position is becoming steadily
worse."[4]

On 21 January, BOAC's Eastern Division director, John
Brancker, wrote to Dan McVey saying that QEA now seemed
to be more enthusiastic about the Comet 2 but that Turner
was implying BOAC was allocating Comets to BCPA that had
been earmarked for Qantas. This was not so, wrote Brancker.
"I am writing to you personally about this particular problem
because I do not want you to feel that we have been unfair to
QEA. We have, in fact, done our best to get them to take an
early decision which they have not done, and the whole time
we have been pointing out that delay in making up their
minds would inevitably leave them at the end of the queue."[5]

By the end of the month, Phillip Hood was able to report
more optimistically to his deputy chairman:

> A fully attended QEA Board Meeting took place on 25 January
> and as a result you may by now have received a note from Hudson
> Fysh containing more satisfactory affirmations on the QEA
> [Comet] participation. Early in the New Year the QEA Manage-
> ment endeavoured unsuccessfully to get Board agreement to defer
> the final decision on Comet 2 for three months . . . However, the
> Directors pressed Hudson Fysh hard — Turner came up with the
> suggestion that BOAC should be asked to hire Comets to QEA
> but the Board firmly rejected the proposal. As a result, the Board
> confirmed unanimously that QEA shall meet its obligations . . .
> Turner was very crestfallen. Mr Hudson Fysh was then asked by
> the Board to write to Sir Miles and say that . . . QEA would like a
> little more time (maybe one to two months) before definitely con-
> firming the proposed purchase of three Comet 2 aircraft.

The source of Hood's information about the details of the QEA
board meeting seemed clear enough. He concluded his confidential memorandum: "Mr McVey is indeed our champion in
this matter and I have been in his confidence completely — as
I am also one of his closest friends."[6]

On the other side of the Australian continent, at 10.00 a.m. on
25 January in Hollywood Hospital near Perth, Western Aust-

ralia, the man whose ability, character, and enthusiasm had persuaded Fergus McMaster to support the foundation in 1920 of Queensland and Northern Territory Aerial Services Limited, died from a heart attack.

Paul McGinness had met Fergus McMaster one hot Sunday afternoon in 1919 in Cloncurry. The former member of the Australian Flying Corps had completed a survey for the Defence Department with Hudson Fysh of an air route between Darwin and Cloncurry for the epic competition, won by Ross and Keith Smith, to be the first to fly from England to Australia; McMaster had been attending a meeting of the Anti Cattle Duffing Association at the Post Office Hotel to thwart the stealing by poddy dodgers of umarked calves. McMaster's car had broken a stub axle crossing the Cloncurry river and McGinness's vigour and alertness in helping repair the car had prepared the ground for McMaster's ready help when McGinness and Hudson Fysh met him again in mid-1920 in Brisbane with proposals to start an aerial service. Paul McGinness stayed with the infant company through the trials and uncertainties of its first two years as it sought and finally obtained a government subsidy to begin regular scheduled services between Charleville and Cloncurry. He flew the opening flight of that service, between Charleville and Longreach, on 2 November 1922 but left Qantas two weeks later.

His reasons for leaving, after achieving the dream that he and Fysh had shared for the creation of a regular air service, were mixed. By temperament he did not accept a board ruling that pilots should "sign the pledge" and abstain completely from alcoholic drinks. He was much more an initiator than an administrator. But, though Fysh wrote that the two never quarrelled, there were growing tensions between them. He was bitter when he left and felt that he had been pushed out of the company.

For a month after his departure, McGinness stayed with relatives on the family property at Framlingham in Victoria (where the family had been amongst the state's earliest settlers). He then joined Clarkson, the man called in to help sell shares in Q.A.N.T.A.S. in Queensland, in a venture in Western Australia to float a primary producers' bank. It opened in Perth's St George's Terrace but quickly failed and was taken over by the state government. (It became the R. and I. Bank.) The local people who invested in the venture lost their money and Clarkson, in disgrace, returned to the east. McGinness, whose people in Victoria had close links with the Country

Party, met Western Australia's minister for agriculture and leader of the state Country Party, Charles Baxter, a member of parliament for thirty-six years. In September 1923 Paul McGinness married Baxter's daughter, Dorothy.

The state government were then resuming parts of big country properties under a scheme to assist returned servicemen settle on the land. McGinness qualified for, and was given, 2,500 acres from Kadji Kadji station, near Pintharooka, north of Morawa, some 280 miles north of Perth. His farm was called "Mount Morawa" and cost two shillings and sixpence an acre. He raised a mortage with the Bank of New South Wales, using his Q.A.N.T.A.S. shares as security, and bought himself two windmills, one tractor, one drill, one harvester, six draft horses, a disc plough, and a second-hand Chevrolet truck. Italians were called in to clear a thousand acres of the land and McGinness began making bricks to build himself a house. It was a modest structure, thirty feet by ten feet with a verandah all round. At the back, and separate from it to create a breezeway, was a ten foot by five foot kitchen and bathroom. There was a rainwater tank but the main water supply was pumped from the valley well below, which lay between three hills. Through the pastoral firm of Elder Smith he stocked the property with 2,000 sheep. The airman, whose youth had been spent on a farm, returned to the land. He bought a riding horse, broke it, then bought a second. For his first child, Dorothy Veronica, born in 1925, he bought a Shetland pony. Though it seemed that the restless McGinness was now settled and secure, tragedy lay ahead.

The international economic depression in the early 1930s, coincided with a succession of drought years. In some desperation, McGinness tried searching for gold, specks of which he had seen in the surrounding country. He used an aircraft to carry out what was probably the first aerial mining survey in Australia and marked on a map likely places to exploit. (One of these later became the site of a prosperous gold mine.) He tried to float a company called the Randwick Gold Mine. "He came very close to the edge there", his second daughter, Helen Pauline, said later. "He could have got into serious trouble but someone — I think grandfather Baxter — pulled him out in time." He began to drink heavily, driving from the farm into the local hotel and staying, day after day, into the early hours of the morning. The strains and anxieties of these years told on his marriage and he parted from his wife. The farm failed completely and he was forced to leave it.

In 1936, Paul McGinness returned to the eastern states and tried for a job in aviation. Hudson Fysh could not give him one and Edgar Johnston had no openings at first, but the secretary, Department of Defence, advised McGinness on 27 February 1936 that he had been appointed as temporary caretaker, Western Junction aerodrome, Tasmania. He reported for duty on 2 March. On 10 November he was advised by the secretary of the Civil Aviation Board, that he had been unsuccessful in his application for permanent employment in that position and his services were terminated on 18 November.

Restless, McGinness wrote to a senior member of the Chinese air force, following the Japanese invasion of China, offering his services as a mercenary. On 3 August 1938 McGinness received a letter from C. J. Pao, Chinese consul-general in Australia, that he had been "instructed by my Government to convey to you its sincere appreciation of your offer of service to China in the present crisis". The consul-general advised him "that the situation has not yet matured and therefore your services will not be required for the present".

Throughout this period his health was poor but by 1939, when he returned to stay with his sister, Vera, at the old property at Framlingham, it had improved. When war broke out, McGinness was forty-three and too old for the Air Force. He tried to get a position in the government's recruiting organization, with McMaster supporting and Fysh opposing his efforts. Finally, McGinness put his age down in an application for the RAAF, was accepted, and was posted to New Guinea. There he was recognized by his old commanding officer from World War I, Air Marshal Richard Williams, and was sent back to a training position at Point Cook in Victoria. During those war years he was divorced from his wife, Dorothy, and met and married Rene Searles, whose father owned a prosperous engineering business. In the late 1940s, after serving since 17 December 1942 as station fire officer in New South Wales at Parkes, McGinness received his discharge from the RAAF.*
His restless temperament then took him to the Northern Territory and involvement, with financial help from his wife Rene, in an ambitious scheme to produce and sell frozen beef to Asian markets. When his second marriage failed and his wife withdrew from the scheme, McGinness tried for a time,

---

* His officer's certificate of discharge No. 1286 shows he was commissioned on 1 July 1940 with the rank of flying officer; he held the temporary rank of squadron leader when his services were terminated on 29 January 1945.

unsuccessfully, to grow tobacco in northern Queensland. Defeated again, he finally returned to Western Australia in 1951 to grow tobacco on a soldier settlement farm at North-cliffe, near Albany. By November 1951, due to continued kidney and cardiovascular troubles, he was very sick. He was admitted to Hollywood Hospital for a time, then discharged. His daughter, Pauline, invited him home for Christmas Day and McGinness agreed to come. But she was never to see him alive again.

On Christmas Day, unbeknownst to his family, McGinness was back in hospital. He did not send word to them because he did not want to spoil their day. For a further month he was in hospital, sick but not in any apparent danger; then without warning, he died from a heart attack. On 26 January, the nation celebrated the Australia Day holiday. On 29 January, at Karrakatta cemetery, Perth, he was buried. His coffin was draped with a flag and there was a single wreath from his second wife, Rene. Apart from the priest, only his first wife, Dorothy, and his daughter, Pauline, were present.*

A reporter on the Perth *Daily News*, Lloyd Marshall, heard of his death from a Bob Giles who had been in the bed beside him at Hollywood Hospital when he had died. Marshall wrote in the *Daily News* on 2 February:

> He was buried unhonoured and unsung in a Repatriation Depart-ment grave at Karrakatta last Tuesday . . . At the graveside were merely the padre, the undertaker's representative conducting the funeral and two women. There was only one wreath and its card said simply "Squadron Leader McGinness with love — Rene". There was no bugle at the graveside last Tuesday but two nights later a Qantas Lancastrian roared an unintentional salute as it went above Karrakatta, gaining height for the first courier flight to Cocos.[7]

Marshall had rung the funeral director to ask the identity of the two women but the company told him they could not iden-tify them.[8]

BOAC took delivery of the first of their fleet of Comet airliners on 4 February and it was flown to London airport next day; Fysh wrote to Sir Miles Thomas that he was most anxious to get Qantas into the Comet picture. "We are having temporary

---

* On 29 January 1952 the deputy commissioner of the Repatriation Commission, Western Australian branch, wrote to Mr H. McGinness at Framlingham, Victoria: "It is with heartfelt regret that the Repatriation Commission learns of the decease of your brother, Paul J. McGinness, No 251538, Squadron Leader RAAF, who died in the Repatriation General Hospital, Hollywood, on 25 January 1952."

Qantas Lancastrian VH-EAT parked near the control tower on Cocos Island, early 1952. No. 2 Airfield Construction Squadron, RAAF was responsible for building the 8,000 foot (2,499 m) runway and work began in December 1951. The two Lancastrians VH-EAT and VH-EAU were well suited to landings on the runway in its early stages of construction, carrying mail, fresh food and a small passenger load. DC-4s took over this service when the runway was finished in mid-1952.

difficulties", he said. "The Minister made it plain that an official approach to him at this stage would be unwelcome and embarrassing . . . and he would have no chance of getting it through Cabinet." The order of Comets by BCPA, he said, was taken as an Australian participation in the introduction of the type. It was agreed, wrote Fysh, that the ideal Qantas-BOAC arrangement would be round-the-world parallel operations on the main trunk routes. "It is felt that the position of Tasman Empire Airways is fast becoming untenable . . . and when the large capital required for re-equipment comes up . . . a crisis in the affairs of that Company will have arisen. It does seem that New Zealand has got to be strong enough to operate her own services across the Tasman." On the political tensions inherent in Australia's domestic airline system, he commented: "The betting in the TAA–ANA affair changes almost daily as one plan is discarded for another, the chief suggestion being that the public will not accept the great monopoly . . . which . . . a merger would result in, and following the outstanding success of TAA."[9]

In his diary in February, Fysh reflected on the possible return of a Labor government at the next election and its effect on his own career.

> 1953 looms up as a year leading to a crisis for me personally in 1954 when my QEA appointment is up and must be renewed by a Labor Government, by the look of it; and a reorganisation of Australian airlines is also overdue. For the past year the Liberal Government has only foozeled [sic] round with the thing with the result that Australia has no proper planning for the future. New jet types appearing one after the other. Enormously increasing

capital cost etc. is making operations very difficult. A clean-up of
TEAL and BCPA also very necessary . . . [10]

He expressed some of his feelings in a letter to the minister,
Anthony, writing that he was increasingly apprehensive about
the circumstances for Qantas that prevented essential long-
range planning.

Organisations like BOAC, KLM, Pan American and Air France
all have clear lines of long range planning and have essential aircraft on order. Even BCPA with only a small percentage of the
routes of Qantas operations has six modern aircraft on order
against three for Qantas . . . The other relevent point is that
though many millions is being spent there is no co-ordination
apparent between such concerns as Qantas, BCPA and TEAL,
Australia owning the first and having an interest in the other two.
I am disturbed . . . [11]

Dan McVey, a firm supporter of the Comet and a persuasive
member of the QEA board, expressed his views in a letter to
BOAC's John Brancker, confirming that the Qantas board had

Following the receipt of government approval to purchase
Super Constellations, Qantas
appointed Ron Yates — right —
resident QEA Engineer at
Burbank. This photograph was
taken soon after his arrival as
he toured the factory with
Lockheed sales administrator,
Walt Wayman. The aircraft is
an Eastern Airlines L.1049A
undergoing final checks before
delivery in February 1952.

unanimously agreed that a definite order should be placed for the Comet 2 but that it could not do so yet.

> The reason is that Government approval is a prerequisite to the placing of an order; and while the Minister personally is agreeable to our recommendation on this subject, he has expressed the view that it would be impolitic for him to take the recommendation to Cabinet so soon after the recent submission he was required to make in favour of the purchase of additional Constellation aircraft. As a Board we have no alternative to accepting the Minister's view on the appropriate timing of the submission to Cabinet for the purchase of the Comet 2 aircraft; and it appears unlikely that the necessary Cabinet approval will be forthcoming before April or May.

McVey went on to make a less than loyal comment about Turner. "BCPA, on the other hand, possessed the necessary Government authority to place an order for Comet 2 aircraft and, Turner's views notwithstanding, BCPA were entitled to the consideration they have received at your hands. QEA, in the circumstances, cannot have any legitimate complaint to make, and I am sure the Board of QEA would endorse that view." McVey said he did not doubt that financial authority to purchase the Comet 2 would be forthcoming. "In anticipation of this you may feel impelled to secure for QEA the best place possible in the queue without prejudicing in any way any other Commonwealth airline or imposing any sacrifice on BOAC. This is the most QEA could hope to expect."[12] That BCPA had not placed any firm order for the Comet, despite the authority of the government to do so, and was still far from doing so, was evident in the chairman's address by Norman Watt to the annual general meeting in Sydney as late as November 1952. It said: "The question of ultimate replacement of the Company's existing fleet of four DC-6 aircraft is at present receiving the active consideration of the Board."

The perception by Qantas that their national role extended beyond airline operations into the strategic defence infrastructure had by no means weakened as commercial operations grew. Fysh used this latent — if ill-defined — defence role to seek support for the pressing commercial necessity of fleet expansion. On 9 May he wrote to the chief of Air Staff, Air Marshal J. D. I. Hardman, with details of the capabilities of the Super Constellation 1049C.

> Unfortunately, the Bristol 175 is not fully developed or tested yet and we do not feel, at this stage, that we can hold our horses and burn our other boats and wait for a problematical aircraft in 1956

or 1957 if all goes well with the tests. As you know QEA and Australia are very short of long range aircraft capable of carrying troops or equipment, and as the responsibility falls on QEA to quite an extent for the provisions of this facility, it does seem to be our duty to keep presenting the position to those in authority, despite the dollar shortage. . . Considerating the position of QEA in the RAAF air transport picture, your help and advice would be greatly appreciated.[13]

In a formal report to the minister on "Defence Aspects of the 1049C Project" on 19 May, QEA drew attention to Australia's desperate shortage of long-range aircraft. There were only twenty-eight aircraft in the whole country capable of military use in an emergency: four DC4s of TAA; nine DC4s of ANA; four DC6s of BCPA; six Constellation 749As, and five DC4s of QEA. The submission said that QEA needed to order a further six Constellation 1049C aircraft to meet minimum needs of overseas services in 1954 — in addition to the three machines already on order. These six aircraft would, said Qantas, cost $12 million with spares, and "we submit that there is justification that this be classified as an urgent defence requirement and taken care of in any new dollar loan".[14]

Ministerial authority and pressure were evident in smaller matters. Fysh wrote to QEA director W. C. Taylor in London: "Seeing the Minister yesterday, I gathered he was not entirely happy about two QEA directors being away on trips at the one time and wanted to know what you were both doing. I have also sent him a list of Directors' attendances which shows your own attendance the highest of all. The Minister is sensitive at present and has just not renewed the term of one of the ABC Commissioners."[15] The other director abroad was Dan McVey, who had had his first experience of QEA standards by flying with his wife to London. He wrote to Fysh: "One thing I may emphasise is that those of us on the Board of QEA who have never travelled on QEA service can have no real knowledge of how well organised the Company is and how good is its service. I say this in the hope that all Directors who have not shared my experience will do so as early as possible.

McVey was particularly impressed with the flying personnel.

Whilst on the subject of air crews, I should say that there was very much in my mind during our trip the discussions we have had at recent Board meetings on the remuneration of pilots. These officers of our flying personnel could not, in my judgement, be too well treated in the way of remuneration. Leaving aside the top administration of the Company, the pilots and flying personnel are the people who really earn the Company's revenues and, in the main, ensure financial success of the Company's operations. In a sense, they are all we have to offer in competition with other airline operators. Whatever we do, Hudson, let us not be niggardly in our treatment of their representations for adequate remuneration. Their responsibilities are greater than is generally imagined. The long sectors over which they operate involving successive day and night flying impose upon them considerable physical fatigue which none but men in first class physical and mental condition could endure; and their active flying life is, as you know, a relatively short one. There is to be borne in mind also, the fact that from the viewpoint of domestic circumstances, their wives and families suffer badly by comparison. Our pension fund arrangements I feel may be on the inadequate side and might justifiably be reviewed; and having regard to the high rate of income taxation their net salaries on existing scales are somewhat low. Men in jobs such as these must be remunerated in a way that will relieve them of all financial worry, both present and future, and I suggest it might prove helpful in reaching a satisfactory solution to the problem if a committee of the Board were appointed to assist the management in looking into the whole question and, if necessary, negotiating directly with the Pilots' Association on the claims that have been submitted to the Company. For the Board to leave such an important matter largely in the hands of the Personnel Department and the Management may savour of shirking responsibility . . . [16]

Qantas's aircraft were given a new colour scheme in 1952. The top surface of the fuselage was painted white, the name Qantas Empire Airways was replaced by QANTAS and the thin blue stripe below the cabin windows changed to a dark red band. Constellation *Ross Smith* demonstrates the "new look" over the sea, off Sydney.

This was to become an important issue for Qantas over many years and one which Turner, with his combative temperament, would pursue with both the board and the pilots. Fysh replied: "I do agree they are a fine lot and that we should do all we can for them. The trouble is that they have got unavoid-

ably mixed up with the Australian Airline Pilots Association
on which they are poorly represented."[17]

Fysh visited New Guinea and on his return advised the acting
area manager for New Guinea, Captain Denny, of his impres-
sions. Denny responded that he gathered the drinking habits
of the staff in New Guinea had concerned Fysh. He had had,
he said, a very serious talk with each member of senior staff at
Lae and Port Moresby.

> I have called the Social Committee (who are responsible for the
> operation of the Staff Mess Bar) together and passed on to them
> the seriousness of operating this bar in keeping with our Com-
> pany policy concerning strong drink. In pointing out to the Com-
> mittee that the drinking habits of our staff in Lae must be curtail-
> ed, I ran into a fair amount of opposition and difficulties. Their
> main defence is that surely they are allowed to do what they like
> in their own time . . . Personally, I am inclined to agree that there
> is something in what they say. In view of their outlook on this
> matter I then had to point out to them the seriousness [sic] that the
> Company takes over indulging in strong drink, whether it be in
> their own time or the Company's time and that unless they show-
> ed very strong control of the Bar and drinking in the Mess, I as
> their Area Manager, will have to intervene and, if necessary, with-
> draw the privilege they have been given.

On operational matters, Denny wrote:

> I fully agree that it is imperative for a conference between the
> Department of Civil Aviation, External Territories, New Guinea
> Administration and QEA Management with the idea to establish
> some clear and better understanding of the part that we are to take
> in the development of the country. . . We certainly overdid our
> expansion in New Guinea but I feel that this was brought about
> by a quick and sudden rehabilitation of the Territory.

On the question raised by Fysh of white lap-laps for the native
servants, particularly those who came in contact with passengers, he promised attention as soon as sufficient white material
could be obtained.[18]

As Denny had commented, QEA's expansion in New Guinea
had been substantial since they had been requested in 1947 to
develop air facilities in the territory. There were fourteen aircraft in 1952, controlled from Lae, Port Moresby, and
Madang, that flew regularly to over a hundred places. There
were twenty-six pilots servicing the hazardous network and just
over thirty-five thousand passengers were carried. Although
the Commonwealth paid Qantas £44,000 for their services,

the company still operated there at a loss of £20,000 on a capital investment of some half a million pounds.[19]

QEA route expansion, increased aircraft utilization, and aircraft conversion work had raised staff numbers at Mascot to a level that could not — as conversion work tailed off and the company found revenue falling while costs increased — be sustained. The efficiency yardstick of capacity ton miles produced per employee was also declining. As a consequence the company now banned recruitment of new staff and implemented a programme to reduce staff in all departments by five per cent. Fysh told the minister that staff to be retrenched would be those considered least efficient by those in charge of their sections. Notices were served to about sixty employees on 27 May, twenty-eight of whom worked at the Mascot hangars. The following day there was a mass meeting of employees at Mascot and overtime bans were imposed. Two days later, at a further mass meeting attended by four hundred employees (but ignored by a further one thousand), a resolution was passed that notices of termination would not be accepted. Fysh advised the minister: "The present trouble at the Mascot Hangars is the culmination of a long record of industrial dispute led by a communist element. . . The moderate unions are on the side of the Company . . . Every possible action must be taken in future to try and eliminate this dangerous and disruptive element".[20]

Norman Watt congratulated Fysh on the way in which the reasons for staff dismissals had been presented.

> The employees themselves couldn't reasonably object to reduction of staff corresponding to the flattening out of the work load [he wrote]. It is now a year since Mr Chifley died and I am reminded of his strongly held views on this problem, that in a democracy things must be settled by the people themselves — and that this principle applies equally to the domestic affairs of the Unions. So . . . the job is to educate the rank and file of the Unions to manage their own affairs and to trust to their native good sense to put the trouble makers out.

Though fleet re-equipment, the particular problems in New Guinea, and industrial unrest at Mascot were preoccupations, there were other issues of importance. One concerned the level of mail rates paid that directly influenced the company's profitability. Fysh wrote to McVey:

> What we are going all out for now is the 3.99 gold franc (per tonne-kilometre) rate to line up with the BOAC rate. Anything

less than what we ask will place us in financial difficulty this year, and more so next year when the South African Service has to be reckoned on — and the introduction of new Services such as the Tourist Services, which look certain to become so popular that public demand will oblige us to act earlier than expected. The attitude of the Treasury on our mail rate has been very tough, and along the lines that we do not get a penny more than what is recovered from air mail surcharges. This is a fine thing to aim at but rarely achieved by any international operating company. If it were adhered to, then we would need special assistance for services such as to South Africa. The Minister has announced that the South African service is to open on 1 September . . . [21]

Fysh was also concerned with impending pilot shortages, and wrote to the director-general of civil aviation:

From 1953 onwards, particularly with the extra personnel needed to man the Constellation 1049Cs, there is a very definite problem confronting us . . . At the present time we are endeavouring to

Perth, 2 September 1952. H. L. Anthony, Minister for Civil Aviation, with his wife by his side arrives at Perth airport on the inaugural Qantas Constellation service between Australia and South Africa.

During the stopover in Perth of Constellation *Charles Kingsford Smith* operating the inaugural Australia–South Africa service, the Speedpak was loaded with fresh and frozen food for Cocos Island, 2 September 1952. During the refuelling stop at Cocos, the Speedpak was removed and it remained on the island while the aircraft flew on to Johannesburg. The empty container was taken back to Perth on the return flight and the process repeated on the next service. Compare the "1947 style" markings on the Speedpak with the new ones on VH-EAD.

help ourselves with a Cadet Pilot Scheme but this is really inadequate to meet our future needs . . . I am quite sure that the other major airlines, TAA, ANA and BCPA, have a similar realisation of the position in Australia today. There would seem full justification for the establishment of a central Flight Training School sponsored by the Federal Government and run by your Department to supply the right type of trained aircrew personnel to the air transport industry.[22]

On 1 September 1952 the inaugural QEA flight for South Africa was farewelled from Sydney by the postmaster general and minister for civil aviation. It flew via Melbourne, where the minister for territories, Paul Hasluck, and Air Marshal Williams joined the aircraft, the Constellation *Charles Kingsford Smith*. The route then took them to Perth, Cocos (where QEA had a staff of fourteen), and Mauritius before their uneventful arrival at Johannesburg on 4 September, a total distance of 8,705 miles in a flying time of thirty-nine hours seventeen minutes. The new route was to be known as the

Wallaby Service. It was important in political and strategic terms but initially attracted low traffic density and, without a subsidy on the mail rate, sustained regular losses.

On the day of inauguration of the new service, Anthony wrote to Fysh on matters of more economic weight. Following discussions in Canberra among representatives of the United Kingdom, New Zealand, and Australian governments, he said, "reference was made to proposals by BOAC to introduce tourist class air services to Australia early in 1953 and to initiate steps to increase substantially the fares on the normal Kangaroo Service at about the same time". The minister obviously envisaged political problems, telling Fysh that QEA should not enter into any commitment without his prior approval.[23] At that same Canberra meeting, Australia and the United Kingdom agreed that drastic changes were needed on the Pacific route. The meeting recorded: "The most effective way of promoting community of interests between Kangaroo Route and Pacific–Atlantic operations would be to entrust the responsibility to one operator. It seemed logical, therefore, that QEA should assume both operational and financial responsibility for the Pacific section of the Pacific–Atlantic route, thereby obviating government grants to this operation."[24] Two and a half years after the QEA board, on 20 April 1950, had formally proposed to T. W. White that they should take over BCPA, there was at last a more hopeful initiative.

At a meeting with Edgar Johnston on 10 September, Turner discussed at length the problem of valuing BCPA's assets. QEA, he said, did not consider the BCPA aircraft worth a million pounds each. The proper way to value them was to calculate a future value for 1954–55 when the introduction of new 1049C aircraft would have relegated them to tourist operations and add the amount that could, in the meantime, be reasonably written off. Turner also considered that the BCPA order for six Comet 2s should be cancelled. (It was not, in fact, a formal order.) QEA, he said, planned to put 1049Cs on the Pacific early in 1954 as an essential move to compete with the DC6Bs of Pan American and Canadian Pacific. Turner strongly criticized TEAL's proposals to order the Bristol 175 as a flying boat replacement in 1955. It would, he said, be financial suicide to accept the Bristols before 1958 as the aircraft were unlikely to be fully developed before then. Johnston agreed that TEAL's only hope of remaining solvent was to maintain a monopoly of the Tasman route until it acquired modern aircraft.[25]

329

H. L. Anthony had formal discussions in London in September with the British government on the two issues of British Commonwealth Pacific Airlines and Tasman Empire Airways Limited. In BCPA Australia had half the capital, New Zealand thirty per cent, and the United Kingdom twenty per cent; in TEAL, New Zealand had fifty per cent, Australia thirty per cent, and the United Kingdom twenty per cent. The time had come to review these arrangements, Anthony told a press conference at Australia House, London, on 25 September. BOAC was proposing to begin operations across the United States between New York and San Francisco and, by linking with the BCPA Pacific service to Australia, operate a round-the-world British route. In his London talks about possible changes to shareholdings in BCPA and TEAL no decisions had been taken, said Anthony; the matter remained fluid. He told the press that he had also discussed the BOAC–QEA parallel partnership of the Kangaroo Route where an important source of revenue came from mail. Readjustments in mail payments had been raised but, he emphasized, there would not be increases in airmail fees to the public.

Anthony reminded the press that although BOAC had US transit rights, Australia did not. The US sector of any round-the-world route would have to be operated by BOAC. Statements about an amalgamation of QEA and BCPA were, he said, premature. Questioned about aircraft types, the minister referred to an "order" by BCPA for six Comet 2s and by QEA for three Constellation 1049Cs for 1954 delivery. Britannias were under consideration for the TEAL service.

The questioning shifted abruptly from aviation. "Is television any closer for Australia?" he was asked. "It is closer than it was", he replied.

"Will it be operating in time for the Royal Tour?"

"I cannot say."

"In time for the Olympic Games?"

"All I can say is I am giving it careful study. I think that television is inescapable but I also feel that it ought to be severely limited in hours."

"You feel that its social effects have to be watched?"

"The Archbishop of Canterbury and Clement Attlee both made statements to that effect this week."

The Qantas attitude towards the Pacific service was set down in a briefing for the minister at the London talks. Possible alterations in the operation of BCPA and TEAL had been, until now, a matter between governments. QEA had not finalized detailed views but had confined themselves to showing, at the request of the Department of Civil Aviation, that there could be considerable operational savings, and capital savings over a period of years. How such a service would operate, said the brief, was now being discussed with the chairman of BOAC. QEA felt it was essential that there be changes in the organization of BCPA and TEAL to allow Australia full control of the large amounts of capital that would be required, as well as due control over revenue and expenditure and future expansion. QEA, operating from Sydney to San Francisco, would link with a BOAC service between London and San Francisco. QEA would absorb BCPA staff, take over their aircraft, and continue operating without dislocation. The brief was firmly against the inclusion of Australian National Airways in any future reorganization. Difficulties were recognized for New Zealand but it was felt she was being given a great deal if the existing monopoly across the Tasman were confirmed.[26]

In a further memorandum from Fysh to the acting minister (Senator G. McLeay) on the impending eighteenth annual general meeting of QEA, set down for 29 September, he was reminded that QEA

is, of course, wholly owned by the Commonwealth, the shares being held by: Hudson Fysh, chairman and managing director, one share; C. O. Turner, general manager, one share; N. Hay, secretary, one share; W. C. Taylor, director, one share; D. McVey, director, one share; G. P. N. Watt, director, one share; Sir Keith Smith director, one share. [The remainder of the shares were held by the Commonwealth of Australia.] Accordingly you would be entitled to attend the Annual General Meeting and vote . . . but some years ago one of your predecessors authorised certain of the Directors of the Company to vote on behalf of the Commonwealth and that authority still stands.

The eighteenth annual report, said Fysh, revealed a gross profit of £373,205. "This is, I believe, a record profit but, contrary to practice over the last few years, the Directors are not proposing to declare a dividend but are proposing to appropriate the money to various reserves and carry forward the remainder." In recent years, he said, the company had declared a five per cent dividend on subscribed share capital which would, in the current yuear, have absorbed £125,000 of the profit made.

It is normal practice for Commonwealth instrumentalities to pay dividends on money subscribed by the Commonwealth or, in the case of Trans-Australia Airlines, to pay interest on advances made, where the profit allows this. . . In the case of QEA the Company operates under a Financial Directive which requires the declaration of dividends when the profit position so allows and I am of the opinion that, before the Directors' Report is adopted by the Annual General Meeting, you would want to know and consider the reasons for the Directors' action in this particular case in failing to declare a dividend and in so doing appear to ignore the provisions of the Financial Directive. Accordingly I have prepared an appropriate letter to the Company . . . for your signature. The letter provides for the suspension of the authority which had been given to exercise your vote.

The Treasury, Fysh added, had expressed the view that QEA had not observed the terms of the financial directive. The letter prepared by QEA for the minister's signature said that the ministerial proxy dated 24 July 1947 "is hereby formally suspended . . . I assume that the Directors had regard to the provisions of paragraphs 18 and 19 of the Financial Directive issued to the Board of Directors in May, 1949". It was, in effect, a letter prepared by Qantas requiring an explanation by Qantas of their action.[27]

The issue was an important one, involving, in the words of N. H. Hay, acting secretary of QEA, "an initial bid to obtain a clarification of the powers of the Directors under the Financial Directive".[28] W. C. Taylor formally replied for Qantas to this ministerial letter, which they had themselves drafted, on 16 October. The directors, it said, "are, and always have been, fully conscious of the obligations which the Financial Directive imposes upon them . . . In this particular instance, however, there has admittedly been an omission to place before you earlier the reasons which prompted the Directors to reach the decision they did. Indeed, viewed in retrospect, it would have been better if the decision had been taken after consultation with you."

The issue of mail rate payments was brought into the argument. Taylor wrote that although profit for the 1951 financial year had been substantial, the position for 1952 was uncertain because

no agreement had been reached with the Commonwealth Government on the rate to be paid for the carriage of mail, notwithstanding the provisions of the Financial Directive that contract arrangements with the Commonwealth Government should be agreed prior to 1 January 1952. The Directors were impelled to take into effect the added fact that, although the Company had applied to the Commonwealth Government for additional capital provisions in the budget to the extent of £1,000,000, advice had been received from the Treasury that no budgetary provision was being made for such extra capital. Those two factors created for the Directors problems of grave financial concern.

Taylor honed the QEA argument more finely. The company, he said, had requested agreement on mail payment rates in December 1951 but

> finalisation of the arrangement apparently depends upon discussions only now taking place between the Minister and the Ministry of Civil Aviation in the United Kingdom [which] illustrates the uncertain financial position in which the Company has been placed. As a result, although nine months of the year 1952 have now passed, the Directors are unable to say with any degree of accuracy whether over this period the Company's operations have resulted in a profit or a loss.

If the 1951 mail rates were applied to 1952 there would, he said, be a substantial loss.

> The Directors trust . . . you will be able to share their view that the passing of a dividend in respect of 1951 is justified, notwithstanding the substantial profit earned in that year . . . the sole purpose of the Directors is to safeguard the Commonwealth Government's investment in the Company . . . The Directors . . . feel their responsibilities more keenly and are anxious to observe both the spirit and the letter of the Financial Directive in the carrying out of their functions.[29]

Turner prepared a brief for directors for an anticipated discussion with the minister on financial matters. The Department of Civil Aviation and Treasury, wrote Turner, "seek to deny Qantas £113,000 of mail payment for 1951 . . . The Directors claim that the £113,000 is legitimate Company revenue as it arises directly from an agreed increase in the pooling rate from 1.47 gold francs per tonne kilometre to 2.43 under our partnership agreement with BOAC. The Commonwealth Treasury is not called upon", he pointed out, "to pay any part of the amount from consolidated revenue." QEA, said Turner, had no alternative but to ask for an increase in mail rates. The airmail rates paid to other international operators were generally much higher than those requested by Qantas.[30] Combined with the pressing need for fleet expansion, the financial problems caused by government delay in agreeing mail rates greatly concerned both board and management.

> Information received [from the director-general] indicates that decisions may take more time [Fysh wrote to Taylor]. Such decisions may involve the discussion of wider QEA problems and considerable delay could result. For instance, a discussion on the 1953 mail rate will involve the operations to South Africa . . . Our

New Guinea operations and Pacific considerations could also come up — and all of these matters then become involved in QEA capital requirements and new aircraft. It is agreed that the first matter to be settled is the 1951 and 1952 mail payments and dividend . . . [31]

On Sunday 26 October 1952 the BOAC Comet C-ALYZ crashed on take-off at Rome but no passenger or crew member was injured (though every seat was occupied) and there was no fire. Though de Havillands, in a letter to Qantas, said that it was not for them at the present stage of inquiries to discuss the cause of the crash, they pointed out that the tail of the aircraft had made contact with the ground some distance before the runway end was reached on take-off, that the aircraft had then swerved or drifted to the left, and that the tailplane and port wing had hit the airfield boundary lights "which, at Ciampino, are mounted on concrete posts". The letter stressed that the chief inspector of accidents of the British Ministry of Civil Aviation had issued a statement saying that the mishap was not caused by any failure or malfunctioning of the aircraft or its engines. It seemed clear that there had been over-rotation of the aircraft by the pilot as it lifted from the runway.

A few days later, Sir Miles Thomas wrote to Sir George Cribbett at the British Ministry of Civil Aviation on Hudson Fysh's attitude to British aircraft as reported in the press after his return to Australia from the London talks. "It strikes me as being rather lukewarm . . . We must have this attitude of his in mind, I think, in considering forward Antipodean planning."[32] Cribbett responded promptly: "Obscurantists seem to have one thing in common with inebriates and pessimists", he wrote. "They are all incurable. As you know, we have firmly stipulated in our discussions as part of the round-the-world route proposal, that any successor to BCPA must assume their liability to purchase Comets. I think we all know that Hudson is temperamentally incapable of much enthusiasm, but I think he might endeavour occasionally to lash himself into a little for the benefit of sterling if not for the sake of Commonwealth sentiment."[33]

Cribbett had every reason to believe that an Australian businessman with Hudson Fysh's background of service would regard Commonwealth sentiment as paramount in such important matters for Britain as the commercial future of her aircraft industry; the success of the Comet was central to this future.

The British were accustomed to Australian expression of commitment to Britain and the Commonwealth at the highest levels. The leader of the Country Party, McEwen, had encapsulated these attitudes in the Parliament's debate on ratification of the charter of the United Nations in 1949. Our safety and our destiny, he said, lay in our membership of the British Commonwealth and our strength was the total strength of the British Commonwealth.[35] In that same debate McEwen pointed out that the Australian ministerial title "minister for external affairs" was not "foreign minister", indicating that the duties involved were mainly concerned with Australia's relations with the United Kingdom and other dominions; that the development by Australia of a separate foreign policy would weaken the British Commonwealth as a whole.[36]

When P. C. Spender had reviewed the foreign policy of the new Menzies government in March 1950, he had emphasized the closest co-operation with the British Commonwealth, especially Britain. (Spender was later to become president of the International Court of Justice at The Hague; he was appointed to Washington in March 1951 and was succeeded by R. G. Casey, who held the external affairs portfolio for ten years.) He had added, however, that co-operation was also important with the United States, as the greatest Pacific power. "Indeed, as far as possible," he had said, "it is our objective to build up with the United States somewhat the same relationship as exists within the British Commonwealth."[37] These emerging sentiments did not disturb the deep-seated British feeling that, in John Curtin's words to a dinner at Greenwich in 1944, "seven million Australians were seven million Britishers".[38] Even the signing and ratification by 1952 of the ANZUS Treaty, though it was resented by some in Britain because it excluded the United Kingdom from what was a military alliance by Australia with a foreign country, did not shake traditional British attitudes. Britain had seen a Labor prime minister, Chifley, make a gift of £25 million to help Britain with her balance of payments in March 1947. Labor, under Chifley, had ensured that Australia had done its bit to conserve dollar funds on behalf of the Commonwealth and help maintain the strength of sterling as an international currency.[39] Above all, Britain heard the compelling oratory of R. G. Menzies expressing his faith in the British Commonwealth. British knights at the Ministry of Supply and at the head of BOAC, as well as the leaders of the British aircraft industry, had good reason to feel puzzled, and even betrayed, as Australia's chosen instrument in international air transport looked with ever-increasing pragmatism towards the United States for their airliners.

On 12 November 1952, the first Super Constellation powered by the new Turbo-Compound engines made its maiden flight from Burbank. The new engines could develop 3,250bhp for take-off compared to the 2,800bhp of the 1049A Super Constellation. The US Navy had priority on deliveries of the Turbo-Compound but during the test programme of the new model (designated the R7V-1) representatives of airlines who had ordered the 1049C were permitted to fly on board and assess the performance. Capt. R. J. Ritchie, Qantas Controller of Technical Development, took the opportunity to fly the R7V during a visit to Burbank in December 1952. From left: Ron Yates of Qantas, Glen Waring of Lockheed, Capt. Ritchie, and Ted Cloherty of Qantas.

Fysh had visited the main aircraft manufacturers in both England and the United States, with the notable exception of Boeing. On his return he reported that the Avon-engined Comet 2 had not come up to expectations in range and speed because of additional weight, higher fuel consumption, and some loss of performance as a result of the Avon installation itself. "It is now admitted by de Havillands that this aircraft, the prototype of which is flying, will not carry its stated pay-load of 13,500 pounds on stages up to 2,500 miles. The Comet 3 is the main centre of interest . . . The power plant will be the Rolls-Royce Conway engine giving 9,000 pounds thrust against 6,500 for the Avon." Nevertheless, wrote Fysh, "public demand to fly Comet is striking enough in Australia but is overwhelming abroad, and will undoubtedly continue to grow unless such misfortune as a series of accidents should occur to the Comet". (Pan American announced on 20 October that it would exercise its option to buy three Comet 3 series

for delivery in 1956.) QEA, wrote Fysh, could not get delivery for any Comet 3 order before 1957. "My main doubt about the Comet 3 is in regard to the length of runway required . . . The type deserves serious consideration."

Fysh also visited Vickers–Armstrongs (Aircraft) at Weybridge where it was intended to fly a prototype of a commercial version of the Valiant bomber by 1954. He did not recommend that QEA should consider it. At Bristol he found that the Proteus 3 version of the Bristol 175, expected to fly in 1953, looked promising but undeveloped. "Providing the development of the Proteus 3 is satisfactory, the aeroplane (at £650,000 sterling) appears a cheap buy and to have outstanding advantages in regard to economy." In New York Fysh noted that at Curtiss Wright "it was admitted as elsewhere in the United States that British jet development was well ahead". At Burbank he regarded the Constellation 1049C as "a lifesaver for us over the years 1954-55-56 and thereafter for some years . . . for tourist traffic, though a close analysis should be made in comparison with the Bristol 175". Both Lockheed and Douglas, he wrote, had each "got out a preliminary suggestion for a straight jet type". It was, he summarized, a difficult transition period with a continuing high rate of aircraft development. The straight jet versus turboprop issue had not been resolved, though the premier public demand was for 500 miles per hour travel. "The problem of QEA action is closely identified with Pacific operations and can only be considered jointly if economic operation is to result. The Australian operator, working in conjunction with BOAC, should have two types: a straight jet [with] consideration given the Comet 3. An intermediate stage would be joining with BOAC in Comet 2 operations; plus continuance with the Constellation 1049C type for the present [with] a close watch on Bristol 175 development.[40]

Fysh made it clear that his comments were superficial and subject to critical analysis by QEA technical experts. The formal Qantas position was put to the minister in a submission on aircraft requirements on 11 December, following a meeting between the minister and QEA directors on 1 December. At that meeting reference was made to discussions in April 1952 when directors had submitted a memorandum requesting that QEA should be permitted to order six additional Constellation 1049Cs and three Comet 2s. At that prior meeting the minister had asked that any official submission for new aircraft be withheld until the then plans for rationalization of the services of

Trans-Australia Airlines and Australian National Airways had been considered and provision made for the aircraft requirements of the internal operators. "Recently," said the QEA submission of 11 December, "Parliament has passed legislation providing funds for purchase of equipment for the Internal airlines, and the Directors therefore feel that consideration should be given as a matter of urgency to the provision of equipment for Australia's International air services." Pending finalization of plans for the reorganization of Pacific services, QEA urgently required that minimum steps be taken to protect their forward position.

The minister's approval was sought to trade in QEA's six existing Constellation 749As for six Constellation 1049Cs, at a net cost estimated at between £9 million and £11 million. Payment arrangements proposed by QEA allowed the aircraft to pay for themselves over a four-year period as they were operated and there would be no call on the government for additional capital to buy the aircraft. (QEA did still require £3 million in additional capital to finance the current order for three Constellation 1049Cs, already approved by the government.) Delivery dates for the proposed new order were two aircraft for December 1954, two in January 1955, and two in February. "The Directors desire to state that they realise we must get back as soon as we are able to the operation of British aircraft on Commonwealth routes in co-operation with BOAC. We believe we have done everything practicable to support the United Kingdom . . . " The paper said that QEA could not proceed with the former proposal to order three Comet 2s. Guaranteed performance data were not yet available and QEA had to take into account the BCPA commitment to Comets in the light of the proposed rationalization of the Pacific services. The Bristol 175 (Britannia) was not, in the view of QEA, available for the period 1954–58 and its success was dependent on the development of an entirely new propeller turbine engine, the Proteus 3. The submission concluded: "The Directors recognise that this is a very difficult problem for the Government in view of the shortage of dollar currency and the general pressure that Australia should get back to the operation of British aircraft. However . . . failure to secure more modern equipment may well mean that eclipse of Qantas Empire Airways as an International operator in the years from 1954 to 1958."[41] (The QEA fleet in December 1952 consisted of six 749A Constellations, five Skymaster DC4s, thirteen

Douglas DC3s, four DHA3 Drovers, five DH84 Dragons, four Sandringham and four Catalina flying boats.)

QEA's general attitude towards aircraft replacement and joint operations with their United Kingdom partner was analysed critically by Phillip Hood only days after this official submission.

Hudson Fysh [wrote Hood] becomes daily more dominated by Turner who, with his clear and determined mind, seems to be assuming his Managing Director's position. The Board meetings themselves are better described as Management Committees where most of the agenda items are supported by reports not previously approved by the management for submission to the Board. McVey and W. C. Taylor are exasperated, Sir Keith Smith contributes little or is absent on Vicker's affairs, while G. P. N. Watt is generally watchful of his own interests in BCPA. McVey particularly understands the need for decisions and would like to correspond with you more often but finds this difficult out of loyalty to Hudson Fysh.

In recent weeks, there has been a meeting on the subject of aircraft with Mr Anthony who is really a sick man and has many worries on his mind, such as television. After a few hours at the meeting, I was told by somebody present, that Mr Anthony seemed unable to cope with the subject matter. The Government as such seems overburdened with major problems and is almost apathetic towards aviation — the general view is that the Government would give much to get out of civil aviation and turn it over to private enterprise. This view should perhaps exclude the Prime Minister who appears alive to the necessity for strength and backing. He has a coalition, however, and is not his own master.

BCPA's intentions to purchase British aircraft, and wavering by QEA, has led to intense activity by Lockheeds. You may know that this Company has submitted a well prepared plan whereby QEA's existing fleet of six 749 Constellations would be turned in against the purchase, for sterling, of a similar number of 1049s.

Turner and Allan, then, have been successful in keeping alive the acquisition of more 1049s and, although my information is that the scheme described above cannot go through, persistence may win the day. QEA continues to plan on the assumption that orders placed by BCPA will be inherited but at the same time reckoning that the fleet of DC6s might be divided up between TEAL and, say, TAA.

This matter has been discussed with Mr McVey and we both feel this is the moment for a vigorous approach to QEA ... McVey will be backing an immediate approach to BOAC and/or the British Industry for Comets and Britannias but, naturally, his name must not be connected with matters discussed in this memo.[42]

It was a perceptive analysis from BOAC's point of view, and

an unusual liaison for a director of Qantas to sustain with such a flow of confidential information on matters of high policy.

Hood wrote a corporate report to BOAC on the same day on southwest Pacific affairs. Turner and Allan, he wrote, continue to advocate the purchase of more Constellations. "Maybe they are nervous of supporting jets in the knowledge that Mr Hudson Fysh is himself apprehensive although, at the same time, he is not backward in reproving them if the full facts about British aircraft are not brought out." Turner and Allan were, in fact, in a fully reciprocated relationship of professional trust and respect. Turner's "clear and determined mind", so perceptively described by Hood, recognized Captain Allan's capacity for technical detail and logical analysis and was, increasingly, to find him a capable and dispassionate executive in all matters relating to aircraft evaluation. Allan, in turn, respected with at least as much fervour Turner's extraordinary abilities in matters of high policy and finance.[43]

Hood ended his report by noting that there was serious indecision in the QEA board and management and that a firm request from BOAC, as partners, on future plans might help clear the air and obtain some decision. "As BOAC Representative," he wrote, "I have done my best in this matter but it will be appreciated there must be a limit to my activities short of plain interference."[44]

Hood's memorandum to his chairman found its way swiftly to the Ministry of Civil Aviation. Sir George Cribbett thanked Sir Miles Thomas for it and commented on 31 December: "This memorandum confirms the suspicion some of us have always held about the predilection of Turner and Allan for American aircraft. Both are forceful personalities and I fear that Hudson Fysh and the Board of QEA will have increasing difficulty in controlling them." It was, in relation to Hudson Fysh's growing problems with his brilliant and single-minded general manager, a most perceptive comment.[45]

Our Own Interests 1953

On 1 January 1953, Sir Miles Thomas moved to force Qantas to a decision on the Comet. He told Sir George Cribbett at the Ministry of Civil Aviation that instructions had been given for QEA to be told BOAC had definitely decided to run Comet 2s on the Kangaroo Route in mid-1954 and that the 749 Constellations would be withdrawn as Comet capacity was introduced and converted to tourist configuration. QEA was also to be told that BOAC would introduce Britannias on the Kangaroo Route in tourist configuration when they were available. "This definite proposal by BOAC", wrote Sir Miles, "will, I hope, bring to an end the shadow boxing that has gone on far too long."[1]

Miles Thomas wrote a personal letter to Dan McVey that same day outlining his plans. McVey responded promptly on 8 January.

> I cannot fault your proposals from BOAC's point of view. Already the Comet service from Singapore to London is evoking praise from those Australians who have travelled on it. The 1049 cannot, in my judgment, hope to compete against the Comet 2 for first class passenger traffic. QEA must acquire Comet 2s for the Kangaroo service . . . It may assist you if I relate the view I advocated a little over a week ago in Hudson Fysh's office — with Fysh, Taylor and myself the only Directors present and Turner and Allan in attendance — and which received acceptance as a framework within which the Management might present their proposals for full Board consideration on Friday next.

QEA, said McVey, "had better give up any thought of purchasing any more dollar aircraft, for the reason that we are not

15

likely to have dollars provided for them, and also because the public will travel in the Comet 2''. In stating QEA's aircraft needs to the government, "QEA should not attempt to take into account at the present juncture any probable Government decisions in respect of BCPA, and TEAL likely to favour QEA with additional aircraft, either existing or on order''. QEA also "must reach an early decision to purchase Comet 2 aircraft, and also get in the queue for Comet 3s". McVey also advocated that "QEA should give up thought of replacing 749s with 1049s and must reach a decision on the replacement of 749s with a British type". He said that these views were strongly supported by W. C. Taylor and finally accepted by Hudson Fysh "as a direction to the Management for the preparation of the statement which is to be submitted to the Board on Friday 16 January".[2] The phrase "as a direction to the Management" was a significant one. Both Turner and Allan opposed the purchase of the Comet 2.

McVey's letter to Sir Miles Thomas was yet another confirmation of his intimate and direct relationship with BOAC on matters of high QEA policy. McVey discussed his letter with Phillip Hood, who wrote to his chairman on 9 January:

> I have talked to Sir Keith Smith (without mention of your correspondence with Mr McVey) and he will support your proposals, as also will W. C. Taylor. In Melbourne a few days ago, Mr G. P. N. Watt told me that BOAC and the British should leave Australia alone to work out aircraft requirements. His attitude is very civil service conscience and, altogether, I think he is quietly sabotaging the Cribbett plan. . . In view of the suggestion in 1951 that the UK had officially intervened in the matter of Comets for QEA may I suggest your proposals to QEA are clearly limited to the partnership route . . . I mention this matter again because it is of a sensitive nature here.[3]

Hood's close relationship with McVey enabled him to inform BOAC on 16 January of the result of the special QEA board meeting that had met that day.

> I am advising you immediately on the main features of the decisions taken, which are very satisfactory and are as follows: 1. Recommendations to purchase two Comet 2s for parallel operation with BOAC on the first class Kangaroo service. 2. The use of three Constellation 1049s as a tourist aircraft as soon as delivered to QEA. 3. Trading in of the existing six Constellation 749s in exchange for four 1049s . . . 4. To make a letter of intent in about a year's time to buy some long fuselage Britannias . . . You will be glad to hear that these decisions were unanimous . . . May I ask that you treat this information in the strictest confidence and

make sure that your approach to QEA does not lead them to sup-
pose that we have prior information on their intentions.[4]

Hudson Fysh, unaware that one of his directors had made
the board decision known to BOAC, wrote to Sir Miles
Thomas on 19 January outlining them. Before his letter arrived in London, Miles Thomas wrote to him on 21 January setting out the BOAC decisions that he had communicated to
Cribbett at the beginning of the month. His letter concluded:
"My suggestions about equipment are, of course, specifically
limited to the partnership route." Phillip Hood's briefing had
been noted. Meanwhile, McVey's correspondence had been
passed on by Sir Miles Thomas to Sir George Cribbett, who
commented on 30 January in acknowledgment: "I agree he
has the right ideas and it is a comforting thought that he is a
friend at court to hold in check the pro-American school of
thought in the management."[5] It appeared that the various
pressures brought to bear by the British had been successful in
confounding what Cribbett saw as "the pro-American school
of thought" but which really constituted the view of Qantas
management under Turner.

The insensitive attempts by the British government to pressure Qantas (by direct correspondence with the Australian
government) into a Comet order was now followed by a clumsy
initiative from BOAC — the unilateral introduction of tourist
fares that threatened Qantas profitability on the Kangaroo
Route. Fare levels, unlike aircraft selection, were matters that
required approval by governments when international routes
were involved; BOAC chose to regard the routes as cabotage
traffic (because they were between British territories) rather
than international routes and took action on its own authority.
A row erupted.

Hudson Fysh had had prolonged discussions with BOAC on
the introduction of tourist fares which Edgar Johnston had
summarized in a cable to the Department of Civil Aviation
from London on 10 October 1952. Qantas, he said, regarded
the introduction of tourist services as inevitable but, "on
account of domestic problems, would prefer to delay their
introduction on the Kangaroo route until 1954". BOAC had
told Fysh that they planned to introduce tourist services at
least as far as Singapore in April 1953. (Estimates showed that
for a combined, Argonaut-DC4 operation through Singapore
on a twice-weekly basis there would be an annual loss of
£213,000, half of which would, under the partnership, be
attributed to Qantas. QEA argued through Turner that BOAC

343

fixed charges such as obsolescence and administration should be excluded and so allow an actual, though small, profit on direct expenditure.) The IATA conference in Cannes, Johnston informed his director-general, "has tentatively agreed on the introduction of tourist class services ... [between] Europe, the Far East and Australia from April 1954" though BOAC had reserved the right to introduce them earlier on an end-to-end basis between London, Singapore, and Hong Kong on the grounds that (these being British territories) this was cabotage traffic. QEA considered that these BOAC tourist class services between London and Singapore would seriously affect the Kangaroo partnership revenue by diverting traffic from the Kangaroo services to the tourist services, and Johnston urged representations from the Australian government to the United Kingdom government.

Despite the Australian concern at the highest level, BOAC announced to the British press on 14 January 1953 — without clearance from their own Ministry of Civil Aviation — the introduction of tourist services to Singapore and Hong Kong from April. The Australian minister officially protested to Alan Lennox-Boyd, the British minister, by telegram. Sir George Cribbett immediately wrote a private and confidential letter to Edgar Johnston:

> The plain truth is that the whole affair is as shattering to us as it must have been to you. We had naturally been expecting a proposal from BOAC if these fares were to be introduced and, after considering them, we should naturally have referred to you. Actually, we were informed at quite junior level on the night of 13 January that the introduction of these tourist services would be included in the general press statement on the introduction of tourist fares to be released on the following morning. By the time this came to notice at a higher level on the morning of 14 January, the release to the home and foreign press had been made and we could not retrieve the situation.
>
> You will naturally ask how this could have happened if the Ministry had the Corporation under proper control. It is due to an unfortunate weakness in the Air Corporations Act which defines the powers of the Minister in relation to the Corporations. There is no specific provision for ministerial approval of fares charged ... but we have hitherto relied on our indirect powers of subsidy control. Since BOAC has ceased to have Exchequeur grants our position has become, to put it no higher, doubtful ... No difficulty arises, of course, on services governed by bilaterial agreements because all fares, as you know, are subject by international treaty to the approval of governments. The problem is really confined to cabotage services ... I need hardly say that a protest in the strongest terms was immediately sent to BOAC and

they have been told to discuss with QEA all practical measures to minimise any effect on the partnership . . . In fairness to Miles Thomas I should explain that he is away in Central Africa.[6]

The first Turbo-Compound engined Super Constellation built for civilian use, the Model 1049C, made its first flight on 17 February 1952. It is seen here during a test flight off the Californian coast; some of the test equipment on board can be seen through the forward windows.

It now appeared that, following British pressures and despite British heavy handedness, Qantas were moving towards acceptance of British jet and turboprop aircraft. Turner wrote to Fysh about the possibility of his accepting a directorship of BCPA and the problem of rationalizing (BCPA and QEA) Comet operations for Australia.*

> The consideration by Qantas and BCPA of separate Comet proposals is obviously wrong in that both companies are likely to end up with heavy losses . . . our approach should now be that QEA should take over the operations of the BCPA routes, under charter to BCPA as a holding company, and the first steps towards achieving this could be worked out through operation of the Comets. It would be an obvious advantage for QEA to hold the Australian Government's shareholding in BCPA as we do in TEAL . . . However, the position now appears that BCPA might make heavy losses, which may be embarrassing for us to provide for, having the present attitude of the Treasury in mind . . . The fact that one of our Board is appointed by the Australian Government to represent the Australian interest in BCPA is the really important point and indicates that the Australian Government's views are already clear that the Pacific and Kangaroo routes should be operated by one Company, but that BCPA as such might have to be carried on for some time until the political position can be cleared.[7]

Fysh also informed St Barbe at de Havillands that there was a proposal before the government that the two Comets held in QEA's name should be taken up. St Barbe extended the option

---

* Fysh was appointed to the BCPA board on 11 June 1953.

date on the aircraft from 31 March to 15 April, writing: "There is no need for me to say that there are several operators anxious to secure advantageous delivery dates, but that we continue to regard Qantas as of the first importance."[8] (Sir Miles had already announced that as "a gesture of friendship" and to help the British aircraft industry in its export drive, it had offered to let QEA have six of the Bristol Britannia airliners on order for BOAC, and to make a similar concession to Pan American with three Comet 3s from the corporation's order.)

Fysh responded to the extended de Havilland option, telling St Barbe he saw little hope of being able to issue a firm order by 15 May, and that he could not "press you to keep open the advantageous delivery position".[9] Phillip Hood did not share Turner's view that Fysh supported the Comet and opposed the technical judgment of Scottie Allan. He wrote to his chairman that

> Hudson Fysh is still apprehensive of the Comet 2 and the recent Comet 1 disaster has really alarmed him. Briefly, he puts his faith in Allan's judgment . . . I heard recently of the possibility of your accompanying the first Comet flight to Tokyo. As you are possibly the only person with the ability to quieten Hudson's fears and urge some action from him, I considered inducing him to meet you somewhere en route. McVey thought the idea sound and prompted Hudson to do so . . . Hudson Fysh is clearly in a hesitant mood and needs to be straightened up before Turner, Allan etc get a further opportunity to swing him away from the agreed Kangaroo plans.[10]

Turner, in fact, was now able to write (with evident satisfaction) to Keith Granville, sales director of BOAC (and later their chairman): "Mr Fysh will be writing Sir Miles telling him of the Government's official reply that our proposals to purchase two Comets must await the clarification of the BCPA position. I think the Minister and our Department of Civil Aviation feel the operation of the Comets on the Pacific is not nearly as clear as it should be and that it may turn out that three will provide far too much first class capacity for the Pacific . . . "[11] Fysh confirmed that "our proposed order of two Comet 2s is not progressing very well" in a letter to Miles Thomas on 9 April. (His meeting with Sir Miles, planned by Hood, did not take place. Sir Miles did not travel on the opening Comet service to Tokyo.) Fysh wrote that approval had been given for QEA to give a letter of intent to order six Bristol 175 aircraft with long fuselages but that any really early decision about the problems of BCPA seemed unlikely. "If

346

this is so it may be some time before we can progress our order
. . . Another point that has arisen is that our proposal to purchase two Comets was placed before our Government with the
suggestion that the aircraft could be integrated and operated as
part of the BOAC fleet on order . . . but from our talks with
Granville we now understand that it would not be possible for
us to integrate our fleet with yours."[12]

While Turner and Allan opposed the purchase of Comets,
they were also aware that the Proteus engine of the Bristol
Britannia was having problems. These problems were referred
to with some acidity in the British weekly, the *Economist*, on
4 April 1953.

> The history of the Proteus engine . . . is fortunately not typical of
> all aero-engine development. The cost of most developmental
> work in the aircraft industry is financed by the Ministry of Supply,
> and the average cost of developing an aero-engine, in these days,
> can be put very roughly at £4 million. By the end of March last
> year, nearly £10 million had been spent on the Proteus project,
> and more than £13 million may have been spent before it is com-
> pleted. The Bristol Aeroplane Company began work in 1944 on
> the Proteus as a turboprop engine for long range operation. It was
> intended to build first a low-powered pilot design (the Theseus)
> and follow this with a full scale engine of 4,000 to 5,000 horse-
> power. The probable cost of developing these engines was expect-
> ed to be rather less than £500,000; they were to power those two
> flying dinosaurs, the Brabazon airliner and the Princess flying
> boat. The engine was not developed as successfully or as speedily
> as was necessary and although this was not the main reason for the
> eventual abandonment of the Brabazon and Princess, it was a con-
> tributing factor . . . The engine now under development, the Pro-
> teus 3, uses a different type of compressor and is for all practical
> purposes a new engine. But a further £3 to £4 million may have
> been spent in addition to the £10 million already accounted for
> before the Proteus 3 is ready for commercial operation in Bristol's
> Britannia airliner in 1955. The cost to the public of developing
> the Brabazon, the Princess and their engines has been probably
> around £30 million, all of it a total loss . . . This is a prolonged
> and expensive way of buying experience. It raises the question
> whether, in such cases, another company fresh to the problems
> might not more profitably be given an opportunity to try its hand
> at projects that have already baffled one group of designers.[13]

Turner had prepared a proposal in March for the trade-in of
QEA's six Constellation 749As and spares for four additional
Super Constellation 1049Es. Qantas already had on order, he
wrote, three 1049Cs for delivery in early 1954 but would have
great difficulty in operating a mixed fleet. The disposal prices
of the older 749As would be high. No additional dollar outlay

was required and Qantas were able to finance the proposed purchase without further capital. "This action", he argued, "will protect the Commonwealth dollar investment because the new Super Constellations will have a good dollar value in 1958 if they are replaced by Britannias."[14] There was a remarkably swift government response. On 23 March Edgar Johnston advised QEA that the minister authorized immediate completion of negotiations for the proposal with the Lockheed Corporation. On the further elements in Turner's aircraft programme relating to British aircraft, Johnston advised that "the Minister decided that consideration of the purchase of Comets must stand over until decision is reached on the proposals in regard to the future of BCPA. However, the Minister has approved the proposal to give a letter of intent to order six Bristol Britannia aircraft, with the lengthened fuselage, on the understanding that this does not constitute a definite commitment to purchase Britannias."[15] Roland Wilson, secretary of the Treasury, wrote to Turner the following day confirming the approval of the Treasurer.[16] Fysh reminded Johnston, however, that if government approval was given for the purchase of two Comet 2s, additional capital finance of £2 million would be required, either by capital subscription from the government or through an extension of the QEA overdraft.[17] In fact, QEA management, on the basis of a Traffic Department analysis, preferred to hire Comet 2 capacity from BOAC as QEA's actual requirement in 1955 showed the need for only one first-class Comet service weekly.

A board memorandum from Turner stated that if BOAC were unable to agree to the proposal for hiring Comet 2s and pressed Qantas to buy them, then the recommendation would be to buy two aircraft on condition that they were operated in pool with them, and that BOAC would absorb any surplus capacity.[18] Traffic Department estimates showed tourist passengers would exceed first-class passengers from the beginning of 1955 by seven to one. Large economic aircraft would be required to carry them and to transport the bulk of mails and cargo.

> We could not reckon with confidence on having the Bristol 175 with the lengthened fuselage available for operation before 1958 and the critical years for which we must provide for further equipment [said the board paper] are 1955, 1956 and 1957 . . . Our analysis shows that in 1955 we need a minimum of seven Constellation 1049Cs, increasing to eight in 1956 and nine in 1957 . . . and we should therefore place orders for at least a fur-

During the Coronation Year, Qantas Constellations were decorated with a commemorative badge. This photograph was taken at Singapore, probably about April or May 1953 judging by the BOAC Argonaut in the background. BOAC began tourist services between UK and Singapore in April 1953.

ther four Constellation 1049Cs for delivery at the end of 1954 to meet our minimum need . . . In the event of disposing of the seven Constellation 1049Cs when the Bristols are available, these aircraft will have a potential dollar value very much in excess of the total net dollar outlay required to cover the current transaction.

The board paper said that the short fuselage Bristols (which BOAC were willing to forego in favour of Qantas) showed no economic improvement on the Constellation 1049C and that though delivery would be twelve months earlier, they had a new engine liable to costly teething troubles. "The Management considers, however, that subject to the engine being proved in actual operation over a period, the Bristol 175 with lengthened fuselage, will be an economic aircraft and meet competition on tourist and freight services over our routes from 1958 onward."[19] Qantas, it seemed, would again become a customer for British aircraft.

At that period the turboprop Bristol Britannia, though slipping in the time scale, was becoming a serious challenger — even in the eyes of Sir Miles Thomas — to the pure jet airliner. Though its planned cruising speed, 450 miles per hour, was 100 miles per hour less than that of pure jet airliners, he believed that with more powerful and economic turbines, the

Britannia could fly London–Japan over the edge of the Arctic in only two stages and to New York or Johannesburg in only one. "Present evidence", he wrote, "is that the so-called propeller is likely to be a good friend to airmen for years to come if only because it gives faster acceleration and can be used as a brake."[20] Despite the emergence of an impressive swept-wing jet design from Boeing, with its engines suspended from the wing on pods for easy access and a projected all-up weight of 85 tons, Britain's jet and turboprop aircraft had a time lead that looked promising for Britain's resurgence as a supplier of long-range airliners for international operations. The Avon-engined Comet, in production at de Havillands (BOAC had ordered twelve), had sparked enthusiasm — even elation — within the British aircraft industry for its prospects. The take-off crash at Rome was not blamed on the aircraft itself but was seen as a result of the excessive tail-down attitude of the aircraft as it rotated to leave the runway.

On 2 May, however, one year after the inaugural BOAC Comet service to Johannesburg, Comet G-ALYV crashed near Calcutta, killing all forty-three on board. Six minutes after take-off there had been a last radio message that said "climbing on track". The wreckage was found twenty-two miles northwest of the airport. Evidence pointed to structural failure but not necessarily to any fault in design or construction. A court of investigation reported that the failure of the airframe had been caused either by severe gusts during a thunderstorm or overcontrol or loss of control by the pilot when flying through the thunderstorm. The court recommended a detailed technical examination to establish the primary failure and consider if any modifications were needed. There was no recommendation to ground the Comet as a type. Less than two months later, the Queen Mother and Princess Margaret flew by Comet to Salisbury in southern Rhodesia. Its passenger appeal was unabated and loads on other Comet services remained high.

Both the Rome and Calcutta accidents had pointed to possible pilot difficulties in flying the Comet. QEA's London manager, Capt. L. R. Ambrose, flew on a six-hour test of the Avon-engined Comet on 8 September (the first high-level, prolonged test flight) and confirmed that from the pilot's point of view the Comet differed from other airliners. In charge of that flight was BOAC's Comet flight superintendent, Captain Cane, who, said Ambrose, was very frank in his comments. Ambrose reported Cane's actual words: " 'It is a beautiful aircraft to handle, but unforgiving. Where one can get away with a foolish mistake in an orthodox aircraft, it is seldom possible to do this in a Comet.'" Cane's attitude, he said, was that he "felt justified in asking for above average pilots, but he was convinced that the younger pilots, raised in Comet techniques, could quite safely be of average standard as they would be unaware of the older technique, which tended to introduce some confusion of mind and the possibility of mistakes".

In the Queen's Coronation Honours List, Hudson Fysh received a knighthood for his long services to aviation. Staff members of Qantas gave a dinner in Sydney on 28 July 1953 at the Wentworth Hotel to celebrate the occasion. Fysh prepared a long address ("Personally and confidentially distributed to those attending the dinner in grateful thanks", said the title page.) In it he referred to the six years since the introduction of Constellations as "the complexity period" and paid a handsome tribute to C.O. Turner. The period that commenced with the operation of modern aircraft saw, he wrote,

> the rise of an important group in Qantas; a group of top officials organised by and under the General Manager. These are the organisers and the drafters, the initiators and indeed the Brains Trust, and unsung backroom boys who are doing great work today. But it is of your General Manager that I particularly want to speak. It is said that in time of necessity the hour always produces the man. At least this is true of successful organisations, and Qantas has been successful. Cedric Turner is a man of great brilliance, determination and ambition. He has burst fully into the Qantas picture after many years of good work, just at a time when he was wanted, and perhaps no one is in a better position than myself to realise the work he is doing . . . The General Manager is doing work which is not recognised yet outside the Company as it should be . . . No tougher man than he when inefficiency lurks about, he supports to the full merit and efficiency . . . and never takes a mean or small attitude.

On himself, Fysh said:

> I regret that I continue to be the centre of great publicity . . . Quite a few people have asked me why I have been so successful . . . Material success and success in the eyes of the public perhaps, yes to a degree, but while riding that tiger called "Qantas" I have not had time to dismount awhile and think as I should on the things that matter most. Religion and ethics, for instance. What is truth? I am still not sure yet . . . Yet these things mean more to me in the possible attaining of them than any material reward. These were the principles taught me in youth. Through illness, I had a very poor schooling and was not educated for a professional career; but as a contra I did have a good character training . . .

351

Qantas, said Fysh reminiscing,

> in its whole long thirty-three years has always stood, and I mean
> really stood, for all those things on which is built a house which
> will last and weather the storm. When the gale blows and the
> house bends over a bit it is the foundations which count. Charac-
> er, reputation, loyalty, confidence, honesty and all those sorts of
> things.[21]

The future of the Tasman and Pacific routes was as pressing
and as important a problem for Qantas in the closing months
of 1953 as the future composition of the aircraft fleet. Discussions on these routes in Christchurch, New Zealand, among
the British, New Zealand, and Australian governments in October had ended with the decision that, the Australian government having taken over the QEA shareholding in TEAL, it
should be owned equally by Australia and New Zealand, with
the aircraft being based in New Zealand. (TEAL was also to
take over BCPA's four DC6s; two weeks after the Christchurch conference one of these aircraft, RMA *Resolution*,
crashed into the hills on its approach to San Francisco airport,
killing all on board.)

Fysh, however, was concerned that there had been no com-
prehensive and authoritative statement on BCPA and the
Pacific route and he expressed concern in a letter to Anthony
on 21 October.

> The long protracted consideration of these problems, extending
> now for over a year, has created a very undesirable state of uncer-
> tainty and unrest in the organisations concerned . . . Much of our
> forward planning of services has been held up awaiting the
> Governments' decisions. For instance, consideration of the QEA–
> BOAC programmes for partnership operations in 1954–55, inclu-
> ding introduction of Comet 2 aircraft and the operation of tourist
> services, has been delayed for some months, while forward plann-
> ing for both BCPA and TEAL has stopped altogether.

Fysh set down the Qantas view on these problems.

> We believe that it is essential to the future development of Austra-
> lia's overseas air services that the operator of the service between
> Australia and the UK [via India] should also control the service
> across the Pacific to the United States . . . We believe that the
> development of these services should be by QEA as the Australian
> operator in partnership with BOAC as the United Kingdom
> operator. It is our understanding that the responsible Minister in
> the United Kingdom Government and the Board and Executives
> of BOAC all share the above view.

Fysh detailed the argument for QEA control of trans-Pacific

services. The existing three-government control would be eliminated; it would allow for an all-British round-the-world service; competition between Commonwealth-owned airlines would be eliminated and a combined front presented to Pan American, KLM, and other large foreign operators; substantial savings in overhead costs would be achieved, converting the existing BCPA loss into a profit; there would be no QEA call for further capital other than the takeover of Australia's share of the assets of BCPA.

> We believe that Australia's primary object must be to obtain control of the Pacific air service and that the trans-Tasman services could continue to be operated from New Zealand, but with landplanes replacing flying boats . . . The proposals that are being put forward as an alternative — i.e. to merge BCPA and TEAL — would, we believe be wrong . . .The other alternative — to do nothing — is equally untenable . . . [The working of the interlocking boards] particularly as between QEA and BCPA, has reached a most embarrassing stage . . . which can only result in inefficiency and injury to either one or the other or both organisations. Your invaluable leadership in this matter is greatly appreciated . . . [22]

Edgar Johnston was addressing problems of a different kind concerning the trans-Tasman route. The government of the United States was pressuring the Australian government on behalf of Pan American World Airways for access to traffic between Auckland and Sydney. A Mr Peck of the US Civil Aeronautics Bureau had discussions with Johnston "as a representative of his Government representing informally his Government's view with the object of ascertaining informally from the Australian Government its attitude towards the representations made".[23] Peck told Johnston "that if we were not prepared to accept his representations on an informal basis, the US Government would take the procedural steps necessary under the consultations provisions of the US–Australia Air Transport Agreement to place the matter before us on a formal basis".[24]

In his talks with Johnston, Peck expressed "the serious concern of the State Department and the CAB at the inequity for the US operator of the route situation at the southern end of the trans-Pacific route". Tasman Empire Airways, Peck claimed, was no longer dependent for its existence on the Auckland–Sydney service and the granting of traffic rights to a US operator on this route would not injure its economics. The weekly frequency contemplated by Pan American would take no more than two to three per cent of the traffic presently carried by TEAL. Trunk operators through Auckland, Peck argued, would tend to increase the amount of traffic between New Zealand and Australia and TEAL would possibly gain from this.

Edgar Johnston's reply was that TEAL was not necessarily better able now to withstand competition than it had been in 1946. He reviewed the history of the US request for rights, made formally in March 1951 by a note from the State Department to the Australian Embassy in Washington, and reminded Peck that in Australia's formal reply it had agreed to the US proposal to include Auckland subject to the US operator carrying no local traffic between Australia and New Zealand. In the Australian government's opinion, there were good grounds for believing that Pan American was already carrying excessive amounts of fifth freedom traffic to and from Australia and that the inclusion of Auckland would simply increase this.

> I summed up the Australian position [wrote Johnston] as I saw it by saying that the Australian Government's policy was one of trying to protect our own interests particularly in relation to traffic between Australia and our near neighbour New Zealand ... I stated that at the time the US–Australia Agreement was negotiated in 1946 the US was left in no doubt as to our position and that I was unaware of any circumstances which would cause the Government to take a different view ... I reminded Mr Peck, however, that at the present time the Governments concerned were making an examination of the overall situation of air transport services in the Pacific and that as the outcome of this examination could have an effect upon the Government's attitude, it was quite possible that the Australian Government would not wish to commit itself one way or the other until decisions regarding this matter had been taken.

Peck responded that if the US request were rejected "the United States authorities might have to give careful consideration to the operation of the Vancouver–San Francisco segment by the Australian airline and determine to what extent Australian operations on this leg represented something to Australia's advantage for which the United States did not receive a comparable quid pro quo".[25]

It was Edgar Johnston's heavy responsibility in such talks to conserve what, by virtue of her geographical position, were Australia's greatest civil aviation assets — the traffic rights to, from, and through Australia on valuable, long-haul routes. That there were technicalities in the bilateral agreements concerned that were not beyond argument was evident in a letter that Edgar Johnston wrote, as a result of his discussion with Peck, to Sir George Cribbett, on 11 November. The Americans have, he said,

> from time to time been nibbling at the New Zealand–Australia traffic and have on two occasions recently . . . endeavoured to talk us into giving them full traffic rights between Australia and New Zealand on Pan American's trans-Pacific service. In accordance with the policy which has been agreed between Australia, the United Kingdom and New Zealand for a number of years we have resisted the United States approaches. During the talks which Peck has had with us we got into discussion of the question of the origin and destination of traffic being picked up and set down by Pan American in Australia. During these discussions Peck advanced the theory of what he described as multiple destination traffic. He claimed that the first destination of such traffic was the United States, the second destination was Europe and that as such it represented for the purpose of carriage to the United States — its first destination — third and fourth freedom traffic for the United States carrier . . . I seem to recollect that during your visit to Australia in August last year you made some reference to discussion you had had with the United States people on the question of the origin and destination of traffic and I had an idea that you said that for the purposes of reviewing operations under the Bermuda Agreement you had achieved some working definition of these terms . . . I would be extremely grateful if you would be so good as to let me have the details again.[26]

One year after the announcement by BCPA that all government approvals had been given it to order Comets, chairman Norman Watt wrote, on 22 December, to Air Marshal Williams that at a BCPA board meeting on 17 December it had been decided that the company should proceed with the purchase of three aircraft. "It is felt", he wrote, "that the assurances now obtained [from de Havillands], coupled with our contract guarantee, fully vindicates the opinion previously expressed that the Comet 2 is suitable for operation on the Pacific route."[27]

At the same time, QEA's United Kingdom representative reported that the second Britannia prototype had been test flown on 23 December and was "even better than the first aircraft as regards handling qualities . . . Both Britannias are at present flying and from my office window it is quite a sight to see the aircraft coming in to land at what appears to be an extremely low speed and short landing run." The report said that there was still optimism that the engine (the Proteus type 705) would turn out very satisfactorily and "although faults were still showing up, they are confident with the progress so far. It is well to note that in severe icing conditions the total engine bleed-off of hot air is very large in terms of power. Maximum bleed affects power by as much as 30 per cent . . . Even so, the advantages of full engine bleed for pressurisation and de-icing . . . offset any disadvantage."[28]

Despite Norman Watt's letter to Air Marshal Williams, with its commitment to a Comet fleet and an innovative future, BCPA's days were numbered. In the face of continuous press speculation and what Norman Watt later described as interminable delays, BCPA staff were fearful and looking for other employment. The government of the day was, he said, proud of Qantas and under strong pressure from Hudson Fysh. BCPA staff saw that their own chairman was linked with the wholly owned Australian corporations, QEA and TAA. BCPA was never, wrote Watt, directly consulted by the Commonwealth government in the negotiations that preceded its demise. There was, he said, a fundamental unsoundness in BCPA, with three governments represented on the board yet only one route to operate, and there was a financial unsoundness due to its small fleet of four aircraft, with one or two of them never fully employed, and with no share of the Australia–UK mail. Normal Watt had particular difficulties as chairman of a three-government board which brought him into conflict with H. L. Anthony, to whom he was responsible directly. He also felt deeply about the San Francisco crash and thought it at least partly due to the low staff morale because of constant speculation about BCPA's future (though the Appeal Court in America ultimately absolved BCPA of any blame or failure of efficiency). Finally, wrote Norman Watt, "the national ego centred in Qantas and the far greater strength of the airline at all levels".[29]

At the end of 1953, Qantas had eight Super Constellations on order for delivery in 1954 and early 1955. Its 749 Constellation fleet operated the services to London and Johannesburg. Skymasters flew to Tokyo (both through Manila and Hong Kong), to Lae, and to Norfolk island, and operated a separate service to Singapore. Sandringham flying boats operated to Suva, to Port Moresby, and to Espiritu Santo via Noumea and Vila. The extensive New Guinea network was operated by Douglas DC3s, Drovers, and a Sandringham. The October conference in Christchurch had cleared the way for a rearrangement of national responsibilities on the Pacific route and a great advance in operational reach for Qantas.

Fysh wrote to his general manager on 22 December: "I want to sincerely thank you for the great work you have done and leadership you have displayed in what has been a most diffi-cult year of 'hair trigger' decisions and complicated actions. I hope that in this year the foundations of a wider Qantas have been laid — and you have taken a leading part in it."[30]

Qantas Pacific Inaugural 1954

16 "I do greatly appreciate your letter", Turner replied to Fysh on 4 January 1954, "and may I say too that your helpful advice and guidance have been of great assistance in any success that I achieved last year. I know only too well that running a large airline is a matter of team work and I have been proud to be one of your team."[1]

Privately, Cedric Turner neither appreciated the guidance of his chairman nor enjoyed fulfilment as one of his team. Turner had the habit of writing (to himself) utterly private notes on small, lined cards. One of these cards was headed "Great Fysh Myth", and accused Fysh, in this postwar period, of committing Qantas to the British Tudor 2 aircraft which, noted Turner, took years to overcome.* It said too that Fysh had, initially, lost the Pacific route to BCPA. Fysh, wrote Turner, ignored management on DC4s and "lost millions". He also, in Turner's view, urged the purchase of Comet 2s against the advice of himself and Scottie Allan which "would have spelt disaster".[2]

None of these feelings was evident in the exchange of letters between managing director and general manager, but Turner's comments on the Tudor, the Comet, and the initial operation of the Pacific by BCPA indicate clearly that, at least from the

---

* There is no evidence in correspondence or documents that Fysh *committed* Qantas to the Tudor 2 aircraft. In February 1946, at the QEA meeting with Lord Knollys, Fysh did say that if the Australian and British governments agreed on the use of the Tudor 2s, such a decision would be acceptable to QEA; but he pointed out that because of the superiority of the Constellation, QEA as operators had no alternative but to recommend them to the Australian government.

early postwar years, he saw himself as seriously at oddds with Fysh on major policy matters. Turner's influence in all Qantas matters increased throughout the 1940s, particularly into those years that Hudson Fysh, in his address to staff at the Wentworth Hotel, had revealingly described as the "complexity period".

As World War II ended, Turner and Lester Brain had replaced Harman, under Fysh himself. Captain Ritchie (who was later to become chief executive but had flown on the Perth Colombo service before involvement in the postwar introduction of Lancasters) sympathized with Brain, and later commented:

> Brain was a very sincere man but his ambitions were not of the same consuming passion as Turner's. Turner was a man of great dominance and, coupled with that dominance, dictatorial and pretty sweeping in everything. But also a brain. There was a great deal of animosity — in fact, enmity — between Turner and Fysh. Turner regarded Fysh as a fool. I regarded Fysh as a sincere, well-meaning, highly ethical man. But a simple man, not able to match with scheming people like Turner — and I do not mean that in a derogatory way. He was a general, seeing his way ahead. Fysh had a quality; W. C. Taylor said that Fysh almost destroyed himself about once a year in regard to Canberra. But he managed to hang on in his simplistic, dogmatic, stupid, irrational way. As the knives would start to go in, always he had the ability to pull his head back as the knife went past.

Brain's resignation, to join Trans-Australia Airlines as its first general manager, left the way clear for Turner, said Ritchie.

Norman Watt, chairman of BCPA and a director of QEA, described Hudson Fysh more succinctly: "He was", said Watt, "an able but not a modern man." Ritchie had affection and respect for Fysh but commented: "The grand strategy in Qantas for many years — certainly in the important years — was the brainchild of Cedric Oban Turner. That is the only way to state it."[3]

Turner's affable new year's letter to Hudson Fysh gave no hint of this growing ill-feeling between the two men. He confirmed his strong loyalty to his management team in the face of possible rearrangements after the incorporation of BCPA.

> I am anxious to protect our top team even after we have taken over the BCPA personnel [he wrote], and in order to do this I feel that some reorganisation of our top management should be effected as soon as possible. We do not, of course, want any violent changes but we do not want our key personnel, like Allan, Derham and Ritchie, superseded in seniority by others from

BCPA. Our other problem, particularly in view of the formidable programme we have [1954 included a royal tour by the new queen and a general election] is to relieve me as far as possible of detailed management work and this means strengthening the executive under Allan . . . It looks as if 1954 will be an exciting year![4]

On 10 January 1954, BOAC Comet G-ALYP, flying from Rome to London, disintegrated over the Mediterranean ten miles south of the island of Elba. There were no survivors. On 12 January, BOAC announced that "as a measure of prudence their normal Comet passenger services were being temporarily suspended to enable a minute and unhurried technical examination of every aircraft in their Comet fleet". Fifteen bodies were recovered and a large part of the wreckage eventually located in deep water and shipped to England.

Allan reported on 22 January on possible causes for both the Calcutta and Elba Comet crashes, stressing that these were speculative and based on the newspaper reports of nontechnical observers.

No firm reasons for the Calcutta accident have been announced [he wrote]. Actions taken as a result of [this] accident were the changing of all tailplanes and strengthening of No 7 wing ribs found cracked in most Comets subsequently examined. There is a possibility of similarity between the Calcutta and Elba accidents in that both occurred soon after take-off, during the climb, with empty centre-section tanks and well below full all-up weight. Ground observers reported explosions, fire and breaking up of the aircraft in the air in both cases, and no radio warning was given.

On the Elba accident he commented that

structural failure must be considered as most likely and caused by straight out failure of a part, overstressing of parts by excessive speed, fatigue and failure of a vital part, overloading by excessive control movement . . . The existing Comets are being examined for defects . . . It would not be satisfactory for QEA to accept an edict that as no weakness was found at these examinations, Comets would be certified to fly. Points required by QEA before acquiring Comets would be: a positive reason for the Calcutta and Elba accidents; a proven remedy for the cause or causes.[5]

De Havillands, under immense pressure, tried with some desperation to maintain confidence in the essential integrity of the Comet design. Only eighteen days after the Elba disaster, a private and confidential bulletin was issued to airline operators.

The minute and unhurried examination of the Comets has almost been completed [it said]. The condition of all the aircraft was found to be excellent and no defect of any significance was dis-

360

closed. Bearing in mind that the Comet 1s have flown 30,000 hours in airline service, we feel entitled to conclude that no defect calling for major re-design is likely to exist . . . Meanwhile flight testing of the Series 2 proceeds without diversion . . . You may be glad to know that all the operators who have ordered Comets have maintained encouraging confidence in the aircraft.[6]

Soon after, the other British airliner under consideration by Qantas suffered a dramatic setback. The second prototype of the Bristol Britannia was flying under test at 9,000 feet above cloud when fire broke out in the inner starboard engine. The extinguishing system was operated but proved ineffective. The aircraft headed back at once for the airfield at Filton but, following an electric short circuit, the other three engines stopped. Specialists on board managed to restart two of the engines but the test pilot, A.J. Pegg, decided to attempt an immediate forced landing on the expanse of low-tide mud in the Severn estuary revealed below when they broke cloud. The Britannia landed on its belly with surprisingly little damage and no serious injuries to those on board but the rising tide quickly swamped it. It was recovered the following day but salt water had so damaged the alloy from which it was made that repairs were impossible. Already badly delayed, the Britannia programme had suffered a disastrous setback.

Fysh advised Sir Miles Thomas in January that Qantas had received a request from Israel that one or more of the Kangaroo Route frequencies should call at Lod. "Undoubtedly there would be a considerable amount of traffic between Israel and Australia if the country could attain to a reasonable state of stability and curb the present inflationary costs of accommodation", he wrote. "But even then we would be up against the local currency difficulties and the difficulty of visiting both Jewish and Arab-dominated States on the same schedule." Miles Thomas replied that BOAC had had similar suggestions from Israel from time to time, all of which had been politely turned down. "For the last two years at least," he wrote, "the BOAC once-weekly service has not been justified but we have kept it on because we regard it as an insurance against a flare-up amongst the Arab peoples." There was an unsatisfactory currency situation and restrictive routing regulations imposed on Israeli nationals. "Even with these artificial handicaps to our selling effort we have collected more Israeli money than we can dispose of, even after investing in better premises, Israeli Government bonds and so on. We have therefore put an artificial restriction on the number of seats which may be sold . . . because we are embarrassed by having too much Israeli currency . . . The other problem is . . . the necessity for duplicate passports for crews as neither Israel nor the Arab countries will accept a passport which has been used for other territories . . . It is a confounded nuisance." He did not support any proposal to route a Kangaroo Route frequency through Lod.[7]

On 22 February 1954, the *Sydney Morning Herald* carried a story from their Melbourne correspondent that began: "Strike threats are fairly common in Australia but few people ever expected one from civil airline pilots, who are regarded as among the most conservative and level-headed men in the community." For the first time in its history, the article continued, the Australian Air Pilots Association was taking a ballot of its 850 members on a proposal for direct action to secure salary increases.

The Australian Air Pilots Association had come into being in April 1944 when its predecessor, the Australian Institute of Air Pilots and Navigators, met and decided to change its name and rules. The new body continued its philosophy and aims of maintaining good relations and understanding between pilots and their employers. In 1945 it applied for registration under the Conciliation and Arbitration act. By November 1950, by direct negotiations, an agreement had been reached between Qantas and the AAPA on salaries and working conditions of pilots and this was formally filed under the act on March 1950.[8] But from 1952 the AAPA decided that it should use arbitration, rather than direct negotiations, in its attempts to better pilots' salaries and working conditions, in the belief that it had a strong and persuasive case to put before an independent body with power to arbitrate.

The AAPA asked the public service arbitrator to investigate its case and determine the rates of pay and conditions for pilots employed by TAA, whose employees mostly came under public service awards. This award was then to be used as the basis for an application to a conciliation commissioner for an award to cover pilots employed by all private airlines. It was a time-consuming process for the pilots. Their application was lodged before the public service arbitrator on 12 August 1952. TAA objected but was overruled. On 15 June 1953 the hearing began and it was not until 18 November that a determination was given. A rate of £2,400 was fixed for top captains and

£1,200 for first officers grade three. TAA gave notice that it would appeal to the Full Arbitration Court and when leave to appeal was granted, TAA pilots threatened to strike.

Coinciding with these drawn-out moves since August 1952 had been what Nicholas Blain in *Industrial Relations in the Air* called "an extremely unusual and unexpected strategy" by Qantas to achieve an industry-wide award for pilots (and thwart the AAPA strategy of building on a TAA victory).[9] On 4 September 1952, Qantas served a log of claims on the AAPA and thirteen other operators. A slow, legalistic ritual followed and by 17 December 1953 the High Court made an order absolute prohibiting the conciliation commissioner from proceeding with the Qantas log in respect of other employers.

On 18 December 1953, the AAPA broadened its own action and served a log of claims on all Australian operators other than TAA but, commented Turner in a memorandum to the board on 25 February, "it is significant to note that . . . it has taken no action to refer it into court for hearing and determination".[10] The AAPA, wrote Turner, "has set its course of endeavouring to obtain an award from the Public Service Arbitrator for TAA pilots only". If this were granted "it is our opinion that this will not satisfy the pilots because they are openly stating 'give us this amount to start with', and they are preparing to lodge very much higher demands — in our view out of all proportion to what the Industry can bear." Despite the pilots' threat of direct action to force early agreement, Turner commented: "The Management believes that there is no other course than to channel the awards through the Arbitration Court and that they are taking this action, which is in line with the Board decision of August 1952."[11]

Turner sent a memorandum to all Qantas pilots, outlining the history of the negotiations.

> The facts show [he told them] that the Association has endeavoured to obtain an Award covering pilots of TAA only in a jurisdiction from which all other operators in Australia are excluded. If the Association had endeavoured to obtain an industry-wide award through the one common arbitral channel, i.e. the Commonwealth Court of Conciliation and Arbitration, it is certain that an Award would have been made many months ago . . . The Press has given prominence to statements . . . made by the Manager of the Pilots' Association which have, in effect, said that because of the long delay in having the claims dealt with, the Association was holding a plebiscite among its members to determine whether the law should be obeyed or a strike should be called. I am disturbed by further announcements that the Pilots have voted overwhelm-

ingly in favour of direct action rather than Arbitration and that a Stop-Work Meeting is being held throughout Australia on 17 March 1954 . . . Qantas is endeavouring to make flying an attractive career. While we will do everything possible to further improve both salary and conditions of service, we consider that this can only be done through the processes of the Commonwealth Court of Conciliation and Arbitration . . . [12]

No strike by Qantas pilots eventuated but the pilots' experience of the arbitration and conciliation process between 1952 and 1954 was a bitter and expensive one. The AAPA spent £20,000 on legal fees in a period of over two years, failed in its attempt to gain an award covering TAA pilots specifically, and by December 1954 (when the decision of the court was finally made) was faced with the very industry-wide award that it had fought against. The court rejected the AAPA arguments involving international pilots pay comparisons and handed down a formula basing pilots' salaries on a calculation involving the margins of a metal trades fitter. (The court's award for pay rates to commence in January 1955 was well below that sought by the AAPA more than two years before its August 1952 claim.) The seeds had been sown for increasing pilot militancy, disillusion with the legalistic processes of the Conciliation and Arbitration Commission, and alienation from management.

While the issue of pilots' salaries and conditions was argued with much emotion and media coverage, that of increases for senior executives, including general manager Turner, was raised directly with the minister. These matters had first been raised in August and September of 1953 when Qantas had recommended that the salary of the general manager be increased by £500 to £3,500 per year (with the assistant general manager's rising by £500 to £3,000). The minister had responded that the basic salaries fixed in July 1950 for QEA's general manager "were not only those for your General Manager, but also for the Public Service and Trans-Australia Airlines and other Commonwealth authorities in similar salary ranges — and there have been no alterations since which have not applied also to your Senior Executive Officers". In February 1954, Hudson Fysh asked the minister to reconsider. "It must be emphasised", he wrote, "that the control and organisation of a world-wide Airline, operating as a commercial organisation, are of a particularly complex and specialised nature, demanding management of the highest calibre. If we are to preserve the Company's high reputation for efficent and realiable overseas services in competition with other countries' operators, we feel there is no alternative but to pay them salaries which are reasonably related to the salary levels of commercial organisations in Australia and International Airlines in other countries".[13] While resisting international comparisons for pilots salaries, there was no reluctance in using them to support the case for senior management salary increases.

Overshadowing these ongoing problems in the first months of 1954* were the interlinked issues of BCPA and the Pacific route and the fate of Britain's pioneering jet airliner, the Comet. Both were central to the future of Qantas.

The year had started with a worried letter from Fysh to Miles Thomas lamenting that Qantas was still without a decision on the future of Pacific operations. "This long protracted delay", he wrote, "is proving distressing and injurious in that planning is halted. TEAL do not know whether they are to be or not to be; BCPA is in nothing less than turmoil, and we in QEA are more or less arrested in mid-planning."[14] Sir Miles blamed the New Zealand government. "Future planning between BOAC and QEA is being held up in a most embarrassing manner, due to the delay of New Zealand in coming to a conclusion on the re-arrangement of airline services."[15] Fysh also wrote directly to Prime Minister Menzies, enclosing press clippings from New Zealand that strongly criticized the delay by New Zealand in ratifying the agreement reached at Christchurch on the future of the Pacific and Tasman services. "The long protracted delay has now reached a critical stage for QEA . . . I feel I am only reiterating what you know when I say that Australia gave way to New Zealand in regard to trans-Tasman arrangements. The United Kingdom gave way to New Zealand in that she is accepting an undervaluation of her shareholding in BCPA . . ."[16]

On 10 March 1954 a meeting was held in the hospital bedroom of the minister at Sydney's Royal Prince Alfred Hospital to discuss the reorganization of the Pacific and Tasman services. The director-general of civil aviation, Air Marshal Sir Richard Williams, was present with his deputy, Capt. Edgar Johnston; Sir Hudson Fysh and C. O. Turner represented

---

* A royal tour of Australia by Queen Elizabeth and the Duke of Edinburgh in February and March involved Qantas in four royal flights and was a brief, colourful distraction. Hudson Fysh and Daniel McVey both received their knighthoods from the queen at a ceremony at Government House, Sydney.

Qantas. Norman Watt and Captain Barlow represented BCPA and officers of the Treasury were present. The meeting confirmed that Australia should acquire the UK and New Zealand interests in BCPA and the UK interest in TEAL as from 1 April 1954. It was realized that formalities of transfer of the operating authorities under the agreements with the United States and Canada would probably make it impossible for QEA to operate the Pacific in its own name from 1 April but that BCPA could do so during the interregnum under the general direction of QEA. This arrangement was also seen as facilitating the absorption by QEA of the BCPA staff. The Treasury representatives proposed that BCPA should make a loan to QEA to enable QEA to purchase the UK and New Zealand interests, thus avoiding any immediate call on Treasury funds.[17]

Scottie Allan issued a memorandum to all Qantas staff, setting out the principles for the integration of BCPA staff and operations into the Qantas organization. The Pacific service would, he said, initially operate as a division of QEA with BCPA's general manager, Alec Barlow, heading it. QEA would assume responsibility for the employment of all BCPA staff. All QEA and BCPA staff would have equal opportunity for promotion within QEA.[18]

Two days after the meeting in the minister's hospital room, Sir Miles Thomas cabled Fysh:

> I have just learned through official channels that the Australian Government has withdrawn approval for BCPA to sign the Comet 2 contract and that Qantas regard themselves as no longer committed to the Christchurch agreement to take them over. The UK Government is likely to take a serious view both in relation to the understanding already reached and in relation to the damaging effect on de Havillands of cancellation of the order. Without prejudice to Government views, however, BOAC would be prepared to take over the Comet 2s provided they have the sole responsibility in the Kangaroo Route partnership for the operation of first class services leaving QEA with all tourist class services until BOAC themselves could take over 50 per cent of tourist class services in Britannias. If you agree suggest you still purchase Comets to avoid damage to de Havillands and we will quietly buy them from you before delivery.[19]

In the weeks following the Comet disaster off Elba no indisputable evidence as to the cause of the aircraft's disintegration had been found but BOAC had embarked on a substantial modification programme to its Comet fleet. Armour plate

shields were fitted between the turbine blades area and the
fuel tanks; a modification was made to allow venting to the
outside atmosphere of the battery so that no hydrogen gas
could accumulate; extra fire warning detectors were installed
and extra lightning conductors fitted. Faith in the Comet remained high. It had not been officially grounded by the
British government; it had simply been agreed with the minister, Alan Lennox-Boyd, that the aircraft would be withdrawn
from service.[20] When all these modifications had been completed, BOAC resumed Comet services on 23 March.

From Qantas's viewpoint, however, the clear and logical requirements that Scottie Allan had set down for identification
of specific causes of the Elba crash and for proven remedies
had not been met. Apart from this overriding concern, Allan
had received information from D. H. Wright, QEA's technical
representative in the United Kingdom, on some critical aspects
of handling the aircraft in the air. "The Comet 1 stall is achieved without much warning and accompanied by a bad shudder
and tail buffet", wrote Wright on 23 March. Wright had, he
said, discussed these matters with the Air Registration Board's
chief test pilot, who was "concerned only with the handling
and flying qualities of the aircraft". At critical Mach number
0.77, said Wright, "it noses down with tail buffet and great
care must be taken in handling the controls . . . Although the
take-off with the drooped leading edge type is good, the
absence of an attitude position indicator could cause a stall
after take-off if the nose is pulled up too soon, particularly at
night . . . The aircraft is easy to fly but care must be exercised
at high speed in handling the controls, as the stick movements
are small." On the Comet 2, Wright said that engine acceleration was not yet acceptable and that the aircraft "will stall
without warning". He had criticism also of the Britannia,
reporting that the cockpit view was bad. "In a turn the pilot
cannot see other aircraft on the same level . . . The controls
are too sensitive, the roll is unstable . . . there is slow response
in recovery from turn or roll. Recovery from a 60-degree bank
takes eleven seconds which is two and a half times slower than
other similar type aircraft . . . It stalls without proper warning
(British Aircraft Corporation test pilots report differently).
There is bad aileron control and response in an 'S' turn on the
approach." Wright reported that de Havilland were advising
an upturn in Comet sales.[21]

Qantas were by now, however, firmly embarked on their
Super Constellation fleet programme. A prim note from the

secretary to the Treasury, Roland Wilson, to Turner in March said:

> You are aware that the Commonwealth has negotiated a third dollar loan with the International Bank and that Super Constellations and spares for QEA are included in items of capital equipment to be purchased from the proceeds . . . To avoid any possible misunderstanding, I want to make it quite clear that these loan arrangements in no way affect the obligation assumed by your Company . . . that dollar expenditure on five of the eight Super Constellations on order is to be covered by dollars (a) derived from sale of aircraft and spares owned by the Company and (b) available from its normal annual allocation of dollars for replacement parts. Your Company's undertaking to this effect was an important factor influencing approvals for the last five aircraft given by the Treasurer in March and September 1953, and is expected to be met in full.[22]

Turner had discussions with Sir Miles Thomas in London and reported to Fysh on 8 April:

The christening of Qantas's first L.1049C Super Constellation, Burbank, 29 March 1954. From right: Carl Squier of Lockheed, Sir Percy Spender the Australian Ambassador to Washington, Lady Spender, C. O. Turner and George Christopher of Lockheed.

He has renewed his cable offer to take over our order for three
Comet 2s, providing we agree to operate 1049s on tourist class
services and allow them [BOAC] to operate all the first class services. When I stated that the proposal to confine our operations to
tourist services only would be unacceptable to our Government
from the prestige angle he suggested that we might operate the
aircraft with a "few" first class passengers. In discussing Comet
2s he emphasised the difficulties we would have in operating only
three aircraft . . . He stated that any "politics" involved in regard
to the necessity to support de Havillands could be overcome and
that BOAC would themselves purchase the aircraft . . . It looks as
if Britannias will not be available for operation on tourist services
until about the end of 1956 and BOAC have no intention of putting on tourist services on the route to Australia until these aircraft are available . . . It is obvious that BOAC are desperately
short of aircraft . . . We are starting detailed talks today but it
looks as if we have quite diverse views on not only how the traffic
will flow, but also as to the frequency and the configuration of the
aircraft to be operated . . . I hope everything is going well with
the take-over of BCPA. My trip via the US to London has again
emphasised the tremendous benefit that it will be to QEA to have
a route both ways . . . I mentioned this to Sir Miles Thomas and
expressed the view that every effort should be made to extend
their services to San Francisco. BOAC have apparently no plans
at all to extend beyond Chicago, at which point they have been
granted rights by the US Government. The recent accidents to
Stratocruisers have very considerably depleted their fleet . . . [23]

Turner wrote again on 16 April in a "strictly confidential"
letter, criticizing BOAC's attitude to the Comet crashes.

The general comment in BOAC is that they are "used to this sort
of thing" and it is one more trouble to get over. Granville and
Tate say there is no reason why the trouble should not be found
and in fact might be some minor trouble, and they can then put
the aircraft back into service again! As an approach to what I
regard as a national tragedy it just about takes the bun. BOAC
asked how we could help . . . I told them we could not delay the
Pacific/Tasman operations . . . Basically the problem is to get
more aircraft into the pool . . . Their views on the six 1049s are
that . . . they would be starting a new operation and as they have
Comet 2s coming forward they can't do it. It is a fine example of
putting one's head in the sand and refusing to face facts . . . The
easiest way to handle their problem on a short term basis is to get
more Constellation 749A aircraft into the picture and they are
casting longing eyes at our machines . . . I emphasised that as a
basic policy we were reluctant to dispose of our Constellation 749
fleet until we had properly proved our new Super Constellations.

The BOAC picture, he wrote, was a grim one.

Comets grounded and seventy crews doing nothing. Threats that
they will have to modify and reinstate the Hermes fleet. Atlantic

VH-EAG, Qantas's first Super Constellation moves out from its parking area at Burbank on a crew training flight in early April 1954.

service inadequate with Boeing Stratocruisers becoming outmoded. Shipping companies buying into the Independents and competing for traffic. South American services suspended. No possibility of making any aircraft purchases until Comets are finally proved or disproved — it may take months. South Africa probably will buy 1049Cs and not Comet 2s, after all initial development on Comet 1s. Against all this, the only paying routes are to the Far East and Australia . . . [24]

Preliminary and explanatory discussions were held in Auckland in March and April between the Australian and New Zealand governments on the reorganization of TEAL. Edgar Johnston told the meeting that Australia would purchase the 20 per cent of TEAL's shares held by the United Kingdom in the name of the Australian government and not in the name of QEA. The Australian government, he said, would ultimately own one hundred per cent of British Commonwealth Pacific Airlines and would transfer the residual assets of BCPA to QEA against the issue of new shares. QEA would transfer to the Australian government all their shares in TEAL and the value of these shares would be taken into consideration in assessing the number of shares to be issued by QEA to the Australian government. Johnston explained that licences from the US and Canadian aviation authorities would not be available for QEA by 1 April 1954 and that BCPA would have to continue in the meantime its present schedule of services. It was expected that one DC6 aircraft could be released by 8 May and the other two about the middle of May when the Super Constellations would be available to take over the trans-Pacific service.[25]

370

The Comet 1 would never carry passengers again following the crash off Italy on 9 April 1954. Exhaustive tests proved that metal fatigue was the cause of the disaster on 10 January 1954 and probably caused the subsequent accident. The fuselages of the surviving Comets remained in open storage at the Royal Aircraft Establishment, Farnborough, until the mid 1960s.

On the morning of 9 April the final blow for the Comet 1 and the aspirations of BOAC and de Havillands fell. A Comet with a South African Airways crew took off from Rome for Cairo and crashed into the sea to the east of Italy without survivors. Sir Miles Thomas instructed the BOAC duty room that all Comet services throughout the world were to be grounded. "Our hopes and the panache that we in British Overseas Airways were the proud pioneers of jet-propelled civil aviation had crashed", he wrote. "We had to face up to the reality that we had failed. We simply did not know what was wrong with the Comet. All we knew was that passengers who had entrusted their lives into our hands, together with some skilful crews, had met with appalling disaster . . . In the meantime, we had to keep the Corporation operating."[26]

Without their Comet fleet, BOAC asked Qantas for assistance. Turner, in London, cabled Fysh:

> As a result of the grounding of Comets it is possible that the UK government has already cabled the Australian and New Zealand governments requesting maximum possible assistance. BOAC is now pressing QEA to delay the introduction of the Super Constellation on the Pacific in favour of the Kangaroo route, which would release some of our present Constellation capacity for other work . . . I have emphasised the urgency of QEA commencing its own Pacific operation for competitive and political reasons; also of removing flying-boats from the Tasman. An alternative proposal being considered is the purchase by BOAC of DC-6 aircraft ex-Philippines to be used on Pacific–Tasman operations until the second batch of Super Constellations is obtained . . . I am unwilling to recommend delay in the introduction of Super Constellations on the Pacific if this would prejudice in any way the absorption of BCPA . . . [27]

On 15 April 1954 the first Qantas L1049 Super Constellation

Sleeping accommodation on a Qantas L.1049C operating on the Pacific service. The berths shown were located on the port side of the rear passenger compartment. The passenger entry door was just out of the photograph to the right.

(named *Southern Constellation*) was delivered to Kingsford Smith Airport, Sydney. It was an elegant aircraft with its triple tail and upswept fuselage and impressive in size. With a length of 116 feet 2 inches and a wingspan of 123 feet 5 inches, its four Wright Cyclone TC 18DA turbo-compound engines of 3,250 horsepower each could achieve a cruise speed of 275 miles per hour with a load of from sixty-three to eighty passengers. (Qantas were to acquire a fleet of sixteen of these Super Constellations.)

One week later, Edgar Johnston sent to Qantas a confidential memo from the United Kingdom high commissioner in Canberra addressed to the prime minister "on the matter of BOAC's problems of aircraft availability following the withdrawal from service of the Comets". The official memorandum on behalf of the UK government said:

> It is understood that there has been discussion between British Overseas Airways Corporation and Mr Turner, the general manager of Qantas Empire Airways, regarding the difficulties which are being experienced by the former Company following recent accidents to their aircraft. BOAC have been authorised to purchase

372

one Constellation 749A in the United States to replace [an] aircraft lost at Singapore. [A BOAC Constellation had crashed at
Singapore on 13 March.] They are considering other means of
supplementing their present resources but there will remain a
serious shortage of capacity and to remedy this BOAC have discussed with Mr Turner a proposal that BOAC should take over
from Qantas Empire Airways up to four Constellation 749As as
soon as they can release them. It is understood that QEA consider
that they could make available two Constellation 749As in August
and two in November if they acquired two additional Constellation 1049Cs (which are available in the USA in October). These
additional aircraft would be required only for a temporary period
because they could be sold on the resinstatement of the Comets.

In these circumstances there would be a requirement for dollars
for a temporary period and a postponement of the realisation of
dollars from the delayed disposal of the Constellation 749s. To
meet this the United Kingdom Government would offer to purchase for dollars the four Constellation 749s and their spares with
a view to selling them again (not, of course, to Australia) when the
Comet situation rights itself . . . It will, of course, be appreciated
that the whole arrangement will depend on the readiness of the
Australian Authorities to authorise QEA to purchase two additional Constellation 1049Cs.[28]

Scottie Allan replied to this request for Qantas in a letter the
following day to the director-general of civil aviation. Qantas,
he wrote, could not release the four Constellation 749s to
BOAC to meet immediate traffic demands. "The future of the
Comet must at present be regarded as doubtful and at best the
delivery of three Comet 2s to Qantas, arising from BCPA's
agreement with the de Havilland company, will be delayed —
and this whole project will now be reviewed", he wrote. Two
additional Super Constellation 1049Cs would, he said, help
strengthen and standardize the fleet. "Provided we receive
£2,000,000 as agreed from BCPA's liquidation, and sell four
Constellation 749s to BOAC, we can purchase the additional
Constellation 1049s without further financial assistance from
the Government."

The director-general advised his minister that the board of
Qantas was anxious to help BOAC. Turner had, in fact, proposed selling the whole Qantas fleet of six 749s and all spares
to BOAC at a price of between $10 and $11 million, but had
then reconsidered. Although financially attractive, wrote Williams, it would have left them in a somewhat precarious position for aircraft, at least over the period when Qantas had a
military commitment to Korea. The director-general said that
the purchase of two 1049s "must therefore be regarded as substitution for the Comet 2 for the time being". The purchase of

US 1049s instead of British Comets will, he wrote, "involve dollars and . . . must be regarded as a new dollar commitment" by Qantas. The amount involved for two aircraft and spares was $5 million. "Although QEA will need a dollar allocation (which possibly could be made from dollars secured from the sale of 749s to BOAC) the Company states that it is in a position to provide the finance without calling on the Treasury as the amount would be in substitution, at least temporarily, for the purchase of three Comet 2s and spares at an estimated £A3.3 million." The proposal, he said, would benefit both BOAC and QEA and "substantially strengthen the competitive position of them both in the light of the Comet difficulties".[29] Anthony supported the proposal and telegraphed the prime minister and treasurer: "Matter is urgent since there is a strong world demand for the Constellations and QEA options on two now available expires Saturday."[30]

The Treasury replied that the sale of four Constellations to BOAC for dollars would be contrary to sterling area policy. However, it said:

> The Treasurer raises no objection to the sale of the four aircraft, the transaction at the moment being settled as between QEA and BOAC in sterling in the normal way. The question of subsequent currency adjustments can be looked at when more time is available . . . The Treasurer considers that the purchase of two additional Super Constellations is a separate issue and should be dealt with on its own . . . This will not involve delay in replying to the UK request for assistance to BOAC. The separate question of outlaying an additional $5 million on two further Super Constellations is a major one which must be fully considered even if extension of options is necessary to do so.[31]

Qantas set out their fleet position the following day in a memorandum to the minister. Prior to the BCPA merger, it said, the aircraft position for the Pacific and Kangaroo routes was to be: for the Pacific, three Comet 2s and two DC6s; for the Kangaroo Route, seven Constellation 1049s and two Comet 2s. This made a total of fourteen aircraft. During the merger negotiations, said the memo, it was accepted that the minimum number of aircraft required for the combined Pacific and Kangaroo Routes was three Comet 2s and eight Super Constellation 1049s, totalling eleven aircraft. However, because of the grounding of the Comets the position changed to one of securing two 1049s instead of three Comet 2s, making the total number of aircraft needed for the combined operation ten Constellation 1049s. "We have therefore", said Qantas, "saved substantial investment of capital funds equivalent to a total of four aircraft." The memo said that QEA were prepared to sell four of their 749s provided two 1049s could be purchased. "The remaining two are required to help cover the defence commitment we have to Japan but we would be prepared to dispose of these next year if this commitment is eliminated . . . The sale of four Constellation 749s and spares will, with credits available from our annual spares allocations and from other sales of DC-3s and spares, fully cover our commitment to Treasury to refund $10.5 million on account of the purchase of four 1049s plus spares." Analysis of expected utilization of aircraft, said Qantas, showed very high annual hours from each type (averaging 2,835 hours per aircraft for the 1049s, 3,246 hours for the 749s, and 3,100 for the five DC4s). Qantas stated that total flying hours for 1955 on the Kangaroo Route was calculated at 33,630, requiring a total then of eleven 1049s, each averaging 3,056 hours per year. "The statement of the Qantas dollar position showed that the dollar cost of the eight Super Constellations was covered by Treasury approvals for the first three, DC-6 sales for one, and the sale of four 749s with spares towards four of the 1049s."[32]

On 21 May, with time running short, the director-general made a final effort to persuade the treasurer to allow the purchase of the two Constellations on which Qantas held an option. He sent a long telegram urging reconsideration of their decision "as further extension of option cannot be expected beyond 26 May".[33] On 25 May the treasurer approved that Qantas be authorized to take up the option on two Super Constellations but, with a federal election imminent, that no further or consequential action be taken until the election results were known.[34] It was not a full commitment. Air Marshal Williams tried again. "In our view the UK Government cannot be given unqualified advice regarding the release from Australia of four Constellations whilst there is only qualified [Treasury] approval . . . We cannot therefore agree with your proposed advice and have so informed the Prime Minister's Department. Now that the election results are broadly known, these difficulties can be overcome." (The Menzies government was returned. The bureaucratic battle continued, however, and it was not until 9 June that Cabinet gave its approval.)

Anthony had written to Fysh on 29 April asking him to press on with all details involving the transfer to Qantas of BCPA staff. "I wish you to proceed on the assumption", he wrote, "that all steps necessary as between the Governments of the

The official opening of Qantas's Pacific service Sydney, 15 May 1954. Minister for Civil Aviation, H. L. Anthony is at the microphone on the dais. Mrs Anthony is seated in the front row nearest to her husband; alongside her are Sir Hudson and Lady Fysh and Qantas director G. P. N. Watt.

Mrs Anthony cuts the ceremonial ribbon to send the inaugural Qantas Pacific service on its way from Sydney on 15 May 1954. The Director of Civil Aviation, Sir Richard Williams releases the ribbon attached to *Southern Constellation*, the L.1049 operating the inaugural.

Commonwealth and of the United States of America and Canada will be taken to permit Qantas Empire Airways Ltd to operate the trans-Pacific service in its own name. In the meantime, the name of BCPA is retained only for the purposes of the existing agreements and it should not in any way hold up the process of integration of staffs etc as planned."[35]

To Norman Watt, the minister wrote:

> In case there may be any doubt in the matter, I wish to make it clear at once that there was never any intention on my part that BCPA, whilst continuing to operate the trans-Pacific service in the name of the company for purposes of the existing agreements between the Commonwealth Government and the Governments of the United States and Canada, should continue to be a self-contained organisation as it was previously ... I stress the point that in my view the integration of staffs can proceed and I wish it to do so without regard to the actual name under which the Pacific service continues to be operated.[36]

On the morning of 15 May 1954, in a ceremony at Mascot, the wife of the minister for civil aviation, Mrs Anthony, cut a ribbon to release QEA's *Southern Constellation* for the inaugural Qantas flight across the Pacific. The British Comet, tragically grounded and discredited, was no longer a contender as an international airliner; the Qantas–American link was made with American aircraft. It was a political and operational development of great significance. Acquisition of the Pacific route finally made Qantas the sole overseas operator in which the Australian government held a financial interest (except for the regional trans-Tasman service). It now brought within Qantas's reach the possibility of achieving the vision of around-the-world services as Australia's chosen instrument.

Appendix A

**Financial Directive from the Minister for Civil Aviation
to the Board of Directors of
Qantas Empire Airways Ltd.**

Preamble:

1.   In assuming full ownership of Qantas Empire Airways Ltd., the Government is fully conscious of the value of taking over as a going concern, an efficient established organisation with many years' experience of international air transport, and it is the desire of the Government that there should be as little change as possible in the existing organisation and the managerial and operating practices in existence prior to government ownership.

2.   With Government ownership, the subscribed share capital becomes an investment of public moneys and consequently subject to the various safeguards imposed by the Constitution and Commonwealth legislation in the public interest.

3.   The Board of Directors appointed by the Government is charged with the responsibility of directing the operations of Qantas Empire Airways Ltd. in accordance with the Government's civil aviation policy, as communicated by the Minister from time to time, and also with the responsibility of ensuring the proper use of public moneys invested in the Company.

4.   The object of the following Directive, is to define responsibilities in financial matters and to lay down, for the guidance of the Board, a financial policy approved by the Government, including matters requiring the specific approval of the Minister prior to action being taken.

5.   Within the framework of this Directive, the Board is authorised to direct the affairs of the Company as it thinks fit, with due regard to the practises in existence prior to Government ownership.

378

Provision of Capital:

6. The Commonwealth is the holder of all the issued share capital of the Company, and additional capital requirements will be met by the Commonwealth by subscription to further issues of share capital. In the raising of such additional capital, the Company will observe normal commercial practice with due regard to the correct capitalisation of a business of this nature.

7. Shares in the Company shall not be issued to or transferred to persons or bodies other than the Commonwealth and its nominees.

Borrowing Powers:

8. To meet commitments of a temporary nature, which do not justify an issue of additional share capital, the Company may, subject to such limitations as to amount as may be intimated by the Treasurer from time to time, borrow moneys on overdraft from the Commonwealth Bank of Australia, and the repayment of such loans both as to principal and interest will, if necessary, be guaranteed by the Treasurer. The Company shall not otherwise borrow except with the approval of the Minister.

Powers of Investment:

9. With due regard to the correct capitalisation of the business, any sums in the hands of the Company which are not immediately required for the purposes of its business may be invested in such manner as the Board thinks proper, provided that the total amount so invested shall at no time exceed £500,000 without the specific approval of the Minister.

Revenue and Expenditure:

10. The revenue of the Company shall be obtained from its normal trading activities, including payments either for the carriage of mails or for operation of special services in accordance with contracts entered into with the Department of Civil Aviation, and other Government and non-Government organisations. Contract arrangements with the Commonwealth Government will be agreed prior to commencing services and be subject to review by either side on expiry of stated periods.

11. Any arrangements requiring the pooling of revenue as between the Company and another operator shall be subject to the approval of the Minister.

12. The Company shall charge to revenue in every year all charges which are proper to be made to revenue, including the cost of earning such revenue, adequate provision for depreciation obsolescence and renewal of assets and reserves for outstanding charges.

Reserves and Provisions:

13. The existing General Reserve shall be retained and added to from time to time from the profits of the Company, provided that the total amount in General Reserve shall not at any time exceed 75% of the subscribed capital of the Company, subject to any direction which may be issued by the Minister from time to time.

14. The General Reserve shall be used in the business of the Company, and shall not be set aside in cash.

16. Provisions for obsolescence of aircraft, engines, wireless, stores and spares shall be kept in a separate account, and moneys so recovered may, at the discretion of the Board, be retained and invested in Commonwealth Government Securities pending the replacement of assets.

17. Normal provisions shall be made for taxation.

Profits and Dividends:

18. The profits of the Company in any year, after proper provisions for taxation liabilities, shall be applied as follows:—
   (a) in writing off any accumulated losses brought forward from previous years;
   (b) in payment of dividends to the Commonwealth on subscribed share capital;
   (c) in building up the Company's General Reserve and such other reserves as may be approved by the Minister;
   (d) in making provision for the writing off of subsequent losses;
   (e) any balance not so applied to be carried forward to the balance of Profit and Loss Appropriation Account in the next year.

19. When the profit position of the Company so allows, dividends will be paid each year on the subscribed share capital at such rate as the Directors think fit; provided that every effort shall be made to ensure a return to the Commonwealth equivalent to at least £3.2.6 per cent on Commonwealth moneys invested in the Company. For the purposes of this proviso, the amount invested by the Commonwealth as at the date of this directive is to be regarded as:

   (a) From 1st April, 1947   £ 850,000
   (b) From 1st July, 1948   2,850,000
   (c) From 1st May, 1949   3,750,000

representing the actual cost to the Commonwealth, on an ex-dividend basis, of the purchase of shares in the Company plus new capital subscribed.

Losses:

20. In the event of the operations of the Company showing a loss in any year, such loss will be charged against unappropriated profits from previous years, the resulting balance being carried forward to subsequent years.

21. If at any time the debit balance in the Profit and Loss Appropriation Account exceeds the amount of the General Reserve, the Minister may, on the advice of the Board, recommend to the Government that a deficiency grant be made to the Company.

Financial Year:

22. As from 1st January, 1949, the Company's financial year shall be the calendar year.

Audit:

23. The accounts of the Company shall be subject to inspection and audit by the Auditor-General of the Commonwealth as from 1st January, 1949,

who will report direct to the Minister, but also submit a copy of such report to the Board of Directors.

Programme and Estimates:

24. At least two months prior to the commencement of each Company financial year, the Board shall submit to the Minister:

    (a) A programme of the air transport services which the Company propose to provide during that year and of other activities in which the Company proposes to engage during that year; and

    (b) An estimate of the revenue to be received by the Company during that year and of the expenditure to be incurred by it on revenue accounting during that year; and

    (c) An estimate of expenditure to be incurred and receipts to be derived by the Company during that year on capital account.

Accounts and Annual Report:

25. The Company shall keep its account in such form as is approved by the Treasurer.

26. The Company shall, as soon as possible after the close of each financial year, submit to the Minister an annual report with respect to its operations, and financial accounts in respect of that year.

27. Every effort will be made to have such Annual Report and Financial Accounts completed in time to be laid before both Houses of Parliament prior to the annual Treasury Estimates, normally in September–October of each year.

28. In order that suitable provision may be made in annual Treasury Estimates for additional capital required by the Company during the coming year, the Company shall, prior to 31st May in each year, submit to the Minister an estimate of expenditure to be incurred on capital account during the year commencing last July, and of any additional share capital which, having regard to estimated revenue and capital receipts and payments, the Board considers will be required to be subscribed by the Commonwealth during the ensuing financial year commencing 1st July.

Capital Expenditure:

29. Notwithstanding any general approval of a programme of capital expenditure as in 28 above, the Company shall not, without the approval of the Minister:

    (a) acquire by purchase any land the cost of acquisition of which exceeds the sum of £5,000;

    (b) enter into any lease of land for a period exceeding five years;

    (c) in any manner dispose of any property, right or privilege having an original or book value exceeding the sum of £5,000;

    (d) enter into any contract in any case where the contract is for the supply, either directly or indirectly, from places outside Australia, or aircraft, equipment or materials of a greater value than £10,000, other than requirements for the maintenance of the Company's Fleet.

General:

30. The following are matters which shall be referred to the Minister for approval:

    (a)   appointments of staff other than aircrew and other staff covered by awards or agreements, where the proposed remuneration exceeds £1,500 per annum;

    (b)   staff pension schemes;

    (c)   any proposal relating to bonus payments to staff of the Company.

Appendix B

McVey's Board Notes on Bilateral Agreements

Since the Nations who attended the International Conference on Civil Aviation at Chicago in November–December 1944 failed to agree upon the provision of a multi-lateral agreement covering the Five Freedoms of the Air — or, for that matter, even failed to reach unanimous agreement in respect of Third and Fourth Freedoms — it was decided by British Commonwealth Countries that bilateral agreement negotiations with other countries should, as a general rule, be related to third and fourth freedom traffic; and that fifth freedom traffic, if conceded in any bilateral agreement, should be subject to strict controls and also to prior consultation with other British Commonwealth Countries which might be affected. It suits Australia, so far as it may, to negotiate agreements relating to third and fourth freedom traffic only.

Australia is a "terminal country" as opposed to a "transit" country, such as India or even the United Kingdom (as in the case of American airlines operating from America through England to Europe and beyond). Few airlines of foreign countries, which might operate to Australia, would be likely legitimately, to seek to operate to territories beyond Australia, except to New Zealand via Australia, their Governments would have to negotiate bilateral agreements with the New Zealand Government; and those bilateral agreements, which would undoubtedly relate to third and fourth freedom traffics only, would confer upon New Zealand traffic rights reciprocal to those they sought from New Zealand. It is unlikely, however, that New Zealand — at least for a long time to come — would wish to operate external airlines other than those in which she is now interested, and would therefore in all probability not feel disposed to grant rights which New Zealand herself would not be likely, reciprocally, to exercise.

Even if New Zealand did agree to negotiate bilateral agreements with certain countries desirous of operating to New Zealand via Australia, Australia is not bound to grant fifth freedom traffic rights to their operators — and would not do so unless Australia were also granted fifth freedom rights in the other countries concerned. The test would be whether Australian operators transited the territories of those countries seeking reciprocal fifth freedom rights; if they didn't, the question of reciprocal fifth freedom rights does not arise and Australia in those circumstances would be justified in withholding fifth freedom rights. New Zealand itself is likely to oppose the granting of fifth freedom rights between Australia and New Zealand if only to protect TEAL; and Australia is bound to support New Zealand under the provisions of the Canberra Agreement [Anzac Pact].

Any suggestion of Australia granting fifth freedom rights for traffic beyond Australia to a territory other than New Zealand could be successfully combated. International airline operations, under bilateral agreements between the Governments concerned, are primarily related to terminal traffics; and, as a rule, the routes traversed are required to be "direct" routes, or fairly so, deviations from the "direct" routes being allowed only to the extent required by the endurance and range of the aircraft employed or by the need to traverse "intermediate" territories in which traffic rights have been obtained. The feature which all countries — or, at least, most countries — represented at the Chicago Conference, sought to eliminate was "tramp traffic" in international airline operations.

Australia could, for example, justifiably deny to the Dutch Government fifth freedom traffic to KLM if that airline wishes to operate from Amsterdam to San Francisco via Australia, since Australia is not on the direct eastabout route from Amsterdam to San Francisco. (Australia could deny this right for the reason also that the Dutch have no reciprocal fifth freedom traffic to offer Australia, except perhaps in the Netherlands East Indies.)

Insofar as Australia is concerned, therefore, bilateral agreements relating to third and fourth freeedom traffics are the type of agreement which, as a general rule, Australia would wish to negotiate. In this respect, Australia's problem is simpler than that of the United Kingdom or of India. Turning now to negotiations with India, with whom both the UK and Australia are in the process of discussing bilateral agreements, it should be kept prominently in mind that BOAC and QEA are operating under a "parallel partnership" arrangement, and that arrangement is so valuable to both operators that it must form the background of the negotiations. India has aspirations to operate international airline services. India is a "transit" country and has much to offer in the way of fifth freedom traffic. India will therefore wish to exact in her negotiations maximum reciprocal fifth freedom rights. But, as far as Australia is concerned, it is suggested that, for the purpose of these negotiations, terminal traffics in India and Australia are the primary considerations. This applies also, but to a somewhat lesser extent, to the negotiations between the UK and India.

Frequencies, under a bilateral agreement, are based upon originating traffics in both countries; and where such traffics are approximately 50–50, the two countries are entitled to establish services of equivalent capacities. The services between Australia and India should be established on the basis of traffic originating in India and terminating in Australia plus traffic originating in Australia and terminating in India. QEA can, of course, add that traffic to the traffic originating and terminating in territories beyond India, to and from which QEA is entitled by agreements to carry traffic. There is also a formula for increasing schedules in an appropriate manner as traffic increases.

If it be possible, the UK should also negotiate a bilateral agreement with India relating to third and fourth freedom traffic only; because, if India proposes to operate services eastabout and westabout to the UK and Australia respectively, the fifth freedom traffic now in India and available to BOAC and QEA will be largely diverted to Indian airlines; and, in any case, in the light of the "parallel partnership" operating arrangements between BOAC and QEA, each can carry the other's traffic into and out of India — which, in a sense, is fifth freedom traffic to both operators in their "through" operations.

No doubt India is well aware of this and will wish the suspension of the "parallel partnership" arrangement insofar as Indian traffic is concerned, so that India may be able to bargain on the basis of reciprocal fifth freedom rights; but India cannot logically demand this, since insofar as the UK–India and Australia–India bilateral agreements are concerned, that traffic is third and fourth freedom traffic.

It would seem most desirable that a strong stand should be taken on this point, and in order to avoid any disturbance of the "parallel partnership" operating arrangement.

If the Indian Government becomes adamant on the suspension of the "parallel partnership" arrangement insofar as Indian traffic is concerned, it would mean that QEA could transport passssengers from Australia to India but could not pick up passengers in India to carry them on to the UK; and that BOAC could transport passengers from the UK to India but could not pick up passengers in India for Australia. At this stage, fifth freedom traffic rights must be considered in the interests of economic operation of the Kangaroo Service; but so far as the reciprocal arrangements in favour of Indian airlines are concerned, the traffic must be legitimate fifth freedom traffic. What fifth freedom traffic in Australia can the Indian airline request? Traffic from Australia to New Zealand? Only if the New Zealand Government grants rights to the Indian Government to operate in and out of New Zealand; and, as stated above, unless New Zealand has in mind operating, by itself, an airline between New Zealand and India, there would be no call for New Zealand to grant to India rights to operate into New Zealand. In any case, the traffic originating in India for New Zealand would be relatively small. It is inconceivable, also, in the light of past experience, that New Zealand would allow any competition with TEAL.

Does India then wish to operate to Fiji via Australia? And requests rights, in return for fifth freedom rights granted to QEA in India, to pick up traffic in Australia for Fiji? It could be argued that, if India wishes to operate a service to Fiji, and the UK grants to India third and fourth freedom rights in Fiji, the normal direct route is not via Sydney, but along a route to the north of Australia. In these negotiations, there is little doubt that political considerations become of important consequence and may outweigh considerations related solely to international airline operations. If it becomes desirable, politically, to concede to India the right to operate from India to Fiji via Australia, the international operators likely to be most affected would be, not QEA, but BCPA and Pan American; and the traffic carried out of Australia to Fiji, and from Fiji to Australia, by the Indian airline may well be negligible (except for Indian nationals), because of prejudice against Indian air crews. Added to which is the important point that India has yet to prove herself capable of efficient and economic international airline operations. BOAC, QEA and BCPA and Pan American have a tremendous advantage in this respect by virtue of their reputation and experience in international airline operations, the support they receive from the public, and the support they are accorded by their respective Governments. India could not continue such a service for long without public support — and this may be lacking.

To sum up:

(i) Australia should strenuously endeavour to limit the bilateral agreement with India to third and fourth freedom traffics. The UK, if possible, should follow a similar course.

(ii) The "parallel partnership" arrangement between BOAC and QEA should not be sacrificed.

(iii) If it becomes necessary, in order to avoid a breakdown in negotiations, to grant reciprocal fifth freedom traffic rights, they should be granted only on the basis of "fill-in" traffic, based on capacities related to available third and fourth freedom traffics, and as a high-level political concession; but, even if it becomes necessary to grant that concessions, it may not, in its incidence over a period, have any materially prejudicial effect upon the international airlines in which Australia is interested.

Appendix C

Qantas Fleet: Aircraft Owned and Operated, 1939–54

Aircraft Type	Registration	Constructor's Number	Aircraft Name	Acquisition	Disposal
Short Empire Flying Boat	VH-ABG	S838	*Coriolanus*	Aug. 1942	8 Jan. 1948
Short S33 Empire Flying Boat	VH-ACD	S1025	*Clifton*	July 1943	18 Jan. 1944
Short S23 Empire Flying Boat	VH-ADU	S844	*Camilla*	Aug. 1942	22 April 1943
DH84 Dragon	VH-URD	6037		3 May 1950	24 Dec. 1951
	VH-URV	6089		25 May 1949	13 Dec. 1951
	VH-URY	6082	*John Flynn*	14 June 1943	24 July 1949
	VH-UZF	6065		April 1940	16 Aug. 1940[a]
	VH-AEF	2057		18 June 1948	14 May 1953
	VH-AIA	2086		July 1948	16 Mar. 1953
	VH-AMN	2059		July 1946	1949
	VH-AOK	2056		6 April 1950	29 Sept. 1950
	VH-AON	2019		26 Mar. 1947	20 Nov. 1952
	VH-AOR	2042		Aug. 1947	9 Mar. 1953
	VH-AOT	2050		2 Jan. 1949	2 Aug. 1952
	VH-AQW	2068		7 Mar. 1949	23 Apr. 1953
	VH-AXL	2093		9 May 1947	21 Sept. 1951
	VH-AYM	2031		1 Nov. 1946	24 Nov. 1948
DH84 Dragon	VH-BAF	2027		28 May 1947	14 July 1947
	VH-BAH	2055		1 June 1948	13 May 1949
	VH-BDS	2081		28 Apr. 1948	14 Nov. 1952
Lockheed Electra 10A	VH-AEC	1034	*Inlander*	8 June 1941	12 Feb. 1948
Lockheed 14H2	VH-ADT	1409		Oct. 1944	22 Jan. 1947

Aircraft Type	Registration	Constructor's Number	Aircraft Name	Acquisition	Disposal
Douglas DC3	VH-AIH	25491/14046	Reg. changed to VH-EBH[a] 24 Feb. 1950	Dec. 1945	27 Nov. 1953
	VH-AII	13622	Reg. changed to VH-EBI 23 Sept. 1949	Dec. 1945	3 Nov. 1950
	VH-AIJ	12667	Reg. changed to VH-EBJ 30 Sept. 1949	Dec. 1945	3 Oct. 1953
	VH-EAK	12872		Dec. 1946	22 Oct. 1953
	VH-EAL	13084	Reg. changed to VH-EBH[b] 19 Aug. 1954 and to VH-EBW on 7 Mar. 1958	Dec. 1946	21 Oct. 1960
	VH-EAM	9286		Jan. 1947	21 July 1953
	VH-EAN	12187	Reg. changed to VH-EBF[b] 10 May 1956 and to VH-EBU on 20 Jan. 1958	Sept. 1949	1 Sept. 1960
	VH-EAO	25367/13922	Reg. changed to VH-EBX 15 Aug. 1957	Dec. 1946	1 Sept. 1960
Douglas DC3	VH-EAP	12873	Reg. changed to VH-EBY 29 Jan. 1957	Apr. 1948	1 Sept. 1960
	VH-EAQ	11870		Apr. 1948	1 Sept. 1960
	VH-EAR	12035		Apr. 1948	Oct. 1960
	VH-EBE	10000	Reg. changed to VH-EBT Feb. 1958	May 1948	1 Sept. 1960
	VH-EBF[a]	12248		May 1948	15 Oct. 1953
	VH-EBF[b]	12187	Originally VH-EAN VH-EBF[b] on 10 May 1956 and later became VH-EBU on 20 Jan. 1958	see VH-EAN	see VH-EAN
	VH-EBG	12541	Reg. changed to VH-EBV Sept. 1957	May 1948	1 Sept. 1960
	VH-EBH[a]	25491/14046	Originally VH-AIH, reg. changed to VH-EBH[a] on 24 Feb. 1950	see VH-AIH	see VH-AIH
	VH-EBH[b]	13084	Originally VH-EAL, reg. changed to VH-EBH[b] on 19 Aug. 1954 and later became VH-EBW on 12 Mar. 1958	see VH-EAL	see VH-EAL
	VH-EBI	13622	Originally VH-AII, reg. changed to VH-EBI on 23 Sept. 1949	see VH-AII	see VH-AII

Aircraft Type	Registration	Constructor's Number	Aircraft Name	Acquisition	Disposal
	VH-EBJ	12667	Originally VH-AIJ, reg. changed to VH-EBJ on 30 Sept. 1949	see VH-AIJ	see VH-AIJ
	VH-EBT	10000	Originally VH-EBE, reg. changed to VH-EBT in Feb. 1958	see VH-EBE	see VH-EBE
	VH-EBU	12187	Originally VH-EAN, reg. changed to VH-EBF[B] on 10 May 1956 and later became VH-EBU on 20 Jan. 1958	see VH-EAN	see VH-EAN
	VH-EBV	12541	Originally VH-EBG, reg. changed to VH-EBV in Sept. 1957	see VH-EBG	see VH-EBG
	VH-EBW	13084	Originally VH-EAL, reg. changed to VH-EBH[b] on 19 Aug. 1954 and later became VH-EBW on 12 Mar. 1958	see VH-EAL	see VH-EAL
	VH-EBX	25367/13922	Originally VH-EAO, reg. changed to VH-EBX on 15 Aug. 1957	see VH-EAO	see VH-EAO
	VH-EBY	12873	Originally VH-EAP, reg. changed to VH-EBY on 29 July 1957	See VH-EAP	see VH-EAP
	VH-EDC	12874		May 1961	15 Nov. 1971
	VH-EDD	25367/13922		Jan. 1964	15 Dec. 1971
Consolidated Vultee Liberator (LB30)	VH-EAI[c]	39		29 Nov. 1945	4 Aug. 1950
	VH-EAJ[C]	22		14 Mar. 1946	Nov. 1950
CAC CA6 Wackett Trainer	VH-EAY	248		Mar. 1947	3 Dec. 1949
	VH-EAZ	317		Mar. 1947	7 Mar. 1951
Avro 691 Lancastrian	VH-EAS	1184		July 1947	7 Apr. 1949
	VH-EAT	1191		Sept. 1947	7 Aug. 1952
	VH-EAU	1180		Nov. 1947	28 Aug. 1952
	VH-EAV	1291		Jan. 1948	17 Nov. 1951
Consolidated Vultee Catalina PB2B2[d]	VH-EAW			17 Aug. 1947	27 Aug. 1949
	VH-EAX			7 Oct. 1947	23 June 1949
	VH-EBA			13 Dec. 1948	Mar. 1954
	VH-EBB[e]				Feb. 1951
	VH-EBC		Island Chieftan	31 Dec. 1948	11 Nov. 1958
	VH-EBD		Island Patrol	29 July 1949	11 Nov. 1958

Aircraft Type	Registration	Constructor's Number	Aircraft Name	Acquisition	Disposal
	VH-EBU		*Island Warrior*	25 Nov. 1949	Mar. 1954
Lockheed	VH-EAA	2562	*Ross Smith*	14 Oct. 1947	15 Feb. 1955
Constellation	VH-EAB	2565	*Lawrence Hargrave*	22 Oct. 1947	26 Feb. 1955
749-79[f]	VH-EAC	2572	*Harry Hawker*	22 Oct. 1947	8 Oct. 1955
	VH-EAD	2573	*Charles Kingsford Smith*	27 Oct. 1947	31 Oct. 1955
	VH-EAE	2505	*Bert Hinkler*	17 Jan. 1950	18 Aug. 1954
	VH-EAF	2504	*Horace Brinsmead*	27 Apr. 1951	23 July 1954
Avro Anson 652A	VH-BBZ			4 Feb. 1949	10 May 1949
Douglas DC4 Skymaster	VH-EBK	42917	*Malayan Trader*	18 Feb. 1949	Reg. changed to changed to VH-EDA, July 1961
	VH-EBL	43067	*Hong Kong Trader*	15 Feb. 1949	13 Jan. 1961
	VH-EBM	42918	*Philippine Trader*	6 May 1949	16 Oct. 1959
	VH-EBN	7458	*New Guinea Trader*	9 July 1949	10 Sept. 1958[g]
			Pacific Trader[h]	Apr. 1960	Reg. changed to VH-EDB, July 1961
	VH-EBO	18347	*Pacific Trader*	Feb. 1949	31 May 1956
	VH-EBP	42920	*Australian Trader*	3 Mar. 1955	29 Oct. 1959
	VH-EDA	42917	*Norfolk Trader*[i]	See VH-EBK	
	VH-EDB	7458	*Pacific Trader*	See VH-EBN	
DHA3 Drover MkI	VH-EAS	5014	Originally VH-EAZ, reg. change to VH-EAS 5 May 1958	See VH-EAZ	1 Sept. 1960
	VH-EAZ	5014		30 July 1952	See VH-EAS
	VH-EBQ[j]	5003		13 Sept. 1950	16 July 1951
	VH-EBR[j]	5005		9 Apr. 1951	11 June 1954
	VH-EBS[j]	5008		28 Sept. 1951	15 Oct. 1954
	VH-EBT[j]	5009		1 Nov. 1951	11 June 1954
Short S25 Sandringham	VH-EBV	SH40C	*Pacific Warrior*	15 July 1951	6 June 1955
	VH-EBW	SH30C		18 Apr. 1950	10 June 1951
	VH-EBX	SH32C	*Pacific Chieftain*	13 Apr. 1950	10 Dec. 1954
	VH-EBY	SH41C	*Pacific Voyager*	Dec. 1951	5 July 1955
	VH-EBZ	SH37C	*Pacific Explorer*	15 July 1951	23 June 1955
Lockheed	VH-EAA[k]	4580	*Southern Sea*	4 Mar. 1955	22 Jan. 1963
Super	VH-EAB[k]	4581	*Southern Horizon*	8 Mar. 1955	27 Mar. 1963
Constellation	VH-EAC[l]	4606	*Southern Wave*	25 Oct. 1955	25 Aug. 1960
L1049	VH-EAD[l]	4607	*Southern Dawn*	26 Nov. 1955	15 Mar. 1960
	VH-EAE[l]	4578	*Southern Moon*	8 Feb. 1955	2 Mar. 1960
	VH-EAF[m]	4579	*Southern Wind*	23 Feb. 1955	22 Apr. 1963
	VH-EAG[n]	4539	*Southern Constellation*	15 Apr. 1955	3 May 1963
	VH-EAH[n]	4545	*Southern Sky*	28 Apr. 1954	3 Nov. 1959
	VH-EAI[n]	4546	*Southern Sun*	24 May 1954	1 Dec. 1959
			Southern Boomerang	Nov. 1960	5 Apr. 1961
	VH-EAJ[m]	4549	*Southern Star*	5 July 1954	2 Jan. 1960

390

Aircraft Type	Registration	Constructor's Number	Aircraft Name	Acquisition	Disposal
	VH-EAK[m]	4573	*Southern Mist*	18 Jan. 1955	2 Feb. 1963
	VH-EAL[m]	4574	*Southern Breeze*	31 Jan. 1955	11 Nov. 1959
	VH-EAM[o]	4801	*Southern Spray*	18 Oct. 1956	24 July 1962
	VH-EAN[o]	4803	*Southern Tide*	20 Nov. 1956	24 July 1962
	VH-EAO	4679	*Southern Aurora*	*28 Oct. 1957*	*14 Oct. 1959*
			Southern Prodigal[q]	18 Aug. 1960	5 Mar. 1963
	VH-EAPP	4680	*Southern Zephr*	21 Nov. 1957	25 Oct. 1959
DHC2 Beaver	VH-EAS	643		7 Dec. 1954	22 Jan. 1958
	VH-EAT	645		7 Dec. 1954	14 Apr. 1958
	VH-EAU	646		7 Dec. 1954	23 Dec. 1958
	VH-EAV	741		7 Feb. 1955	16 Apr. 1959

Note: Table includes aircraft acquired in 1938 but operated in subsequent years.

Between 1949 and 1958, eleven changes of registration were made to nine aircraft of the Qantas DC3 fleet. The reasons for the changes are as follows: September 1949 and February 1950 — To consolidate all Qantas aircraft registrations into the VH-EA-/VH-EB- groups; August 1954 — Transfer of registration VH-EAL to an L1049 Super Constellation due to delivery in January 1955; May 1956 — Transfer of registration VH-EAN to an L1049H due for delivery in November 1956; January and August 1957 — Transfer of registrations VH-EAO and EAP to two L1049Gs due for delivery in late 1957; and September 1957, January, February, and March 1958 — Transfer of registrations VH-EBE to VH-EBH inclusive to four Boeing 707s due for delivery in 1959 and 1961.

[a] Impressed by RAAF.
[b] Returned from impressment.
[c] These two aircraft commenced operations under UK registrations G-AGTI (-EAI) and G-AGTJ (-EAJ). They came onto the Australian register in June (-EAI) and April (-EAJ) of 1947.
[d] Although the Catalina was originally designed by Consolidated Vultee, all seven Catalinas shown were manufactured by Boeing Aircraft of Canada.
[e] Registration allotted but aircraft broken up for spares.
[f] All six aircraft were modified to L749A-79 specifications.
[g] Chartered to Malayan Airways.
[h] Renamed on return from charter.
[i] Change of name.
[j] Modified to MkIF and later to MkII.
[k] Delivered as L1049E-55; modified to L1049E-01-55; later modified to L1049G; subsequently fitted with L1049H loading door at rear only for freighter use.
[l] Delivered as L1049E-55; modified to L1049E-01-55; later modified to L1049G.
[m] Delivered as L1049E-55; modified to L1049E-01-55.
[n] Delivered as L1049C-55-81; modified to L1049E-01-55.
[o] L1049H-82-133.
[p] L1049G-82-118.
[q] Repurchased and renamed.
[r] On lease and renamed.

Appendix D

QEA Summary of Aircraft Accidents, 1939–54

Date	Aircraft	Crew	Location	Category	Nature of Accident	Damage to Aircraft	Cause of Accident	Injuries Sustained
19 June 1941	DH90 UN-UXB	C.H.C.	Alexandra	Serious	Propeller failure during flight required a forced landing	Broken engine mountings, cowls and propeller	Defective propeller	Nil
30 Jan. 1942	Empire Flying Boat GAEUH	A.A. Koch and Lyne	Koepang	Destroyed	During flight between Sourabaya and Darwin, shot down by Japanese fighter aircraft	Destroyed	Enemy action	Crew: 3 killed, 1 seriously hurt; Passengers: 10 killed, 1 slightly hurt
20 Feb. 1942	DH86 VH-USE	C.H.C. Swaffield	Belmont, Brisbane	Destroyed	Shortly after takeoff, fell out of low clouds and crashed	Destroyed	Loss of control owing to either failure of instruments or inability of pilot to fly on instruments	Crew: 2 killed; Passengers: 7 killed
27 Feb. 1942	Empire Flying Boat VH-ABC	RAAF crew F/Ltr. Love	Townsville	Destroyed	Crashed during alighting at Townsville on completion of test flight	Destroyed	Unknown; aircraft under charter to RAAF	Crew: RAAF killed
28 Feb. 1942	Empire Flying Boat GAETZ	W.B. Purton	Tjilatjap Broome	Destroyed	Lost during flight between Tjilatjap and Broome	Destroyed	Unknown, probably enemy action	Crew: 4 killed; Passengers: 16 killed
3 Mar. 1942	Empire Flying Boat G-AEUC	RAAF	Broome	Destroyed	Destroyed at mooring in Broome Harbour owing to enemy aircraft action	Destroyed	Enemy action	Nil

Date	Aircraft	Pilot	Location	Severity	Description	Damage	Cause	Casualties
	Flying Boat G-ADUT				in Broome Harbour owing to enemy aircraft action			
22 Mar. 1942	Empire Flying Boat G-AEUF	L.R. Ambrose	Darwin	Destroyed	Shortly after alighting at Darwin the planing bottom broke up and flying boat capsized.	Destroyed	Loading error; believed to have been caused by shifting of heavy freight in forward lower compartment, resulting in splitting of the hull	Crew: 1 seriously hurt, 2 slightly hurt, Passengers: 2 killed, 2 seriously hurt, 7 slightly hurt
30 June 1942	DH83 VHUZD	D.M. Elphinstone	Helen Springs	Serious	Struck tree during takeoff	Both mainplanes and undercarriage badly damaged; propeller broken; other minor damage	Pilot error; attempted takeoff down wind	Nil
29 Jan. 1943	Loadster VHCAA	O.F.Y. Thomas	Townsville	Serious	During takeoff, first officer retracted the undercarriage prematurely	Fuselage skin, propellers, engine cowl, and undercarriage structure damaged	Crew error	Nil
22 Apr. 1943	Empire Flying Boat VH-ADU	A.A. Koch and Peak	Near Port Moresby	Destroyed	Caught in bad weather and darkness and crashed carrying out emergency landing in open sea	Destroyed	Weather and restricted radio aids preventing pilot locating flare path	Nil
6 May 1943	DH90 VH-UTJ	G.T. Morgan	Breddon	Serious	After landing, starboard wheel locked causing aircraft to swing violently	Port undercarriage badly damaged; main centre section spar broken	Structural failure; sudden seizure of starboard brake (penetration of dirt)	Nil
8 May 1943	DH90 VH-UXB	W. Forgen-Smith	Daly Waters	Serious	Cabin filled with smoke and forced landing on clay-pan	Stern post and tail plane damaged	Generator defect	Nil
23 June 1943	DH86 VH-USC	D. Tennent	Longreach	Propeller accident	Apprentice engineer Drinkall struck by propeller	Nil	During starting of engines	1 fatality
13 July 1943	DH90 VH UXB	Sloane	Archerfield	Serious	During takeoff aircraft developed a swing to starboard	Both spars cracked, undercarriage and cowlings damaged	Inexperience of pilot on the type of aircraft	Nil
4 Aug. 1943	Empire Flying Boat VH-ABC	E.R. Nicholl	Rose Bay	Destroyed	During flight landings at Rose Bay a floating object was struck	Planing bottom torn	Unswept waters	Nil

Date	Aircraft	Crew	Location	Category	Nature of Accident	Damage to Aircraft	Cause of Accident	Injuries Sustained
21 Sept. 1943	DH86 VH-USF	I. Flynn	Roma	Serious	During takeoff, aircraft swung to port and failed to respond to corrective action with rudder, and the undercarriage collapsed	Undercarriage severely damaged and starboard lower main spar broken	Mishandling during takeoff due largely to inexperience of pilot	Nil
1 Oct. 1943	DH86 VH-USC	Capt. Hosie	Dalby/ Roma	Serious	Struck by eagle hawk during flight	Fin, rudder, and empennage	Bird strike	Nil
4 Oct. 1943	DH84 VH-URY	R.I. Flynn	Cloncurry	Serious	Shortly after landing the aircraft swung violently to port, causing the undercarriage to collapse	Undercarriage badly damaged; damage to lower mainplane and fuselage	Inability of pilot to control swing after landing	Nil
13 Oct. 1943	DH86 VH-USC	D.A. Tennent	Brisbane	Serious	Shortly after landing, aircraft swung violently to port and starboard undercarriage collapsed	Undercarriage severely damaged, both propellers broken, minor damage lower mainplane	Poor landing and inability of the pilot to control resultant swing	Nil
21 Oct. 1943	DH90 VH-UTJ	T.J. Keirnan	Breddon	Serious	Crashed during landing owing to swing	Undercarriage and spar damaged	Inability of pilot to maintain control during swing owing to jammed throttle	Nil
26 Nov. 1943	Lockheed Lodestar VH-CAB	W.G. Campbell	Near Port Moresby	Destroyed	Approximately 10 miles from aerodrome of departure (Ward's Strip), aircraft flew into hillside 30 to 40 feet from its summit	Destroyed by impact and fire	Aircraft climbed at an insufficient rate after takeoff due to either a structural or personal factor	Crew: 4 killed; Passengers: 11 killed
10 Jan. 1944	Empire Flying Boat VH-ABB	F.A. Reeve	Rathmines	Serious	After entering a storm near Newcastle the flying boat, without warning, dropped hundreds of feet causing some passengers to strike their heads on the roof of the cabin	Serious interior damage	Flying into a storm and experiencing severe turbulence	Passengers: 3 seriously hurt, 4 slight hurt
18 Jan. 1944	Empire Flying Boat VH-ACD	H.B. Hussey and A.L. Ashley	Rose Bay	Destroyed	Shortly after alighting the flying boat "porpoised" on surface of water for about 100 yards, and stalled after rising into the air again	Destroyed by impact and water damage	Poor landing, causing collapse of the planing surface of the hull	Crew: 1 slightly hurt
28 Jan. 1944	Lodestar VH-CAF	C.F. Moore	Brisbane	Serious	While taxing the aircraft struck a tree stump	Underside of fuselage torn	Poor aerodrome lighting combined with inadequate briefing of	Nil

Date	Aircraft	Pilot	Location	Result	Circumstances	Damage	Cause	Casualties
	VH-USF	Smith			outer engine cut, causing aircraft to swing violently and starboard undercarriage leg collapsed	to starboard undercarriage, starboard lower mainplane and 2 starboard propellers	during takeoff after having been reported on 3 occasions for cutting out during flight	Nil
9 Oct. 1944	DH86 VH-USC	D.A. Tennent	Darwin	Destroyed	Carrying out crosswind landing at Darwin, aircraft swung off runway and struck a ditch	Major damage to undercarriage; lower main spar broken and ailerons damaged	Pilot unable to control the aircraft in strong crosswind	Nil
11 Oct. 1944	Empire Flying Boat VH-ABB	L.J. Brain and K.C. Caldwell	Rose Bay	Destroyed	Approximately 20 minutes after takeoff oil pressure commenced to drop (starboard inner engine). On return to Rose Bay flying boat stalled 10 to 12 feet from water and on impact the planing bottom of the hull failed, resulting in an extensive break-up of the aircraft	Destroyed	Flying boat stalled 10 to 12 feet from the water	Crew: 2 seriously hurt, 1 severe shock; Passengers: 1 killed, 2 seriously hurt, 1 slightly hurt
13 Nov. 1944	Lockheed 14 VH-ADT	K.G. Jackson	Mascot	Serious	After landing at Mascot the starboard undercarriage leg collapsed	Starboard undercarriage assembly extensively damaged; little other damage	Structural failure; failure of the lower drag strut; there were indications that the strut had been cracked before this accident	Nil
28 Jan. 1945	Lockheed 14 VH-ADT	A. Myers	Mascot	Serious	After bursting a main hydraulic pipe line it was impossible to lock the undercarriage down; aircraft was landed and brought to a half but on turning to taxi the starboard leg collapsed	Starboard wing extensively damaged; lower starboard rudder and fin damaged; starboard airscrew blades bent; starboard undercarriage structure damaged	Structural and pilot error: (1) bursting of main hydraulic pipeline; (2) failure of the emergency system to extend the undercarriage into fully down position; (3) pilot's action in taxiing knowing undercarriage was not locked	Nil
27 Feb. 1945	Empire Flying Boat VH-ABG	N/A	Rose Bay	Serious	During slipping operations aircraft collided with a tractor	Hull frames, planing bottom, chine, various stringers and hull plates damaged	Slipping methods unsatisfactory; negligence of supervisory staff	Nil
14 Oct. 1945	DH90 VH-UTJ	L.L. McNeill	Cloncurry	Serious	During landing the aircraft swing slightly to port and swung violently to starboard collapsing the starboard undercarriage	Undercarriage and port propeller severely damaged; damaged port lower mainplane	Mishandling during landing	Nil

Date	Aircraft	Crew	Location	Category	Nature of Accident	Damage to Aircraft	Cause of Accident	Injuries Sustained
21 Oct. 1945	DH83 VH-UZD	E.R. Robinson	Creswell Downs	Serious	During taxiing struck post	Main spar fractured	Inexperience of pilot plus tendency of aircraft to swing	Nil
23 Jan. 1946	DH83 VH-URI	E.R. Robinson	Wandoola	Serious	During takeoff the port tyre blew causing the port compression strut to be loosened or torn from its mountings; aircraft left the ground but on touching down again the undercarriage collapsed	Severely damaged undercarriage; lower wing spars either broken or strained, engine cowlings dented and propeller broken	Structural failure; probably tyre being staked by some sharp object during takeoff	Nil
28 Jan. 1946	DH90 VH-UXB	I.F. McSparron	Cloncurry	Serious	Towards the end of the landing run the aircraft swung slightly to starboard; application of port brake failed to stop the turn and aircraft swung violently collapsing the port undercarriage assembly	Port undercarriage assembly collapsed; port airscrew tip broken; port outer interplane strut slightly damaged	Structural failure; failure of the brakes during landing run	Nil
23 Mar. 1946	Lancastrian G-AGLX	O.F.Y. Thomas	Probably vicinity Cocos Is.	Destroyed	Aircraft disappeared in flight between Colombo and Cocos Island.	No wreckage located	Lost at sea	Crew: 5 killed; Passengers: 5 killed
2 May 1946	Lancastrian G-AGMC	J.J. Griffith	Mascot	Serious	During landing attempt aircraft struck sandbank 60 yards from end of runway collapsing undercarriage	Starboard mainplane, engines, undercarriage and tailplane extensively damaged; fuselage slight damaged	Undershot by inexperienced pilot on training flight	Nil
16 Jan. 1947	DH90 VH-UXB	E. Morton and W. Forgen-Smith	Cloncurry	Serious	Aircraft swung slightly to port during takeoff and then swung violently to starboard collapsing the undercarriage	Port undercarriage damaged beyond repair, centre section spar fractured, port propeller broken	Pilot error; failed to control swing during takeoff (training)	Nil
22 Jan. 1947	Lockheed 14 VH-ADT	K.G. Jackson	Schofields	Destroyed	During takeoff the aircraft swung slightly to port and then violently to starboard; aircraft left the runway and port undercarriage collapsed after striking small log; fire broke out immediately	Damaged beyond repair by impact and fire	Failure of the port engine to develop full power during early stages of takeoff; inexperienced pilot on type of aircraft	Nil

Date	Aircraft	Pilot	Location	Severity	Damage	Circumstances	Cause	Casualties
	G-AGMB	Morris			destroyed, starboard engine badly damaged, lower portion of fuselage extensively damaged; all propellers bent; nose portion of aircraft dented and twisted	swung to port violently and the undercarriage was torn off when it sank into soft sand	technique while making crosswind landing; overcorrection combined with tendency of aircraft to swing, caused it to develop an uncontrollable swing	Nil
10 Apr. 1947	DH84 VH-AON	F.S. Furniss	Kainantu	Serious	Both undercarriage legs collapsed; mainplane slightly	After landing aircraft overshot the runway and fell into a deep ditch damaged; nose of aircraft damaged; port propeller broken.	Approached aerodrome too high and with too great a forward speed	Nil
14 July 1947	DH84 VH-BAF	R.K. Crabbe	Wampit River	Destroyed	Aircraft damaged beyond repair	Owing to low cloud aircraft entered valley unknown to pilot, with insufficient height to clear rising ground and continued on until crashing into trees	Weather-flying at insufficient height to clear terrain in an endeavour to avoid low cloud	Crew: 1 slightly hurt; Passengers: 1 seriously hurt, 1 slightly hurt
9 Aug. 1947	Grumman Widgeon VH-AZO	P.L. Oakley	Kariava	Serious	Port float torn off, trailing edge port flap and port aileron bent, starboard tailplane fractured and fabric on port wing damaged	Aircraft bounced twice on alighting; on third and final impact with the water the port wing dropped and aircraft swung violently to port	1. Pilot permitted aircraft to bounce owing to misjudging height from water 2. Port wheel became unlocked causing aircraft to swing violently	Nil
10 Jan. 1948	DH83 VH-UZD	W.D. Young	Burketown	Serious	Front spar lower port mainplane fractured; tailwheel and rudder king posts slightly damaged, several wing ribs broken	Aircraft struck aerodrome boundary fence after abandoning takeoff, owing to severe crosswind	Inability of pilot to control the aircraft in a crosswind	Nil
12 Feb. 1948	Lockheed 10A VH-AEC	D.A. Tennent and R. Crabbe	Condamine	Destroyed	Damaged beyond repair	Aircraft crashed 3 miles south of Condamine while making a forced landing after failure of starboard engine	Failure in flight of starboard engine; flight could not be continued on remaining engine forcing landing on unprepared field	Crew: 1 slightly hurt; Passengers: 1 slightly hurt

Date	Aircraft	Crew	Location	Category	Nature of Accident	Damage to Aircraft	Cause of Accident	Injuries Sustained
18 May 1948	Douglas DC3 VH-EAO	S.A. Roggenkemp	Camooweal	Serious	While taxiing to dispersal area after landing the port mainplane and propeller came in contact with small buildings and 2 utility trucks	Port mainplane extensively damaged and starboard propeller blades bent	1. Brakes not operating normally 2. Pilot aware of this fact continued service 3. Tailwheel lock failed to disengage when attempt was made to turn the aircraft	Nil
19 Aug. 1948	Douglas DC3 VH-EAM	D.A. Tennent	Archerfield	Serious	Aircraft crashed during takeoff on test flight for renewal of C. of A.	Aircraft extensively damaged requiring complete rebuilding	Aileron controls operating in reverse sense due to malassembly of the aileron control cables	Nil
27 Aug. 1948	Lancastrian G-AGMB	Garside	Tengah	Destroyed	One hour after departure aircraft returned to Tengah with No. 4 propeller feathered; during landing the aircraft swung to port and collided with an embankment	Total loss	High approach and speed excessive	Passengers: 2 injured
9 Sept. 1948	Hythe Flying Boat G-AGEW	I.C. Peirce	Sourabaya	Destroyed	Flying boat suffered damage to port float while attempting takeoff and subsequently capsized and sank	Total loss	Swung during takeoff in difficult sea conditions and pilot allowed port wing to to enter water after damage had occurred to float	Nil
21 Nov. 1948	DH84 VH-AMN	G.F. Macrae	Cloncurry	Serious	Whilst parked, aircraft was caught in high wind and blow distance of 100 yards	Both undercarriage assemblies broken; both lower mainplanes and ailerons extensively damaged	Weather: due to wind of gale force the tiedown ropes were cut through by the tiedown lugs on the wings	Nil
24 Nov. 1948	DH84 VH-AYM	P.R.C. Buchanan	Canobie	Destroyed	During engine starting, fire that could not be controlled started in the starboard engine	Aircraft destroyed by fire	Broken fuel line in front of the fireproof bulkhead	Nil
22 Mar. 1949	DH84	J.R. Rose	Kerowagi to Garoka	Serious	In bad weather Rose flew along a road under construction, at a low altitude; he had just completed a turn to the left and was commencing a right hand turn when he became aware of a rending noise; he immediately throttled back and	Wing damage	When flying at a low altitude aircraft struck a tree or some other object	Nil

Date / Aircraft	Pilot	Location	Severity	Description	Damage	Cause	Casualties
VH-EAS	and J.A. Furze			could not be brought to a stop within the limits of the runway; undercarriage collapsed during deliberate ground loop and fire broke out	impact and fire	flapless landing under unsuitable meteorological and wind conditions	
10 May 1949 Anson VH-BBZ	D.N. Mitchell	Kerowagi	Destroyed	During takeoff aircraft swung off runway and was extensively damaged when port undercarriage collapsed on striking a small drain	Mainplane front and rear spars fractured; tailplane rear spar fractured and port undercarriage torn away	Inability of pilot to control aircraft during takeoff, location of strip necessitating downwind takeoff	Crew: 1 slight hurt
23 June 1949 Catalina VH-EAX	L.W. Clark	Lord Howe Island	Destroyed	During night and while unattended VH-EAX broke adrift from its buoy and ran aground on a rocky beach	Aircraft extensively Aircraft extensively damaged and considered a total loss	Third party error; Third party error; failure of D.C.A. storm pennant (during windstorm) due to corrosion	Nil Nil
27 Aug. 1949 Catalina VH-EAW	N.A.	Rose Bay	Destroyed	Internal explosion by infernal machine	Total loss	Sabotage	Nil
15 Sept. 1949 Lancastrian VH-EAV	J.H. Coles	Mascot	Serious	During landing a deliberate ground loop to port was carried out but during this manoeuvre the starboard and then the port undercarriage struts collapsed	Aircraft extensively damaged	Caused by the ground loop resulting in collapse of undercarriage	Nil
16 Sept. 1949 Douglas DC4 VH-EBM	N/A	Kai Tek Hong Kong	Serious	During maintenance by Jardine Aircraft Maintenance Co. Ltd., contract engineer released the parking brake during engine run-up	Aircraft fuselage extensively damaged	Ground engineer's error	Nil
3 Oct. 1949 DH83 Fox Moth VH-UZD	L.L. McNeill	Tarpini	Serious	During approach the strip was lost sight of and in endeavouring to locate it the aircraft was allowed to sink; throttle was immediately opened and although the engine responded immediately, the aircraft struck the ground	Aircraft extensively damaged and due mainly to inaccessibility, salvage	Error of judgment by a good pilot under difficult circumstances	Passengers: 1 slightly hurt
30 Oct. 1949 L1049 VH-EAA	J.P. Shields	Darwin	Serious	Flap panels extensively damaged during retraction by coming into contact with a loading rostrum	Extensive	Incorrect technique and insufficient co-operation between ground and flight crew	Nil

Date	Aircraft	Crew	Location	Category	Nature of Accident	Damage to Aircraft	Cause of Accident	Injuries Sustained
3 Sept. 1951	Sandringham VH-EBX	L.W. Clarke	Rose Bay	Serious	Port wing severely damaged when landing at Rose Bay was being carried out and a collision occurred with the D.C.A. control launch	Port wing extensively damaged	Control launch being out of position and obstructing the aircraft during the approach to the flare path	Nil
21 Sept. 1951	DH84 Dragon VH-AXL	F.G. Barlogie	Karanka	Destroyed	During flight the aircraft crashed near Kamvaira village, about half-a-mile from the eastern end of Karanka airstrip, New Guinea	Total loss	Aircraft entered Wanton Gap at a low altitude in restricted visibility and whilst endeavouring to maintain visual flight failed to clear a ridge covered in heavy fog	Crew: 1 killed
8 Nov. 1951	Douglas DC4 VH-EBM	G.A. Condell	Mascot	Serious	Nose wheel retracted at end of landing run on 04 runway at Mascot	Front fuselage extensively damaged	First officer mistakenly placed the undercarriage selector level in the UP position towards the end of the landing run	Passengers: 1 minor abrasion
17 Nov. 1951	Lancastrian VH-EAV	R.M. Mullins	Mascot	Destroyed	Crashed during takeoff	Damaged beyond repair	Failure of No. 1 engine at critical stage of takeoff; failure initiated a violent swing to port which could not be controlled by the pilot	Crew: 1 killed; Passengers: 2 killed
13 Dec. 1951	Dragon DH84 VH-URV	S.W. Peebles	Yaramanda	Destroyed	Aircraft after having flown over Yaramanda airstrip at low altitude flew into rising ground and was forced to enter the Minyemba River Gorge until it could no longer clear rising terrain	Total loss	An error of judgment by pilot by flying into rising terrain, which was beyond the capabilities of the aircraft	Crew: 1 killed; Passengers: 2 killed
24 Dec. 1951	DH84 VH-URD	R.J. Davies	Menyamya	Destroyed	Aircraft when flying into Menyamya airstrip, was unable to maintain height and crashed; pilot failed to appreciate the descending air after having observed that there was a wind at sufficient strength at ground level to prohibit landing	Damage extensive and economical repair not possible	Pilot failed to take proper corrective action in early stages of descent and permitted the aircraft to get into such a position that he was compelled to fly towards rising ground	Crew: 1 slight abrasions

Date	Aircraft	Pilot	Location	Classification	Description	Damage	Cause	Casualties
	VH-AJO	Fox	Moresby		moorings at the marine base, having a damaged port float		resulted in the port wing entering the water, permitting water to enter the hull through the port cockpit windows and the top hatch	Nil
31 Jan. 1952	Sandringham VH-EBY	J.W. Solly	Rose Bay	Serious	Shortly after commencing takeoff run the flying boat swung to port and in attempting to correct the swing the pilot inadvertently closed No. 3 throttle	Extensively damaged	Incorrect pilot technique	Nil
23 July 1952	DC3 VH-EAL	L. Purkiss McKillop	Kaviang	Serious	During land with flaps fully down the aircraft entered a water area on the strip resulting in extensive damage to the flap system	Extensive	Runway condition	Nil
2 Sept. 1952	Douglas DC4 VH-EBK	J.G. Morton	Anderson Field, Guam	Propeller Accident Serious	First Officer T.E. Poole was killed when struck by No. 3 propeller	Nil	First Officer Poole whilst assisting in aircraft despatch procedures walked into No. 3 propeller	Crew: 1 killed
11 Sept. 1952	DHA3 Drover VH-EBS	R.S. Cuthbertson	Mackay	Serious	Centre propeller of DHA3 aircraft failed during takeoff	Centre engine installation and engine cowlings extensively damaged as a result of the blade failure	Fracture of No. 2 blade retaining nut	Nil
8 Feb. 1953	DC4 VH-EBO	F.T. Bryce and F.M. Twemblow	Labuan Darwin	Serious	On arrival at Darwin it was found that outer panel of port wing was extensively damaged owing to a low pressure area within No. 1 main petrol tank	Extensive wing and fuel tank damage	Main tank vent blocked by a cork, this lowered the pressure within the tank owing to the consumption of fuel	Nil
8 Dec. 1953	DC3 VH-EAO	J.C. Johnson and T.E.W. Howes	Yandina	Serious	Aircraft swung off the runway and port wing collided with a palm growing alongside the strip	Port wing tip suffered severe damage	The captain temporarily lost directional control while landing in a gusty, turbulent wind	Nil
10 Dec. 1949	DH84 VH-AOR	R.E. Biddolph	Chimbu	Serious	Undercarriage extensively damaged when landing	Extensive	Loss of lift resulted from a katabatic wind and inexperience of pilot at high altitude	Nil

Date	Aircraft	Crew	Location	Category	Nature of Accident	Damage to Aircraft	Cause of Accident	Injuries Sustained
17 Feb. 1950	DH84 VH-AXL	L.W. Purkiss	Banz	Serious	After landing the aircraft swung to starboard; an attempt to prevent this was of no avail as the rudder was jammed	Extensive wing and fuselage damage	Structural failure of timber members owing to the effects of moisture and strain imposed during landing and takeoff	Nil
9 Mar. 1950	DC3 VH-EAR	Twenblow O'Malley	Hayfields	Serious	When landing it became apparent that the surface of the strip was greasy; brakes were ineffective and with no wind there was insufficient space to stop	Wing damage	Unusual greasy surface of the strip and poor brakes; captain was blameless	Nil
17 Mar. 1950	DH84 VH-AOT	L.W. Purkiss	Chimbu	Serious	When the engines were being started by the pilot, aircraft commenced to move forward and pivoted on the port wheel; all efforts to stop the aircraft failed and it ran off the strip	Wings, fuselage, and undercarriage damaged	Poor pilot technique and nonadherence to company instructions	Nil
9 June 1950	DH84 VH-AIA	L.R.T. Ballard	Archerfield	Serious	During a taxi test to prove brake efficiency, aircraft was stopped suddenly and the tail lifted until the propellers struck the ground	Propeller damaged	Test carried out down wind and insufficient care taken when applying brakes	Nil
24 Nov. 1950	DH83 VH-URI	W.H. Carter	Boana	Serious	After the takeoff was abandoned the aircraft entered kunai grass at the end of the strip and nosed over	Extensive	Engine failure during takeoff and inability of pilot to stop the aircraft within the limits of the airstrip	Passengers: 1 seriously hurt
4 Apr. 1951	Sandringham VH-EBW	H.M. Birch and R.R.	Rose Bay	Serious	During a landing run the starboard float was carried away and the wing entered the water; aircraft saved by crew members and passengers on the port wing tip	Extensive wing and float damage	Failure of the port stay wire which resulted from a split swage fitting	Nil
13 Apr. 1951	Lancastrian VH-EAV	G. Jakimov	Singapore	Serious	Towards the end of the landing run a ground loop resulted in undercarriage	Aircraft extensively damaged	Pilot overshot and landed too far down runway	Nil

Aircraft	Pilot	Location	Damage	Circumstances	Damage description	Cause	Casualties
VH-EBW	Shields	New Hebrides		to takeoff, VH-EBW struck a coral nigger head	below the water line at several places between the keel and chine in "A" compartment	object in an area slightly north of that normally used for water manoeuvring at Vila	Nil
19 June 1951 DC3 VH-EAO	Jacobson Quinn	Lae	Serious	Starboard engine caught fire while being taxied to the takeoff position; it was not until the aircraft had moved another 150 yards that they became aware of it; fire was extinguished by ground staff	Extensive engine and bulkhead damage	Main fuel-line from the pump to the carburettor had split circumferentially	
16 July 1951 DHA3 Drover VH-EBQ	J.W. Speire	Lae	Destroyed	Aircraft crashed into the sea approximately 4.5 miles south of the mouth of the Markham River, and about one mile offshore	Total loss	Loss of control resulting from structural failure of the centre propeller during flight	Crew: 1 killed; Passengers: 6 killed

Notes

In citing sources in the notes, abbreviations have generally been used. Sources frequently cited have been identified by the following:

McMP   McMaster Papers (in the possession of Qantas)
HFP   Hudson Fysh Papers (Mitchell Library, Sydney)
EJP   Edgar Johnston Papers (in the possession of
       Edgar Johnston)
QAW *Qantas at War*
BA   British Airways archives; RAF Museum,
       Hendon, London
AA   Australian Archives

Introduction

1.   Watt, *Evolution of Australian Foreign Policy*, p. 20.
2.   Fysh to Sir John Reith, 15 September 1939, HFP.
3.   Draft chairman's address to Nineteenth Annual General Meeting of Qantas, 27 September 1939, McMP.

Chapter 1

1.   Fysh to McMaster, 9 October 1939, HFP.
2.   McMaster to Fysh, 12 January 1940, HFP.
3.   Fysh to McMaster, 11 October 1939, HFP.
4.   McMaster to Fysh, 16 October 1939, HFP.
5.   Fysh to Reith, 24 October 1939, HFP.
6.   Fysh to Reith, 18 March 1939, HFP.
7.   Fysh to F.J. Smith, 24 November 1939, HFP.
8.   Fysh to Menzies, 5 December 1939, HFP.

9. Fysh to Menzies, 23 November 1939, HFP.
10. Fysh to McMaster, 8 January 1940, HFP.
11. McMaster to Fysh, 4 December 1939, HFP.
12. McMaster to Loxton, 11 January 1940, HFP.
13. McMaster to Fysh, 11 January 1940, HFP.
14. Loxton to McMaster, 16 January 1940, HFP.
15. Fysh to McMaster, 17 January 191940, HFP.
16. McGinness to McMaster, 23 January 1940, HFP.
17. McMaster to Fysh, 26 January 1940, HFP.
18. Fysh to McMaster, 30 January 1940, HFP.
19. Fysh to McMaster, 23 February 1940, HFP.
20. McMaster to Rudder, 11 March 1940, HFP.
21. McMaster to Fys, 2 February 1940, HFP.
22. *QAS*, p. 210-11.
23. Fysh to McMaster, 24 January 1940, HFP.
24. McMaster to Fysh, 26 March 1940, HFP.
25. Fysh to McMaster, 29 March 1940, HFP.
26. McMaster to Fysh, 7 March 1940, HFP.
27. *QAW*, p. 277-30.
28. McMaster to Fysh, 7 March 1940, HFP.
29. Hocking and Haddon-Cave, *Air Transport in Australia*, p. 23.
30. Johnston to McMaster, 10 May 1940, HFP.
31. Fysh board report, 16 May 1940, HFP.
32. McMaster to Fysh, 14 June 1940, HFP.
33. Fysh to McMaster, 19 June 1940, HFP.
34. McMaster to Fysh, 8 January 1940, HFP.
35. Fysh to McMaster, 30 March 1940, HFP.
36. Thorby to McMaster, 29 May 1940, McMP.
37. McMaster to Foll, 29 May 1940, HFP.
38. McMaster to Fysh, 14 June 1940, HFP.
39. Dismore to Fysh, 4 June 1940, HFP.
40. Fysh to Runciman, 24 June 1940, HFP.
41. Runciman to Fysh, 15 August 1940, HFP.
42. McMaster to Fysh, 18 June 1940, HFP.
43. Fysh to McMaster, 25 June 1940, HFP.
44. McMaster to Fysh, 27 June 1940, HFP.
45. Chairman's address, 4 July 1940, Qantas Annual Report.
46. McMaster to Fysh, 24 June 1940, HFP.
47. Fysh to Fairbairn, 6 July 1940, HFP.
48. Fairbairn to Fysh, 9 July 1940, HFP.
49. McMaster to Fysh, 8 July 1940, HFP.
50. Fysh to McMaster, 11 July 1940, HFP.
51. QEA gazette *Empire Airways*, June 1940.
52. War Cabinet Agendum 406, 11 July 1940, EJP.
53. War Cabinet Agendum 94/1940, 27 April 1940, EJP.
54. Fairbairn to chief of Air Staff, 11 July 1940, EJP.
55. Johnston to Fairbairn, 23 September 1940, EJP.
56. Johnston to Fairbairn, 4 October 1940, EJP.
57. Johnston to chief of Air Staff, 4 October 1940, EJP.
58. Fysh to Fairbairn, 11 July 1940, HFP.
59. Fysh to Trippe, 16 July 1940, HFP.
60. *Empire Airways*, September 1940.
61. McMaster to Fysh, 23 July 1940.
62. Fysh to Runciman, 27 August 1940, HFP.
63. Fysh to Runciman, 30 July 1940, HFP.
64. Runciman to Rudder, 30 August 1940, HFP.
65. McMaster to Fysh, 5 September 1940, HFP.
66. McMaster to Fysh, 9 September 1940, HFP.
67. Runciman to Fysh, 6 September and 7 October 1940, HFP.
68. Corbett memorandum quoted by Fysh to McMaster, 12 November 1940, HFP.
69. The Brisbane Clinic to McMaster, 15 October 1940, McMP.
70. Grey to Fysh, EJP.
71. *QAW*, p. 111.

Chapter 2

1. Fysh to Menzies, 23 January 1941, HFP.
2. Brain to Johnston, 5 February 1941, EJP.
3. Ibid.
4. Brain official report, HFP.
5. Runciman to Fysh, 4 June 1941, HFP.
6. Australian minister, Washington, cable, Department of Defence Co-ordination No. CS 208, 13 March 1941, EJP.
7. Fadden to Menzies, 26 March 1941, No. 164, EJP.
8. Menzies to Fadden as acting prime minister, 25 April 1941, EJP.
9. McMaster to Rudder, 8 May 1941, HFP.
10. Twenty-first Qantas Annual Report.
11. McMaster to Fysh, 25 July 1941, HFP.
12. McMaster to Harman, 1 August 1941, HFP.
13. Runciman to McMaster, 22 August 1941, HFP.
14. Watt, *Evolution of Australian Foreign Policy*, p. 42.
15. Corbett to Fysh, 8 August 1941, HFP.
16. Corbett to Fysh, 15 August 1941, HFP.
17. Corbett to Fysh, 3 September 1941, HFP.
18. Fysh to Corbett, September 1941, HFP.
19. Fysh memo to management, 22 July 1941, HFP.
20. Fysh to McMaster, 11 August 1941, HFP.
21. McMaster to Fysh, 15 September 1941, HFP.
22. Chairman's address, twenty-first Annual General Meeting of Qantas, 14 October 1941.
23. Fysh to Burnett, 25 October 1941, HFP.
24. Watt, *Evolution of Australian Foreign Policy*, p. 49.

Chapter 3

1. Summary of Qantas war work by Fysh, 28 January 1943, HFP.
2. *QAW*, p. 125.
3. Fysh to McMaster, 26 December 1941, HFP.
4. Bennett-Bremner, *Front-Line Airline*, p. 37.
5. Ibid., p. 44.
6. *QAW*, p. 130.
7. Qantas general memo, No. 1, 1942, HFP.
8. Fysh to Runciman, 10 January 1942, HFP.
9. Runciman to Fysh, 7 January 1942, HFP.
10. Brancker to Runciman, 10 January 1942, BA.
11. *QAW*, p. 128.
12. Drakeford to McMaster, 14 January 1942, HFP.
13. Corbett to Fysh, 14 January 1942, McMP.
14. Fysh to Corbett, 16 January 1942, McMP.
15. Corbett to Fysh, 21 January 1942, McMP.
16. Fysh to McMaster, 21 January 1942, McMP.
17. Fysh to McMaster, 21 January 1942, McMP.
18. Corbett to Fysh, 21 January 1942, McMP.
19. Handwritten comment on above letter by McMaster, McMP.
20. Brancker to McMaster, 16 February 1942, McMP.
21. Bennett-Bremner, *Front-Line Airline*, p. 21.
22. Interview with author.
23. Bennett-Bremner, *Front-Line Airline*, p. 64-66.
24. Ibid., p. 71-72.
25. Ibid., p. 85.
26. *QAW*, p. 145.
27. Lester Brain diary notes, 2 March 1942, HFP.
28. *QAW*, p. 142.
29. Lester Brain diary, HFP.

30. *QAW*, p. 150.
31. Ibid., p. 150.
32. Lester Brain diary, HFP.
33. Ibid.

Chapter 4

1.   *QAW*, p. 156.
2.   Gilpin to McMaster, 10 April 1942, HFP.
3.   BOAC memo to department heads from P. Wimbush, 10 August 1942, based on information received in April 1942, BA.
4.   Tapp interview with author.
5.   *QAW*, p. 158.
6.   QEA general memo, No. 1, 22 March 1942, HFP.
7.   QEA war summary, 1942, HFP.
8.   Ibid.
9.   Fysh to Burnett, 6 March 1942, HFP.
10. Jones to Fysh, 27 May 1942, HFP.
11. Fysh to Corbett, 8 April 1942, HFP.
12. *QAW*, p. 161.
13. QEA war chronology, 31 August 1943, compiled by I. Isaacs, HFP.
14. McMaster to Fysh, 30 April 1942, HFP.
15. *QAW*, p. 162.
16. Corbett to Fysh, 1 May 1942, McMP.
17. Fysh to Bostock, 7 and 14 May 1942, HFP.
18. Bennett-Bremner, *Front-Line Airline*, p. 110.
19. Fysh to McMaster, 5 May 1942, HFP.
20. Fysh to drakeford, 15 May 1942, HFP.
21. Drakeford to Fysh, 13 June 1942, HFP.
22. Fysh to McMaster, 15 May 1942, HFP.
23. McMaster to Fysh, 15 May 1942, HFP.
24. Fysh to McMaster, 9 June 1942, HFP.
25. McMaster to Fysh, 11 June 1942, HFP.
26. Melbourne *Herald*, 27 December 1941.
27. Watt, *Evolution of Australian Foreign Policy*, p. 57.
28. Ibid., p. 60. P. Hasluck quoted by Watt.
29. Runciman to McMaster, 6 July 1942, McMP.
30. McMaster to Bruce, 3 July 1942, McMP.
31. Courtenay to Allied Newspapers, 23 July 1942, HFP.
32. Courtenay to Attlee, 23 July 1942, HFP.
33. McMaster to Fadden, 29 June 1942, HFP.
34. Drakeford to Fysh, 3 July 1942, HFP.
35. Corbett to Fysh, 13 July 1942, HFP.
36. Johnston interdepartmental committee summary, 12 August 1942, EJP.
37. Fysh to McMaster, 24 July 1942, HFP.
38. McMaster speech in Brisbane, 28 July 1942, McMP.
39. McMaster to Drakeford, 29 July 1942, McMP.
40. The *Times*, London, 3 August 1942.
41. *Courier-Mail*, Brisbane, 2 August 1942.
42. Fysh to McMaster, 12 August 1942, HFP.
43. McMaster to Fysh, 20 and 25 August 1942, HFP.
44. Fysh to Holyman, 20 June and 27 August 1942, HFP.
45. Holyman to Fysh, 27 June 1942, HFP.
46. Fysh to Holyman, 26 September 1942, HFP.
47. Bennett-Bremner, *Front-Line Airline*, p. 128.
48. QEA war chronology compiled by I. Isaacs, 31 August 1943, HFP.
49. Fysh to Gowrie, 22 August 1942, HFP.
50. Official secretary to Fysh, August 1942, HFP.
51. Corbett to Fysh, 31 August 1942, HFP.
52. Fysh to Corbett, 1 September 1942, HFP.
53. McMaster to Fysh, 25 August 1942, HFP.

54. McMaster to Page, 2 September 1942, McMP.
55. Corbett to Fysh, 17 September 1942, HFP.
56. Corbett to Fysh, 15 September 1942, HFP.
57. McMaster to Fysh, 17 September 1942, HFP.
58. McMaster to Fysh, 25 August 1942, HFP.
59. Fysh to McMaster, 16 September 1942, HFP.
60. McMaster to Watt, 22 September 1942, HFP.
61. McMaster to Curtin, 22 September 1942.
62. Baird to McMaster, 26 September 1942, McMP.
63. Fysh to McMaster, 26 September 1942, HFP.
64. Fysh to McMaster, 30 September 1942, HFP.
65. McMaster to Fysh, 2 October 1942 and McMaster notes 8 October 1942, HFP.
66. Bennett-Bremner, *Front-Line Airline*, p. 125.
67. Fysh to Corbett, 21 October 1942, HFP.
68. Corbett to Fysh, 21 October 1942, HFP.
69. McMaster to Fysh, 26 October 1942, HFP.
70. Managing Director's Report, 11 November 1942, HFP.
71. McMaster to Fysh, 26 October 1942, HFP.
72. Corbett to Fysh, 9 November 1942, HFP.
73. Corbett to Fysh, 11 November 1942, HFP.
74. Fysh to Corbett, 16 November 1942, HFP.
75. Corbett to Fysh, 22 November 1942, HFP.
76. QEA war chronology compiled by I. Isaacs, 31 August 1943, HFP.
77. Fysh report, 28 January 1943, HFP.
78. Operations Department report to managing director, 16 February 1943, HFP.
79. McMaster to Forde, 5 November 1942, McMP.
80. McMaster to Rudder, 26 October 1942, McMP.
81. Pearson to Fysh, 19 November 1942, HFP.
82. Watt, *Evolution of Australian Foreign Policy*, p. 71.
83. Fysh to McMaster, 5 December 1942, HFP.
84. McMaster to Drakeford, 22 December 1942, McMP.
85. McMaster to Fysh, 24 December 1942, HFP.
86. Runciman to Fysh, 25 November 1942, HFP.
87. McMaster to Pearson, 23 December 1942, McMP.
88. Chairman's address, twenty-second Annual General Meeting, 16 December 1942.
89. Fysh memo to executives, 23 December 1942, HFP.
90. *Sydney Morning Herald*, 31 December 1942.

Chapter 5

1. Fysh to McMaster, 4 January 1943, HFP.
2. Corbett plan, 11 January 1943, EJP.
3. McMaster to Fysh, 20 January 1943, HFP.
4. Fysh to McMaster, 26 January 1943, HFP.
5. Kenney to QEA, 15 January 1943, HFP.
6. *QAW*, p. 196.
7. Fysh to McMaster, 13 January 1943, HFP.
8. Fysh to Woods Humphrey, 5 January 1943, HFP.
9. McMaster to Fysh, 8 January 1943, HFP.
10. McMaster to Fysh, 11 January 1943, HFP.
11. Fysh to Holyman, 26 February 1943, HFP.
12. Holyman to Fysh, 1 March 1943, HFP.
13. Fysh to Holyman, 10 March 1943, HFP.
14. Fysh to McMaster, 10 March 1943, HFP.
15. Fysh to McMaster, 9 March 1943, HFP.
16. Fysh to McMaster, 5 January 1943, HFP.
17. Fysh to McMaster, 18 February 1943, HFP.
18. McMaster to Fysh, 23 February 1943, HFP.

19. McMaster to Fysh, 24 February 1943, HFP.
20. Fysh to McMaster, 6 January 1943, HFP.
21. Fysh to McMaster, 16 February 1943, HFP.
22. Fysh to McMaster, 22 January 1943, HFP.
23. Johnston to Fysh, 9 March 1943, HFP.
24. Report by Lester Brain, 30 April 1943, HFP.
25. *QAW*, p. 175.
26. Pattison and Goodall, *Indian Ocean Service*, p. 12.
27. Ibid.
28. Author's interview with Capt. R.J. Ritchie.
29. Pattison and Goodall, *Indian Ocean Service*, p. 15.
30. Interview with author.
31. Pattison and Goodall, *Indian Ocean Service*, p. 14.
32. Crowther report, 25 September 1943, quoted by Pattison and Goodall, *Indian Ocean Service*, p. 18.
33. *QAW*, p. 184.
34. Ibid., p. 185.
35. Ibid., p. 175.
36. Ibid., p. 177.
37. Appendix B to report of interdepartmental committee, December 1943.
38. War Carbinet Agendum, No. 381/1943, EJP.
39. Ibid.
40. Fysh submission to government, 25 September 1943, HFP.
41. Corbett: first meeting of IDC, October 1943, EJP.
42. Para 93, report of IDC, EJP.
43. Fysh to McMaster, 18 October 1943, HFP.
44. Menzies broadcast speech, sent to McMaster, 15 October 1943, McMP.
45. Fysh to Curtin, 19 October 1943, HFP.
46. McMaster to Knollys, 9 November 1943, McMP.
47. Menzies to McMaster, 22 December 1943, McMP.

Chapter 6

1. *Civil Aviation Policy Organisation During the War and Post-war Period*: Interdepartmental Committee Report, December 1943, para 34, EJP.
2. Ibid., para 25.
3. Ibid., Appendix 6.
4. McMaster to Menzies, 4 January 1944, McMP.
5. Fysh to McMaster, 5 January 1944, HFP.
6. Fysh to McMaster, 6 January 1944, HFP.
7. McMaster to Fysh, 10 January 1944, HFP.
8. McMaster to Fysh, 1 February 1944, HFP.
9. Fysh to McMaster, 7 February 1944, HFP.
10. Fysh to McMaster, 2 February 1944, HFP.
11. Fysh to McMaster, 7 February 1944, HFP.
12. Fysh to McMaster, 8 February 1944, HFP.
13. Fysh to McMaster, 11 February 1944, HFP.
14. Fysh to McMaster, 16 February 1944, HFP.
15. Fysh to McMaster, 9 March 1944, HFP.
16. *QAW*, p. 201.
17. Fysh to McMaster, 22 March 1944, HFP.
18. McMaster to Fysh, 24 March 1944, HFP.
19. Fysh to Knollys, 29 March 1944, HFP.
20. McMaster to Dismore, 30 March 1944, McMP.
21. Fysh paper, *Post-war Overseas Air Transport as Affecting Australia*, 19 April 1944, HFP.
22. QEA paper, 25 July 1944, HFP.
23. McMaster to Drakeford, 28 April 1944, McMP.
24. Fysh to McMaster, 26 April 1944, HFP.
25. McMaster to Fysh, 28 April 1944, HFP.
26. Fysh to McMaster, 3 May 1944, HFP.

27. McMaster to Fysh, 2 May 1944, HFP.
28. Fysh to McMaster, 8 May 1944, HFP.
29. Fysh to Corbett, 29 May 1944, HFP.
30. McMaster to Knollys, 31 May 1944, McMP.
31. McMaster to Knollys, 31 May 1944, McMP.
32. Pattison and Goodall, *Indian Ocean Service*, pp. 41-42.
33. Knollys to Fysh, 10 June 1944, HFP.
34. Fysh to McMaster, 31 May and 21 June 1944, HFP.
35. McMaster to Fysh, 23 June 1944, HFP.
36. McMaster to Fysh, 2 June 1944, HFP.
37. Turner to Fysh, 13 April 1944, HFP.
38. *QAW*, p. 202.
39. Notes of McMaster talks with Chifley sent by Fysh to Drakeford on 27 July 1944, HFP.
40. *QAW*, p. 202.
41. McMaster to Watt, 1 August 1944, McMP.
42. Fysh to McMaster, 3 August 1944, HFP.
43. McMaster to Fysh, 3 August 1944, HFP.
43. McMaster to Fysh, 9 August 1944, HFP.
44. Fysh to Knollys, 4 August 1944, HFP.
45. Watt to Fysh, 10 August 1944, HFP.
46. Watt to McMaster, 10 August 1944, McMP.
47. McMaster to Knollys, 25 August 1944, McMP.
48. McMaster to Fysh, 30 August 1944, HFP.
49. Fysh to McMaster, 29 August 1944, HFP.
50. McMaster to Fysh, 9 September 1944, HFP.
51. Fysh to Knollys, 31 August 1944, HFP.
52. Fysh to Watt, 2 September 1944, HFP.
53. McMaster to Knollys, 9 September 1944, McMP.
54. Fysh to McVey, 16 September 1944, HFP.
55. McVey to Fysh, 25 October 1944, HFP.
56. Fysh to McMaster, 11 September 1944, HFP.
57. Fysh to McVey, 16 September 1944, HFP.
58. Smith to McMaster, 11 September 1944, McMP.
59. Watt to McMaster, 18 September 1944, McMP.
60. McMaster to Watt, 28 September 1944, McMP.
61. Grey to Fysh, 25 September 1944, HFP.
62. McMaster to Harman, 27 September 1944, McMP.
63. HQ RAF Transport Command to BOAC, 10 October 1944, BA, file RSI/1178.
64. Internal BOAC memorandum 10 October 1944, BA.
65. *QAW*, p. 204.
66. Hocking and Haddon-Cave, *Air Transport in Australia*, p. 97.
67. Commonwealth of Australia, Parliamentary Debates, 1944, p. 1737.
68. *QAW*, p. 205.
69. BA, file 1180.
70. Rudder to McMaster, 22 November 1944, McMP.
71. Fysh to McMaster, 23 November 1944, HFP.
72. McMaster to Fysh, 4 December 1944, HFP.
73. Harman to McMaster, 7 June 1944, McMP.
74. Qantas Annual Meeting, Brisbane, 9 November 1944.
75. McMaster to Fysh, 2 December 1944, HFP.
76. McMaster to Fysh, 4 December 1944, HFP.
77. McMaster to Fysh, 15 December 1944, HFP.
78. Fysh to McMaster, 30 December 1944, HFP.
79. Fysh to McMaster, 29 December 1944, HFP.
80. Fysh to McMaster, 3 January 1945, HFP.

Chapter 7

1. Fysh to McMaster, 24 February 1945, HFP.
2. Fysh to Drakeford, 19 February 1945, HFP.

410

3. McMaster to Fysh, 26 February 1945, HFP.
4. Fysh to McMaster, 28 February 1945, HFP.
5. McMaster to Fysh, 6 March 1945, HFP.
6. Fysh to McMaster, 7 March 1945, HFP.
7. Drakeford to Fysh, 13 March 1945, HFP.
8. Report on No. 2 delivery flight by Capt. O.F. Thomas, 24-30 April 1945, HFP.
9. McMaster to Fysh, 15 June 1945, HFP.
10. Fysh to McMaster, 16 June 1945, HFP.
11. Harman to Fysh, 6 July 1945, HFP.
12. Harman to Fysh, 13 July 1945, HFP.
13. Fysh notes on UK trip, 23 June to 9 August 1945, HFP.
14. Fysh to Knollys, 18 July 1945, HFP.
15. Harman to Tapp, 28 July 1945, HFP.
16. Harman to Fysh, 20 July 1945, HFP.
17. Hocking and Haddon-Cave, *Air Transport in Australia*, pp. 79-80.
18. Knollys to McMaster, 9 August 1945, McMP.
19. Fysh to McMaster, 14 August 1945, HFP.
20. Fysh to Knollys, 24 August 1945, HFP.
21. Fysh to Johnston, 27 August 1945, HFP.
22. Fysh to Drakeford, 18 September 1945, HFP.
23. Fysh to McMaster, 26 September 1945, HFP.
24. Fysh, *Wings to the World*, p. 16.
25. McMaster statement, 28 September 1945, McMP.
26. Fysh to Harman, 14 November 1945, HFP.
27. McVey to Fysh, 19 November 1945, HFP.
28. McVey to McMaster, 27 November 1945, McMP.
29. Fysh to Knollys, 3 December 1945, HFP.
30. Notes on London conference, 6 December 1945, HFP.
31. Fysh board report, 22 December 1945, HFP.
32. Fysh board report, 24 December 1945, HFP.
33. Air Ministry letter to P.J.B. Wimbush, BOAC, 12 December 1944, BA, file RSI/1178.
34. Fysh to Rudder, 6 September 1945, HFP.

Chapter 8

1. Fysh to McVey, 5 January 1946, HFP.
2. Ibid.
3. Knollys to Fysh, 16 January 1946, HFP.
4. Fysh to Mcmaster, 22 January 1946, HFP.
5. McMaster to Fysh, 24 January 1946, HFP.
6. McMaster to McVey, 30 January 1946, McMP.
7. McVey to McMaster, 9 February 1946, McMP.
8. McMaster to Knollys, 11 February 1946, McMP.
9. Knollys memo, 5 May 1946, HFP.
10. *QAW*, p. 17.
11. McMaster to Fysh, 3 April 1946, HFP.
12. Fysh to McMaster, 12 April 1946, HFP.
13. Fysh to McMaster, 3 April 1946, HFP.
14. Fysh to McMaster, 12 April 1946, HFP.
15. Fysh to Allan, 9 May 1946, HFP.
16. Fysh to McMaster, 10 May 1946, HFP.
17. Fysh to McMaster, 27 May 1946, HFP.
18. *QAW*, p. 24.
19. Williams to Fysh, 2 July 1946, HFP.
20. Fysh to Gross, 6 July 1946, HFP.
21. Fysh to McMaster, 13 July 1946, HFP.
22. McMaster to Fysh, 17 July 1946, HFP.
23. QEA board minutes, 26 July 1946, HFP.
24. Fysh to McMaster, 1 August 1946, HFP.

25. Fysh to McMaster, 6 August 1946, HFP.
26. McMaster to Fysh, 5 August 1946, HFP.
27. McMaster to Fysh, 8 August 1946, HFP.
28. QEA cable to BOAC, 27 July 1946, HFP.
29. Williams to Fysh, 8 August 1946, HFP.
30. McMaster to Fysh, 9 August 1946, HFP.
31. Fysh to McMaster, 9 August 1946, HFP.
32. McMaster to Fysh, 12 August 1946, HFP.
33. Turner memo, 19 August 1946, HFP.
34. Fysh to BOAC, 14 August 1946, HFP.
35. BOAC Morning Meeting Case Book, 9 August 1946, BA.
36. BOAC cable to QEA, 16 August 1946, HFP.
37. Fysh, *Wings to the World*, p. 29.
38. *Sydney Morning Herald*, August 1946.
39. Fysh, *Wings to the World*, p. 30.
40. Cable No. 331, Chifley to Dominions Office, 10 September 1946, BA.
41. Drakeford to Fysh, 10 September 1946, HFP.
42. Fysh to Chifley, 5 September 1946, HFP.
43. Fysh to Drakeford, 25 September 1946, HFP.
44. Harman to Williams, 4 October 1946, HFP.
45. Arnold to Fysh, 25 September 1946, HFP.
46. McMaster to Fysh, 17 October 1946, HFP.
47. Fysh to Loxton, 18 October 1946, HFP.
48. Fysh to McMaster, 18 October 1946, HFP.
49. Fysh to Drakeford, 19 October 1946, HFP.
50. McMaster to Fysh, 4 November 1946, HFP.
51. Rudder to McMaster, 13 November 1946, McMP.
52. McMaster to Harman, 20 November 1946, McMP.
53. Rudder to McMaster, 25 November 1946, McMP.
54. Fysh to Drakeford, 25 November 1946, HFP.
55. Fysh to Knollys, 6 December 1946, HFP.
56. Fysh to Loxton, 6 December 1946, HFP.
57. Fysh to Williams, 9 December 1946, HFP.
58. BCPA First Annual Report, 5 December 1946.

Chapter 9

1. Confidential QEA memorandum, 7 January 1947, HFP.
2. Gross to Fysh, 17 January 1947, HFP.
3. Fysh to McMaster, 20 January 1947, HFP.
4. McMaster to Fysh, 4 February 1947, HFP.
5. Fysh to McMaster, 6 February 1947, HFP.
6. Fysh to McMaster, 24 February 1947, HFP.
7. Fysh to McMaster, 10 March 1947, HFP.
8. Fysh to McMaster, 24 March 1947, HFP.
9. Watt interview with author.
10. Fysh to Loxton, 28 March 1947, HFP.
11. Watt interview with author.
12. Fysh, *Wings to the World*, p. 34.
13. Loxton to Fysh, 8 April 1947, HFP.
14. Tait to Fysh, 14 April 1947, HFP.
15. Turner to Fysh, 1 May 1947, HFP.
16. Barnard to Fysh, 15 May 1947, HFP.
17. Fysh to Chifley, 6 May 1947, HFP.
18. QEA press release, 26 May 1947, HFP.
19. Fysh, *Wings to the World*, p. 40.
20. Ibid., p. 41.
21. Ibid., p. 41.
22. QEA circular, 11 June 1947, HFP.
23. McMaster to Fysh, 18 June 1947, HFP.
24. McMaster to Knollys, 10 May 1946, McMP.

25. Watt handwritten notes in possession of author.
26. Drakeford to Fysh, 3 July 1947, HFP.
27. Campbell letter to directors, 8 July 1947, HFP.
28. Fysh to Campbell, 14 July 1947, HFP.
29. Fysh to McMaster, 8 September 1947, HFP.
30. McMaster to Fysh, 29 September 1947, HFP.
31. Fysh, *Wings to the World*, p. 43-45.
32. Ibid., p. 45.
33. Ibid., p. 45.
34. Fysh note, 1947, HFP.
35. Fysh to McMaster, 7 October 1947, HFP.
36. Fysh to Drakeford, 3 October 1947, HFP.
37. Fysh to Gross, 11 December 1947, HFP.

Chapter 10

1. Fysh to Hartley, 1 January 1948, HFP.
2. Fysh to Straight, 2 January 1948, HFP.
3. Taylor to Fysh, 22 May 1948, HFP.
4. Handwritten notes by Norman Watt in author's possession.
5. Taylor toFysh, 22 April 1948, HFP.
5. Fysh to Chifley, April 1948, HFP.
7. Board minutes, 23 April 1948, HFP.
8. Ibid.
9. Hood to BOAC, May 1948, HFP.
10. QEA board papers, 1948, HFP.
11. Fysh, *Wings to the World*, p. 105.
12. Fysh to McVey, 11 August 1948, HFP.
13. Fysh to Drakeford, 7 December 1948, HFP.
14. Financial Directive, 1 May 1949, HFP.
15. QEA fifteenth Annual Report to 31 December 1948, HFP.

Chapter 11

1. Fysh to Hartley, 30 December 1948, HFP.
2. QEA board minutes, 14 January 1949, HFP.
3. Department of Aviation, Qantas file SP1844, AA.
4. QEA sixteenth Annual Report to 31 December 1949.
5. Ibid.
6. Fysh report, 22 October 1948, HFP.
7. QEA-BOAC discussions, 1-2 February 1949, EJP.
8. Penrose, *Wings Across the World*, p. 162.
9. Moody, *Qantas and the Kangaroo Route*, Ph.D. thesis, p. 10.
10. Fysh, *Wings to the World*, p. 63.
11. BCPA fourth Annual Report on 30 June 1949.
12. Fysh to Watt, 7 January 1949, HFP.
13. Drakeford to Fysh, 11 March 1949, file SP1844, AA.
14. Fysh to Drakeford, 4 March 1949, file SP1844, AA.
15. Askew to Fysh, 20 May 1949, file SP1844, AA.
16. Drakeford to Fysh, 31 May 1949, file SP1844, AA.
17. Fysh to Hartley, 8 April, 1949, BA.
18. Fysh, 1949 diary, 12 May entry, HFP.
19. Fysh, 1950 diary, 25 January entry, HFP.
20. Fysh, *Wings to the World*, p. 123.
21. McVey to Turner, 27 June 1949, HFP.
22. Ibid.
23. Turner to McVey, 1 July 1949, HFP.
24. Birch to Fysh, 1 April 1968, HFP.
25. Straight to Hood, 4 July 1949, AW/1/1315, BA.
26. Drakeford to Fysh, 5 July 1949, file SP1844, AA.

27. Chifley to Drakeford, 13 July 1949, file SP1844, AA.
28. Fysh to Drakeford, 6 July 1949, file SP1844, AA.
29. Hood to Straight, 13 July 1949, file AW/1/1315, BA.
30. Hood to Straight, 16 March 1949, file AW/1/1315, BA.
31. Fysh to Straight, 8 July 1949, HFP.
32. Hood to Straight, 13 July 1949, BA.
33. QEA Staff Magazine, Vol. 1, No. 1, September-November 1949; QEA board minutes, 29 July 1949.
34. Fysh to McVey, 5 August 1949, HFP.
35. Ibid.
36. Fysh to Askew, 4 August 1949, file SP1844, AA.
37. Fysh, *Wings to the World*, p. 71.
38. Fysh to Thomas, 6 September 1949, HFP.
39. QEA board minutes, 14 October 1949.
40. Paper by Hudson Shaw, Qantas, 1970.
41. Ibid.
42. Ibid.
43. Fysh, 1949 diary, 8 November entry, HFP.
44. Ibid.
45. QEA sixteenth Annual Report to 31 December 1949.

Chapter 12

1. Thomas, *Out on a Wing, p. 283.*
2. *Ibid., p. 284.*
3. *Ibid., p. 274.*
4. *Ibid., p. 276.*
5. *Ibid., p. 277.*
6. *Hasluck, Government and the People*, p. 115.
7. Watt, *Evolution of Australian Foreign Policy*, p. 109.
8. Clark, *Short History of Australia*, p. 218-19.
9. Fysh, *Wings to the World*, p. 77.
10. Ibid., p. 81.
11. White to Fysh, 16 January 1950, HFP.
12. Fysh, *Wings to the World*, p. 81.
13. Fysh to Turner, 20 January 1950, HFP.
14. Turner to Fysh, 20 January 1950, HFP.
15. Minutes of meeting, 22 February 1950, HFP.
16. Amended report by Allan to Fysh, 23 January 1950, HFP.
17. QEA board minutes, 27 January 1950.
18. Schedule of Qantas aircraft, Technical Development Department.
19. Fysh, 1950 diary, 20 February entry, HFP.
20. Fysh, 1950 diary, 27 February entry, HFP.
21. Thomas to Straight, 22 February 1950, BA.
22. Turner to Fysh, 20 January 1950, HFP.
23. Fysh, *Wings to the World*, p. 131.
24. Fysh, 1950 diary, 13 July entry, HFP.
25. Handwritten notes to Watt in author's possession.
26. Fysh to Smith, 3 February 1950, HFP.
27. QEA press release, 3 April 1950, HFP.
28. Fysh to Drakeford, 14 April 1950, file SP1844, AA.
29. Minutes of meeting, 14 April 1950, file SP1782, AA.
30. Memo to QEA board, 20 April 1950, HFP.
31. QEA report to minister, 2 May 1950, file SP1844, AA.
32. Government press statement, 14 June 1950, file SP1844, AA.
33. Minutes of QEA-BOAC meeting, 14 June 1950, file SP1782, AA.
34. Thomas to Fysh, 16 June 1950, file SP1844, AA.
35. Hood to QEA, June 1950, file SP1844, AA.
36. Allan to Fysh, 23 June 1950, file SP1844, AA.
37. Fysh to Drakeford, 22 May 1950, HFP.
38. Fysh to Turner, 12 May 1950, HFP.

39.   QEA memo, 25 May 1950, HFP.
40.   Fysh to Menzies, 23 June 1950, HFP.
41.   Fysh to White, 3 July 1950, HFP.
42.   Fysh, *Wings to the World*, p. 127.
43.   South Pacific survey report by operations manager, 5 August 1950, file SP1782, AA.
44.   QEA submission to government, 28 July 1950, HFP.
45.   Fysh to McVey, 13 July 1950, HFP.
46.   Report by controller of technical development, 21 August 1950, file SP1782, AA.
47.   Allan report, 19 September 1950, file SP1782 AA.
48.   QEA board memo, 23 August 1950, file SP1782 AA.
49.   Fysh to McVey, 13 July 1950, HFP.
50.   Fysh, 1950 diary, 13 July entry, HFP.
51.   Drakeford to Fysh, 15 September 1950, HFP.
52.   Fysh to White, 21 August 1950, HFP.
53.   Final submission on Wentworth for government, 18 August 1950, HFP.
54.   Fysh to Menzies, 29 August 1950, HFP.
55.   Fysh, *Wings to the World*, p. 63.
56.   White to Fysh, 19 September 1950, HFP.
57.   Ibid.
58.   Menzies to Fysh, 12 September 1950, HFP.
59.   De Havilland *Gazette*, December 1950.
60.   QEA board minutes, 24 November 1950.
61.   Allan to Fysh, 16 November 1950, HFP.
62.   Minutes of meeting, 1-2 November 1950, file SP1844, AA.
63.   Fysh to Williams, 9 November 1950, file SP1844, AA.
64.   Notes to J. Somerville, former Qantas economics research officer, in author's possession.
65.   Fysh to Jones, 30 November 1950, HFP.
66.   Fysh to Menzies, 20 December 1950, HFP.
67.   Submission, 25 November 1950.
68.   Fysh to Williams, 30 November 1950, file SP1844, AA.
69.   Crowther to Allan, 30 November 1950, file SP1844, AA.
70.   Fysh to Turner, 22 December 1950, HFP.
71.   Letter to Fysh from Graham, "Answer Downs", McKinley, Queensland, 19 December 1950, HFP.

Chapter 13

1.   Second Sir Ross and Keith Smith Memorial Lecture by D.G. Anderson CBE, director-general of civil aviation, Department of Aviation Library.
2.   Shaw, R., "The Essential Ingredient", 1961, HFP.
3.   Campbell Orde to Fysh, 29 December 1950, BA.
4.   Thomas to St. Barbe, 21 December 1950, BA.
5.   Fysh to White, 2 January 1951, file SP1844, AA.
6.   Turner to Fysh, 9 January 1951, file SP1844 AA.
7.   Hood to Thomas, 19 January 1951, BA.
8.   Fysh to Thomas, 2 April 1951, BA.
9.   QEA submission, 28 February 1951, file SP1844, AA.
10.   Fysh to Thomas, 2 April 1950, BA.
11.   Hood to Thomas, 3 April 1950, BA.
12.   Straight to Fysh, 30 April 1950, HFP.
13.   Heymanson to Watkins, 3 May 1951, G.P.N. Watt papers.
14.   Lloyd to Thom, de Havillands, 5 May 1951, BA.
15.   Lloyd to Thom, 12 May 1951, BA.
16.   Fysh to Thomas, 9 February 1951, HFP.
17.   Notes by Fysh, 16 February 1951, HFP.
18.   Hood to BOAC deputy chairman, 22 May 1951, BA.
19.   Straight to Hood, 29 May 1951, BA.
20.   St. Barbe to Thomas, 31 May 1951, BA.

21. Dunnet (UK Ministry of Supply) to Thomas, 31 May 1951, BA.
22. Fysh to Thomas, 1 June 1951, BA.
23. Minutes of Ministry of Supply meeting, London, 6 June 1951, BA.
24. Thomas to Fysh, 8 June 1951, BA.
25. Thomas to Fysh, 8 June 1951, BA.
26. St. Barbe to Thomas, 11 June 1951, BA.
27. Thomas to Hood, 11 June 1951, BA.
28. Fysh to Watt, 13 June 1951, BA.
29. Hood to BOAC general manager, international affairs, 21 June 1951, BA.
30. Fysh to McVey, 2 July 1951, HFP.
31. Internal BOAC memo, 23 July 1951, TP423 from sales planning manager to sales director, BA.
32. Watt to Fysh, 8 August 1951, G.P.N. Watt papers.
33. Fysh to Anthony, 25 June 1951, file SP1844, AA.
34. QEA application to the minister, 11 July 1951, file SP1844, AA.
35. Fysh to Williams, 6 July 1951, file SP1844, AA.
36. Acting UK high commissioner to Anthony, 12 July 1951, file SP1844, AA.
37. UK High Commission to Anthony, 17 July 1951, file SP1844, AA.
38. Fysh to Anthony, 3 August 1951, file SP1844, AA.
39. Fysh to Air Marshal Jones, 3 August 1951, file SP1844, AA.
40. Farnes, Bristol Aeroplane Co., to Turner, 25 July 1951, file SP1844, AA.
41. QEA report of Bristol 175, 26 July 1951, file SP1844, AA.
42. Fysh notes, 2 August 1951, file SP1844, AA.
43. QEA notes, 27 September 1951, file SP1844, AA.
44. Hood to Straight, 18 July 1951, BA.
45. Hood to Thomas, 31 July 1951, BA.
46. Cribbett to Thomas, October 1951, BA.
47. Thomas to Cribbett, 18 October 1951, BA.
48. Turner to Straight, 5 December 1951, and Straight to Turner, 28 December 1951, HFP.
49. Fysh to Anthony, 18 October 1951, file SP1844, AA.
50. Fysh to Anthony, 3 December 1951, file SP1844, AA.
51. Hood to Thomas, 7 December 1951, BA.
52. Turner to DGCA, 6 December 1951, file SP1844, AA.
53. Fysh to Murray, 18 December 1951, HFP.
54. Murray to Fysh, 24 December 1951, HFP.

Chapter 14

1. Hood to Thomas, 2 and 8 January 1952, BA.
2. Hood to Thomas, 10 January 1952, BA.
3. Turner to Straight, 11 January 1952, HFP.
4. Fysh to Williams, 30 January 1952, HFP.
5. Brancker to McVey, 21 January 1952, BA.
6. Hood to deputy chairman BOAC, 30 January 1952, BA.
7. Perth *Daily News*, 2 February 1952.
8. This account of Paul McGinness's life was given to the author in 1985 by his first wife, Dorothy, and his daughter, Pauline. Originals of McGinness's discharge certificate and some of his correspondence are in the Battye Library, Perth.
9. Fysh to Thomas, 4 February 1952, HFP.
10. Fysh, 1952 diary, 24 February entry, HFP.
11. Fysh to Anthony, 7 March 1952, HFP.
12. McVey to Brancker, 18 February 1952, BA.
13. Fysh to Hardman, 9 May 1952, file SP1844, AA.
14. QEA report, 19 May 1952, file SP1844, AA.
15. Fysh to Taylor, 20 May 1952, HFP.
16. McVey to Fysh, 5 May 1952, HFP.
17. Fysh to McVey, 20 May 1952, HFP.
18. Denny to Fysh, 22 May 1952, HFP.
19. Fysh, *Wings to the World*, p. 99.

20. Fysh to Anthony, 3 June 1952, HFP.
21. Fysh to McVey, 2 June 1952, HFP.
22. Fysh to Williams, 4 July 1952, HFP.
23. Anthony to Fysh, 1 September 1952, HFP.
24. Fysh, *Wings to the World*, p. 132.
25. Notes of meeting between Johnston and Turner, 10 September 1952, HFP.
26. QEA brief to minister, London talks, 1952, file SP1844, AA.
27. Memo to the minister, 26 September 1952, HFP.
28. Hay to QEA directors, 7 October 1952, HFP.
29. Taylor to acting minister G. McLeay, 16 October 1952, HFP.
30. Turner memo to board, 27 November 1952, HFP.
31. Fysh to Taylor, 11 December 1952, HFP.
32. Thomas to Cribbett, 17 November 1952, BA.
33. Cribbett to Thomas, 8 November 1952, BA.
34. St. Barbe to Thomas, 31 May 1951, BA.
35. Commonwealth Parliamentary Debates, Vol. 184, quoted by Watt, *Evolution of Australian Foreign Policy* p. 97.
36. Ibid.
37. Watt, *Evolution of Australian Foreign Policy*, p. 113.
38. John Curtin speech, Painted Hall, Greenwich, London, 1944; attended by the author.
39. Watt, *Evolution of Australian Foreign Policy*, p. 274.
40. Fysh report, 22 October 1952, HFP.
41. QEA submission to minister, 11 December 1952, HFP.
42. Hood to Thomas, 17 December 1952, BA.
43. Interview with Allan by the author.
44. Hood report *Civil aviation development — Australia*, 17 December 1952, BA.
45. Cribbett to Thomas, 31 December 1952, BA.

Chapter 15

1. Thomas to Cribbett, 1 January 1953, BA.
2. McVey to Thomas, 8 January 1953, BA.
3. Hood to Thomas, 9 January 1953, BA.
4. Hood to sales director, BOAC, 16 January 1953, BA.
5. Cribbett to Thomas, 30 January 1953, BA.
6. Cribbett to Johnston, 15 January 1953, EJP
7. Turner to Fysh, 20 February 1951, HFP.
8. St. Barbe to Fysh, 23 March 1953, HFP.
9. Fysh to St. Barbe, 9 April 1953, HFP.
10. Hood to Thomas, 1 April 1953, BA.
11. Turner to Granville, 8 April 1953, BA.
12. Fysh to Thomas, 9 April 1953, BA.
13. The *Economist*, 4 April 1953.
14. Turner, *Aircraft Programme*, 2 March 1953, file SP1844, AA.
15. Johnston to Fysh, 23 March 1953, file SP1844, AA.
16. Wilson to Turner, 24 March 1953, file SP1844, AA.
17. Fysh to Johnston, 20 March 1953, file SP1844, AA.
18. Board memo, 15 January 1953, file SP1844, AA.
19. Ibid.
20. Penrose, *Wings Across the World*, p. 182.
21. Fysh address, 28 July 1953, HFP.
22. Fysh to Anthony, 21 October 1953, file SP1844, AA.
23. Johnston memo to minister, file SP1844, AA.
24. Ibid.
25. Ibid.
26. Johnston to Cribbett, 11 November 1953, file SP1842, AA.
27. Watt to Williams, 22 December 1953, file SP1844, AA.
28. QEA representative's monthly report, December 1953, HFP.
29. Handwritten notes by G.P.N. Watt given to the author.
30. Fysh to Turner, 22 December 1952, HFP.

Chapter 16

1.   Turner to Fysh, 4 January 1954, HFP.
2.   Handwritten cards by Turner in author's possession.
3.   Interviews with Captain Ritchie and G.P.N. Watt by the author.
4.   Turner to Fysh, 4 January 1954, HFP.
5.   Allan report, 22 January 1954, HFP.
6.   De Havilland Bulletin, 28 January 1954, HFP.
7.   Thomas to Fysh, 21 January 1954, file SP1844, AA.
8.   Blain, *Industrial Relations in the Air*, p. 18.
9.   Ibid., p. 20.
10.   Turner board memo, 25 February 1954, file SP1844, AA.
11.   Ibid.
12.   Turner memo to pilots, 2 March 1954, HFP.
13.   Fysh to Anthony, 25 February 1954, file SP1844, AA.
14.   Fysh to Thomas, 4 January 1954, HFP.
15.   Thomas to Fysh, 8 January 1954, HFP.
16.   Fysh to Menzies, 4 March 1954, HFP.
17.   Summary of discussions, QEA meeting with minister, 10 March 1954, file SP1844, AA.
18.   QEA staff memo, 12 April 1954, file SP1844, AA.
19.   Thomas to Fysh, 12 March 1954, HFP.
20.   Thomas, *Out on a Wing*, p. 319.
21.   Wright to Allan, 23 March 1954, HFP.
22.   Wilson to Turner, March 1954, HFP.
23.   Turner to Fysh, 8 April 1954, HFP.
24.   Turner to Fysh, 16 April 1954, HFP.
25.   Johnston report on Auckland conference, March–April 1954, HFP.
26.   Thomas, *Out on a Wing*, p. 321-22.
27.   Turner to Fysh, 13 April 1954, HFP.
28.   Whitehead, United Kingdom High Commission to prime minister, SP1844.
29.   Williams to Anthony, 14 May 1954, HFP.
30.   Anthony telegram, HFP.
31.   Treasury memo to director-general of civil aviation, 19 May 1954, HFP.
32.   QEA memo, 20 May 1954, HFP.
33.   Director-general of civil aviation to treasurer, 21 May 1954, file SP1844, AA.
34.   Treasurer to director-general of civil aviation, 25 May 1954, file SP1844, AA.
35.   Anthony to Fysh, 29 April 1954, file SP1844, AA.
36.   Anthony to Watt, 29 April 1954, file SP1844, AA.

General Bibliography

Alexander, F. *Australia Since Federation.* 3rd ed. London: Nelson, 1976.

Allen, R. *Pictorial History of K.L.M. Royal Dutch Airlines.* London: Ian Allan, 1978.

Baitsell, J.M. *Airline Industrial Relations: Pilots and Flight Engineers.* Boston: Harvard University, 1966.

Behr, J. *Royal Flying Doctor Service in Australia 1928-1979.* Manuscript in the possession of Federal Council of the Royal Flying Doctor Service of Australia.

Bennett-Bremner, E. *Front-Line Airline: The War Story of Qantas Empire Airways Limited.* Sydney: Angus and Robertson, 1944.

Blain, N. *Industrial Relations in the Air.* St Lucia: University of Queensland Press, 1984.

Brackley, F.H., comp. *Brackles: Memoirs of a Pioneer of Civil Aviation.* Chatham: W. & J. Mackay, 1952.

Brogden, S. *Australia's Two-Airline Policy.* Carlton, Vic.: Melbourne University Press, 1968.

Butler, C.A. *Flying Start: The History of the First Five Decades of Civil Aviation in Australia.* Sydney: Edwards & Shaw, 1971.

Carter, I.R. *Southern Cloud.* Melbourne: Landsdown Press, 1963.

Clark, C.M.H. *A Short History of Australia.* New York: New American Library, 1963.

Corbett, D. *Politics and the Airlines.* London: George Allan & Unwin, 1965.

Crome, E.A. *Qantas Aeriana.* Edited by N.C. Baldwin. Sutton Coldfild: Francis J. Field, 1955.

Davis R.E.G. *A History of the World's Airlines.* London: Oxford University Press, 1964.

Donne, M. *Leader of the Skies: Rolls-Royce: The First Seventy-Five Years.* London: Frederick Muller, 1981.

Friedman, J.A. *A New Air Transport Policy for the North Atlantic: Saving an Endangered System.* New York: Atheneum, 1967.

Fysh, H. *Qantas at War*. Unedited manuscript. Mitchell Library, Sydney.

Fysh, H. *Qantas Rising*. Sydney: Angus and Robertson, 1965.

Fysh, H. *Taming the North*. Rev. and enl. ed. Sydney: Angus and Robertson, 1950.

Fysh, H. *Wings to the World: The Story of Qantas 1945–1966*. Sydney: Angus and Robertson, 1970.

Gibson, R.J. *Australia and Australians in Civil Aviation: An Index to Events from 1832 to 1920*. Vol. 1. Sydney: Qantas Airways Ltd., 1971.

Harvey-Bailey, A. *Rolls-Royce — the Formative Years 1906–1939*. Historical Series no. 1. Derby: Rolls-Royce Heritage Trust, 1982.

Higham, R. *Britain's Imperial Air Routes 1918 to 1939: The Story of Britain's Overseas Airlines*. London: G.T. Foutlis & Co. Ltd., 1960.

Hocking, D.M. and Haddon-Cave, C.P. *Air Transport in Australia*. Sydney: Angus and Robertson, 1951.

Jackson, A.J. *Avro Aircraft Since 1908*. London: Putnam, 1965.

Mackenzie, R.D. *Solo: The Bert Hinkler Story*. Sydney: Jacaranda Press, 1962.

Miller, H.C. *Early Birds*. Adelaide: Rigby, 1968.

Mollison, J. *Playboy of the Air*. London: Michael Joseph, 1937.

Moody, J.D. *Qantas and the Kangaroo Route*. Ph.D. thesis, Australian National University, Canberra, 1981.

Munson, K. *Pictorial History of BOAC and Imperial Airways*. London: Ian Allan, 1970.

Pattison, B. and Goodall, G. *Qantas Empire Airways Indian Ocean Service 1943–1946*. Footscray, Vic.: Aviation Historical Society of Australia, 1979.

Penrose, H. *Wings across the World: An Illustrated History of British Airways*. London: Cassell, 1980.

Scott, C.W.A. *Scott's Book: The Life and Mildenhall–Melbourne Flight of C.W.A. Scott*. London: Hodder and Stoughton, 1934.

Shaw, A.G.L. *The Story of Australia*. London: Faber & Faber, 1955.

Smith, C.B. *Amy Johnson*. London: Collins, 1967.

Stroud, J. *Annals of British and Commonwealth Air Transport 1919–1960*. London: Putnam, 1962.

Thomas, M. *Out on a Wing: An Autobiography*. London: Michael Joseph, 1964.

Turner, P. St. J. *Pictorial History of Pan American World Airways*. London: Ian Allan, 1973.

Ward, R. *A Nation for a Continent*. London: Heinemann, 1979.

Watt, A. *The Evolution of Australian Foreign Policy 1938–1965*. London: Cambridge University Press, 1967.

Younger, R.M. *Australia and the Australians: A New Concise History*. Adelaide: Rigby, 1970.

Index

421

424

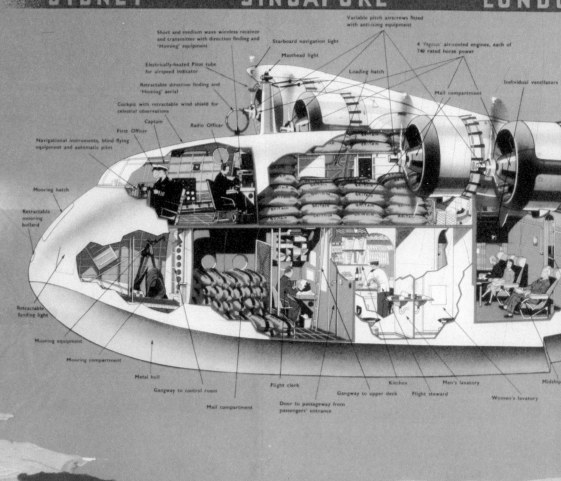